THE NEW LEGAL REALISM, VOLUME II

Studying Law Globally

This is the second of two volumes announcing the emergence of the New Legal Realism. At a time when the legal academy is turning to social science for new approaches, these volumes chart a new course for interdisciplinary research by synthesizing law on the ground, empirical research, and theory.

Volume II explores the integration of global perspectives and information into our understanding of law. Increasingly, local experiences of law are informed by broader interactions of national, international, and global law. Lawyers, judges, and other legal actors often have to respond to these broader contexts, while those pursuing justice in various global contexts must wrestle with the specific problems of translation that emerge when different concepts of law and local circumstances interact. Using empirical research, the authors in this path-breaking volume shed light on current developments in law at a global level.

HEINZ KLUG is Evjue-Bascom Professor of Law at the University of Wisconsin Law School. Having grown up in South Africa, he participated in the anti-apartheid struggle, spent eleven years in exile, and returned in 1990 as a member of the ANC Land Commission. Professor Klug's book on South Africa's democratic transition, *Constituting Democracy*, was published by Cambridge University Press in 2000.

SALLY ENGLE MERRY is Silver Professor of Anthropology at New York University. She is the author or editor of nine books, including the J. Willard Hurst Prize-winning *Colonizing Hawai'i: The Cultural Power of Law* (2000). Her most recent book is *The Quiet Power of Indicators* (2015), co-edited with Kevin Davis, Angelina Fisher, and Benedict Kingsbury.

The New Legal Realism, Volume II

STUDYING LAW GLOBALLY

Edited by

HEINZ KLUG

University of Wisconsin School of Law

SALLY ENGLE MERRY

New York University

CAMBRIDGE
UNIVERSITY PRESS

CAMBRIDGE
UNIVERSITY PRESS

University Printing House, Cambridge CB2 8BS, United Kingdom

One Liberty Plaza, 20th Floor, New York, NY 10006, USA

477 Williamstown Road, Port Melbourne, VIC 3207, Australia

4843/24, 2nd Floor, Ansari Road, Daryaganj, Delhi - 110002, India

79 Anson Road, #06-04/06, Singapore 079906

Cambridge University Press is part of the University of Cambridge.

It furthers the University's mission by disseminating knowledge in the pursuit of education, learning and research at the highest international levels of excellence.

www.cambridge.org
Information on this title: www.cambridge.org/9781107422988

First published 2016
First paperback edition 2017

A catalogue record for this publication is available from the British Library

Library of Congress Cataloging in Publication data
The new legal realism : translating law-and-society for today's legal practice / Stewart Macaulay, University of Wisconsin, Madison; Elizabeth Mertz, American Bar Foundation and University of Wisconsin School of Law; Thomas W. Mitchell, University of Wisconsin School of Law.
volumes cm
ISBN 978-1-107-07319-7 (hardback)
1. Law – United States – Philosophy. 2. Realism. 3. Law – Study and teaching – United States. I. Macaulay, Stewart, 1931– editor. II. Mertz, Elizabeth, editor. III. Mitchell, Thomas W, editor.
KF379.N49 2016
340′.10973–dc23 2015032311

ISBN 978-1-107-07319-7 Hardback
ISBN 978-1-107-42298-8 Paperback

To Elizabeth Mertz, a creative and tireless advocate for New Legal Realism

Contents

Contributors

Martin Chanock is Emeritus Professor at La Trobe Law School in Melbourne, Australia. A renowned legal historian, he is the author of *The Making of South African Legal Culture, 1902–1936: Fear, Favour and Prejudice* (2001); *Law, Custom, and Social Order: The Colonial Experience in Malawi and Zambia* (1998); and *Unconsummated Union: Britain, Rhodesia, and South Africa, 1900–1945* (1977). Chanock's work locates law in discourse as well as society, while also, in the words of one reviewer, revealing "law's failure to protect against arbitrary power" and providing "a distressing lesson in legal realism."

Carol A. Heimer is Professor of Sociology at Northwestern University, Research Professor at the American Bar Foundation, and 2015–2016 Lenore Annenberg and Wallis Annenberg Fellow in Communication at the Center for Advanced Study in the Behavioral Sciences, Stanford University. Her current research focuses on overlapping normative systems, including especially the normative systems of law and medicine in the world of HIV/AIDS. She is currently completing a book project based on her ethnographic work in HIV clinics in the United States, Thailand, Uganda, and South Africa. Recent publications from this project include: "'Wicked' Ethics" (*Social Science and Medicine*); "Inert Facts and the Illusion of Knowledge" (*Economy and Society*, winner of the 2014 Star-Nelkin Award); and "Extending the Rails" (with J. Petty, *Social Studies of Science*). Her previous works include *For the Sake of the Children* (with L.R. Staffen, 1998), *Reactive Risk and Rational Action* (1985), and *Organization Theory and Project Management* (with A.L. Stinchcombe, 1985). Professor Heimer received her BA from Reed College and her PhD from the University of Chicago.

Alexandra Huneeus is Associate Professor of Law at the University of Wisconsin–Madison. She was previously a fellow at the Center on Democracy, Development, and the Rule of Law at Stanford University. Professor Huneeus's research focuses on international law, courts, and politics, with an emphasis on human rights. She is currently working on a project examining the evolution of regional human rights systems, in particular the Inter-American System for Human Rights. Her article "International Criminal Law by Other Means: The Quasi-Criminal Jurisdiction of the Human Rights Courts" (2013) won the Association of American Law Schools (AALS) 2013 Scholarly Papers Competition. She also edited *Culture of Legality: Judicialization and Political Activism in Latin America* (Cambridge University Press, 2010). She received her PhD and JD from the University of California, Berkeley. Prior to studying law, Professor Huneeus was an editor and journalist in Santiago, Chile, and in San Francisco.

Heinz Klug is Evjue-Bascom Professor of Law at the University of Wisconsin Law School and Honorary Senior Research Associate in the School of Law at the University of the Witwatersrand, Johannesburg, South Africa. Growing up in Durban, South Africa, he participated in the anti-apartheid struggle. After spending eleven years in exile, he returned to South Africa as a member of the ANC Land Commission, and has been involved in post-apartheid South Africa in a number of capacities. His research focuses on constitutional transitions, constitution building, human rights, international legal regimes, and natural resources. His publications include *The Constitution of South Africa: A Contextual Analysis* (2010) and *Constituting Democracy: Law, Globalism and South Africa's Political Reconstruction* (Cambridge University Press, 2000).

Bronwyn Leebaw is Associate Professor in the Department of Political Science at the University of California, Riverside. She currently serves on the editorial board of *Humanity: An Interdisciplinary Journal of Human Rights* and as co-organizer of the UC Human Rights Collaboration funded by the UC Humanities Research Institute. Leebaw's articles on human rights, humanitarianism, and transitional justice have been published in journals such as *Perspectives on Politics, Human Rights Quarterly, Polity, Humanity*, and the *Journal of Human Rights*. Her first book, *Judging State-Sponsored Violence, Imagining Political Change* (Cambridge University Press, 2011), won the 2012 award for best book on ethics and international politics, given by the International Ethics Section of the International Studies Association. Leebaw received a PhD in political science from the University of California, Berkeley.

Sida Liu is Assistant Professor of Sociology and Law at the University of Wisconsin–Madison. He is also Faculty Fellow at the American Bar Foundation. His research focuses on historical change, social structure, political mobilization, and globalization of the legal profession. Recent publications include *The Logic of Fragmentation: An Ecological Analysis of the Chinese Legal Services Market* (in Chinese, 2011), "The Legal Profession as a Social Process: A Theory on Lawyers and Globalization" (2013), and "Law's Social Forms: A Powerless Approach to the Sociology of Law" (2015). He graduated from Peking University (LLB) and the University of Chicago (MA, PhD).

Mark Fathi Massoud is Associate Professor of Politics and Legal Studies at the University of California, Santa Cruz, and a 2015–2016 Law and Public Affairs Fellow at Princeton University. He has done extensive work on the institutionalization of law and human rights in conflict settings and authoritarian states. His first book, *Law's Fragile State: Colonial, Authoritarian, and Humanitarian Legacies in Sudan* (Cambridge University Press), received prizes from the Law and Society Association and American Political Science Association. Massoud received a Guggenheim Fellowship in 2015.

Michael McCann is Gordon Hirabayashi Professor for the Advancement of Citizenship at the University of Washington (UW). Professor McCann was the Founding Director of the Law, Societies, and Justice program as well as the Comparative Law and Society Studies (CLASS) Center at the University of Washington for more than a dozen years. He is the author of more than sixty article-length publications and numerous books, including *Rights at Work: Pay Equity Reform and the Politics of Legal Mobilization* (1994) and (with William Haltom) *Distorting the Law: Politics, Media, and the Litigation Crisis* (2004); both books have won multiple professional awards. His current research, with George Lovell, documents and analyzes the history of struggles for socioeconomic rights and social justice by Filipino immigrant workers in the western United States over the twentieth century. Professor McCann has won a Guggenheim Fellowship (2008), a Law and Public Affairs Program Fellowship at Princeton (2011–2012), and numerous National Science Foundation (NSF) and other research grants; he was elected President of the Law and Society Association for 2011–2013. In 2014, he assumed a new leadership role as Director of the Harry Bridges Center for Labor Studies at the University of Washington.

Sally Engle Merry is Silver Professor of Anthropology at New York University. Her recent books include *Colonizing Hawai'i, Human Rights and Gender Violence, Gender Violence: A Cultural Perspective,* and *The Practice of Human Rights* (co-edited with Mark Goodale; Cambridge, 2007). Her forthcoming book, *The Seductions of Quantification: Measuring Human Rights, Gender Violence, and Sex Trafficking,* examines indicators as a technology of knowledge used for human rights monitoring and global governance. She has recently co-edited *The Quiet Power of Indicators* with Kevin Davis and Benedict Kingsbury (Cambridge University Press, 2015) and *A World of Indicators* with Richard Rottenburg, Song-Joon Park, and Johanna Mugler (Cambridge University Press 2015). She received the Hurst Prize for *Colonizing Hawai'i* in 2002, the Kalven Prize for scholarly contributions to sociolegal scholarship in 2007, and the J.I. Staley Prize for *Human Rights and Gender Violence* in 2010.

Sindiso Mnisi Weeks is Assistant Professor at the School for Global Inclusion and Social Development at the University of Massachusetts, Boston. She was formerly a lecturer in legal studies at the University of Massachusetts, Amherst, and a resident scholar at the University of New Hampshire School of Law. She was also previously a senior lecturer in the Department of Private Law and a senior researcher at the

Centre for Law and Society at the University of Cape Town, where she worked on the Rural Women's Action Research Project. Professor Mnisi Weeks is a co-author of *African Customary Law in South Africa: Post-Apartheid and Living Law Perspectives* (2013). Her areas of expertise include women's rights, traditional courts, the relationship between culture and human rights, public policy, the institutionalization of traditional authorities, the relationship between property and authority, the law of succession, and comparative epistemology. Professor Mnisi Weeks received her BA and LLB from the University of Cape Town and her doctorate in law from Oxford University, where she was a Rhodes Scholar. She also previously clerked for the Deputy Chief Justice of the Constitutional Court of South Africa, Dikgang Moseneke.

Jaimie Morse is a PhD candidate in sociology at Northwestern University, where she is a Presidential Fellow, Mellon Interdisciplinary Cluster Fellow in Science Studies, and Graduate Fellow in Legal Studies. Her research lies at the intersection of law, medicine, human rights, and science and technology studies. Her current research traces the history and use of medical evidence as a means of human rights advocacy to document political and sexual violence; it has been published in *Genocide Studies and Prevention*. She worked with Professor Carol Heimer at the American Bar Foundation as part of her comparative study of the role of law in medicine and the use of rules in HIV/AIDS clinics in the United States, Uganda, South Africa, and Thailand. Morse was a Fulbright Scholar in Malawi, Central Africa, and also received an MA in public health from the University of California, Los Angeles.

Sol Picciotto (BA Oxford, JD Chicago) is Emeritus Professor of Lancaster University, a Senior Adviser of the Tax Justice Network, coordinator of the BEPS Monitoring Group, and a member of the Advisory Group of the International Centre for Tax and Development, where he coordinates and carries out research on taxation of transnational corporations with special reference to developing countries. He has taught at the Universities of Dar es Salaam (1964–1968), Warwick (1968–1992), and Lancaster (1992–2007); and was Scientific Director of the Oñati International Institute for the Sociology of Law (2009–2011). He is the author of *International Business Taxation* (1992), *Regulating Global Corporate Capitalism* (2011), several co-written books including *Corporate Control and Accountability* (1993), *International Regulatory Competition and Coordination* (1996), and *Regulating International Business: Beyond Liberalization* (1999), and numerous chapters and articles on various aspects of international business and economic law, and social theory of law.

Susan K. Sell is Professor of Political Science and International Affairs at George Washington University. She is author *of Power and Ideas: The North-South Politics of Intellectual Property and Antitrust; Private Power, Public Law*, and with Christopher May, *Intellectual Property: A Critical History*. She is co-editor of *Who Governs the*

Globe? She has published numerous articles and book chapters on intellectual property, including "Revenge of the 'Nerds': Collective Action against Intellectual Property Maximalism in the Global Information Age" (*International Studies Review*, 2013); and "TRIPS was Never Enough: Vertical Forum-Shifting, FTAs, ACTA, and TPP" (*Journal of Intellectual Property Law*, 2011). She earned her BA in political science at Colorado College; her M.A. at University of California, Santa Barbara, and her PhD at University of California, Berkeley.

Gregory Shaffer is Chancellor's Professor at the University of California at Irvine School of Law. Professor Shaffer's publications include *Transnational Legal Orders* (Cambridge University Press, 2015, co-edited with Terence Halliday); *Transnational Legal Ordering and State Change* (Cambridge University Press, 2013); *Dispute Settlement at the WTO: The Developing Country Experience* (Cambridge University Press, 2011); *Regulating Risk in the Global Economy: The Law and Politics of Genetically Modified Foods* (2008); *Defending Interests: Public-Private Partnerships in WTO Litigation* (2003); *Transatlantic Governance in the Global Economy* (2001); and more than ninety articles and book chapters on international trade law, global governance, and globalization's impact on domestic regulation. His work has been published in the main law reviews or international law reviews at Harvard, Yale, Stanford, Columbia, NYU, Virginia, Michigan, Duke, and Cornell, as well as numerous peer-reviewed journals. Previously, he was the Melvin C. Steen Professor of Law at the University of Minnesota Law School, Wing Tat Lee Chair at Loyola University Chicago, and Professor of Law at the University of Wisconsin and Director of the University's Center on World Affairs and the Global Economy, and of its European Union Center. He is Vice President of the American Society of International Law. He received his JD from Stanford Law School and his BA from Dartmouth College.

Richard A. Wilson is the Gladstein Distinguished Chair of Human Rights and Professor of Law and Anthropology at the University of Connecticut Law School, and founding director of the Human Rights Institute at UConn. Wilson studies international human rights, and in particular post-conflict justice institutions such as truth and reconciliation commissions and international criminal tribunals. Having received his BSc and PhD from the London School of Economics and Political Science, Professor Wilson held full-time faculty positions at the Universities of Essex and Sussex, as well as fellowships from the National Endowment for the Humanities and the Institute for Advanced Studies Princeton. He has consulted for various policy agencies including UNICEF in Sierra Leone, and he served as Chair of the Connecticut State Advisory Committee of the U.S. Commission on Civil Rights from 2009 to 2013. His ten books include *The Politics of Truth and Reconciliation in South Africa* (2001); *Culture and Rights* (ed., 2001); *Human Rights in the "War on Terror"* (ed., 2005); and *Humanitarianism and Suffering* (ed., 2009). His most recent book, *Writing History in International*

Criminal Trials, selected by *Choice* in 2012 as an "Outstanding Academic Title," analyzed the ways in which international prosecutors and defense attorneys marshal historical evidence to advance their case. He is currently writing a book on the international law and social science of speech crimes titled *Propaganda on Trial* (Cambridge University Press).

Preface to *The New Legal Realism*, Volumes I and II

Michael McCann

The publication of this two-volume set by New Legal Realist (NLR) scholars marks an important moment in sociolegal development. To a large extent, NLR scholars follow the original Realists in pushing to integrate social science with study and research about law in action. But NLR scholars do so with an astute grasp of fundamental developments in the character of both contemporary sociolegal scholarship and the legal academy. From the start, scholars involved in this movement have been concerned in particular about the limitations and arguable myopia of law school fascination with other movements like Empirical Legal Studies (ELS) or Law and Economics (L&E) in recent years. NLR offers a compelling alternative vision that engages these and other approaches while expanding beyond their limitations. These two volumes make the substantive intellectual case, by argument and example, for the value of such a comprehensive, multidimensional approach to sociolegal studies within the legal academy. The timing of these two new volumes is also propitious and marks a new self-conscious form of engagement. Law schools are in a moment of heightened panic about the crisis of their professional mission, and these volumes outline new directions in both research and teaching that can help to reconcile contradictory pressures that mark the current uncertain situation.

The internal logic of each volume is both sensible and exciting. Volume I's essays focus on practices in U.S. law school teaching, conceptualization, and research about "real-life" law. The key goal is to encourage more successful integration of theoretically sophisticated empirical research from the law-and-society tradition into law school agendas. The collection begins by addressing analytical and epistemological dimensions of law school teaching, conceptualizations, and preparation; then shifts to method; and concludes by offering various "translations" of NLR into specific research questions. This volume is very much a project by and for law school professors who aim to "make law real." Volume II focuses on "studying law globally." It proposes to focus "translation" of NLR approaches on "diverse global, national, and local sites of law." The collection begins with two chapters exploring the concept of "globalism" in relation to specific legal phenomena, and then shifts to questions of global norm transfer (globalism is all about flows, about exports and imports); it then proceeds to institutions and actors, and ends up with inquiries into normative issues of global justice.

It is worth underlining at the outset that both the editors and the individual essay contributors are very distinguished scholars; they include some of the most accomplished sociolegal scholars of the past half century. It is very tempting for me to review and engage the outstanding essays in the collection on their individual merits. But it is to the whole of the enterprise rather than the distinguished parts of this new volume that I choose to direct the remainder of my prefatory comments.

I. WHAT IS NEW LEGAL REALISM?

The core commitment of New Legal Realism to date has been summarized by its advocates as theory-driven empirical research about law in action that values qualitative as well as quantitative and experimental methods.[1] This could be contrasted with the most hard-core adherents of Empirical Legal Studies (ELS), who have tended to limit the scope of empiricism to quantitative data with very little theory, and classical Law and Economics (L&E) scholars, who tend to focus on deductive theory with limited attention to grounding in systematic data collection. (Of course one could point to notable exceptions in each case.)

While I do not disagree with any of these claims, I propose a slightly altered framing of what the New Legal Realist effort is advancing. I begin with the observation that the law-and-society experiment fifty years ago aimed for a partnership and exchange between law professors and social scientists committed to replacing the traditional case law focus of legal scholarship and teaching with more sophisticated analysis of legal behavior. The exchange was generally reciprocal, although the common commitment to social science study of law animated both sides of the joint effort. Over time, the behavioral focus of early sociolegal study was joined by attention to legal practices, legal discourse, constructions of legal meanings, post-structural analysis of legal institutions, law and social change, sociology of legal fields, and much more. New Legal Realists have rightly pointed out, however, that the cross-disciplinary sociolegal partnerships, and especially the new interpretive turns, have not influenced the broader legal academy as much as many had originally hoped. NLR scholars thus aspire to repackage the cutting-edge insights of sociolegal research, amplify their significance, and revitalize their impact for law

1 Suchman and Mertz write in a classic essay comparing and contrasting New Legal Realism to Empirical Legal Studies: "From the outset, the group focused on building an integrative model for studying law – one that would bring together multiple empirical methodologies to be used in service of resolving theoretically-informed questions.... Rather than prejudging what kind of method would be used (quantitative, qualitative, experimental), these scholars argued that research methods should be chosen based on the kinds of questions being asked. This approach emulates the inclusive approach of the law-and-society movement – and, indeed, NLR remains closely allied with Law-and-Society still." (2010, 562).

school teaching and research. But will this repackaging of sociolegal scholarship as NLR make a difference?

I very much think that NLR scholarship does have something concrete, simple, and fundamental to offer. In short, L&E and ELS refashion in new ways old-fashioned realism in that they generally aim to use microeconomic or behavioral methods to identify the nonlegal independent variables causing or determining law defined as a dependent variable. In these frameworks generally, law has relatively little power, or its limited independent power matters only when bolstered by other independent, intervening extralegal factors (as in judicial or legal impact studies).[2] By contrast, NLR tends to encompass a wide variety of approaches that recognize that law itself – as language/discourse, as institutional practices, as aspirational ideals, as actual or potential enforcement by state violence, and so on – actually matters as power, and is interrelated with other dimensions of extralegal or mutually constitutive power. Most NLR studies view this power complexly, attending to the "constitutive" role of law, or how legal meaning matters, or how legal actors perform legal practices, or how institutional norms and pressures interact with other factors. The focus is on more relational, contingent, context-sensitive, or process-based understandings of law, where law is both dependent variable and independent variable (and hence neither in the classic linear causal logic). This is not true for all NLR scholarship, but the generalization at least points to something distinctive about much of the broader NLR sensibility. And declaring and demonstrating that "law matters" (even in these complex, qualified ways) would seem to be a great mantra to preach in law schools.

For the preceding reasons, I urge more attention to epistemology and analytical theory (of law/power) as the key to how NLR differs from ELS and L&E. In this regard, the familiar qualitative and/versus quantitative relationship strikes me as ill-conceived and misleading, or at least overemphasized. After all, many scholars use qualitative study to make linear causal claims in the positivist mode, and some very quantitatively oriented studies are self-consciously postpositivist and noncausal (and, as such, reject regression). Much L&E scholarship refers to little or no data at all; it is all deductive theory. ELS tends to be all data and little theory, or theory that is presumed rather than directly addressed in critical ways. While NLR embraces both economic theory and quantitative methods – and thus much of the work emerging from ELS and L&E – it tends to insist on more attention to background theories and assumptions regarding how best to translate between different kinds of social science understandings of law and (or in) social context. Hence, it is not the types of data that mark NLR, but the differences in the relationships among theorization, analytical premises, and empirical data.

2 This claim may understate the commitment of ELS scholars to assessing how much law matters. But most ELS studies follow the gap tradition of impact studies and tend to confirm that law is a limited resource for changing power relations in society.

It is quite possible that my effort to push for clearer delineation of the NLR project in these ways narrows the enterprise too much, mutes big differences among NLR scholars, and deflates the big tent. And I do think that the NLR is a big tent, in at least two ways. First, NLR is self-consciously the ambassador to contemporary law schools for a tradition of law-and-society scholarship that itself has expanded dramatically in recent decades to include diverse interpretive as well as behavioral research, qualitative as well as quantitative research methods, and a host of critical theoretical frameworks applied to an ever-expanding array of legally constituted phenomena around the entire globe. We should celebrate this robust, dynamic expansion of analytical formats and topics of study. Second, NLR may distinguish its general orientation from ELS and L&E, but the former advocates have consistently reached out, welcomed, and engaged the latter in a host of ways, sometimes critical but always friendly. There is no reason to exaggerate conflict, when in fact there is a lot of vigorous, constructive engagement going on. NLR scholars tend to shrink the tent a bit only in an effort to define its boundaries in coherent ways, a dilemma that has long been shared and perhaps abandoned by spokespeople for the law-and-society tradition and its professional association, the Law and Society Association (LSA).

II. ADDRESSING THE CURRENT LAW SCHOOL CRISIS: JUDGMENT, GLOBALISM, AND ACCESSIBILITY

The "crisis" that has beset contemporary law schools has received a great deal of attention. My primary faculty appointment is not in a law school, but I have viewed the development of panic in law schools with some interest and concern. The core challenge, as I see it, has been in defining clearly the mission of contemporary law schools in a rapidly changing environment. Law schools have long experienced tensions and been subject to disagreements about their various academic, practical, and professional credentialing roles. These tensions have remained unresolved for many decades, but they have been compounded and forced to the forefront by changing fiscal pressures. Law school tuitions have increased dramatically at the same time that demand for legal services generally, and entry jobs specifically for new lawyers, have declined, thus resulting in substantial declines in law school applications and enrollments as well as forced termination of some programs. Old tensions about the mission and role of law schools have been intensified and multiplied as these fiscal pressures have escalated.

New Legal Realism as a movement does not, as far as I know, offer unique solutions to the economic challenges of legal education. But it seems to me that NLR can contribute to reconciling some of the competing pressures for academic excellence and practical skill development, and thus for clarifying the mission, activity, and standards of law school practice. I offer three points on this matter. The first point transforms a common critique of NLR into a virtue. One objection by some sophisticated critics has been that some leading NLR scholarship has withdrawn from or failed to realize the positivist goal of linear causal analysis and prediction. NLR scholars should, I think, answer, "Yes, and so much the better!" After all, identifying the indeterminate, contingent, context-specific character of legal meaning and practice is a hallmark of much NLR research. Most NLR scholars do not reject attention to instrumental or linear dimensions of power so much as integrate them into more complex modes of analysis that are attentive to nonlinear, interactive, and constitutive dimensions of institutional and ideological power (see McCann 2007). Indeed, the commitment to understanding contextual contingency is arguably a practical virtue that underlines the relevance of NLR approaches for law school teaching and research.[3] Rather than a specious promise of certainty, NLR scholarship approaches offer to develop capacities of analysts and practitioners alike to exercise sophisticated judgment amid the complexity of multiple interacting institutional, discursive, and instrumental forces. Much NLR scholarship does not offer the simple, confident explanations of the kind that ELS and L&E tend to offer, but for many analysts that is its appeal; it questions the sufficiency of numerical representations and simplistic causal explanation, offering instead rich intellectual analysis and practical skills of informed interpretation and assessment in sorting out complex, contingent, dynamic, multidimensional features of real-life situations. Is this not what lawyers most need? And is this not what we look for in analytical scholarship? In many ways, this commitment recalls Holmes's famous realist claim that the "life of the law has not been logic; it has been experience" (Holmes 1881, 1). Whether NLR is consistent with the old realism is largely irrelevant, not least because, as Brian Tamanaha (Vol. I) has demonstrated, the old realism was rather more variable, complex, and subtle than is often alleged. What matters most is the contribution of NLR now, and I think that the movement is timely in its appeal.

Second, NLR scholarship generally has been ahead of the curve in pressing for study of legal institutions and practices outside the United States, and especially for addressing important dimensions of growing global interdependence. NLR scholars have helped to underline why these commitments are important, even for scholars and lawyers who plan to focus their energies within the United States. For example, one of the signal contributions of recent sociolegal scholarship has been to show how U.S. law has been shaped by global/international forces, by U.S. involvement in the world, and by relationships beyond unilateral U.S. control. This is the thrust of the expansive scholarship on how World War II and the Cold War were critical to creating pressures supporting the civil rights movement, the War on Poverty, and the Great Society in the United States (Dudziak 2011; Tani 2012). Late–Cold War human rights campaigns against the Soviets were similarly critical to narrowing the scope of rights talk in the United States, including the emphasis on legal procedure and rights of the accused that went hand in hand with the rise of the mass incarceration state,

[3] See the discussion by Erlanger, Garth, Larson, Mertz, Nourse, and Wilkins (2005) on the "situated knowledge" that NLR emphasizes.

and fed into neoliberalism's key currents of marketization, contracts, and the like. The entire history of citizenship rights, the right to have rights, was shaped by U.S. struggles against Europe, slave importation from Africa, removal of Native Americans from their traditional homelands, and immigration from all directions; U.S. law was forged out of these engagements with peoples, states, and forces from beyond our borders. Moreover, laws of war continuously shape domestic law and policy, and vice versa, right up through issues with enemy combatants. In addition, U. S. commercial and intellectual property law has evolved to deal with participation in an increasingly globalized economy. And U.S. law schools have been a persistent force in proselytizing (often very misleadingly) for versions of "rule of law" and specific legal techniques around the world, arguably in imperial fashion. In short, the international and global have been critical parts of the context of American domestic law development, and the United States has been a formative force shaping international relations and globalism since its origins. One promise of NLR scholarship is to bring attention about the great power and problematic impacts of American law and lawyers more directly into U.S. teaching of aspiring young legal professionals and academics.

The NLR editors of these volumes are sophisticated and integrate these understandings very well; these are lessons that much of their research well documents. By contrast, demonstrating and interrogating global interdependency is not a focus of much L&E or ELS study, which is largely U.S. centered and often are not methodologically attuned to the complexities of global "interdependence." Indeed, those approaches can be complicit in exporting U.S.–derived models, techniques, and assumptions in quasi-imperial fashion.[4] Volume II of *The New Legal Realism* collection in particular is committed to recognizing the theme of the "U.S. shaping and shaped by the world." One might quibble with the separation of volumes according to a local/domestic U.S. focus or a global focus. Again, the United States and its legal system have always been connected to and shaped by global interdependencies. But the editors fully recognize this connection, and the two-volume pairing underlines integration of the local and global in important, sophisticated ways.

Finally, the strong emphasis of much NLR scholarship on interpretive and qualitative methods, attention to legal discourse and meaning, and sensitivity to institutional context promises to add sophistication and rigor to enterprises in which most traditional law scholars already engage. Whereas ELS and L&E offer exotic, somewhat esoteric methodologies that are foreign to most conventional legal scholarship, much of the NLR scholarship aims primarily to sharpen, refine, and elevate theoretically, analytically, and empirically modes of scholarship that are familiar,

4 The copious scholarship of Yves Dezalay and Bryant Garth (2002) has raised these and related questions in theoretically sophisticated and empirically rigorous ways. A rich literature on U.S. colonial ventures that were formative in the development of empire also exists. See, for one brilliant example, Merry (2000).

accessible for literate readers, and realistically practicable with only moderate retooling of scholarly skills. There is much sophisticated method involved in good ethnography, qualitative case study, historical narrative, and analytical theory, but it is more accessible than formal modeling or advanced statistical regression. The latter may be attractive for some legal scholars and students, but the former are likely to be much more appealing and available for effective use among a larger number and range of scholars in the law school world.

Together, these virtues of refining capacity for legal judgment in dynamic and complex institutional relations, of viewing local legal practices in comparative and global terms, and of accessibility all offer important value to legal scholars struggling to make modern law schools relevant and effective.

III. REACHING ACROSS DIVIDES: WHY SOCIAL SCIENTISTS SHOULD CARE

One of the most promising aspects of the New Legal Realism project is the clarity of focus on a targeted audience. The project has been developed mostly by law school professors, with varying degrees and kinds of disciplinary or interdisciplinary connection, writing to and for other law school professor colleagues. This targeting is rather more evident in Volume I, which focuses clearly on U.S. law schools and audiences, than in Volume II, but both seem to aim more for law school audiences than for scholars anchored in social science or humanities units or in other intellectual communities largely outside law school orbits. While a virtue, however, this specification of audience can also be narrowing in potentially problematic ways. In short, to the extent that the New Legal Realism is an interdisciplinary sociolegal project that emanates from debates primarily within law schools, then it may offer little of intellectual or professional value to sociolegal scholars largely outside law schools. In that case, the NLR campaign could be viewed as simply the latest campaign in the "palace wars" of contemporary law schools and largely irrelevant to social scientists or humanities scholars. Indeed, at worst, it might exacerbate the split between law professors and those in social science disciplines and interdisciplinary units (not to mention humanities scholars), undermining any sense of common commitments that once existed in the law-and-society traditions.

I again think this potential tension is not a great problem, and in fact it can be viewed as an opportunity. At least three points of productive connection between NLR and social science (and humanities) scholars strike me as promising. First, there is still much *intellectual* reason for continued exchanges and collaboration among law school faculty, social scientists, and humanities scholars. While those scholars outside law schools do not have a direct interest in the relative institutional influence of NLR inside law schools, we still have an intellectual stake in the interaction. After all, the old realist and postrealist sociolegal projects overcame the challenges of different institutional demands, as they imagined (perhaps naively) a two-way partnership between law professors and social scientists. There is no reason to devalue the aim of partnership now because NLR is repackaging the long collaborative tradition of interdisciplinary law-and-society scholarship for law schools facing new challenges. Indeed, my own experience confirms that we social scientists still have as much to learn from colleagues in law schools as they can learn from us.

Second, many social scientists have become more interested in and involved with law schools, as law schools have become more interested in PhDs. The numbers of PhDs hired in law schools have grown over the past decades, and many PhDs (like me) are adjuncts, affiliates, or just close colleagues with law school faculty. Social scientists in turn often welcome the larger salaries, expanded audiences, elevated public stages, reduced teaching loads, and better food that come with participation in law school activities. Moreover, engagement with law schools can expand the range of venues, terrains, and types of policy or political engagement that many social scientists and humanities scholars value. The New Legal Realism project thus can be viewed as indirectly enhancing these opportunities and inclinations for scholars with a PhD within law schools.

Finally, we should not forget that many faculty members in the social sciences and humanities routinely teach, mentor, and counsel undergraduates who are considering or committed to attending law schools as well as PhD students who may seek employment in law schools. Those of us who believe that an increased role of NLR scholarship would enhance the research and teaching agendas of law schools may find our interests served in these other ways as well. If I knew that NLR approaches were welcomed at some schools, I might be more comfortable recommending professional legal education to students. If NLR approaches became more welcomed overall, my routine and increasing reservations about recommending applications to law schools might be relaxed a bit. And if NLR can create more opportunities for my PhD students, then more power to them, and I am happy to be an ally. In all these regards, intellectual principle and professional interest converge for sociolegal social scientists and humanities scholars.

In sum, there is much to be said on behalf of the New Legal Realism project intellectually and professionally. I find the release of these two volumes to signal an important moment for understanding better, assessing more fully, and advancing the NLR agenda at this historical moment.

REFERENCES

Dezalay, Yves, and Bryant G. Garth. 2002. *The Internationalization of Palace Wars: Lawyers, Economists, and the Contest to Transform Latin American States*. Chicago: University of Chicago Press.

Dudziak, Mary L. 2011. *Cold War, Civil Rights Race and the Image of American Democracy*. Princeton: Princeton University Press.

Erlanger, Howard, Bryant Garth, Jane E. Larson, Elizabeth Mertz, Victoria Nourse, and David B. Wilkins. 2005. "Is It Time for a New Legal Realism?" *Wisconsin Law Review* 2005 (2): 335–363.

Holmes, Oliver Wendell. 1881. *The Common Law*. Boston: Little, Brown.

McCann, Michael. 2007. "Dr. Strangelove: Or How I Learned to Stop Worrying and Love Methodology." In *Studies in Law, Politics, and Society*, edited by Austin Sarat, 19–60. Boston: JAI/Elsevier Press.

Merry, Sally Engle. 2000. *Colonizing Hawai'i: The Cultural Power of Law*. Princeton: Princeton University Press.

Suchman, Mark C., and Elizabeth Mertz. 2010. "Toward a New Legal Empiricism: Empirical Legal Studies and the New Legal Realism." *Annual Review of Law and Social Science* 6: 555–579.

Tani, Karen M. 2012. "Welfare and Rights before the Movement: Rights as a Language of the State." *Yale Law Journal* 122: 314–383.

1

Introduction

Heinz Klug and Sally Engle Merry

Studying law globally is both necessary to understanding the arc of law and justice in the twenty-first century as well as a challenge to explore how law manifests itself across cultures, institutional arrangements, and economic contexts. While legal formalism still dominates the doctrinal study of law, the emergence of legal realism in the first quarter of the twentieth century opened up the study of law to a wider range of approaches, including those of social science. Today there is a healthy debate over the different approaches and meanings of legal realism, or what is now described as New Legal Realism (NLR). However, there is little doubt that our understanding of law in all its dimensions has been enhanced by the multidisciplinary contributions of social scientists and lawyers who have explored not only the logic of the law but also the multiple ways in which law manifests itself in society, whether local or global.

For a new legal realism, the understanding of law is rooted not only in an empirical knowledge of how law works in context but also in drawing attention to the relationship between the use of law and other ways of understanding and studying law, whether doctrinal or jurisprudential. Concerned with ensuring an open yet reflexive approach to the study of law, a new legal realism embraces a multidisciplinary approach yet remains concerned with ensuring a careful translation between law and empirical research. It is this concern that makes studying law globally such a challenge as well as an opportunity to understand the role law might play in achieving the goals of justice and stability sought by communities across the globe.

In order to think about what a new legal realist approach to studying law globally might help us to do, we must first reflect on what we understand new legal realism to be. Confronting this question, our colleague Alexandra Huneeus has suggested three possible ways of understanding what new legal realism might mean in the academy today, especially when we try to think of new legal realism as an approach to the study of law that is distinct from regular social science scholarship that focuses on understanding how law works in society. First, it might simply refer to sociolegal scholarship created by law professors; in Huneeus's words, "just as a gamer adopts an avatar to enter a virtual world, Law and Society scholarship appears in the legal academy as NLR, an identity arguably better suited to the mores and palace wars of that peculiar world" (Huneeus 2014). Another possibility, she notes, is premised on the source of the questions that are asked. NLR scholars use empirical methods to answer questions that emerge from the practice of law rather than from debates in the disciplines of sociology, political science, or anthropology. Thus it is less vested in theory building for the social sciences and is rather more motivated by questions of practice, and in using social science methods to facilitate practice. The problem, as Huneeus points out, is that through the borrowing of methods, legal scholars are importing into their work the concepts and categories developed by means of social science theorizing. This requires greater attention to questions of translation between the research methods of law and of social science. It also requires greater attention to social science methodologies.

Finally, Huneeus identifies a third, more robust version of new legal realism. She argues that while the "borrowing and translation view" of NLR depicts legal scholarship as derivative – legal academics learn from social scientists how to pose and answer their questions through empirical inquiry – the challenge is whether, as Shai Lavi argues, it is possible to "bring the logic of other disciplines under the critical scrutiny of jurisprudence" (2011, 812). This third option seems to point toward an engagement with what Hanoch Dagan (2013) identifies as the normativity of legal realism. Even if we do not fully embrace the reincorporation of normativity, we might still distinguish a new legal realist approach from a purely social science approach to law in three ways: (1) it is a body of scholarship, usually based in law schools, driven primarily by problems that arise in legal practice; (2) it places a greater theoretical emphasis on doctrine and legal processes to explain legal outcomes, and it takes seriously law as a somewhat autonomous phenomenon not reducible to other social phenomena; and finally (3) it is a field of study sustained by constant dialogue between scholars working in law schools and social scientists. As such, it might be described, for the purposes of studying law globally, as one among many scholarly approaches to law that make up the broader Law and Society tradition.

In his book *Reconstructing American Legal Realism & Rethinking Private Law Theory*, Hanoch Dagan (2013) draws upon the early realists, including Oliver Wendell Holmes, Karl Llewellyn, Felix Cohen, and Benjamin Cardozo, to argue that the realists did not merely posit the interpretation of legal doctrine as indeterminate or ascribe legal meaning to the exercise of raw judicial power, but rather advanced a conception of law as an ongoing institution that accommodates three constitutive sets of tensions: "power and reason, science and craft, and tradition and progress" (Dagan 2013, 28). Repudiating the "equation of law with doctrine," this approach highlights the interconnections between an understanding of law that acknowledges both the coercive and the normative aspects of law – but also requires any understanding of law to be grounded in empirical knowledge of law in action.

Recognizing the problems of both a purely assimilationist approach in which the study of law is merely incorporated into the different disciplines within social science and an inward turn in which an understanding of law is built upon the logic of legal processes or the craft of lawyers, Dagan argues for a revitalization of legal theory as a genus of jurisprudential approaches to the study of law as a "set of coercive normative institutions" (2013, 93) within which legal realism is an important species of legal theory. Given the expansion of methodologies and the embrace by social scientists of the study of legal phenomena, we would argue that the distinctive contribution of a new legal realism is its emphasis on multidisciplinarity, its openness to multiple methods, and a recognition of the importance of theory in the fields of both social science and law. The uniqueness of the new legal realist approach is its close attention to the translation between law and empirical research so that both lawyers and social scientists recognize and appreciate the complex interactions among different empirical approaches to understanding law and traditional legal approaches – as well as the institutional and normative dimensions of law in action. Studying law globally only adds additional layers of complexity to this endeavor. This collection does not simply use social science methods to address problems of legal practice, but includes many chapters by social scientists using social science theory and methods to understand law in a global context. Thus it embodies the new legal realist ideals of interdisciplinary communication and translation that take seriously the concerns, theories, methods, and core questions of both law and the social sciences.

The initial legal realist movement of the early twentieth century argued that it was insufficient to study law through doctrine, and urged a mode of understanding that stretched to the social life of courtrooms and everyday practices outside the law (Macaulay 2005; Tamanaha 2016, in Volume I). This analytic approach was revolutionary at the time, transforming the way law was understood. It is even more important today. As the international dimension of law grows in importance, it is valuable to see law as a set of practices with histories, habitual ways of doing things, and systems of cultural meaning. While this was always true of national legal systems, in the contemporary era these practices, habits, and meanings are often radically plural. They may emerge from distinct legal and cultural traditions, or from quite different assumptions about the role of law and the state. Colonialism pitted such diverse systems against each other, forcing them to coexist, always within the framework of unequal power (Sharafi 2007; Benton 2002; Chanock 2001; Merry 2000; Shamir 2000). Such plurality is now enhanced by development-linked legal reforms, military takeovers and the imposition of new legal orders, transnational legal regimes from trade agreements to international criminal courts, embedded sovereignties such as indigenous or ethnic communities, and overarching legal norms such as human rights. In all of these fields of contestation among systems of law, analyzing the historical, cultural, and social systems that constitute them is essential to understanding what kind of law exists. Doctrine will not explain why some laws are followed and others resisted or how compromises are reached between local systems of ordering and national and transnational ones. As the chapters in this book indicate, specific situations vary greatly in the way confrontations take place among various ideas of what law is and what its norms are.

The new legal realist perspective not only is attentive to pluralism and diversity; it also asserts the importance of historical, contextual, and sociocultural approaches to understanding how law works. The term "empirical" is sometimes claimed to refer only to quantitative studies of law that focus on economic or psychological modes of analysis, but in the new legal realist frame, empirical research covers a broad array of quantitative and qualitative approaches to knowledge. For example, in order to understand the way law produces order and disorder in the Sudan, as Massoud shows in his chapter, it is necessary to trace its colonial and Islamic origins and the contemporary intersections with human rights law. In another example, Merry shows in her chapter that countries react differently to the admonitions of human rights treaty committees depending on the sphere of social life and law that is being criticized. When human rights committees critique practices that are strongly supported culturally and/or are politically essential, such as Turkey's insistence that Kurds are not a minority, they are energetically resisted by countries. At the same time, the same country may readily acknowledge the need for more education for its people.

Our version of a new legal realism examines the relationship between law and culture. Law embodies cultural principles and reflects them, while the procedures and practices of law articulate and construct culture. In the context of an increasingly interrelated transnational society, law can take on new importance as an index of culture and peoplehood: as a way to assert identity and difference. This role of law is particularly visible in the efforts of small, relatively powerless indigenous communities to control their own legal systems as a way to assert sovereignty. The persistence of systems of normative ordering within ethnic communities is another example. Conversely, forcibly transforming a society's legal system, as the United States did in Iraq after ousting Saddam Hussein, is a powerful tool to change the society itself. These examples show the importance of a longitudinal approach to analyzing law that incorporates historical analysis, of analyzing the plurality and complexity of law under conditions of contemporary globalization and struggles over sovereignty, and of the need for a cultural analysis that recognizes the link between normative orders and a community's definition of itself. This is not a narrow paradigm of analysis, but instead an open set of questions, methods of research, and possibilities of explanation.

This volume brings together scholars from across the academy – historians, lawyers, and social scientists – whose work is deeply rooted in an empirically informed understanding of the terrain of law in order to demonstrate how a new legal realist approach is able to inform our understanding of law across the globe. Using multiple methods, including ethnography, comparative historical analysis, interviews, and participatory research, these contributions reflect the combined value of interdisciplinary and mixed methods applied reflexively and with close attention to issues of translation between law and empirical research. While the individual chapters cover subject matter as distinct as constitutionalism, human rights, legal pluralism, and the regulation of international finance and trade, they are all grounded in deeply empirical understandings of legal institutions and practice in these different realms. At the same time, they do not flinch from exploring the normative implications of this understanding, nor do they assume that their individual methods are the sole means of understanding the law in their different domains. It is this reflexive openness and awareness of the difficulties of translation between social science and law, as well as between law and legal institutions in different contexts, that has become the hallmark of the new legal realist approach.

Studying law globally in the twenty-first century requires us simultaneously both to embrace the processes of globalization, in which law has played a significant role, as well as to understand how law and legal institutions continue to be rooted in local practices and contexts. To this end we have divided the contributions to this volume into four sections focusing on: the globalization of law, the global transfer of norms, global institutions and the changing roles of legal professionals, and finally, global justice. While this is not a comprehensive set of lenses through which to study law globally, these different foci do identify different realms or locations in which the practice and hence study of the global dimensions of law may be framed.

The first section, on the globalization of law, incorporates studies that focus on the complex interactions among traditional international law, national rules, and a comparative perspective on the rules and roles of law. This initial section provides a broad perspective on the historical and continuing interactions among global rules, norms, and local agency. Martin Chanock's chapter on postcolonial African constitutionalism explores the relationship between global developments and ideas – including colonialism, decolonization, modernization (of both the capitalist and socialist varieties), the Cold War, and neoliberalism – and the struggle to build an African constitutionalism that is rooted in the embrace of the rule of law by African societies and not imposed from above. Sally Engle Merry, in her chapter on human rights monitoring, deploys an ethnographic analysis of the content of expectations, the political and economic situation of the countries under investigation, and the willingness or resistance of a country to accept treaty obligations, as a means of exploring forms of quantification and the use of indicators in the global management of human rights and legal globalization more generally. Susan Sell's chapter explores the dynamic interplay among domestic politics, international institutions, and state and nonstate actors in the production of global rules protecting intellectual property. Together these three chapters provide a deeply contextualized yet broad overview of the globalization of law, highlighting the multifaceted character of a process that is central to any understanding of global law.

Section II on the global transfer of norms recognizes that as law travels globally, scholars are uncovering many tacit ways that unrecognized norms are also being exported and imported. In this section, the contributors explore the diffusion of norms through the interaction of local and global rules. In their chapter, Carol Heimer and Jaimie Morse explore the transnational diffusion of norms through a rich comparative ethnography of HIV clinics in the United States, South Africa, Thailand, and Uganda, highlighting how law moves simultaneously across two boundaries as it moves from the global north to the global south and from legal arenas into medical settings. Mark Fathi Massoud's chapter on Islamic law and human rights in Sudan explores the local experiences of the poor and marginalized as they are confronted with the imposition of different legal orders, whether state-imposed forms of Islamic law or the norms of international human rights as offered by nongovernmental organizations responding to humanitarian crises. Sindiso Mnisi Weeks, in her chapter, uses a focus on the interaction between vernacular and state law and courts in two traditional rural communities in South Africa, exploring a broader context of social relationships, values, politics, and economics in order to understand how justice and security are accessed and negotiated in a context in which both indigenous law and human rights are legally recognized and celebrated. These three chapters offer rich and compelling examples of the interaction of global and local norms and demonstrate how the diffusion of norms over multiple boundaries may be fruitfully explored to understand the mechanisms, processes, and impacts associated with legal globalization.

The third section explores what roles institutions, conceived and functioning at a global or regional level, are playing in shaping law and regulating activities – from the flow of capital to the trade in goods – as well as the policy and practice options available to states. While there is strong empirical evidence of the global harmonization of law – the conscious adoption of identical or nearly identical rules – this section also explores the changing role of judges and lawyers in international and local contexts. Gregory Shaffer's chapter reflects on the distinction between the new and old legal realisms as well as the realism of the international relations literature to highlight the value of a new legal realist approach to international law. Using the example of his own work on the World Trade Organization, Shaffer concludes that a new legal realist approach takes international law seriously but also demonstrates a healthy skepticism regarding the social forces, inequalities, and ideological factors that pervade this field by relying, for its own evaluations, on an empirically grounded understanding of the relevant institutions and processes.

In his chapter, Sol Picciotto explores the regulatory construction of the offshore financial system and tax avoidance, especially by multinational corporations, to highlight the tangled interactions of national and international laws. Picciotto uses the personal odyssey of a whistle-blower and the wider systemic context of the post–financial crisis battles to combat bank secrecy, for understanding the interplay of agency and structure in the development of legal and social institutions. Sida Liu's chapter on the legal profession in China uses a national case study to explore how the changing role of lawyers reflects the engagement of China with global markets and norms. Liu argues that since its revival in the 1980s the Chinese legal profession has been transformed from state bureaucrats into market brokers and political activists – and that while the three roles coexist, it is the interaction among them that is shaping the future of the profession in China. Through their exploration of the role of global institutions, the harmonization of rules, and the agency of lawyers in an era of global law, the authors in this section demonstrate how an empirically grounded understanding of legal institutions and participants provides both clearer understandings and alternative normative and institutional examples that might be fruitfully deployed in debates over the future of legal processes, institutions, and lawyers at both the international and the national levels in a constantly changing global context.

Finally, the fourth section recognizes that achieving justice has become both an emblem of the new century as well as an increasingly complex problem as different forms of justice, from international criminal liability to local forms of amnesty and reconciliation or transitional justice, vie for global recognition and acceptance. Contributors to this last section explore efforts to achieve justice in the global context, from the local performance of justice to the creation of global institutions and the diffuse practices of transitional justice. In her chapter on the irreconcilable goals of transitional justice, Bronwyn Leebaw contrasts the ambitious goals of transitional justice institutions with the tension created by the dual roles of law in regulating violence on the one hand and legitimating power on the other. Leebaw argues that a better understanding of this tension will shed light on the central aspirations of transitional justice institutions and practices to condemn past violations while simultaneously providing a path to reconciliation by conflating political compromise and stability with the establishment of a political community based on principles of human rights and the rule of law. Instead, Leebaw contends that it is important to root any understanding of transitional justice in an empirical understanding of the role of particular transitional justice institutions and the political dynamics associated with their often irreconcilable goals.

In her chapter, Alexandra Huneeus uses the experience of the Inter-American Court to inform the debate over the future of the International Criminal Court (ICC), demonstrating how a particular set of techniques of oversight and supervision may provide a path through which the ICC might evolve its complementarity regime to address some of the criticisms the court now faces but also to foster increased accountability for international crimes at the national level. Richard Wilson completes this volume with his chapter on the relationship between law and social science in the context of international criminal tribunals by exploring the evolution of the legal framework of criminal accountability for direct and public incitement to commit genocide. Focusing on the issue of causation in the jurisprudence of the International Criminal Tribunal for Rwanda (ICTR), Wilson demonstrates how the insistence on causation in international criminal law's formulation of the crime of "incitement to commit genocide," based on a model of causation developed by the International Military Tribunal and the ICTR that has been discredited by four decades of social science research, was the product of the difficulty the jurists – prosecutors and judges – had in proving the special intent required to commit genocide. In demonstrating how organizational culture can dramatically transform legal thinking in these contexts, Wilson argues that a legal realist approach holds the promise of "unearth[ing] the ways in which international criminal court decisions result as much from the quotidian dimensions of the law – the courtroom conventions, rules of procedure and evidence, and assumptions and beliefs of legal actors – as they do from the black letter of the law and established legal reasoning."

Whether from the perspective of historians, lawyers, or social scientists, the contributors to this volume demonstrate how the study of law globally may be advanced through the conscious embrace of a new legal realist approach. Consistent with the realist ethos, there is no attempt to claim a singular approach but rather a recognition of the complexities of translating the social, political, economic, and institutional contexts as they are elucidated by different social science methodologies into an understanding of law as an ongoing institution that accommodates, as Dagan notes, three constitutive sets of tensions: power and reason, science and craft, and tradition and progress. By paying close attention to the issues of translation – between social science and law, across boundaries, and within the realm of international law – these new realist perspectives on the studying of law globally make an important contribution to the broader law-and-society tradition by opening up the relationship between the normative claims of global law and more contextual and social scientific understandings of the role of law as it moves across boundaries of professions, states, and disciplines.

REFERENCES

Benton, Lauren. 2002. *Law and Colonial Cultures: Legal Regimes in World History, 1400–1900*. New York: Cambridge University Press.

Chanock, Martin. 2001. *The Making of South African Legal Culture 1902–1936: Fear, Favour and Prejudice*. Cambridge: Cambridge University Press.

Dagan, Hanoch. 2013. *Reconstructing American Legal Realism & Rethinking Private Legal Theory*. New York: Oxford University Press.

Huneeus, Alexandra. 2014. *Legal Realism and Law and Society in Latin America*. Draft on file with authors.

Lavi, Shai. 2011. "Turning the Tables on 'Law and . . .': A Jurisprudential Inquiry into Contemporary Legal Theory." *Cornell Law Review* 96: 811–836.

Macaulay, Stewart. 2005. "The New versus the Old Legal Realism: 'Things Ain't What They Used to Be.'" *Wisconsin Law Review* 2005: 365–403.

Merry, Sally Engel. 2000. *Colonizing Hawai'i: The Cultural Power of Law*. Princeton: Princeton University Press.

Shamir, Ronen. 2000. *The Colonies of Law: Colonialism, Zionism and Law in Early Mandate Palestine*. Cambridge: Cambridge University Press.

Sharafi, Mitra. 2007. "A New History of Colonial Lawyering: Likhovski and Legal Identities in the British Empire." *Law and Social Inquiry* 32(4): 1059–1094.

Tamanaha, Brian Z. 2016. "Legal Realism in Context." In *The New Legal Realism, Volume I: Translating Law-and-Society for Today's Legal Practice*, edited by Elizabeth Mertz, Stewart Macaulay, and Thomas W. Mitchell. 147–168. New York: Cambridge University Press.

SECTION I

The Globalization of Law

2

African Constitutionalism From the Bottom Up

Martin Chanock[1]

I. INTRODUCTION: CONSTITUTIONALISM UPSIDE DOWN

Failure to establish democratic constitutionalist states is not a peculiarly African failure. Working constitutionalist democracies are rare. And in the African context they will be very difficult to build. Four things must be kept in mind from the outset. The first is that the story of constitutionalism in Africa must begin with violence. The second is that the new African states were, after decolonisation, very weak. The legacy of colonial domination left them both without workable institutions and economically powerless; for the first three decades they were used ruthlessly as pawns in the Cold War; and in the last two, as areas for experiments in neoliberalism. The third is that African leaders had agency and choices; some worked to build democratic institutions; others made the decisions that led to the coups, incited the violence and genocide, and profited from the corruption. The fourth is that fifty years of African experience grounds us in a history of multiple (legally skilled, imaginative, and politically brave) attempts to create and to re-create constitutions for democracies and a history of their failures. But in the foreground of our minds must be the enormous numbers of lives lost and the many long terms of imprisonment served, which lie behind the term 'comparative constitutional law'. The price paid for institutional failure in Africa has been extraordinarily high – the Congo, Nigeria, Sierra Leone, Uganda, Liberia, Ivory Coast, Zimbabwe, Rwanda, Angola, Mozambique, and others. Extremes of political violence, and also famine, are a necessary part of the story of the failure to achieve government by consent.

It may seem odd to start a discussion of constitutionalism by focusing on the violent consequences of its failure, but this is more than a rhetorical flourish. No kind of 'law' – constitutional, common, customary, or local, or international human rights law – provides a solution to the violence produced by predation, a disintegrating social compromise, and collapsing states. Over the past half century large numbers of African states have failed to establish legitimate and peaceful governance. This

[1] An earlier version of this chapter appeared in *Law in Context* 28(2). I am grateful for the contribution of Steve Ellmann to the first version, and of Heinz Klug in the writing of the second.

perspective usually leads to a focus, particularly from the standpoint of a lawyer's analysis, on the framework and methods of government, constitutional law, and the culture of constitutionalism, as well as issues of legitimacy and democracy. But, as I shall suggest, this may not be the best starting point.

This chapter will argue that the bulk of legal and political literature and actual political practice regarding the search for constitutional democracy is upside down. In the most recent example, a comprehensive volume on comparative constitutional law (Ginsburg and Dixon 2011), there is only one chapter which refers to the relationship between new constitutions and the existing common law, and it draws attention to the weeding out and 'constitutional colonisation' of common law (Michelman in Ginsburg and Dixon 2011). The habit in academia and, more sadly, in practice has been to start at the top, with the writing of increasingly complex constitutions, with increasingly sophisticated institutions and rights guarantees, which have, as has been shown time and time again, floated meaninglessly above the societies for which they have been designated, until the bubble bursts in outbreaks of violence.

Instead, this chapter will suggest that the quest for constitutionalism must be based on a rule of law that builds from the bottom up, rather than a bill of rights handed down. Like successful Western constitutionalism, African constitutionalism must be based on a common law with which people identify. This will mean a basic intellectual and institutional reengagement with the legal forms and processes with which *Africans* identify. Claude Ake wrote years ago:

> One of the most urgent tasks of democratisation in Africa is to democratise in such a manner that law and the rule of law are relevant to social experience. ... Law defines the realm of freedom. ... It is extremely alienating for people to live under a system of law which does not connect to their social experience; it gives a pervasive sense of helplessness amid a chaos of arbitrariness. (1996, 178–180)

Taking an interdisciplinary approach, this chapter considers constitutional developments in Africa since decolonisation in the light of comparative constitutional law; the political science of new states and the democratisation projects both during and after the Cold War, as well as development studies. It relies on a historical narrative which focuses on the Anglophone states of Africa, and, while it deals with significant developments in many states, it considers in particular Nigeria (the largest and most complex), Ghana (which was emblematic), Tanzania (the attempt at difference), and South Africa (the belated constitutional exemplar). Inherent in writing a historical narrative of democratisation are the temptations of teleology. *Each failure seems, to many writers, to point towards an inevitable success*. Indeed, it is hard, given the very admirable attempts to establish democratic states, not to will history on towards this goal.

II. CONSTITUTIONALISM IN CONTEXT

The persistent failure of constitutional government in Africa over the past fifty years raises critical questions in a world which is has strong trends towards legal and constitutional universalism. There has been globally an extraordinary narrowing of the constitutional repertoire. After each failure in Africa, another variation of this repertoire has been chosen on which to rebuild. In the meantime political scientists tell us that development of sustainable constitutional democracy is dependent on other economic, social, and political developments such as a particular level of gross domestic product (GDP), the existence of a middle class, and an independent 'civil society'. These developments have not yet taken place in Africa, and may not, but the crucial question of how Africa is to be governed will still remain. This question must also be approached in the context of the world external to Africa, which continues to structure the environment in which Africans can make decisions about themselves.

The existing literature on African constitutionalism was for a long time sparse, consisting of a series of legalist books by Nwabueze (see 1973, 1974, 1977, 1985; see also Amissah 1981 and Prempeh 1999) and a single classic (on Kenya by Ghai and McAuslan 1970). As interest in comparative constitutional law has revived, there has been a developing legal literature. There is a large political science literature on the undemocratic postcolonial period and one which focuses on the revival of democracy but they largely completely ignore law in general, including constitutional law and constitutionalism. So does the development literature, which conveys little sense of the effect of development strategies on the legal means by which governments will bring them into being. It is thus important to consider both past and recent developments in comparative constitutional law and the migration of constitutional ideas, placing the African story in the context of longer-term world history, the creation of post–First World War 'democracies' in multiethnic states in Eastern Europe, and, in particular, the migration of Western constitutions to Asia after World War II. Important, too, are the growth of the international human rights movement and the development of bills of rights as the touchstones for constitutional maturity and the consequent advance of juristocracy. This chapter describes the long-term search for the ideal constitution and concepts of the rule of law and the separation of powers; it frames these with consideration of changes in theorising the state and in development theory. Underpinning these developments was the concept of democracy as majority rule, which was, and is, unworkable in multiethnic states.

A. INDEPENDENCE AND THE DEVOLUTION OF THE WESTMINSTER SYSTEM

A focus on Anglophone Africa would seem in the first instance to be a simple task of trying to work out what the British thought they were doing with regard to the creation of the constitutions of the African states in the process of decolonisation. But one cannot understand the devolution of the so-called Westminster constitutions without the prior Asian stories. A series of 'truths' were created for the Colonial Office in the process of the decolonisation of India, Pakistan, Ceylon, and Malaya. Perhaps the most important of these truths is one which is often overlooked – and that concerns ideas about representation in a democracy. All of the successor states to the British Empire were multiethnic. How were representative institutions to be built for these? Early developments in India and Ceylon focused on representation of communities: common rolls were supplemented by communal rolls to ensure effective communal representation. But these were abandoned, by the Indians themselves, and by the British in Ceylon, in favour of single voters' rolls. The ruling idea was that a true citizenship of the new state could never be created on a basis of communalism. This 'truth' carried over into Africa.

In Africa this 'truth' played into both a local history of denied or restricted franchises in which communal voters' roles had been used in the transition processes in East and Central Africa to give white settlers hugely inflated representation, but also into the demands of African nationalists whose suspicion of colonial motives reinforced demands for immediate universal suffrage and majority rule (Young 2012, 94). Instead of communal representation, Africa's multiethnic states were to be given various forms of regionalism and federalism and, ultimately, bills of rights. The colonial attempts to govern through traditional elites were abandoned in favour of universal franchise. At no point was proportional representation considered. Efforts were made to reproduce Westminster 'conventions' (such as the nonpolitical civil service, military, and police, and the independence of the judiciary) by constitutional mechanisms. I have two overriding impressions from the reading of the British government's documents of this period. The first, of course, is the swiftness of the pace of decolonisation once the decision to liquidate the African empire had been made. The second was (with few exceptions) how irresponsible the process was and how shallow the thought given to it by the relevant officials, including the law officers of the Crown.

B. POST INDEPENDENCE: THE COLLAPSE OF DEVOLVED INSTITUTIONS AND THE GROWTH OF SINGLE-PARTY STATES

Despite the brutality of the colonial state, anointed 'Bula Matari' (he who crushes rocks) by its Congolese victims (Young 1994, 1), the postcolonial states which emerged in midcentury were not strong states. Within the first few years following independence there was a spectacular collapse of constitutional democracies across Africa. From Nkrumah's authoritarian revolution in Ghana to the crises leading to the first, and violent, military takeover in Nigeria, and on to the creation of the one-party 'socialist state' in Tanzania, as well as collapses in Kenya and Uganda, the promise of constitutionalism was soon betrayed. This history, often told from the perspective of political intrigue and venal ambition, can also be approached with an emphasis on constitutional factors such as the repudiation of plural democracy in Ghana and Tanzania and elsewhere in British Africa. While there were serious attempts made by African jurists to think through the problems of the restoration of constitutional government, the most obvious African contribution to constitutional development in these years was the rejection of the idea of 'opposition' as divisive and wasteful, and the creation of single-party states. Three basic justifications were given: they were justified in terms of traditional African political ideas, by the need to drive development, and by the goal of socialism. The constitutional safeguards in the original constitutions were abandoned, including constitutional constraints such as devolution; rights; as well as the insulation of the judiciary, civil service, and armed forces from politics. In several cases one-party states were constitutionalised with the party taking precedence over the parliament. The role of the judiciary during this process and the effect of the judges' reliance on English constitutional and administrative law and legal precedents, all of which had been developed in the United Kingdom in order to limit the possibility of judicial supervision of politics and parliament, is not an insignificant element in constitutional failure. The African judiciary in this period accepted these English judicial precedents, the use of narrow English interpretative methods to limit the meaning of bills of rights, and the use of Britain's limited concepts of administrative law.

C. THE COLD WAR AND RIVAL DEVELOPMENT PARADIGMS

All of the these developments need to be considered in the light of the world political environment and the political science relating to third-world states that developed during the Cold War. The political science of development accepted that modernisation and economic development must come before democracy. It was said both by academic economists and political scientists and by important Western political figures that democracy could inhibit development – that a strong state not compromised by democratic instability and by demands and entitlements which sapped capital was needed to achieve an economic level which might sustain democracy. The modernisation paradigm dominated and the democracy project was postponed. The emergence of development economics is contemporaneous with the Cold War and had both socialist and capitalist paradigms. The Cold War is vital to understanding the development of African states in this period. The United States was suspicious and fearful about the effects of African decolonisation, just as it feared the possible emergence of democracies in Latin America. In the West generally 'development' was linked to the avoidance of communism and was seen as requiring strong, if necessary, authoritarian or military government. These views were most congenial to the African elites.

D. THE FAILURE TO ESTABLISH AN UNDERLYING RULE OF LAW

Before we can understand the failures at the apex level of public law, we must also consider the legal system underlying the new constitutional frameworks. There are three aspects of the rule of law and other basic elements of the postindependence context which inhibited its establishment in the new African states. First, there is the question of the legal profession and lawyers in African states at the time of independence. A political culture oriented to the rule of law requires a well-developed and independent legal profession. But lawyers were scarce in Africa (except in parts of West Africa). Most were trained in English common law, with its impoverished culture of public law. Many African lawyers, especially those trained after independence, were soon caught up with government work. In East Africa a largely white and Asian profession devoted its attention to commercial matters. Nigeria stands out as the country in which there were enough independent lawyers for them to take positions in regard to constitutional issues, and, unsurprisingly, it was there that the most sophisticated thinking and institutions developed. Furthermore, the postindependence judiciary across the continent remained largely non-African for many years, drawing often from judges from the broader British Commonwealth.

Of greater importance to the failure to develop a rule of law culture in Africa was the growth of the 'development state' in Africa in which the states, whether they followed capitalist or socialist models, dominated their economies. The proliferation of parastatals led to the growth of an economic bureaucracy endowed with the far-reaching discretions necessary for economic tasks which ran entire economies that transcended the reach of ordinary administrative law. A huge range of decision making by state bodies was in effect outside of legal parameters. The nature of the inflated state bureaucracies was also anything but Weberian. They were not built on the notion of rational state neutrality between equal citizens, but as means of dividing the spoils of the state between kin and other networks of this kind. Nowhere was a 'legal rational' model developed. Okoth-Ogendo (1993) wrote that to understand law and its relationship to power in Africa we must depart from the Weberian model of the state, of law, and of bureaucracy. Law in these states was not based on determinate rules which provided bases for predicting or evaluating authoritative decisions. He identifies two features of both the colonial and the postcolonial state in Africa – bureaucracy and coercion. Bureaucracy, he writes, is completely dominant in a context in which there is no such thing as civil service neutrality. Ghai confirms that in developing countries 'general norms play a secondary role'. Both socialist and capitalist economies in developing countries, he writes, 'are essentially administered economies, where the license is king and discretion is the norm. . . . As the state is the primary instrument of accumulation, corruption is endemic, woven into the very fabric of the apparatus of the state'. Clientelism, sustained by regular favours, is the basis of political support; public control and accountability are absent (Ghai 1993, 192–193).

A third aspect is the inheritance of legal pluralism made up of customary and common law sectors in the new states and the ambition to unify legal systems under a Western legal model (Chanock 1985, 48–67). The effect of the shifting nature of African law and the absence of a shared common law, and the view that African law could not be the ultimate source of citizens' rights, hugely inhibited the growth of societies oriented to the rule of law. Much of what I have written has concerned the ways in which customs and traditions relating to law and culture had been manufactured in colonial and postcolonial Africa. In my first book on African law (Chanock 1985), I aimed not only to write about the ways in which Africans developed their law in the spaces provided by British colonialism, but to illustrate the social experience of law under colonialism. That study called into question the definition of African law as 'customary' and has been followed over the years by a literature which interrogates the ideas about the customary and its closely linked companion, the cultural. In a later book I focused on the role of law in the creation of Africa's most comprehensive, ruthless, and racist colonial state, the Union of South Africa (Chanock 2001). Africans had little space here to define their law, and, indeed, a special African system of law, oppressive in content and intent, was defined for them by the colonial state. But my scepticism regarding 'customary law' in its colonial presentations does not mean that I am sceptical about the ways in which Africa's changing social formations have been developing legal cultures and ideas that are more meaningful to them than the legal categories of Justinian, which are the basis of Western systems of common law. It is in this direction, towards an understanding of an African common law in a new context, that we might fruitfully look to ground the constitutionalising of Africa (see also Chanock 2008).

We should also consider in this context the effect of the customary law of property, with its basis of administrative discretion rather than fixed property rights, on the rule of law more generally. We do not have to accept any version of a neoliberal philosophy on the importance of property rights to democracy to see that when access to the most important part of livelihood, land, is dependent on the discretion of authorities, rather than legal rights, it has an effect on the idea of a rule of law. All African peasants were dependents rather than rights holders. In the decades after the end of empire, which was a period of emphasis on economic development through statist expansion and control, African law was marginalised even further, being identified with obstinate opposition to developmental objectives and the nation-state and its nation-building priorities. But the spectacular failures of the development states and the collapse of both their economic models and the ineffectiveness of their bureaucratic structures have reopened the field for the displaced law once known as customary law. Simultaneously, there is an increased tendency to look to the market for solutions to the problems of resource distribution and management.

The issue here is different from that of finding a place for regional and local ways of doing things within the ordered and functioning states to the north. Where states do not function, custom competes not with 'law' or with 'market' but with corruption, anarchy, and resource expropriation by uncontrollable nonstate actors. Custom contends not with 'law' or 'market', but with organised kleptocracy, with collapsing states, and with bandit economies (Chanock 2005). The extent to which indigenous African law, its language, ideas, and in particular its *processes*, can become the basis of a rule of law for Africa remains crucial.

E. ATTEMPTS TO RETURN TO CONSTITUTIONAL DEMOCRACY

In Ghana and Nigeria there were several efforts, accompanied by considerable violence, to replace military rule and the one-party state. This was a period in which West African politicians and lawyers focused creatively on ways to reconstitute a democratic state. Here it is worth considering the constitutional debates, the new constitutions developed in both Ghana (though with a mooted attempt to give local government traditional roots) and Nigeria, and the roles of the courts and judiciaries in both countries. Take for example the period following on the end of the Gowan regime in Nigeria, and the attempt to rebuild a new, complex constitutional state and the reasons for its failure in 1984. The Nigerian judiciary in this period displayed both courage and creativity as it worked with the new bill of rights, but the constitution itself collapsed under the weight of political corruption and conflict. This period in the Nigerian state remains as a stark warning to those who think that constitutions, bills of rights, and constitutional courts must necessarily remain permanent features of a polity once they are introduced. Instead we need to understand 'military constitutionalism' in West Africa, as well as constitutional debate and the new constitutional designs (Hutchful 1991). Two important features are worth commenting on: one is the reproduction of existing models of constitution, relatively uncritically in Ghana and after long and very well-informed consideration in Nigeria. Another is the failure of political parties to develop in Africa. Here Nigeria provides a story of exceptional interest in relation to the failure of party politics to develop – for example, in the amazing creation by the military government, prior to relinquishing power, of two entirely artificial parties, one to the left of centre and one to the right. We should also recall that in the 1980s, attempts to reach consensus on a new constitution collapsed over the question of the place of *shari'a* law. More generally, the end of the African one-party systems did not result in successful two-party or multiparty systems, but rather a series of stolen elections, and the hypocritical no-party regimes in Ghana and Uganda (and, ironically, in Africa's self-proclaimed constitutionalist success, South Africa, which is in effect a one-party state).

F. NEOLIBERALISM AND THE NEW ARCHITECTURE OF CONSTITUTIONALISM

After the Cold War, Africa experienced dramatic constitutional change, which returns us to a focus on the relationship between the international environment and state form in Africa. This period is marked by changes in the external environment and the effects of the so-called Washington consensus, with its determined effort to shrink the state and impose neoliberal economics to replace the various forms of African 'socialism'. The collapse of the socialist option and the end of state-dominated development changed the relationship between state and market. The shrinking state frames the development of a new constitutionalism. Once again there are attempts to revive constitutional states in Nigeria and Ghana, and there are changes in Tanzania moving from one-party socialist 'democracy' to a multiparty constitution (though it remains dominated by the same single party). This period also witnesses the reemergence of the human rights paradigm in African constitutionalism and the new roles of courts and bills of rights in these transitions (see Chanock 1999). Oddly, the latter were disappointingly weak in Nigeria, but for a while surprisingly strong in Tanzania (Peters 1997). Significantly, a different form of constitutional architecture, influenced by Lijphartian principles, becomes fashionable. Proportional representation and independent constitutional courts enter onto the African stage, so long dominated by Westminster's forms, along with the reality of one-party states and military rule (see Reynolds 2002). We also see the spectacular emergence of this form of constitutionalism in South Africa as apartheid collapses, as well as successes in democratisation in other parts of the world, (chiefly Asia) as well as failures (the Middle East).

G. FAILING STATES

This new era of African constitutionalism has been haunted, from its inception, by the spectre of failing states, from Somalia at one extreme to the genocide and conflicts of central Africa. Given this environment, it is important to review the place of an African constitutionalist tradition in attempts to create African democracies. Here we might consider the varying languages of African postcolonial politics ranging through the languages of revolution, the language of rights, and the languages of indigeneity. In contrast to the first wave of constitution-making, the later processes of constitution-making involve various forms of elite negotiation as well as attempts to involve citizens in processes in South Africa, Uganda, and Kenya. How might these renewed goals and values of constitutionalism play out in the post–Washington consensus era, considering issues such as what the goals are and whose they might be, the roles of the democratisation and rights industries, the influence of development experts and nongovernmental organisations (NGOs), and the emerging rule of law-based governance paradigm. Attention must be paid to the pressures of donor governments and the emergence of corruption as a major issue. There is particular need to focus on the role of lawyers and courts in fashioning the political discourse in what has been called 'democracy without choice' (see, e.g., Abrahamsen 2000). The differences between formalist and transformative judiciaries in South Africa and the rest of Africa are also important considerations to be assessed. In relation to difficulties of building the rule of law in weak and failing states, consideration must be given to issues of criminal justice and property rights. And, as the silver bullet of the South African constitutional example becomes tarnished, we need to consider the unresolved issues of one-partyism and opposition in African polities and their effects on the building of constitutionalism.

III. TOWARDS A CONCLUSION

What can be said constructively now? One cannot simply pretend that the past half century has not happened. Each new attempt at reconstructing the state must start from here and not from a blank page. One cannot undo the weak and artificial states, the corrupt patrimonial tradition of politics, or the legacies of genocide and poverty. But are there pathways to constitutionalism not yet fully explored?

The most obvious African idea about constitutionalism has been a rejection of multipartyism. First it was based on the simple proposition that it was a waste of scarce resources, and also that it undermined nation building. Then added to this was the proposition that it was contrary to indigenous and customary ways of dealing with conflicts, which were portrayed as essentially consensual. Dictatorial regimes made much of this deliberately fantasised version of an African past which was in reality filled with bloody conflict and domestic oppressions. This version of indigenous political thinking needs to be discarded.

A. WHAT ABOUT OTHERS?

1. *Cul-de-sacs*

Bertrand Badie has written, 'The years following decolonisation clearly revealed the failure of all mimicry in the constitutional area. Everything indicates, however, that mimicry has not ceased and that it has even intensified. . . . It is as if the logic of globalisation goes from error to error, depriving political societies of the means to correct themselves.' Escape from the prison of imported institutions seems all but impossible (Badie 2000, 2–3). In addition we must ask whether African elites want constitutional democracy despite the current lip service paid to it. Michael Crowder (1987) noted more than twenty years ago that the dream of liberal democracy in Africa was a Western one, not shared by the postcolonial elites. Paul Collier (2009/2010; Collier and Sambanis 2005) has observed that in 'impoverished little countries' (2009/2010, 1) democracy has had the opposite effect than it had in rich ones, in that it increased the risk of political violence rather than diminishing it (20). Presidents for life; 'no-party' states, the new version of one-party states (Uganda) and Western-accepted pin-up military regimes (Rwanda) remain features of the African scene. Constitutionalism, the establishing of a state in which power is limited by law, has not been the focus of constitutional scholars. Instead human rights scholars focus on the idea of transformative judiciaries delivering rights, including social and economic rights, while societies experience rising violence and states are disintegrating into arenas of endemic corruption. South Africa is a prime example here. Across the continent new 'democratic' and openly undemocratic regimes are partners in the international race to alienate and exploit Africa's mineral and land resources. Enhanced revenues from these developments, as well as the continuation of aid to African states, maintains the states' freedom from the political constraints imposed by having to seek revenues from their populations and therefore to govern by consent. At the same time, the US-inspired structures of security laws and extralegal actions provide space for governments to inhibit civil liberties regardless of the ambits of bills of rights.

2. *Directions*

One of the conclusions that can be drawn from the story is that constitutional design should be far less relevant than it was thought to be during the 1990s when it became such a fashion. Creating perfect institutions, necessary as they may be, is not sufficient to make them work. From a lawyer's point of view, it is the lack of any underlying sense of a rule of law that concerns me. I say from a lawyer's point of view because there are so many other powerful issues relating to poverty, the still-unsolved issues of identity, and the winner-takes-all – including life – attitudes towards political conflict and elections. The rule of law cannot be built from the top down, but some attachment to it must inhere in the society itself. A starting point to write in a meaningful way about democracy and an African constitutionalist tradition may be awareness of the issues surrounding the *languages* and *translation strategies* in which this can be expressed.

In law language is often used 'not to find the truth but to serve interests' (Kantorowicz, quoted in Grossfeld 2003, 156). In nearly all African countries only a very small proportion of the people speak or are literate in the languages of constitutions, bills of rights, and constitutional discourse. For most, these are meaningless. Mazrui writes that 'the continued reliance on imperial languages may itself have become a primary cause in the failure of democracy and human rights culture to take root on the continent' (2004). Missionaries were well aware that translation of the Bible was the key to conversions, and it is odd that lawyers and human rights activists have not seen that local languages are the key to the rule of law. One might think of the South African case in which just one African word, *ubuntu*, has given rise to a wave of consequential thinking for constitutional jurists. One must wonder what effects there would be if Constitutional Court judges in South Africa gave judgements in African languages. Neither constitutionalist concepts nor the languages of rights have until now been grounded in local languages.

At the beginning of my story, the dominant African *political* language was one of anticolonial revolution. It had little to say about how Africans would govern themselves. When it did, it was in an imported language – that of socialism – which became the dominant discourse of politics for many African states quite regardless of whether they followed socialist policies or practices. There also came into being a kind of language of indigeneity, which was used to defend or to promote an imagined tradition of African democracy that was based on consensus. The purpose of this traditional discourse was, like that of the socialist discourse, to justify and support authoritarian regimes. The language of liberal democracy, according to which the constitutions were framed, was virtually absent from politics, as was a language of individual rights and human rights. These become common among elites only in the post–structural adjustment era. But the discourse of human rights, like the discourse of socialism, is primarily an imported discourse, which is not easily and with transparency translated into vernacular languages (Englund 2006). Very little of the African statute book, which is remarkably similar from country to country, is available in any vernacular.

The weakness of the African states, most especially in the post-restructuring period, ushered in an invasion of foreign NGOs, funded often by former colonial powers, and entrusted with both quasi-governmental functions and the task of spreading the new political concepts of individual rights which the neoliberal world demanded. The NGO/bill of rights discourse also replaces the language of politics (Englund 2006; Krige 2011). The NGOs' forms of transnational governance, again drawing on foreign languages and concepts, have not connected well with communities. As Englund writes, 'empowerment through relationships with others is rendered unthinkable. Individuals and communities are expected to be self-sufficient and free subjects, rights bearing, even when those rights yield few material entitlements' (2006, 10). British colonialism brought the common law to Africa; international human rights law brought another wave of implacable individualist concepts. Rights discourse is not easily integrated into the indigenous concepts of relationships that it must connect to if it is to be the basis of a rule of law. It is by no means original to insist on the importance of establishing the rule of law in third-world states. The United States and the World Bank, for example, have spent copiously on rule of law programs, which concentrated on the building of court-houses, the provision of computers, and the training of court personnel (Carothers 1998). But the motivation has been the desire to find security for property rights and capital investment, not to focus on the underlying concepts of law in the affected societies.

What must be done is to reopen, seriously, what were open questions at the time of decolonisation: the role of African law and the issue of legal pluralism. The earlier failure was based on basic misconceptions about customary law. The first was that it was archaic and that it must (or would) disappear in a necessarily modernising state and society. The second was that it was a system of ancient *rules* and less about *processes* for settling disputes, and still less a way of expressing ideas about relation-ships: ideas that would change as a changing economy and society produces new ideas about relationships. If we abandon the idea of past and rule-bound custom, what can be said? There is little doubt that growing integration into varying forms of capitalism has individualised many African law concepts. Nor, I think, is there doubt that social change is changing gender relationships and therefore law. African law as common law would have the inestimable advantages of being linguistically comprehensible, and closer to local ideas of identity, and of relationships, than foreign common law. It has the potential, particularly as threats to the limited security provided by customary land law have intensified, to spread a more general sense that security might lie in law.

African states like Ghana and Tanzania have already experienced false and violent experiments with returns to traditional ways of governing. I do not advocate yet another such turn. But if we understand 'custom' as newly and continuously produced by ongoing economic and political processes, one can see what a powerful force it is in the kinds of democratic polities that may be built in Africa. It is about democratic assertions and attempts at control of the lower levels of politics in countries in which the paper institutions of Western forms of local government do not work except as the means of corrupt accumulation of public funds by those who control them. Constitutionalism, in the sense of a government limited by law, cannot just float above (and indeed contradict) the ways in which laws are actually administered, and the perceptions of lawfulness in the society as a whole. An African common law might increasingly provide the link between the worlds of the constitutional forms and the democratic practices that these forms are supposed to provide.

In this context we can consider Tully's *Strange Multiplicity* (1995) in which the basic question raised is whether a modern constitution can 'recognise and accommodate cultural diversity' (1). There is, he notes, widespread constitutional nationalism as well as the idea that a constitution can 'avoid recognising any culture' – 'Esperanto constitutionalism' (7). This has led to wars of repression, forced assimilation, exile, extermination, and genocide. He contrasts the 'historical formation of modern constitutionalism: the empire of uniformity' (58) with the 'ancient' constitution, which was a 'historical assemblage of laws and customs' (59–60). The new constitutionalism, based on the popular sovereignty of equal individuals, eliminated 'cultural diversity as a constitutive aspect of politics'. Over the past three centuries, the 'extremely complex language' of constitutionalism – 'a vast network of conventions, . . . a relatively narrow range of familiar uses of these terms' (government, popular sovereignty, people, self-government, citizen, rule of law, rights, equality, recognition, and nation) 'has come to be accepted as the authoritative political tradition of interpretation of modern constitutional societies' (36). This 'prevailing language' of modern political theory has 'elbowed aside entire areas of the broader language of constitutionalism' (37).

As a result, Tully continues, within the dominant language of modern constitutionalism, 'it is difficult to conceptualise the sovereign people as already constituted in customary ways by the authority of their different cultures because culture is conceived as relative to a stage of historical development. ... It is even more difficult to conceptualise the people as agreeing to establish a constitutional association that recognises and accommodates cultural diversity by arrangements of legal and political pluralism. ... It is taken for granted that the unity of constitutional association consists in a centralised and uniform system of legal and political authority ...'(83).

When we think about law in Africa today, we must do so in the context of a population which is overwhelmingly young, and societies in which Islam and forms of evangelical Christianity, neither of which are focused on human rights and gender equality, are growing far faster than engagement with the states' politics of democracy and law. The enactment of the spectacular and internationally lauded bills of rights, and the role of distinguished jurists on the newly established Constitutional Courts, has been primarily responsible for the illusions which lawyers have fostered about the nature of African government. But I do not think that anyone needs reminding that providing for rights in this manner is not reflected in the social practices and daily lives of the rights bearers except in exceptional circumstances. High rates of violent crime (and high rates of incarceration), high rates of homophobic violence, and violence against women persist. Policing has in many states essentially lost the trust of citizens who prefer the private security offered by gangs or, in upmarket zones, security firms (Joireman 2011). States have been indifferent to or unable to deal with the spread of HIV/AIDS for many years. On the level of government administration, corruption is endemic. The problematic relationship between constitutionalised rights and the lives experienced by those who are allegedly governed by them is a primary part of addressing the question of the problematic relationship between African law and constitutionalism. Indeed, taking the area of rights out of the activist political arena and handing it to an imagined apolitical apex judiciary may be one of the reasons for its weakness.

Nonetheless, as long as African languages are spoken, legal ideas which are not derived from the Western tradition will persist and develop. In her recent study, Oomen (2005) shows how in rural South Africa 'law' is not a systematisable set of rules and prescriptions. While there has developed a form of legal pluralism, the law that is invoked cannot really be described as 'customary' if that means a return to the past. It is a melange of old, new, and political (see esp. ch. 6). Oomen writes of 'the importance of the local political arena in the creation of living law, the willingness to invoke state laws and procedures in some cases and to set them side in others, the essentially negotiated character of local law and its embedment in soil and political circumstances' (202). She rejects the word 'customary' in describing living or local law, and observes that 'ideal norms ... more often than not turn out to be exceptions rather than rules' (203).

De Sousa Santos has observed that the 'recovery of the traditional in Africa today is, in general, a very modern exercise. Far from being an alternative to modernity, it is the expression of a claim to an alternative modernity. It is a form of globalisation which presents itself as a resistance to globalisation' (de Sousa Santos, Trindade, and Meneses 2003, 34). From a slightly different perspective, Appadurai has urged that we think of cultures' orientation towards the future. He writes that in taking this approach 'we run into some deeply held counter conceptions. For more than a century culture has been viewed as a matter of one or other kind of pastness – the key worlds are habit, custom, heritage, tradition. . . . In other words the cultural actor is a person from and of the past . . .' (Appadurai 2004, 60). His emphasis instead is on present actors, on cultural dissensus, on the leaky boundaries of cultures, and on the 'deeply ambivalent relations' that the poor have to the dominant norms of their cultures (61–65). He suggests instead that we '*place futurity, rather than pastness, at the heart of our thinking about culture*', and that 'Culture is a dialogue between aspirations and sedimented traditions' (84; my italics). It is from this dialogue, including a dialogue with the imported individualising discourse and centralising ambitions of bills of rights, that we might find the basis for a rule of law and, ultimately, a constitutional democracy. Grossfeld writes, '*Law is a part of a wider web of communications, references, experiences, and hopes, within a culture, the participants in which instinctively feel their place at any given moment*' (Grossfeld 2003, 156; my italics). Until Africans approach this instinctive feeling of place within their law, a rule of law, and therefore constitutionalism, is chimerical. It can be approached best, I think, through *legal processes* with which people are culturally and linguistically familiar and that are a part of participatory democracy, rather than imposed instruments of a nominally representative state and a globalised human rights law.

The pachyderm present in the room in relation to discussions of local law and human rights is the issue of gender. The primary suspicion of those who question plural legal orders, whether they be religious or customary culturally based laws, is that these will betray the gender equality that is now supposed to be sustained by the new constitutional and human rights orders. This creates an ahistorical opposition between modern state legal orders which promote gender equality and traditional ones which sustain gender inequalities. It also places the issues related to gender into the legal rather than the political realm. Gender equality is not intrinsically related to modern constitutionalism, or even to the evolution of human rights statements. It is the product of long and intense political struggles to establish such things as the rights of women to franchise, equality of rights in family law, and protection against discrimination in the workplace. In the Western world these are not old rights, but not wholly established ones, and have, over the past few decades, been fiercely contested. Thus they are not culturally embedded in Western constitutional or legal forms or religions, but are a part of an ongoing struggle produced by specific political and economic developments.

Again, I do not anticipate that there are many who would not recognize the novelty of legal and ideological support for gender equality in the contemporary

Western world whose ideas of constitutional rights have now become, in form, universal. I would expect also that the complexity of the struggles, and the differing ideologies and institutions – religious and secular – which have brought about these changes, would be clearly acknowledged. But this appears not to be the case when the same eyes are cast upon cultures, religions, and societies which appear to stand in the way of implementing gender equality. These are essentialised and unified and placed outside of history and political conflict. But, like Western societies, they are within history and multivocal. The subordinated legal orders, which appear to have a problematic relationship with constitutionalism, are the products of history and change, and reflect the political and economic forces, and the goals, which people experience and pursue. They are not the legal orders of the economically powerful and prosperous, and represent, therefore, the efforts of the poorer parts of societies to express their interests. They are ideologically various and open to change, change which is more likely to be embedded in changed behaviour than brought about by the edicts of the judiciaries of violent and kleptocratic states.

It may have struck readers attentive enough to have reached this point that there is something paradoxical in arguing that the way to constitutionalism is through a rule of law, and not simply through a bill of rights, while also arguing that the law needs to be less of a foreign-inspired, rule-oriented law and more of a process- and context-oriented one embedded in local cultures. Instead of thinking of African culture as static or represented by those claiming a particular form of traditionalism, we must be prepared to acknowledge the dramatic shifts that are evidenced in the increased competition for rural resources, the explosive urbanisation of African societies, the power of new religious formations, the growth of violence, and the increasing cosmopolitisation of Africa's cities as Africans migrate across Africa and around the world. Thinking about a role for law, traditionally conceived, to contend with these forces is difficult. But just raising this issue helps us to ask the crucial question about how law has been conceived in the colonial and postcolonial eras in Africa. Colonial administrators were not lawyers, but they ran courts. They thought of law as being made up of simple rules to be applied to disputes, and of courts as institutions to be obeyed. They were full of contempt for what Weber had called 'Khadi courts', which were substantively oriented, rather than formalistic. The successor states thought in the same way, and this conception was behind the poorly conceptualised restatements of customary law which were done in ex-British colonies. But the whole trajectory of the law and society movement has been away from the identification of 'law' with rule certainty and force. So can we think of a rule of law which is not a rule of rules?

We might instead think of a rule of law on at least three levels. One 'law' will be a developing set of ideas which may be usable in the processual settling of disputes in the violently contending economic and social world described earlier. A second would be a more formal and forceful law to constrain the power of politicians and bureaucracies, while a third would be the combination of the formal and the informal which characterises international economic and human rights law. Indeed, a process- and context-oriented law at the first level may well be a necessary part of the creation of a rule of law culture, which must underlie a rights culture, precisely because it is one which people can fully inhabit, and one which is less a creature of postimperial national and international elites. For more than half a century, human rights lawyers globally have facilitated and celebrated the migration of human rights from the realms of political ideas and common law upwards into 'constitutionalised' instruments at both national and international levels. This has taken rights out of the realms of political culture and underlying law, and placed them in the hands of legal elites, national and international. For those who care about human rights, this migration should be a matter of serious concern.

Having rethought 'law', we must also rethink 'democracy'. Now is the time to come back to Collier's observations about how democracy can increase political violence, and Tully's remarks about the exclusion of pluralism from constitutional thinking. The form of democracy that has increased violence has been the one exported primarily from the United Kingdom, France, and the United States (see, for example the *Journal of Democracy*): thinking oriented around central government is the core of the failure. We need to focus more, in this age of post-sovereignty, on democracy that is not based on violently contested winner-takes-all central elections, but which is functional in localities, and in which the constitutional structures are founded on real power at local levels. These are by no means new thoughts. However, a strong central state has for too long been identified by progressive thought as being the agency through which the transformation of the lives of the poor and oppressed will be accomplished. It is time to let go of this model, just as it is time to let go of the idea that law and rights are about enforceable rules.

REFERENCES

Abrahamsen, Rita. 2000. *Disciplining Democracy: Development Discourse and Good Governance in Africa*. London: Zed Books.

Ake, Claude. 1996. *Democracy and Development in Africa*. Washington, DC: Brookings Institution.

Amissah, Austin. 1981. *The Contribution of the Courts to Government: A West African View*. Oxford: Clarendon Press.

Appadurai, Arjun. 2004. "The Capacity to Aspire." In *Culture and Public Action*, edited by Vijayendra Rao and Michael Walton, 59–84. Stanford: Stanford University Press.

Badie, Bertrand. 1992/2000. *The Imported State: The Westernisation of the Political Order*. Translated by Claudia Royal. Stanford: Stanford University Press.

Carothers, Thomas. 1998. "The Rule of Law Revival." *Foreign Affairs* 77(2): 95–106.

Chanock, Martin. 1985. *Law, Custom, and Social Order: The Colonial Experience in Malawi and Zambia*. Cambridge: Cambridge University Press.

Chanock, Martin. 1999. "A Post-Calvinist Catechism or a Post-Communist Manifesto? Intersecting Narratives in the South African Bill of Rights Debate." In *Promoting Human*

Rights through Bills of Rights, edited by Philip Alston, 392–428. Oxford: Oxford University Press.
Chanock, Martin. 2001. *The Making of South African Legal Culture, 1900–1936: Fear, Favour and Prejudice*. Cambridge: Cambridge University Press.
Chanock, Martin. 2005. "Customary Law, Sustainable Development and the Failing State." In *The Role of Customary Law in Sustainable Development*, edited by Peter Oreback, Fred Bosselman, Jes Bjarup, David Callies, Martin Chanock, and Hanne Petersen, 338–383. Cambridge: Cambridge University Press.
Chanock, Martin. 2008. "Cutting and Sewing: Goals and Means in the Constitutionalist Project in Africa." In *Law and Rights: Global Perspectives on Constitutionalism and Governance*, edited by Penelope E. Andrews and Susan Bazilli, 47–63. Lake Mary, FL: Vandenplas.
Collier, Paul. 2009/2010. *War, Guns and Votes: Democracy in Dangerous Places*. London: Vintage.
Collier, Paul, and Nicholas Sambanis, eds. 2005. *Understanding Civil War: Evidence and Analysis, Vol. 1: Africa*. Washington, DC: World Bank Publications.
Crowder, Michael. 1987. "Whose Dream Was It Anyway? Twenty-Five Years of African Independence." *African Affairs* 86(342): 7–24.
de Sousa Santos, Boaventura, Joao Carlos Trindade, and Maria Paula Meneses, eds. 2003. *The Landscapes of Justices in Mozambique*. Coimbra: Centre for Social Studies.
Englund, Harri. 2006. *Prisoners of Freedom: Human Right and the African Poor*. Berkeley: University of California Press.
Ghai, Yash. 1993. "The Theory of the State in the Third World and the Problematics of Constitutionalism." In *Constitutionalism and Democracy: Transitions in the Contemporary World*, edited by Douglas Greenberg, Stanley Katz, Melanie Beth Oliviero, and Steven C. Wheatley, 186–196. Oxford: Oxford University Press.
Ghai, Yash, and J. P. W. B. McAuslan. 1970. *Public Law and Political Change in Kenya*. London: Oxford University Press.
Ginsburg, Tom, and Rosalind Dixon, eds. 2011. *Comparative Constitutional Law*. Cheltenham, UK: Edward Elgar Publication (e-book).
Grossfeld, Bernhard. 2003. "Comparatists and Languages." In *Comparative Legal Studies: Traditions and Transitions*, edited by Pierre Legrand and Roderick Munday, 154–194. Cambridge: Cambridge University Press.
Hutchful, Eboe. 1991. "Reconstructing Political Space: Militarism and Constitutionalism." In *State and Constitutionalism: An African Debate on Democracy*, edited by Issa G. Shivji, 183–201. Harare: SAPES Books.
Joireman, Sandra F. 2011. *Where There Is No Government*. New York: Oxford University Press.
Journal of Democracy. 1990–2013. Baltimore: Johns Hopkins University Press.
Krige, Detlev. 2011. "Review of Steven L. Robins, *From Revolution to Rights in South Africa: Social Movements, NGOs and Popular Politics after Apartheid*." H-Net Reviews. https://www.hnet.org/reviews/showrev.php?id=32880.
Mazrui, Alamin. 2004. "Globalisation and Some Linguistic Dimensions in Africa." In *Human Rights, the Rule of Law, and Development in Africa*, edited by Paul Tiyambe Zeleza and Phil McConnaughay, 52–70. Philadelphia: University of Pennsylvania Press.
Nwabueze, Benjamin O. 1973. *A Constitutionalism in the Emerging States*. London: C. Hurst.
Nwabueze, Benjamin O. 1974. *Presidentialism in Commonwealth Africa*. London: C. Hurst.
Nwabueze, Benjamin O. 1977. *Judicialism in Commonwealth Africa*. London: C. Hurst.
Nwabueze, Benjamin O. 1985. *Nigeria's Presidential Constitution 1979–1983: The Second Experiment in Constitutional Democracy*. London: Longman.

Okoth-Ogendo, H. W. O. 1993. "Constitutions without Constitutionalism: Reflections on an African Political Paradox." In *Constitutionalism and Democracy*, edited by Douglas Greenberg, Stanley Katz, Melanie Beth Oliviero, and Steven C. Wheatley, 65–82. Oxford: Oxford University Press.

Oomen, Barbara. 2005. *Chiefs in South Africa: Law, Power and Culture in the Post-Apartheid Era*. Oxford: James Currey.

Peters, Chris Maina. 1997. *Human Rights in Tanzania: Selected Cases and Materials*. Koln: Rudiger Koppe Verlag.

Prempeh, H. Kwasi. 1999. "A New Jurisprudence for Africa." *Journal of Democracy* 10(3): 135–149.

Reynolds, Andrew, ed. 2002. *The Architecture of Democracy: Constitutional Design, Conflict Management and Democracy*. New York: Oxford University Press.

Tully, James. 1995. *Strange Multiplicity: Constitutionalism in an Age of Diversity*. Cambridge: Cambridge University Press.

Young, Crawford. 1994. *The African Colonial State in Comparative Perspective*. New Haven: Yale University Press.

Young, Crawford. 2012. *The Postcolonial State in Africa: Fifty Years of Independence, 1960–2010*. Madison: University of Wisconsin Press.

3

Human Rights Monitoring, State Compliance, and the Problem of Information

Sally Engle Merry[1]

How does ratifying a human rights convention affect a state's human rights compliance? This critically important question has inspired considerable scholarship in the past decade, some of it using sophisticated statistical techniques and a nuanced political analysis. Although the earliest work, by Oona Hathaway (2002), indicated that ratification had little impact on compliance based on a large, quantitative study, Beth Simmons's more recent quantitative work shows that there are improvements in compliance in certain kinds of states, based in part on the role of domestic actors (2009). It is, of course, very hard to answer this question, since state behavior depends on a wide variety of considerations, interests, and actors with their own concerns and motivations. The promotion or neglect of human rights is determined by multiple factors, and ratification of a treaty and the effect of its associated monitoring process can only be one of many determinants of compliance.

However, from the perspective of New Legal Realism, this is a question that cannot be answered only in terms of the laws themselves or the formal procedures of monitoring through treaty body hearings (the meetings between country representatives and the small committee of experts charged with monitoring compliance with the treaty, called a treaty body). Instead, it requires an analysis of the content of expectations, the political and economic situation of the countries under investigation, and the willingness or resistance of a country to accept treaty obligations. I argue that ethnographic observation of hearings and the analysis of texts and contexts of committee hearings on states' compliance with the terms of human rights treaties show that states differ in their enthusiasm for the various obligations in human rights treaties. These hearings offer clues to states' willingness to comply with the treaties and areas of resistance. Compliance may well be related to the situated responses of countries to the particular demands of treaty body committees. This is

1 I am grateful to the National Science Foundation, Law and Social Sciences Program and Science, Technology, and Society Program for support for this research, #SES-0921368. I appreciate the insights I have gained from my collaboration with Benedict Kingsbury and Kevin Davis in our work on indicators and global governance and the comments of Ryan Goodman.

an approach that can be productively applied to understanding forms of quantification and indicators more broadly (Merry 2016).

I observed most of the treaty body hearings on the Convention on the Elimination of All Forms of Discrimination against Women (CEDAW) during 2001 and 2002 as well as three country reports in 2012, three country reports of the International Covenant on Economic, Social and Cultural Rights (ICESCR) in 2011, and one country report of the International Covenant on Civil and Political Rights (ICCPR) in 2006. Here I examine the interaction between members of treaty bodies, referred to as experts, and state delegations in hearings on two countries' periodic reports. The experts pose questions and critiques to the state delegation on a variety of topics, and delegations respond to the questions. The hearings last from six to nine hours, and often involve pointed questions as the treaty body committee grills the state delegation about their policies, programs, and success in complying with the treaty. This is a moment in the monitoring process when the state delegation grapples with the committee's numerous questions and critiques, often framed as requests for more information. My approach does not measure the effect of the treaty on state behavior, but does suggest that there are a variety of state reactions that reveal more and less willingness to comply with the demands of the treaty body. While the actions and comments of state delegations in New York or Geneva do not determine what states will actually do, they do provide some insight into the way states view these obligations.

My ethnography of country reports and hearings shows that states are more willing to accept some obligations than others. Those that represent development and modernity are often accepted, while those that deal with gender or minority discrimination can elicit resistance. Resistance occurs around issues that pose significant political challenges to the status quo or where there is little domestic interest in the issue. Acquiescence to the demands of the treaty is more common concerning issues such as improving health, education, and economic development. Such issues are politically popular for states seeking to become more modern.

Resistance sometimes takes the form of explicit refusal, but more often is expressed through failure to provide information about compliance in the report, failure to address the issue in the country report at all, or failure to respond to direct questions about the issue posed by the committee. The treaty monitoring process is, in effect, a struggle over information. Human rights monitoring depends on accurate and complete information in order to hold states accountable. Insofar as the major source of pressure for compliance comes from information on human rights performance, acquiring accurate and relevant information is essential. However, it is states that provide this information. The committee monitoring each treaty is largely dependent on the information a state provides in its country report and in its answers to questions posed by the committee in presessional queries and during the face-to-face meetings. This information is supplemented by international data collection efforts such as Multiple Indicator Cluster Surveys (MICSs) by UNICEF and

Demographic and Health Surveys (DHSs) funded by USAID. Committee members and reporting guidelines constantly press for more statistical data on performance. However, an examination of country reports and reporting guidelines, discussed later, shows very uneven use of this form of information by treaty bodies and by regions. Moreover, the human rights community itself is deeply divided about the use of indicators, particularly the composite forms that join multiple data sources together. Such measurements produce readily comparable measures that permit ranking and shaming, but at the price of a simplification and decontextualization that runs counter to human rights thinking.

Quantitative data plays a critical role in the monitoring process. Statistics such as the rate of maternal mortality for minorities or the number of prosecutions for trafficking provide an opening for questions. When this information is not provided, the experts on the committee must use other sources or are unable to ask pointed questions about discrimination or failure to prosecute traffickers. Country reports often fail to disaggregate data in the categories human rights bodies care about, such as gender or minority status. Thus, the ways countries do or do not provide data reveal the dynamics of resistance and acceptance of human rights obligations. Simply failing to provide disaggregated data is an effective way of concealing systemic discrimination.

After describing the treaty body process and its characteristic struggle over information, I will discuss several examples of resistance and acquiescence in treaty body hearings. I will then draw some conclusions about how the struggle over information and the practices of resistance and acceptance in the monitoring process provide insights into state compliance with human rights.

I. INFORMATION AND HUMAN RIGHTS MONITORING

At the center of human rights monitoring is a set of human rights treaties and committees whose task is to examine to what extent countries are complying with the terms of the treaties they have ratified. The system of human rights conventions developed after 1969 is a multilateral treaty regime with expert committees authorized to receive periodic reports from ratifying countries about their performance with relation to the conventions. Monitoring involves both hearing individual complaints sent to the committees for each convention and receiving and commenting on periodic reports filed by countries that have ratified these conventions. Treaty bodies hold hearings to discuss and respond to country reports, issuing concluding comments indicating areas of progress and problems yet to be resolved. During the 1980s and 1990s, treaty bodies developed their jurisprudence and working methods, gradually claiming more power and critical voice with relation to the state parties they were monitoring. Particularly during the post–Cold War period, treaty bodies were able to be slightly more critical of state performance. For example, since 1992 the Human Rights Committee, the treaty body that monitors compliance with the

ICCPR, has issued concluding observations that sometimes express the committee's "concern" or "deep concern" about state actions (e.g., Kretzmer 2010, 30).

Treaties cover a wide range of civil, political, social, economic, and cultural rights as well as the special situation of vulnerable groups such as racial minorities, women, children, migrants, and the disabled. The fundamental principles of all the treaties are equality, nondiscrimination, and protection of human dignity. A basic tenet of the human rights system is that the set of rights delineated in these conventions are interconnected and must be considered together. International human rights law is a system of multilateral treaties, in which states commit themselves to the terms of a treaty by ratification. Most treaties are ratified by 150 or more states out of a total of 196 (as of June 2014). The first treaty to come into force was the Convention on the Elimination of Racial Discrimination (CERD) in 1969, whose treaty body was created the same year. The Human Rights Committee to monitor the International Covenant on Civil and Political Rights (ICCPR) was formed in 1976, the committee to monitor the Convention on the Elimination of All Forms of Discrimination against Women (CEDAW) in 1982, the committees for the Convention against Torture (CAT) and the International Covenant on Economic, Social and Cultural Rights (ICESCR) in 1987, the committee for the Convention on the Rights of the Child (CRC) in 1990, Migrant Workers' Rights (MWR) in 2004, the Convention on the Rights of Persons with Disabilities (CRPD) in 2009, and the Convention for the Protection of All Persons from Enforced Disappearance in 2011. As of 2014 there were nine treaties in force with committees in operation.

After countries submit their periodic reports, they appear at a treaty body meeting in New York or Geneva to present the report and answer questions from the committee. Committees consist of ten to twenty-three members who are individual experts and do not represent their countries of origin, although they are chosen to be geographically representative. Experts are elected for four-year terms and participate in meetings of two or three weeks, twice or three times a year. They are chosen on the basis of their expertise in the subject of the treaty. They receive expense money but little or no salary. Some are academics, some have civil society experience, and some work for governments, often in the foreign service.

States that ratify human rights conventions voluntarily consent to the terms of the treaty, but retain their sovereignty. They have the option of not ratifying some of the terms of the treaty that they do not wish to accept at the time of ratification. Once a country has ratified a treaty, however, it is expected to adopt it into its domestic legal system. This does not always take place. Despite the parallels between national and international law, international law generally lacks some of the direct enforcement capacity of national law even though it exerts a similar moral and ethical power. The treaty body process is, consequently, a dance between the power and influence of the international legal order and the claims to sovereignty of nation states. Lines of power are ambiguous, and the authority of the committee is always subject to question. Sovereign states voluntarily subject themselves to public scrutiny and critique by a small, international group of individuals whose primary commitments are to the treaty itself, yet they sometimes resist this control. Although the exercise is intended to be a "constructive dialogue" and the treaty body does not render enforceable judgments, it does criticize states that have a poor human rights record. Yet the treaty body's arsenal is largely persuasion and a country's desire to maintain a good reputation for protecting human rights. Domestic organizations and actors play a critical role in promoting state compliance, both by providing information to the committee and by carrying its conclusions back to the country to use to pressure state officials (Simmons 2009). The tense contestation over authority and control in the treaty body process is a central feature of the process of monitoring state compliance with international human rights law. The hearings themselves, while very important in substance, sometimes become very detailed and tedious.

Information is the heart of the process. Ratifying countries are required to report their compliance with the terms of the treaty to the treaty body on a regular basis every four or five years. They satisfy this obligation through a country report that runs to 100 pages or more. The treaty body assesses the country's compliance with the treaty and issues a statement concerning areas where a country is doing well and areas that need further effort. In David Kretzmer's study of the development of the Human Rights Committee, he argues that one of its main accomplishments is creating accurate records of state parties' compliance with the ICCPR (Kretzmer 2010, 47). Yet, the treaty body is largely dependent on the country to provide information about its performance. Most treaty bodies invite reports and participation from nongovernmental organizations (NGOs) and receive some information from other United Nations agencies. They also rely on the knowledge of committee members, theoretically chosen on the basis of their expertise in the treaty. Since experts are selected to be geographically representative, some come from the same region as the reporting country and have regional knowledge. By and large, the details of a country's compliance with its legal obligations such as providing access to food, housing, health care, or protection from torture come from the country itself. The committees see their task as evaluating compliance with legal standards based on the data presented by states, civil society, international organizations, and their own expert knowledge of the country and region. They lack the resources to gather data themselves. The treaty body looks for problems that require state attention, usually focusing on vulnerable and marginal populations, while most countries endeavor to provide the most favorable account of their performance they can.

These are opposing goals that often lead to distrust (see Rosga and Satterthwaite 2009). In order to hold countries accountable, the treaty body needs reliable and extensive information. To avoid scrutiny and criticism, a country needs to withhold damaging information. Thus, acquiring accurate and relevant information is at the heart of the struggle over human rights monitoring. The treaty body cannot compel countries to provide accurate and relevant information, but can undermine a country's reputation as a human rights–respecting nation. In order to win that reputation, a country has to make some effort to provide information. In this delicate dance, the production and analysis of information take center stage.

Over the past thirty years, as the human rights legal system has matured, treaty bodies have constantly grappled with this problem of knowledge. Since the early 1990s, human rights scholars and treaty body members have advocated for greater reliance on indicators, primarily in the area of social, economic, and cultural rights rather than civil and political rights. Many of the treaty bodies routinely request statistical information, disaggregated into relevant categories such as gender for the convention on women (CEDAW) and age for the convention on the rights of the child (CRC). The committee monitoring the International Covenant on Economic, Social and Cultural Rights (ICESCR) asked for indicators in twelve of its twenty-one General Comments written between 1989 and 2009. Health, food, education, and social security are phenomena long subject to measurement, so it makes sense that indicators moved into human rights along this path. Committees working on discrimination against the rights of subgroups such as racial minorities, women, and children have also advocated using indicators. The Convention on the Rights of the Child (CRC) General Comment 5, for example, asks for indicators (Scheinin 2005, 13). Most of these indicators are simple ratios such as maternal mortality rates or rates of school enrollment disaggregated by gender and ethnicity rather than a composite human rights index. The Human Rights Committee that monitors the International Covenant on Civil and Political Rights (ICCPR) has been far less active in developing indicators and, even in recent meetings, rarely refers to them. Of the thirty-one General Comments on ICCPR, for example, only two ask for statistics in state party reporting (Scheinin 2005, 14). In its concluding observations, CERD has often said that a small number of complaints does not necessarily reflect the absence of a problem of ethnic discrimination (Scheinin 2005, 14). Since 2005, the Office of the High Commissioner for Human Rights (OHCHR) has worked with experts to create a more simplified and elaborate composite set of what are referred to as "illustrative indicators" (UN International Human Rights Instruments 2006, 2008; UN OHCHR 2012). Recommendations to use these indicators appear in the 2009 harmonized reporting guidelines for ICESCR and in the 2010 guidelines for the Human Rights Committee and the Committee for the Convention on the Rights of People with Disabilities. Most of the treaties' reporting guidelines advocate the use of disaggregated statistics.

Countries vary greatly in their provision of statistical data, however. A survey I did of the frequency of references to indicators in the country reports to the six major conventions over a recent three years indicates that reports to CRC, ICESCR, and CEDAW are much more likely to contain statistical data than reports to CAT, CERD, and ICCPR, and that countries in Latin America and Eastern Europe provide reports particularly rich in statistical data. This survey covered all country reports to the six major treaty bodies between 2007 and 2011 looking at the frequency of using the word "indicator" not in a title or table. These are mostly counts and ratios. On average, these 365 country reports included 4.6 references to indicators, but this varied greatly by treaty. ICESCR reports included an average of 9.2 indicators in each report, closely followed by CRC at 8.7 and CEDAW at 7.2. The reference to indicators by the civil/political rights treaties was far lower, with 2.5 for ICCPR and 0.4 for CAT. Surprisingly, CERD reports had a similarly low rate of 2.5. There are clearly differences in treaty body interest in statistics and in their encouragement to use them. ICCPR and CAT focus more strongly on legal issues and are less concerned with the number of violations than with their existence at all. At the same time, there are also variations in availability of relevant statistics. CRC is supported by UNICEF and its MICS surveys, intended in part to provide data relevant to CRC reporting. The social and economic data relevant to the rights in ICESCR and CEDAW are often provided for developing countries by DHS surveys as well as other development-focused or public health surveys.

Countries with more resources are better able to generate national data, either by census, survey, or administrative records. However, a cross-tabulation of frequency of indicator use and score on the Human Development Index (HDI) revealed no relationship. In fact, the lowest reference to indicators of any region is Europe, which has highly developed domestic statistics but chooses not to include them in reports. Instead, it appears that developing countries, perhaps eager to show how sophisticated their quantitative knowledge is, are most likely to use indicators.

Data by region support this argument. The highest average reference to indicators comes from Latin American countries and the Middle East, which included an average of 6.0 indicators per report between 2007 and 2011, followed by the Pacific including Australia and New Zealand at 4.7, Eastern Europe at 4.6, Asia at 4.2, Africa at 4.0, and Europe at a surprisingly low 2.6. This regional variation again suggests the importance of internationally generated indicators rather than national ones and the use of development-related indicators. Most of the indicators cited referred to social and economic factors.

Considering the treaty bodies separately, even stronger regional variations appear. For 2008–2011, ICESCR country reports varied from 14.8 indicator mentions in Latin America and 12.2 in Eastern Europe to 6.0 in the Pacific, 5.3 in the Middle East, 4.8 in Asia, 4.5 in Europe, and 3.8 in Africa. In contrast, the ICCPR country reports for the same time period ranged from 6.0 in the Pacific to 4.2 in Africa, 2.8 in the Middle East, 2.1 in Latin America, 2.0 in Asia, 1.9 in Eastern Europe, and 1.7 in Europe. Latin America and Eastern Europe are most likely to use indicators for CRC, and Eastern Europe and the Middle East for CEDAW. An examination of the relationship between these variations by region and the DHS and MICS surveys suggests that the use of indicators is higher among countries that have participated in these international survey regimes.

Indicators that specify the statistical and specific content of the broad obligations of the treaties serve to translate the general terms of the treaty into appropriate expectations given the specific histories, conditions, and resources of each country.

Countries differ greatly in their resources and institutional capacity to protect and promote human rights. Treaty body experts do not expect Sudan to provide the same level of education to its people as Switzerland, for example, but they do ask both countries to work on improving their educational systems and to avoid discrimination against particular populations such as women, the rural poor, or ethnic minorities. Regardless of a country's wealth, it has an obligation not to torture its members or to discriminate against racial minorities in its laws. Using indicators to translate the broad expectations of human rights treaties into specific state obligations facilitates monitoring. Indicators can be used to specify programs, policies, and outcomes that make sense for a particular country given its level of development and history, whether for badly treated minorities or inequalities in the position of women. Experts seek indicators on the condition of the Roma in Eastern Europe, for example, whether or not they appear in the country report. Finally, by using apparently objective, scientifically produced statistical data, treaty bodies can enhance their authority in rendering judgments about human rights compliance (see Rosga and Satterthwaite 2009, 289–293). Judgments are typically expressed through concluding comments, which provide the committee's assessment of each country's level of compliance with the terms of the treaty. Quantitative measures facilitate assessment of country effort and comparisons over time. They strengthen the authority of the treaty body, but at the cost of antagonizing countries.

Indicators as a technology of knowledge production do not fit easily into human rights monitoring (see Davis, Kingsbury, and Merry 2012). In many ways, treaty body monitoring is a tantalizing but difficult site for indicator use (see Landman and Carvalho 2010). Although treaty bodies use indicators to control more powerful states, states resist this control. They fail to provide indicators or offer ones that are not adequately disaggregated. Indicators provide a technology of power but not one divorced from other relations of power. Governance by indicators is more difficult when a weaker party mobilizes them to control a stronger party than when a stronger party uses them to control a weaker one. It is less effective when the monitor cannot itself connect the data to the indicator to produce charts and ranks. Human rights monitoring by treaty bodies is a situation in which the monitor is less powerful than the subject of scrutiny and is dependent on the governed for the information it requires. The monitor seeks to hold the country accountable, but does not have the power to enforce compliance or withhold resources. Instead, treaty bodies must rely on persuasion and threats to a country's reputation.

The power of the treaty body vis-à-vis any state varies with the state's vulnerability to international pressures such as aid and trade and domestic pressures within a country that might use a treaty body's report to mobilize opinion. The international setting can provide a space for NGOs to challenge their governments, and may exert pressure on some states, particularly those with active civil society, but the treaty body's ability to exert power over states is highly indirect and contingent. As Beth Simmons shows, countries with partially democratic transitional regimes are more vulnerable to domestic human rights mobilization than either stable autocracies or stable democracies (2009, 153). Without reliable information about a country's performance in relation to its treaty obligations, however, the committee can do little. Consequently, most of the discussion during the treaty body hearings consists of requests for further information, which the government delegation duly provides, at least to some extent. Some questions are not answered, and much of the requested data, disaggregated by race, gender, age, disability, and other criteria necessary to highlight the situation of vulnerable groups, is not even available.

II. THREE ORDERS OF INDICATORS

Indicators can be roughly divided into three orders, in a framework building on Michael Power's distinction between first- and second-order numbers (1999). As numerical representations, indicators range from simple counts of events or people to ratios to composites with greater interpretive depth and theoretical elaboration. First-order numbers are counts, as in population censuses or counts of unemployed workers or racial minorities. They are interpreted to the extent that they are organized into categories. Racial categories, for example, are classifications based on socially defined collections of individual traits. They vary in different contexts. Through the process of classification, naming, and counting, the categories become fixed and often naturalized. Bowker and Star show how widespread such classificatory systems are, and how often they are ignored or naturalized rather than understood as systems of ordering that shape the way people understand their worlds (1999). Yet, these systems are creations of particular actors who develop cultural categories by which others order their worlds.

Second-order numbers are ratios or percentages, such as maternal mortality, years of expected schooling per person, gross domestic product (GDP) per capita, or incidents of intimate partner violence per woman in a relationship over 12 months. These are essentially counts described in relation to other counts. However, they incorporate more interpretive work than do simple tabulations and make possible comparisons across countries. While it is hard to do a meaningful comparison of the raw number of maternal deaths among countries, it easy to compare rates of maternal death per birth. Ratios depend on the categorizations already created for first-order numbers.

Third-order numbers are composites made up of multiple data sources blended together and weighted to produce a single number or rank. They use different sources of data on the same thing and data on different characteristics merged into a single index or number. For example, the Human Development Index combines health, education, and income into a single score. The Doing Business Index relies on ten distinct measurements. The World Bank Global Governance indicators combine six aggregate indicator sets that reflect different dimensions of good governance: control of corruption, rule of law, voice and accountability, government effectiveness, political stability and absence of violence, and quality of regulation. Composite indicators define a concept, such as rule of law, and join multiple measures, which are sometimes of quite different things. It then merges them into a single score, tier, or rank.

Clearly, there is a trade-off: the simpler the end product, the more easily it is understood and digested and the greater its impact but the less well it reflects various facets of what it claims to measure. First- or second-order indicators are closer to the phenomena they claim to measure and require less interpretive work. GDP per capita, for example, depends on developing a concept of gross domestic product and an interpretive framework that emphasizes average income rather than variations in income per person. Composite indicators define more complicated concepts such as "human rights performance," "human development," or "freedom." They make significant theoretical claims based on substantial interpretive work. When a composite indicator attaches a concept such as "rule of law" to a series of measurements, it defines which concepts are relevant, how they are weighted in relation to each other, and what data sets should serve to measure these concepts. In other words, the indicator incorporates a theory about the rule of law. If composites are then presented in an ordinal or ranking system, the indicator defines a scale of variation and locates particular countries or organizations on that scale. Composites offer a good deal of information packaged together in a convenient way. They permit broad comparisons using scores, tiers, or ranks. When they are arranged in a ranked hierarchy, composite indicators are a zero-sum game in which one country's advance produces another's decline. Most of the indicators included in country reports are counts and ratios, although those who can cite favorable rankings on composite indicators often do so as well. The strategic use of these different, more and less comparable, forms of statistical knowledge is part of the dance of knowledge production and resistance.

III. TREATY BODY HEARINGS: RESISTANCE AND ACQUIESCENCE

On July 19, 2012, the country delegation from Samoa presented its combined fourth and fifth periodic report to the Committee on the Elimination of All Forms of Discrimination against Women (2011), which monitors compliance with CEDAW, in the UN buildings in New York. The report, 84 pages long, responded to the concluding comments from Samoa's previous report and presented its accomplishments since then (CEDAW 2011). I sat in the cavernous room with perhaps forty people present, including NGO representatives as well as the twenty-three experts. The government delegation of seven individuals was led by the Associate Minister for Women, Community, and Development along with the chief executive officers of this ministry and the ministry of health. The executive director of the Samoa Law Reform Commission also attended. They were joined by three members of the Permanent Mission of Samoa to the United Nations. All were women except the head of the Permanent Mission. The hearing lasted about three and a half hours, largely taken up with questions posed by the experts and answers provided by the country delegation. After the hearing, the committee prepares Concluding Comments that assess the country's compliance with the terms of the treaty.

Although the state delegation replied to many of the questions it received with assurances that they were working on the problem by drafting legislation, creating a commission, establishing public awareness campaigns, or other strategies, one issue elicited resistance from the delegation: the low number of women in parliament. Article 7 of the convention specifies, in part:

> States Parties shall take all appropriate measures to eliminate discrimination against women in the political and public life of the country and, in particular, shall ensure to women, on equal terms with men, the right:
>
> a. To vote in all elections and public referenda and to be eligible for election to all publicly elected bodies;
> b. To participate in the formulation of government policy and the implementation thereof and to hold public office and perform all public functions at all levels of government.

However, the experts noted that the law states that in order to be elected to parliament, a person must achieve the status of *matai*, a chiefly title awarded within local communities. Relatively few women achieve this status. Only 15 to 20 percent of chiefly title holders are women. According to the report, as of 2009, only four out of forty-nine members of parliament were women (table 47.1, p. 29). Even though universal suffrage was instituted in 1991, relatively few women can run for parliamentary office, because few achieve *matai* status. In some villages, no woman can receive chiefly rank. The experts asked many questions about the *matai* system, arguing that it was plainly discriminatory against women and a violation of the terms of the treaty that the country had ratified. Although the experts criticized Samoa for many shortfalls, such as a lack of information on trafficking or any law prohibiting it, the delegation accepted these criticisms and pointed to its efforts and incremental progress. It noted, for example, that there is a crimes bill in process that will cover trafficking. The *matai* issue was different. Several experts noted that the law requiring *matai* status to run for parliament was clearly discriminatory given the low proportion of women with this status.

However, some members of the delegation took exception to the attack on the *matai* system. They argued that the awarding of chiefly status is a decision of the family and village. The system of self-governance by village councils and chiefs (*fono* and *matai*) had served well to maintain stability in the country. The village council and *matai* have a lot of responsibility for village affairs, and take care of victims of violence, for example. Villagers run their own communities, and although the government recognizes that the *matai* requirement for parliamentary election is a problem and is making an effort to communicate that women can take this role, they are not planning to change the legal requirement. The senior minister from Samoa, an elegant, gray-haired woman with the status of both political position and age, noted that if a woman comes from a village that does not allow women *matai* holders, she can go to another village that does where she also has roots and kin ties, and acquire the title that way. She pointed out that it is the family that decides who merits the title based on respect and the person's qualities, and the family decides if it should be given to a man or a woman without discrimination.

The head of the Samoan Permanent Mission to the UN, the only male member of the delegation and one of the very few men in the room, began by noting nervously that he was in a great minority. He defended the *matai* system as based on democracy and promoting stability. He said that at independence, Samoans voted for a mixture of traditional and modern features in their governance, and that keeping tradition has maintained stability. He argued that it is necessary to move step-by-step as people adjust to the convention. At the end of the day, women are part of the household, he said. He acknowledged that his wife takes care of his children and all the things in his life. It would take two days, he said, to explain to the committee the structure of the Samoan family and community in order for them to understand how it works. Samoa is happy to be part of the international community, he concluded, but it cannot move too fast. The head of the Law Reform Commission noted that they had not been asked to deal with the *matai* question.

One of the experts challenged the delegation, noting that this system undermines the legal rights of women and violates the convention that Samoa ratified without reservations. Another pointed out that when a country ratifies a treaty, it takes responsibility for conforming to the terms of that treaty. Although she acknowledged that conforming to the treaty can be a challenge, she said the committee was ready to help. One of the experts asked, "What is to be done? Either we insist that the *matai* requirement be abolished right away and face destabilization, or Samoa continues its practices which explicitly violate CEDAW." Another expert noted that women in Samoa are making demands for change themselves, asking for greater participation in village councils and parliament. The NGO shadow report from Samoa, shared with the committee before the hearing, made a similar argument. The report noted the abysmally small number of women in parliament, and pointed out that the ratio of female to male *matai* holders is one to three and that some villages prohibit women from holding titles while others ban even women title holders from participating in village council meetings. The NGO report argues that these village laws violate the rights of women to enter politics (NGO Shadow Report on the Status of Women in Samoa 2012, 10).

The ambassador responded to this set of critiques by pointing out that at independence, only people with chiefly titles could vote at all, and now all can vote. The restriction holds only for standing for election. Moreover, not all men hold titles, either. In response to the obligations of the convention, he argued that Samoans know they have responsibilities to the convention, but that it has to be localized so that people will own it. "We aren't dragging our feet," he insisted, "but we have to move at our own pace and develop home-grown solutions to our problems." He said that the prime minister himself said that he wanted to amend the constitution to get more women in parliament, an idea that came to him at a UN General Assembly meeting when he felt ashamed of his region when the Secretary General said that six of the nine countries with no women in parliament were from the Pacific. The prime minister is thinking about a constitutional amendment guaranteeing that 10 percent of members of parliament should be women. (This would mean, in effect, that there would be 4.9 women in parliament instead of the current 4.0, not a major transformation by any stretch.)

The committee reiterated its concerns in its concluding comments, drawing on the information presented in the NGO shadow report as well as the country report (CEDAW 2012). It complained that the promised quota of 10 percent of women in parliament was too low, that women were underrepresented at all levels of political and public life, and that the committee had "serious concern ... about the persistence of harmful norms, practices, traditions, patriarchal attitudes, and deep-rooted stereotypes regarding the roles, responsibilities and identities of women and men in all spheres of life, in addition to the State party's limited efforts to tackle such discriminatory practices" (CEDAW Concluding Observations 2012, 7; see also 4–5). The committee recommended that all women, whether or not they have a chiefly title, be given equal opportunities to participate in political and public life (CEDAW Concluding Observations 2012, 7).

Thus, the experts sought to pressure the delegation to change, but some of them resisted, in various ways. It is instructive that much of the critique hinged on the claim that only about 20 percent of *matai* holders were women. Here, the number opened up the state policy for critique, and allowed the committee to appreciate the sharp gap between 20 percent and 50 percent if there were no discrimination. Delegations that wish to escape such scrutiny can simply avoid providing the number, or even discussing the issue at all. I did not find the percentage in the report, but it did come up in the hearing. Thus, numbers enable critique. A strategy to resist scrutiny is to avoid providing numbers altogether. Other strategies are to provide so many that the readers are lost in the minutiae, or to frame the numbers to show improvement even if the initial situation is poor. In contrast to the *matai* issue, the committee's other suggestions were accepted with apparent agreement and a willingness to work on the problem. In particular, issues such as the high school dropout rate of teenage girls and the impossibility of abortion even for rape or incest were acknowledged as problems that the state is working on. The Crimes Bill of 2012, for example, if it passes, would allow abortion if a medical professional says there is a danger to the mother or the child. The state may raise the age of marriage from 16 to 18 for girls. While the delegation acknowledged a lack of information on rural women, it promised to try to improve.

Thus, the delegation responded quite differently to the various critiques of the committee. Most comments were accepted and the delegation promised to do more. In the case of women holding *matai* titles, however, there was clearly resistance and unwillingness to change. Not all of the delegation members were resistant, but all who spoke about it were. The head of the law reform commission could be read as regretting that she had not been asked to work on the problem. The NGO report shows that at least seventeen civil society organizations were concerned about women's political exclusion through the *matai* system. This example suggests that international scrutiny of women's subordination can strengthen the hands of those advocating for women's greater prominence in the government. Such scrutiny challenges ideas about chiefly titles and gender. However, the resistance of the delegation's leaders suggests that scrutiny alone will not necessarily change behavior. If scholars are interested in assessing how compliance with human rights treaties works, they need to consider how delegations respond to critiques. Clearly, some suggestions are more welcome than others. In this case, it appears that challenges to political traditions of village governance challenged conceptions of stability, the value of tradition, and patriarchal values held dear by at least some political leaders. On the other hand, there are rarely challenges to the demand for policies that promote development and modernity, goals that seem less politically charged and where winners and losers are less obvious.

A second example shows the significance of political considerations in resistance to human rights treaties. On May 2, 2011, Turkey presented its periodic report to the committee that monitors the ICESCR. Six representatives from Turkey sat together behind a raised desk at the front of an elegant room in the Palais Wilson in Geneva, overlooking the lake and the Swiss Alps beyond. I was part of a small audience of fifteen to twenty people. One committee member commended Turkey for its detailed report (158 pages long) and for following recent guidelines on report writing (Committee on Economic, Social, and Cultural Rights 2009). After this friendly beginning, however, he and the rest of the eighteen-person committee spent most of the nine hours of the hearing peppering the Turkish delegation with questions, some of which were quite pointed. They complained that the report was Turkey's first, and quite late, for example. While many questions received positive replies from the delegation, some evoked resistance. For example, when the committee asked Turkey to lift some of the reservations it declared when ratifying the convention, the delegation refused, saying that it was a matter of national sovereignty.

One of the issues that elicited particular concern from the committee was Turkey's declaration that the only minorities it recognized were Armenians, Greeks, and Jews. Many experts challenged this limited designation of minority status, saying that it was a serious problem. Several experts asked why Kurds, a large minority, were not included in minority status. Some queried the neglect of Roma as well. The experts were concerned about whether Kurdish people could complain about discrimination. One asked why the opportunity to have their own schools was limited to Greeks, Armenians, and Jews. Many of the questions used the statistics provided in the country report to highlight the issue. For example, one member asked: "Why do you have no laws on discrimination against minorities, particularly the Kurdish minority? The Turkish statistical office says that the Kurdish region has a lower proportion of women who work, higher maternal mortality rates, and lower health indicators than the rest of the country." The government delegation responded that it does not plan to change its policy, but that it does try to protect the rights of all minorities. The committee members replied that the Kurds needed more protection of their rights as a minority and that it was not sufficient to assert general rights for all citizens to protect minorities' rights. The experts insisted that Turkey expand its concept of minorities, but it was clear that the government was not willing to do this.

In their concluding comments, the committee repeated its critique of the limited scope of minority designation in Turkey and the denial of rights for unrecognized communities such as the Kurds, Roma, and Aramaeans. It urged the state party to recognize all its minorities and to provide them with equal opportunities (CESCR Concluding Observations 2011b, 3). However, Turkey objected to this comment, going so far as to publish an addendum to the concluding observations. This document states that Turkey regrets that the committee has not taken the information it provided adequately into account, especially with regard to minorities, and that it cannot accept the recommendation about naming new minorities as it is counter to the Treaty of Lausanne of July 24, 1923. Finally, the addendum adds that the Covenant on Economic, Social and Cultural Rights does not have any provisions about minorities (CESCR Comments by the Government of Turkey 2011a, 1). Thus, Turkey explicitly rejected this charge by the committee.

Another issue encountered similar resistance from the state delegation. A group of NGO representatives met with the ICESCR committee in advance of the country hearing and complained about the impact of a system of dams being built in Anatolia, in the eastern part of the country. They pointed to inadequate compensation, failure to restore livelihoods, and violations of rights to food and housing. The experts raised questions with the state delegation about the displacement of populations, the rights of those affected, the lack of concern with resettlement, the environmental damage, and the impacts on cultural heritage. One noted that Germany, Austria, and Switzerland withdrew from the project because conditions were not met and that there were many legal cases surrounding the dams. The delegation responded that this region needs development, but that they were not able to satisfy some of the groups who came to complain to this treaty body. They are taking into account legal opinions that Turkey was guilty of violations. However, they complained that because of their inability to satisfy those who were moved, they lost the foreign investors they had in the first place and had to turn to Turkish investors. This made it harder to compensate those who were moved. One delegate said that there is now a judicial process for compensation in place and he was confident that the compensation will be adequate. He argued that providing energy will help this underdeveloped region, and that this was the main object of the project. Thus, while the government acknowledged some problems in compensation, it resisted the wider set of complaints raised by the committee experts.

Sometimes resistance takes the form of a failure to provide information, particularly statistics. For example, when the committee urged Turkey to provide more information on its national action plan for gender equality and its efforts toward combating violence against women, two experts complained that their questions were not answered. One expert asked about whether the government would draw up a law on equality of opportunity given women's low participation in government and the labor force. She said that a plan of action is not enough. Several complained about a lack of information about women's status. For example, some asked for information about the effect of a development program on women's participation in the labor force. Some complained that the report provided no information about the extent of violence against women.

The delegation responded to concerns about domestic violence by describing new policies and laws, and noted that early marriage was allowed only with court or parental permission and that a new law banning forced marriage had been introduced for discussion five months ago. When the delegation provided statistics on domestic violence applications and guilty findings for 2009 and 2010, however, there were clearly very few (526 applications for domestic violence cases in 2009, 556 in 2010). A committee member from South Korea pointed out that these numbers were very low, and that South Korea has tens of thousands of domestic violence complaints every year. The delegation also defended its practices concerning honor killings by pointing to a new penal code that gives life imprisonment for honor crimes, with honor killing no longer considered a mitigating factor since 2005. It is now viewed as an aggravating element. One delegate said that there were twenty-three applications in 2009 and twenty were found guilty. Thus, the statistics provide an important supplement to the state's claim that it is dealing with such gender problems. Even if the numbers suggest that the success so far is small, the state acknowledges that it needs to make an effort to deal with these issues. In contrast, the delegation was clear that it would not change its policies on minorities or dam construction.

In contrast, when the committee pointed out that Turkey needed to have more women in parliament, more consultation with NGOs in the preparation of the report, more punctual reporting, and a more human-rights-focused foreign policy, the Turkish delegation readily agreed and described its efforts. They said that there will be elections in a month and that the number of women candidates is higher than in the past. One delegate noted that his boss, a woman, was working on a global summit meeting on gender equality.

Similarly, when Moldova reported to the ICESCR committee the day after Turkey, the committee used the information it provided in the country report to point out that Moldova's problems included having too many pensioners in its population, a low birth rate, a shortage of water and sewer systems, a high infant mortality rate, and widespread domestic violence. It urged the government to tackle these problems by building new water and sewer systems, passing a law against domestic violence, and other steps. The delegates accepted these comments and indicated it was working on these problems. They made clear that they sought greater integration with Europe and wanted to pursue policies that would make Moldova more like Europe. While Moldova does not have the resources to provide adequate services for its population, it accepts that it is a good idea to provide health care, social security, food, housing, and education.

Another example of resistance to treaty body comments by a country delegation occurred in the early 2000s CEDAW hearing of Fiji's country report. The committee expressed concern about the use of the traditional practice of reconciliation among families, called *bulubulu*, for rape. While the concern in the country report was that this practice was being used by defendants to pull their cases out of court and into informal processes, the committee complained more broadly about the use of a traditional reconciliation process for rape. It appears that the committee misunderstood the country report. The reaction of the state delegation, both at the time and in subsequent conversations with me, was that *bulubulu* was a fundamental feature of Fijian village life, rarely used for rape in the village context, and should not be eliminated (see Merry 2006 for more details). This hearing took place during a period of growing Fijian nationalism and hostility toward the immigrant Indian population in the country. Fijian nationalism included a celebration of traditional Fijian cultural practices. Thus, support for *bulubulu* from the delegation reflected the political situation of the time. Similarly, when the CEDAW committee pressed India to develop a uniform civil code for marriage during a period in which this long-standing feminist demand was being mobilized by the Hindu right to foment anti-Muslim sentiments in the country, the state delegation resisted the demand by failing to answer the questions about it (Merry 2006).

In the case of Turkey and Samoa, as with these other countries, some criticisms engender opposition, some reveal small and not particularly effective efforts, and some elicit a strong commitment. Commitment seems greater when the actions further the creation of an economically and politically modern state. These examples indicate that it is possible to see, in the texture and flow of country reports and human rights hearings, where countries accept these suggestions and where they resist them. If we are to understand compliance with human rights norms, it seems useful to examine these specific reactions to the conventions. Resistance occurs where changes would destabilize political relationships, particularly along the lines of gender inequality or minority subordination. Focusing on sites of resistance highlights the otherwise widespread acquiescence to the ideas of the treaties, particularly those of development and improvements in health, education, and well-being of a population. Acceptance of these goals does not mean effective efforts, of course, but it does suggest that there is a normative agreement with some – but not all – of the goals.

This comparison also indicates that there are differing modes of resistance to the terms of the conventions. One is explicit refusal to change policies. A second is a failure to provide information, particularly statistical information. It is notable that the availability of statistical data provides an opening for committee members to ask about the effects of a law or program, or to compare one country's performance with another. Obviously, ratios accomplish this goal more effectively than counts, and composites and ranks even more so. Even when a country accepts the goals of the treaty, statements about efforts to pass laws or the existence of a program fail to reveal the extent of an effort as well as a statistic does. Statistics are, of course, themselves constructs that reflect particular practices of data collection and analysis and the interests and categories of those collecting the information. They are hardly free of politics (Merry 2011; Davis, Kingsbury, and Merry 2012), yet they represent a way to move past resistance based on a lack of information, even if they are in many ways flawed.

Monitoring compliance with human rights treaties is always a struggle over information, an effort to change state behavior based on the information provided by the states. Under these conditions, states have opportunities for resistance and noncompliance even when they do produce a periodic report. Experts are always skeptical, and many of the questions they ask seek more information, statistics, and disaggregated data that reveal patterns of discrimination. In this game of monitoring and resistance, information stands at the center. It appears that efforts to promote compliance are most likely to succeed in those areas where countries share goals, and monitoring is most likely to be successful when accurate and comprehensive data are available.

IV. CONCLUSION

Examining the interactions between countries and the committees that monitor compliance with human rights conventions offers a different perspective on state compliance with human rights norms. There are clearly areas where states share the goals of the treaties but have not invested adequate resources in achieving them. There are other areas where states resist the goals or find them politically difficult to achieve. This resistance takes the form of direct refusal or failure to provide adequate information. By looking more specifically at how states respond to the wide variety of obligations in human rights treaties, it is possible to develop a more nuanced analysis of compliance and resistance. Some goals of human rights treaties are readily accepted, whereas others appear to be politically difficult or to contradict widely held values. Those that conform to state aspirations will be more readily acknowledged than those that raise political problems for governing elites. Insofar as issues are contested among state and civil society organizations, as those discussed here clearly are, the international perspective will add fuel to one or another side of the debate. Examining interactions within the human rights monitoring process and the central role of information in these interactions provides a way to think about compliance in a way that can facilitate asking whether – and how – ratifying human rights conventions changes state behavior. At this same time, this approach to monitoring compliance highlights the value of an empirical, ethnographic focus on moments of debate and discussion, the reactions of people in the middle, and the importance of incorporating the social world into an analysis of law.

REFERENCES

Committee on Economic, Social and Cultural Rights (CESCR). 2009. "Initial Reports Submitted by States Parties under Articles 16 and 17 of the Covenant: Turkey." January 28, 2009. E/C.12/TUR/1. 158 pp.

Committee on Economic, Social and Cultural Rights (CESCR). 2011a. "Comments by the Government of Turkey on the Concluding Observations of the Committee on Economic, Social and Cultural Rights (E/C.12/TUR/CO/1)." E/C.12/TUR/CO/1/Add.1, June 17, 2011.

Committee on Economic, Social and Cultural Rights (CESCR). 2011b. "Concluding Observations of the Committee on Economic, Social and Cultural Rights, Turkey." E/C.12/TUR/CO/1. July 12, 2011.

Committee on the Elimination of All Forms of Discrimination against Women (CEDAW). 2011. "Combined Fourth and Fifth Periodic Reports of States Parties: Samoa." CEDAW/C/WSM/4–5.

Committee on the Elimination of All Forms of Discrimination against Women (CEDAW). 2012. "Concluding Observations of the Committee on the Elimination of Discrimination against Women, Samoa." CEDAW/C/WSM/CO/4–5. July 27, 2012.

Davis, Kevin, Benedict Kingsbury, and Sally Engle Merry. 2012. "Indicators as a Technology of Global Governance." *Law and Society Review* 46(1): 71–104.

Hathaway, Oona A. 2002. "Do Human Rights Treaties Make a Difference?" *Yale Law Journal* 111: 1935–2042.

Kretzmer, David. 2010. "The UN Human Rights Committee and International Human Rights Monitoring." Presented at IILJ International Legal Theory Colloquium Spring 2010, New York University School of Law.

Landman, Todd, and Edzia Carvalho. 2010. *Measuring Human Rights*. New York: Routledge.

Merry, Sally Engle. 2006. *Human Rights and Gender Violence: Translating International Law into Local Justice*. Chicago: University of Chicago Press.

Merry, Sally Engle. 2011. "Measuring the World: Indicators, Human Rights, and Global Governance." *Current Anthropology (Corporate Lives: New Perspectives on the Social Life of the Corporate Form)* 52(3): S83–S95.

Merry, Sally Engle. 2016. *The Seductions of Quantification: Measuring Gender Violence, Human Rights, and Sex Trafficking*. Chicago: University of Chicago Press.

NGO Shadow. 2012. "Report on the Status of Women in Samoa, 4th and 5th Periodic Reports of States Parties (2005–2009)," May. http://www2.ohchr.org/english/bodies/cedaw/docs/ngos/JointNGOsSubmission_for_the_session_Samoa_CEDAW52.pdf

Power, Michael. 1999. *The Audit Society: Rituals of Verification*. Oxford: Oxford University Press.

Rosga, AnnJanette, and Margaret L. Satterthwaite. 2009. "The Trust in Indicators: Measuring Human Rights." *Berkeley Journal of International Law* 27(2): 253–315.

Scheinin, Martin. 2005. "Use of Indicators by Human Rights Treaty Bodies – Experiences and Potentials." Paper for the Turku/Åbo Expert Meeting on Human Rights Indicators – Background Paper no. 3. March 11–13, 2005. On file with author.

Simmons, Beth A. 2009. *Mobilizing for Human Rights: International Law in Domestic Politics*. Cambridge: Cambridge University Press.

UN International Human Rights Instruments, OHCHR. 2006. "Report on Indicators for Monitoring Compliance with International Human Rights Instruments." Eighteenth meeting of chairpersons of the human rights treaty bodies, Geneva, June 22–23, 2006. HRI/MC/2006/7.

UN International Human Rights Instruments, OHCHR. 2008. "Report on Indicators for Promoting and Monitoring the Implementation of Human Rights." HRI/MC/2008/3, June 6, 2008.

UN OHCHR (Office of the High Commissioner for Human Rights). 2012. *Human Rights Indicators: A Guide to Measurement and Implementation*. HR/PUB/12/5. New York and Geneva: Office of the High Commissioner for Human Rights.

4

Intellectual Property and the Creation of Global Rules

Susan K. Sell

I. INTRODUCTION

A traditional focus on states and black-letter law provides a misleading picture of intellectual property (IP) lawmaking. It obscures the dynamism that animates this policy space. International intellectual property lawmaking is a fluid and dynamic process in which a multitude of diverse actors struggle to inscribe their preferences into institutions and law. Actors, including states, nongovernmental organizations (NGOs), and firms, wield various forms of economic, discursive, and institutional power. They use institutions strategically in promoting and contesting policy. The international spread of intellectual property policies is a recursive process both in time and in space. It is recursive in time insofar as iterations at Time One alter the playing field, enrolling new actors and institutions and altering the dynamic at Time Two. As Peter Drahos states, in the politics of intellectual property, "negotiations are never really over" (Drahos 2007). It is recursive in space as a process "in which the transnational and local are held in tension, the actors engaged in transnational legal processes seek to influence local lawmaking and practice, and the national legal norms, adaptations, and resistances provide models for the feedback into transnational lawmaking" (Shaffer 2012, 238).

The concept of recursivity highlights the politics of regulatory transformations in three dimensions: within international and transnational processes, within domestic processes, and between them (Shaffer 2012, 239). They intersect and are connected by agents whom Sidney Tarrow refers to as "rooted cosmopolitans" (Tarrow 2010). Rooted cosmopolitans have their feet firmly planted in the domestic political realm but can engage freely transnationally and provide interfaces between the different realms. They can act as intermediaries advocating across and translating between domains. As Shaffer suggests, to be effective these intermediaries must be "cognizant of transnational lawmaking and national settings" (Shaffer 2012, 254). In the politics of intellectual property, these intermediaries include trade lawyers, government officials, rights holders, academics, nongovernmental organizations, and consumers (Morin 2014, 275–309). Contestation between various intermediaries provides dynamism in this process.

Implementing intellectual property laws requires regulatory infrastructure, expertise, and substantial investment in resources. Adopting (and enforcing) intellectual property laws is costly and may challenge domestic political bargains. It may alter the distribution of benefits and lead to disputes. Intellectual property policies are deeply political. At the end of the day, the domestic political context profoundly affects the implementation of intellectual property policies. As Shaffer points out, "weak actors at the level of international negotiations and domestic ratification can become quite strong in foiling actual implementation of transnational prescriptions" (Shaffer 2012, 256–257). Indeed, rights holders continue to press for new standards of intellectual property enforcement because they remain dissatisfied with most developing countries' implementation and enforcement.

This chapter proceeds in three sections. It first examines the origins of international intellectual property law in the domestic politics of the United States. In important respects this is where the Agreement on Trade-Related Aspects of Intellectual Property Rights (TRIPS) began. The second section discusses post-TRIPS developments, including forum proliferation and forum shifting. Since TRIPS, international intellectual property lawmaking has become much more complicated and contested. This section covers the battles over access to generic medicines, and the US efforts to ratchet up intellectual property protection standards and enforcement in the Anti-Counterfeiting Trade Agreement (ACTA) and two domestic laws, the Stop Online Piracy Act (SOPA) and the Protect Intellectual Property Act (PIPA). The final section briefly discusses the ongoing Trans-Pacific Partnership (TPP) negotiations and concludes the chapter. Above all, this chapter unpacks the recursive and dynamic politics driving intellectual property policy making.

II. TIME ONE: THE DOMESTIC ORIGINS OF INTERNATIONAL INTELLECTUAL PROPERTY LAW

"Time One" begins with domestic politics in the United States in the early to mid 1970s. The United States is particularly important, as it has been the leading and relentless demander of ever-stronger intellectual property rights and enforcement worldwide. Producers of luxury goods first raised the issue of trademark counterfeiting as hurting their businesses. They succeeded at getting the United States to raise the issue in the Tokyo Round of the General Agreement on Tariffs and Trade (GATT) in 1974. Negotiators were unable to finalize an agreement, but intellectual property had landed in the trade regime.

US-based producers of entertainment products, movies, and music, along with book publishers, began to complain to Congress that their businesses were losing millions of dollars from foreign copyright piracy. The Motion Picture Association of America's former president Jack Valenti was a powerful advocate for his association members' quest for adoption and enforcement of US intellectual property rights abroad. US-based rights holders appealed to the government for help in achieving this quest by asking it to adopt amendments to US trade laws and preferential treatment policies that would impose trade sanctions on offending countries. Beginning with the Caribbean Basin Initiative in 1983, the US Congress began to pass legislation aimed at protecting US-held intellectual property abroad using trade leverage. The Congress also amended trade legislation to expand the authority of the Office of the United States Trade Representative (USTR) to initiate investigations of intellectual property infringement and to take action against infringing countries. At the behest of intellectual property rights holders, the US Congress passed legislation, including Section 301 of the Trade and Tariff Act of 1984, linking foreign intellectual property protection to US trade retaliation. Amended again in 1988, it strengthened the link between intellectual property and trade and further empowered the USTR to take swift action against reported infractions against US rights holders. The USTR's dependence on data that rights holders provided helped to forge a symbiotic relationship between rights holders and the USTR. Rights holders lobbied to get more resources for USTR, and, in turn, USTR pressed forward with the rights holders' crusade (Sell 2010).

The US government was particularly receptive to the rights holders' demands in the late 1970s and early 1980s. It was facing twin budget and trade deficits and was preoccupied with economic competition from Japan and East Asia. The rights holders were able to demonstrate that their intellectual property–based industries had positive export balances, in contrast to formerly strong industries such as steel. They argued that intellectual property was the key to the country's economic future and the source of the US economy's comparative advantage. The USTR engaged in numerous bilateral consultations with countries such as Hungary, Singapore, South Korea, and Taiwan in the 1970s and early 1980s. Accompanied by rights holders, the USTR extracted pledges from these governments to adopt stronger laws protecting US intellectual property. The USTR and the rights holders found that bilateral trade leverage – the stick of trade sanctions and the carrot of market access – was a promising tool to increase intellectual property protection abroad.

During this same period, the US government engaged in multilateral negotiations in the World Intellectual Property Organization (WIPO) on possible revisions to the Paris Convention for the Protection of Industrial Property. Prominent developing countries such as India and Brazil argued for special and differential treatment and more lax standards of protection for countries at earlier stages of industrial development. For instance, India had developed a robust generic medicines industry after it abolished patents on pharmaceutical products in its Patent Act of 1970. The United States rejected developing countries' demands and became frustrated by the multilateral negotiations at WIPO. These ended in a deadlock in 1985 with no new revisions.

John Opel, the CEO of International Business Machines (IBM), was well aware of the ongoing bilateral negotiations and saw the promise of the trade-based approach to securing stronger protection abroad. He commissioned the economist Jacques Gorlin to draft a paper outlining what a multilateral trade agreement that would protect US-held copyrights would need to include. Gorlin's 1985 paper (Gorlin, 1985) became the basis of a rights holders' consensus to press for a broader trade-based approach to intellectual property protection.

Then-USTR Clayton Yeutter reached out to the business community and asked for its help in getting European and Japanese support for including intellectual property protection in the upcoming Uruguay Round of the General Agreement on Tariffs and Trade (GATT). John Opel and Edmund Pratt, CEO of Pfizer Pharmaceuticals, served on the Executive Branch's private-sector advisory board on trade (the Industry Functional Advisory Committee on Intellectual Property Rights for Trade Policy Matters). They joined forces to press for a multilateral trade-based approach to intellectual property protection. WIPO had no enforcement power, but economic coercion through trade leverage seemed to produce results. Jacques Gorlin established the Intellectual Property Committee (IPC), made up of CEOs from twelve multinational US-based firms representing both patent and copyright interests, to develop and pursue a multilateral trade proposal for the upcoming round of GATT negotiations.

This private-sector group achieved an important horizontal multilateral forum shift from the World Intellectual Property Organization to the General Agreement on Tariffs and Trade negotiating forum. The Intellectual Property Committee met with its counterparts in Europe and Japan and persuaded these firms, and ultimately their governments, to stand with the United States in pressing for a multilateral intellectual property treaty in the trade regime. It was a strategic move designed to maximize rights holders' leverage over foreign governments through government-backed trade sanctions and market access. This was an opportunity for rights holders to inscribe their domestically crafted approach of amending US trade law into the multilateral trade regime. In many respects the resulting multilateral agreement resembles the United States' Section 301 of the Trade and Tariff Act provisions writ large. The symbiosis between US rights holders and USTR became sharply apparent. The US government distributed an Intellectual Property Committee's "trilateral document" that reflected the desires of European, US, and Japanese rights holders as its official position.

As negotiations got under way in March 1986 developing countries such as India and Brazil objected to the inclusion of intellectual property in GATT and insisted that it belonged in WIPO. They tried to resist this horizontal forum shift. Throughout the negotiations, the US Congress continued to respond to rights holders' demands for stronger action against foreign infringers, and in 1988 the United States passed the Omnibus Trade and Competitiveness Act that included "Special 301" explicitly covering intellectual property protection and expanding the USTR's authority to take action against violators of US intellectual property rights abroad. At rights holders' behest, USTR threatened numerous countries with trade sanctions, especially those countries that were objecting to incorporating intellectual property into the trade regime (Matthews 2002, 30–31). Initially, developing countries thought that their choice was between intellectual property in WIPO and intellectual property in GATT. By 1989 it was clear that their actual options were either intellectual property in GATT or continued US bilateral bullying. In 1989 India, the last holdout, finally withdrew its objections.

Private power drove the emergence of public international law. The economic and political power of the United States facilitated this outcome. What began as a US-based private-sector rights holders' crusade for public help to protect private rights abroad became a fully enforceable multilateral treaty incorporated into a new trade institution, the World Trade Organization (WTO). While developing countries had no inherent interest in intellectual property protection, the Organization for Economic Cooperation and Development (OECD) countries promised both an end to textile protection by phasing out the Multi-Fibre Arrangement in GATT and increased market access for developing countries' agricultural exports. This was the quid pro quo that helped to induce developing countries to assent to incorporating intellectual property into the Uruguay Round agreements.

TRIPS is a comprehensive, binding, multilateral intellectual property agreement. TRIPS binds all WTO member countries. Member states are required to implement its provisions in national legislation. TRIPS mandates implementation of protections for patents, copyrights, trademarks, plant breeders' rights, industrial designs, and trade secrets. Member states must extend intellectual property protection to a broad range of subject matters, including pharmaceutical products. States must establish intellectual property enforcement procedures and administering institutions. TRIPS is fully enforceable through the WTO Dispute Settlement Understanding; infractions may be punished by imposition of trade sanctions.

Significantly the United States, Europe, and Japan saw TRIPS as a floor, an absolute minimum standard. By contrast, developing countries saw it as a ceiling or set of maximum standards. These different perceptions have both fueled and haunted subsequent developments at every turn.

A recursive spatial dynamic that originated in the concerns of US-based private rights holders as expressed through domestic political processes produced the multilateral TRIPS. Rights holders' lobbying, their institutional access via official advisory boards, their ability to provide data to the USTR, their economic clout, and their Congressional testimony all helped to produce TRIPS. Legislative changes that linked trade to intellectual property protection seemed to bring desired results. These rights holders and the US government worked to inscribe their homegrown approach into the multilateral trade regime. Private actors representing both patent and copyright interests compromised to present a united front in the multilateral arena. Private actors' preferences moved from the domestic arena to the multilateral level and were backed by state power. By their own admission, they were surprised by their success; Gorlin declared that rights holders got 95 percent of what they wanted (Sell 2003, 48).

Once states agreed to TRIPS, the recursive spatial dynamic worked from the multilateral level back down to the domestic level. WTO member states, and those aspiring to accede to the WTO, worked to implement TRIPS in their national legislation (Deere 2009). This profoundly altered the game and ushered in unintended consequences that would raise questions about TRIPS's merits.

III. TIME TWO: POST-TRIPS FORUM PROLIFERATION AND FORUM SHIFTING

Governments have frequently engaged in forum shifting. As intellectual property rights have been expanded to cover drugs, seeds, and digital media, these rights increasingly impinge upon consumers and users of public health services, agricultural products, software, and the Internet. This broader reach means that intellectual property policy issues are now included in multiple multilateral forums, including the World Health Organization (WHO), the Food and Agricultural Organization, and the Convention on Biodiversity (among others). With a proliferation of forums that now address intellectual property, the opportunities for using institutions to strategic advantage have multiplied (Helfer 2004). Governments have shifted *horizontally*, across multilateral forums, to increase the odds that they can achieve their goals. Different forums have different mandates and value orientations, and actors can manipulate these differences to alter outcomes. In the politics of intellectual property, the first important horizontal multilateral forum shift was the US shift from WIPO to GATT for the Uruguay Round. Governments have shifted from WIPO to GATT, from WHO to WTO, and from WTO back to WIPO. I will discuss each of these in turn. While intellectual property rights holders initiated the 1986 WIPO-to-GATT shift, a different set of actors, concerned about public health, promoted the 2001 WHO-to-WTO horizontal forum shift.

The first big post-TRIPS challenge came in the throes of an HIV/AIDS pandemic in the late 1990s. HIV/AIDS infection rates skyrocketed throughout sub-Saharan Africa, Thailand, and Brazil. When South Africa passed its 1997 Medicines Act that included TRIPS-compliant parallel importation and compulsory licensing provisions to increase access to affordable medicines, US-based brand-name pharmaceutical firms sued Nelson Mandela's government. The Clinton administration backed the firms and pressured South Africa to change its law. South Africa's Treatment Access Campaign mobilized to protest this pressure and publicized how changing the Medicines Act as the United States desired would sharply reduce access to medicines.[1] Conforming to US pressure would keep the desperately needed anti-retroviral drugs unaffordable for the majority of the population ravaged by HIV/AIDS. In the United States, the advocacy group ACT UP mobilized to protest the

[1] For a documentary film about this episode, see Dylan Mohan Gray's Fire in the Blood: fireintheblood.com.

high prices of antiretroviral medicines for HIV/AIDS. African governments, along with Brazil, Thailand, and India, worked with nongovernmental organizations, including Doctors Without Borders, Health Action International, and the US-based Consumer Project on Technology to promote access to generic medicines. These rooted cosmopolitans worked together in WHO to highlight the public health consequences of TRIPS.

The World Health Assembly of WHO unanimously enacted resolution WHA 52.19 in May 1999 that called upon member states to ensure equitable access to essential drugs and to review options under international agreements to safeguard access to these medicines. Member states passed the resolution in the wake of extensive discussions of compulsory licensing and its permissibility under TRIPS. The United States continued to press South Africa to amend its Medicines Act. It also criticized Thailand for trying to avail itself of TRIPS flexibilities under TRIPS Articles 30 and 31 that permit countries to issue compulsory licenses on patented antiretroviral drugs. The USTR threatened Thailand with trade sanctions if it went forward with plans to produce a more affordable generic antiretroviral drug. In June 1999 ACT UP engaged in disruptive displays that interrupted then–Vice President Albert Gore's presidential campaign events to protest US policy of supporting brand-name pharmaceutical firms in the South African and Thai cases. Displaying banners that read "Gore's Greed Kills" and using noisemakers, their antics had quite an impact on live television. The very week that Gore announced his candidacy, the Clinton administration withdrew two years' worth of objections to South Africa's Medicines Act and in September removed South Africa from the USTR 301 Watch List (Gellman 2000).

The WTO Doha trade round started in November 2001, and the African governments, Brazil, India, and Thailand pressed their access to medicines agenda. They insisted that without a declaration on the priority of public health over trade they would refuse to negotiate anything else. Their proposed declaration came directly from the WHO deliberations and the World Health Assembly resolution. Thus, in a horizontal forum shift they brought the activities from an institution that promotes public health into the trade regime to underscore the availability of flexibilities under TRIPS. They sought clarification that their actions to promote access to generic drugs were, in fact, entirely permissible under TRIPS. Their hard negotiating stance led states to unanimously adopt the Doha Declaration of TRIPS and Public Health.

Public health concerns also animated the only amendment to TRIPS. In August 2003 WTO members negotiated the so-called Paragraph 6 agreement. While TRIPS permitted makers of generic drugs made under compulsory licenses to provide them for *domestic* consumption, only a handful of developing countries had generic production capacity. After contentious negotiations between member states representing intellectual property rights holders and multinational brand-name pharmaceutical firms on one side, and member states advocating for public health flexibilities on the other side, parties finally agreed to a provision that would allow generic drug makers to export generic drugs produced under compulsory licenses to countries without domestic generic capacity. Member states finally adopted the amendment in December 2005. Initially embraced as a victory for public health, it proved to be a disappointing and convoluted arrangement that has been used only one time since its adoption.

Countries representing intellectual property rights holders had always seen TRIPS as a floor; TRIPS was never enough for them. The United States and the European Union pursued bilateral and regional free trade agreements, economic partnership agreements, and investment agreements that invariably exceeded the requirements of TRIPS and reduced the flexibilities that TRIPS allowed (Drahos 2001). Not satisfied with TRIPS-level protections and enforcement provisions, these countries aggressively pursued *vertical* forum shifts, negotiating with relatively weaker partners to maximize rights holders' bargaining leverage. Top-down vertical forum shifting (from multilateral to bilateral forums, for example) allows stronger parties to exploit power asymmetries to achieve deals in their favor. Strong states that believe that their vital interests are at stake and that their preferences are distinctly at odds with the vast majority of other states often engage in vertical forum shifting (Benvenisti and Downs 2004).

The high political profile of public health and intellectual property concerns in the World Trade Organization underscored how difficult it would be for rights holders to obtain stronger protection there. Peter Yu points out that, since the TRIPS agreement, "developed countries have had very limited success in pushing for higher intellectual property standards" within the WTO (Yu 2011, 511). Member states representing rights holders engaged in yet another strategic horizontal forum shift by trying to revive the Substantive Patent Law harmonization negotiations in the World Intellectual Property Organization. In 2000 WIPO's Standing Committee on Patents began to consider the draft Substantive Patent Law Treaty that rights holders wanted. Discussions continued and in 2004 the United States, Japan, and the European Patent Office put forward a joint proposal for harmonization (WIPO 2004). Developing countries successfully rebuffed these efforts and insisted that before engaging in any discussions about harmonizing standards upward, WIPO member states needed to address development issues. The United States and European countries had been pressuring them to adopt ever-higher standards of protection and enforcement. Now developing countries pushed back.

Developing country member states proposed a Development Agenda in 2004 (WIPO 2005). Three years later, WIPO members adopted a watered-down Development Agenda, and just two weeks later the Office of the United States Trade Representative (USTR) announced yet another vertical forum shift. Insofar as weaker states had begun to shape WIPO to better reflect their interests (in development rather than more protection), the more powerful member states switched out of WIPO to pursue their goals of increased intellectual property protection and enforcement. Unhappy with the Development Agenda, these states decided to "exploit their agenda-setting power to set up a parallel and competing set of negotiations with other powerful states" (Benvenisti and Downs 2004, 615).

In October 2007, USTR Susan Schwab announced that the United States, Japan, and the European Union would "seek to negotiate ... [a] new, higher benchmark for [IP] enforcement and ... the negotiations would not be part of any existing international organizations" (Schwab, quoted in Ayoob 2010, 175, 179; USTR 2007).

The Anti-Counterfeiting Trade Agreement (ACTA) deliberations were a vertical forum shift from the multilateral level to the plurilateral level (more than two countries but less than a multilateral level).

The Anti-Counterfeiting Trade Agreement negotiations included the United States, Japan, the European Union, and countries already tethered to TRIPS-plus standards in bilateral and regional agreements. The participating countries included Jordan, South Korea, Mexico, Morocco, Singapore, and the United Arab Emirates. Negotiating governments conducted the talks in utmost secrecy; deliberations were completely nontransparent. Only negotiators and "cleared advisors" (e.g., rights holders in the United States) were permitted to see negotiating texts. The USTR rejected numerous Freedom of Information Act requests for text based on "national security" grounds (Levine 2012). When leaked text chapters became available on WikiLeaks, NGOs, Internet users, and European Parliamentarians became alarmed at the TRIPS-plus provisions. To many it looked like an overreaching, draconian agreement. ACTA's critics raised issues of censorship, free speech, and threats to the integrity of the Internet.

The agreement was not a trade agreement, but rather an intellectual property agreement designed to address the digital realm and copyright interests. Many of the proposed provisions focused on enforcement. ACTA's backers sought to require Internet service providers (ISPs) to police and control their systems for infringing content (Gross 2008). Shifting enforcement burdens to ISPs raises important questions about data privacy and reporting requirements. ACTA also would raise substantially the criminal penalties for copyright infringement (Kaminski 2012, 526–527) It would permit customs officials to take action against suspected intellectual property infringers even without complaints from rights holders. Infringement standards in ACTA are quite broad, including "non-commercial use" and "personal use." While some of the substantive provisions are TRIPS-plus, it is also TRIPS-minus insofar as it omits TRIPS flexibilities and is US-minus because it lacks provisions for fair use, limitations and exceptions to copyright, and due process provisions to protect the innocent.[2]

ACTA also would create an additional international intellectual property governance layer atop an already remarkably complex and increasingly incoherent intellectual property regime. One chapter of the ACTA text is devoted to new

[2] I thank Jonathan Band for this point.

institutional arrangements, including a Secretariat. There is no discussion of how such an institution would mesh with, or stand apart from, WIPO and/or WTO.

Many expressed concern about the secrecy of the process. As David S. Levine points out, "international IP agreements like ACTA . . . are now supplanting domestic lawmaking by placing pressure on domestic law to conform to international standards that may be more stringent than what could be politically achieved in Congress" (Levine 2012, 117). The contrast between the international IP lawmaking with ACTA and the domestic IP lawmaking in the United States could not be sharper.

The Stop Online Piracy Act (SOPA)/Protect Intellectual Property Act (PIPA)/ ACTA story demonstrates the dynamic, recursive nature of transnational lawmaking. Ironically, democratic deliberation in the United States over SOPA and PIPA actually helped to undermine the US ACTA initiative. Domestic resistance to proposed US laws SOPA and PIPA undermined support for ACTA in Europe, and triggered heightened concern over the intellectual property provisions of the Trans-Pacific Partnership (TPP) negotiations (Band 2013). The SOPA/PIPA rejection inspired Europeans to protest over ACTA, "spurring a new counterpolitics of transnational coordination, organization and lawmaking" (Shaffer 2012, 258). US national dynamics generated new politics that undermined the transnational legal norms enshrined in ACTA. This time the causal arrow pointed from the bottom up; US domestic dynamics undermined its foreign economic policy. This case exemplified recursivity both in space (a multilevel dynamic) and in time.

The US government went forward with the nontransparent ACTA negotiations and in 2010 signed the agreement that the copyright industries (motion picture, music, and software) had vigorously promoted. Simultaneously, the Motion Picture Association of America, the Recording Industry Association of America, and companies like EMI, Disney, and Time Warner were pressing for domestic legislation to update copyright for the digital age. They expected smooth legislative sailing owing to their unbroken track record in achieving ever-higher standards of intellectual property protection over the previous thirty years. The cozy relationship between Congress and copyright content industries is long-standing and well known. Indeed, in 2011 former Senator Christopher Dodd headed the Motion Picture Association of America (MPAA) that presses for expanded copyright protection and enforcement. The two proposed laws were the SOPA in the House of Representatives and the PIPA in the Senate. SOPA was introduced in the House of Representatives in September 2011.

SOPA targeted foreign "pirate" websites that host copyright-infringing content. SOPA was to block US Internet users' access to such sites, and block online payment processing services such as PayPal from transferring money to the sites. In contrast to ACTA's secrecy, policy makers deliberated on SOPA transparently in the US House of Representatives. Internet users and founders of sites featuring user-generated content, such as Reddit and I Can Has Cheezburger?, mobilized quickly to protest the bill. Open Internet champions Aaron Swartz and Alexis Ohanian (cofounders of Reddit) made extensive use of Web 2.0 interactive technologies to notify Internet users and the technology community of the dangers that the bill posed to Internet freedom, privacy, and free speech. They framed their mobilizing campaign around "stop censorship," and posted information, initiated online petitions, and organized boycotts against the bill's supporters (such as the website host GoDaddy).

The anti-SOPA coalition worked with blogs (e.g., Boingboing and Tech Dirt[3]), government partners, European Pirate Party, the European Parliament, European Green Party, US domestic NGOs (such as Electronic Frontier Foundation and Public Knowledge), foreign NGOs (such as France's La Quadrature du Net), and a handful of US Congress members (Ron Wyden, Darrell Issa, Zoe Lofgren, Jason Caffetz, and Jared Polis) to stop the bill. Google posted an online petition that gathered millions of signatures. Posted links to Congress members' phone lines generated hundreds of thousands of calls, jamming switchboards. The hacktivist group Anonymous even got involved, posting embarrassing personal information about some of the bill's supporters.

In this case, a transnational hybrid coalition of Internet pioneers, users, technology companies, and citizens worked together. These rooted cosmopolitans succeeded in killing domestic US antipiracy laws. Jimmy Wales, Wikipedia's founder, used his "talk page" to solicit community members' opinions on whether to black out their websites to protest the antipiracy bills. The community responded with a resounding "yes" (Sell 2013). On Wednesday, January 18, 2012, more than 15,000 websites went dark for 24 hours, including Wikipedia, Mozilla, and Reddit, to protest the legislation and underscore the consequences if the bill was passed. Millions of users got the message; Google and Craigslist featured censor bars on their home pages. Before the web blackout, the House members were 80 to 31 in favor of SOPA; 24 hours later House members had switched and the count was 65 in favor and 101 opposed (Cho 2012; Pro Publica, 2012). By January 20, 2012, the bills (both SOPA and PIPA) were dead.

Rights holders were flabbergasted. Christopher Dodd of the Motion Picture Association of America stated that opponents' "'ability to organize and communicate directly with consumers was a game-changing phenomenon' that he hadn't seen in more than three decades in public office" (Hollywood Reporter 2012).

As surprising as the anti-SOPA/PIPA coalition's victory was, even more surprising was the ripple effect that the SOPA/PIPA defeat had on the Anti-Counterfeiting Trade Agreement (ACTA). Inspired by David's victory over the rights holders' Goliath, this transnational coalition now mobilized to kill the USTR's and rights holders' plurilateral export: ACTA. In late January and February 2012 a number of countries expressed grave doubts and regrets over

3 boingboing.net and http://www.techdirt.com.

having participated in the ACTA negotiations. Massive online and offline public protests in more than 200 European cities threw ACTA's future into doubt. The February 11, 2012, protests "led to the resignation of the EU Parliament's rapporteur on ACTA, who criticized the public process as a 'masquerade.' And also to the resignation of the Slovenian Ambassador to Japan who signed ACTA – who left office apologizing to her country and her children" (Sean Flynn, quoted in Levine 2012, 136). The fact that it had been negotiated in secret profoundly undermined its legitimacy in the eyes of the public (Weatherall 2012, 238). Bulgaria, the Czech Republic, Slovakia, Latvia, Estonia, Austria, Germany, Poland, the Netherlands, and Cyprus have suspended ratification of ACTA. The European Union has suspended ratification of ACTA, so that now twenty-two of the twenty-seven EU countries that signed ACTA will not be able to ratify it. The Mexican Senate also rejected ACTA; a Twitter campaign derailed it there (Haggart 2014).

IV. WHAT NEXT? THE TRANS-PACIFIC PARTNERSHIP NEGOTIATIONS

Another recent secret rights holders' gambit is the plurilateral Trans-Pacific Partnership (TPP) negotiations. This again is a vertical forum shift in which rights holders seek an advantage that they can no longer obtain at the multilateral level. ACTA was not a trade agreement but rather an intellectual property agreement (Weatherall 2012, 233–234); by contrast, TPP is an actual trade negotiation. In addition to intellectual property, negotiators also are addressing traditional trade issues, such as market access and agricultural subsidies.

Trans-Pacific Partnership negotiations began in 2010 and include the United States, Australia, New Zealand, Chile, Brunei, Singapore, Peru, Malaysia, and Vietnam. Negotiators finally agreed on the treaty text in October 2015, although signatures and ratification battles lie ahead. The intellectual property chapter makes clear that ACTA did not go nearly far enough to satisfy intellectual property rights holders.Other controversial elements include the US's demand for data exclusivity provisions for biologic drugs and provisions that will delay generic competition. The anti-SOPA/PIPA/ACTA coalition is working to draw parallels between troubling procedural and substantive aspects of TPP to kill the intellectual property provisions (Levine 2012). It remains to be seen whether the coalition will succeed. As TPP covers multiple issues, one should expect issue linkage and trade-offs across various proposals as we saw in the Uruguay Round with intellectual property, agricultural, and textile market access commitments.

In November 2013 WikiLeaks released an updated TPP intellectual property chapter that identified the various countries' negotiating positions. Invariably the United States insisted on the most draconian measures for protection and enforcement. The documents revealed how isolated the United States is on intellectual property issues. It is too soon to tell whether the consumer and user protests that buried SOPA and PIPA in the United States, and ACTA in Europe and Mexico, will rise again to jeopardize the TPP's momentum. TPP is more complicated insofar as there is a broad menu of trade provisions included and geostrategic imperatives seeking to shape the future of Asia. Nonetheless, the US-preferred intellectual property and investor–state dispute settlement provisions are quite controversial.

V. CONCLUSION

Tracing the transnational lawmaking process for intellectual property reveals a recursive and complex dynamic. Scale shifting, from domestic and bilateral to regional to multilateral and plurilateral forums, highlights recursivity in space. It demonstrates multidirectional causal mechanisms, including economic power, domestic law, multilateral norm setting and lawmaking, and national and transnational social activism. TRIPS shows how powerful economic actors can shape domestic policies (US trade law), and how those policies may be inscribed into the multilateral regime. TRIPS also shows how multilateral processes alter domestic practices through implementation (Deere 2009). The SOPA/PIPA rejection demonstrates how domestic policies and transnational activism can undermine both domestic and plurilateral efforts.

The thickening of available forums and the broadening of implicated policies highlight recursivity in time. Outcomes at Time One altered the playing field at Time Two, enrolling a new set of actors (e.g., public health advocates after TRIPS). Those resisting higher intellectual property standards forced those seeking to ratchet up intellectual property standards and their enforcement to abandon multilateral forums for plurilateral deliberations cloaked in secrecy. In an era of WikiLeaks it seems as though secrecy is likely to backfire, and with many more citizens now paying attention to intellectual property policies it is not clear that the intellectual property maximalists are destined to win the day.

This chapter has provided an analysis that brings to the foreground the ongoing political contestation over intellectual property. Examining recursivity in time and space reveals a rich, dynamic, and deeply contested policy space. It highlights agency, and powerful economic actors' and rooted cosmopolitans' strategic deployment of discourse, law, and institutions in order to alter regulatory outcomes. According to Peter Gourevitch, "the choice made among conflicting policy proposals emerges out of politics. The victorious interpretation will be the one whose adherents have the power to transfer their opinion into the force of law" (Gourevitch 1986, 17). Power is not always economic might, as we saw in the SOPA/PIPA case. Power can come from effective mobilization as well.

This analysis suggests that examining negotiations as a one-off process, or as confined to one particular level of governance, is bound to provide a misleading picture. Focusing on black-letter law or institutional architecture tends to obscure important aspects of both substance and process. The substance of law matters; if it conflicts with other salient public goals such as access to lifesaving drugs, it is unlikely to be enforced. At the very least it is bound to lose legitimacy and be contested. The process of constructing law is vital as well; if those most affected by law are excluded from the process and are directly harmed by it, one should expect them to challenge the legitimacy of the process. These factors drive the evolution of the politics of law and should not be ignored. Clearly, a consensual and stable equilibrium in this policy space is a long way off.

REFERENCES

Ayoob, Emily. 2010. "The Anti-Counterfeiting Trade Agreement." *Cardozo Arts & Entertainment Law Journal* 28: 175–193.

Band, Jonathan. 2013. "The SOPA-TPP Nexus." PIJIP Research Paper no. 2012–06. *American University International Law Review* 28(1).

Benvenisti, Eyal, and George Downs. 2004. "Distributive Politics and International Institutions: The Case of Drugs." *Case Western Reserve Journal of International Law* 36: 21–51.

Cho, Minhee. 2012. "Podcast: SOPA Opera." Last modified January 27. http://www.propublica.org/podcast/item/podcast-sopa-opera/.

Deere, Caroline. 2009. *The Implementation Game: The TRIPS Agreement and the Global Politics of Intellectual Property Reform in Developing Countries*. Oxford: Oxford University Press.

Drahos, Peter. 2001. "BITs and BIPs: Bilateralism in Intellectual Property." *Journal of World Intellectual Property* 4(6): 791–808.

Drahos, Peter. 2007. "Four Lessons for Developing Countries from Trade Negotiations over Access to Medicines." *Liverpool Law Review* 28: 11–39.

Gellman, Barton. 2000. "A Conflict of Health and Profit; Gore at the Center of Trade Policy Reversal on AIDS Drugs to S. Africa." *Washington Post*, May 21, A1.

Gorlin, Jacques. 1985. "A trade-based approach for intellectual property protection for computer software'" unpublished. On file with author.

Gourevitch, Peter. 1986. *Politics in Hard Times: Comparative Responses to International Economic Crises*. Ithaca: Cornell University Press.

Gross, Robin. 2008. "IP Justice White Paper on the Proposed Anti-Counterfeiting Trade Agreement (ACTA)." http://ipjustice.org/wp/2008/03/25/ipj-white-paper-acta-2008/.

Haggart, Blayne. 2014. "Birth of a Movement: The Anti-Counterfeiting Trade Agreement and the Politicization of Mexican Copyright." *Policy & Internet* 6(1) (March): 69–88.

Helfer, Laurence. 2004. "Regime-Shifting: The TRIPS Agreement and the New Dynamics of Intellectual Property Policymaking." *Yale Journal of International Law* 29(1): 1–84.

Hollywood Reporter. 2012. "Sundance 2012: MPAA's Chris Dodd Calls Piracy Defeat a 'Watershed Event.'" Last modified January 24. http://hollywoodreporter.com/risky-business/sundance-2012-chris-dodd-mpaa-piracy-284190.

Kaminski, Margot. 2012. "The U.S. Trade Representative's (USTR's) Democracy Problem." *Suffolk Transnational Law Review* 35(3): 519–550.

Levine, David S. 2012. "Bring in the Nerds: Secrecy, National Security, and the Creation of International Intellectual Property Law." *Cardozo Arts & Entertainment Law Journal* 30: 105–151.

Matthews, Duncan. 2002. *Globalising Intellectual Property Rights: The TRIPS Agreement*. London: Routledge.

Morin, Jean-Frederic. 2014. "Paradigm Shift in the Global IP Regime: The Agency of Academics." *Review of International Political Economy* 21(2): 275–309.

ProPublica. 2012. "SOPA Opera Update: Opposition Surges." January 19. https://www.propublica.org/nerds/item/sopa-opera-update.

Sell, Susan K. 2003. *Private Power, Public Law: The Globalization of Intellectual Property Rights*. Cambridge: Cambridge University Press.

Sell, Susan K. 2010. "The Rise and Rule of a Trade-Based Strategy: Historical Institutionalism and the Regulation of Intellectual Property." *Review of International Political Economy* 17(4): 762–790.

Sell, Susan K. 2013. "Revenge of the 'Nerds': Collective Action against Intellectual Property Maximalism in the Global Information Age." *International Studies Review* 15: 67–85.

Shaffer, Gregory. 2012. "Transnational Legal Processes and State Change." *Law and Social Inquiry* 37(2): 229–264.

Tarrow, Sidney. 2010. "Outsiders Inside and Insiders Outside: Linking Transnational and Domestic Public Action for Human Rights." *Human Rights Quarterly* 11: 171–182.

United States Trade Representative. 2007. "Ambassador Schwab Announces U.S. Will Seek New Trade Agreement to Fight Fakes." Last modified October 23. http://www.ustr.gov/ambassador-schwab-announces-us-will-seek-new-trade-agreement-fight-fakes.

Weatherall, Kimberlee. 2012. "Politics, Compromise, Text and the Failures of the Anti-Counterfeiting Trade Agreement." *Sydney Law Review* 33: 229–263.

World Intellectual Property Organization. 2004. "Draft Substantive Patent Law Treaty." http://www.wipo.int/patent-law/en/harmonization.htm.

World Intellectual Property Organization. 2005. "Proposal to Establish a Development Agenda for WIPO: An Elaboration of Issues Raised in Document WO/GA/31/11." IIM/1/4 (April 6). http://www.wipo.int/edocs/mdocs/en/iim1/iim14.pdf.

Yu, Peter. 2011. "TRIPS and Its Achilles' Heel." *Journal of Intellectual Property Law* 18(2): 479–532.

SECTION II

The Global Transfer of Norms

5

Colonizing the Clinic: The Adventures of Law in HIV Treatment and Research

Carol A. Heimer and Jaimie Morse

I. INTRODUCTION

Sociolegal scholars have been sensitive to the variety of ways that law in action differs from law on the books. Gaps between the two are especially likely to arise when law moves across boundaries. This chapter looks at the use of law in HIV clinics (in the United States, South Africa, Thailand, and Uganda) that are involved in both treatment and research. In this case, law moves simultaneously across two boundaries when it is transported from legal arenas to medical settings and from the global North to the global South. Because the (new) legal forms are arriving in settings that already have rules, guidelines, and norms, the process of importation is quite complex. Moreover, medical conventions about how to work with rules are different than lawyerly ways of using rules, necessitating further adjustments.

To explore these processes of transnational diffusion of rules and their associated norms, we focus on the role of staff in key intermediary organizations who act as "regulatory wranglers" (Heimer 2013a) both to adapt rules to local realities and to make local realities appear more legible to and in line with what the rules require, thereby contributing to "regulatory success." Their roles in facilitating organizational and normative change recall the work of Merry's (2006a) "translators," Silbey's (2011) "sociological citizens," and Sturm's (2006) "organizational catalysts" who enable uptake and modification of new norms and conventions originally developed at a distance from sites of implementation.

In this way, our research offers a new lens through which to explore mechanisms, processes, and impacts associated with the globalization of law. To date, much of the work in this field of scholarship has taken up processes through which transnational laws, regulations, standards, and norms emerge, diffuse across national borders, and are adopted as national policy, with a focus on state change (Shaffer 2012, 242–243) through national statutes, cases, and regulations (Halliday and Osinsky 2006) and across a variety of legal domains. Further,

This research was supported by the American Bar Foundation, the National Science Foundation (NSF SES-0319560, PI Carol Heimer), and the Russell Sage Foundation.

as Munger (2012) notes, much of this scholarship has focused on formal institutions of law and elite lawyers – and, we would add, elites generally – who create, resist, or facilitate adoption of new national laws, regulations, or governance structures (cf. Dezaley and Garth 1996, 2002, 2010; Halliday and Carruthers 2007). In contrast, scholarship on domestic and transnational social movements in processes of democratic transitions and rights claiming highlights the role of nonelites and activists (cf. Kay 2011; Klug 2000; Merry 2006b; Munger 2008–2009). These nonelites and activists – who may act in concert with elites or who are themselves elites in their local settings – prompt adoption of new laws, legal reforms, and legal frameworks.

These processes of transnational diffusion, adoption, and adaptation occur within fundamentally unequal governance systems in which norms, rules, and resources often move from the global North to the global South (Silbey 1997). Additionally, as we will show, South–South and South–North transfers have increasingly characterized the circulation of normative frameworks and model laws as well. In the midst of these transfers, all too often rules, priorities, and policies crafted in the places marked as "global" (e.g., Geneva, where the World Health Organization [WHO] sits) come to be interpreted by those power holders as "universal" ideals that should govern practice globally. However, these new laws and norms reflect what Santos (1995) has called "a globalized localism" – something (an object, a law, a language) that is in fact the product of a very specific place and time that serves the interests of particular power holders but that is described as global or universal once it has spread transnationally. As we will demonstrate, many of the new laws and norms developed in the global North and introduced under the banner of universal best practices are revealed to be quite specific and laden with moral and cultural assumptions that may not resonate with or complement preexisting norms and routines.

Yet, as Klug demonstrates, actors in particular settings – both elites and nonelites – may strategically use, adapt, and deploy norms and laws originating in distant locales for their own purposes, a process that results in hybrid rules, which in turn influence global discourse. Klug argues for "a dialectical understanding of the relationship between the global and local in which local agency deploys global forms and is both reshaped in the process and contributes to the continuing reformulation of global alternatives" (2002, 277). Klug's hybrid rules recall the mutually constitutive processes of transfer, uptake, and iterative modification that Halliday and Carruthers (2007) have called the "recursivity" of law. Indeed, even presumptuous colonial agents must contend with the people and the realities of the environments they seek to study and change, as Tilley (2011) shows in her account of medical and scientific discoveries made in the context of British colonization. The resulting interactions between the metropole and the colony inevitably transformed both, as she demonstrates, fundamentally shaping science and medicine as they evolved in the early twentieth century.

This project extends this area of scholarship to a new setting (medicine) with a focus on meso and micro levels of analysis that operate below the level of the nation-state and suggest new mechanisms of transfer, sources of authority, and enforcement. First, we explore how law operates in a new domain outside of the formal institutions of law (medicine) that to date has largely been neglected within the scholarship on the globalization of law. In this new domain, mechanisms of transfer, sources of authority, and enforcement often do not require formal national policy adoption and may bypass the nation-state altogether, particularly when both the creator and the enforcer of new rules and norms lies outside the national jurisdiction (e.g., US Food and Drug Administration [FDA]).

Second, the invocation of law in the domain of medicine often involves a transformation of law and a rethinking of the meaning and relevance of traditional categories of "hard law" and "soft law." The rules governing the practice of medicine involve both hard law and soft law, and sometimes also a conversion of hard law into soft law in the absence of enforcement mechanisms within this new domain. Formal law may involve the police and surveillance powers associated with the public health functions of the state, such as mandatory reporting of new infections or forcible quarantine of individuals exposed to highly infectious, untreatable, and/or fatal viruses. Formal law may also involve threats of medical malpractice lawsuits or legal determinations of who may consent to medical procedures on behalf of dependents or those with cognitive impairments.

However, more influential in many ways in the routine practice of medicine are the pressures to recognize, attend to, and comply with the soft law associated with rules, reporting requirements, and anticipated sanctions of a variety of entities that govern subparts of medicine through legislative, interpretive, and oversight activities and have government-like functions. In this chapter we focus on the more subtle, processual effects of adoption, adaptation, compliance, and sometimes resistance to new forms of soft law that influence medical decision making and in turn impact patient care and treatment in the crucible of the clinic.

Third, by training attention on meso and micro levels of analysis, we highlight processes of adoption, adaptation, resistance, and sometimes mutual adjustment at the "messy leading edge of institutionalization" (Heimer 2013a, 142) in particular organizations (HIV clinics in four countries) and their impacts on patient care and treatment. We focus on the more subtle but consequential effects of soft law that transform the daily routines and practice of medicine and have a direct impact on patient care and treatment, even in the absence of strong enforcement mechanisms.

Our central purpose in this chapter is to highlight six processes that characterize clinic-level responses to new rules, laws, and legal regimes. These processes include making preexisting routines legible to outsiders, adoption and compliance, adaptation, resistance, mutual influence, and mutual adjustment. We provide empirical evidence of preexisting norms and rules and how these must be transformed to be legible to outsiders and brought into rough compliance with new regulations. We argue that the result is an unsettled and often incoherent structure of governance that requires continual tinkering as clinic workers weigh priorities and adjust to local circumstances. The legal colonization of the clinic is thus an unfinished project.

The remainder of the chapter is divided into four sections. We first describe our methods and the data on which we draw. We then provide an overview of the incursion of law into the new substantive setting of medicine. We next discuss each of the six processes that describe how HIV clinics in Uganda, South Africa, and Thailand respond to the introduction of new rules and legal regimes. In concluding, we compare substantive and geographic boundary crossings and discuss implications for the globalization of law.

II. BACKGROUND: THE PROJECT, THE SITES, AND THE DATA

To support our argument, we draw on ethnographic data and interviews gathered for a project on the legalization of medicine. With clinical guidelines, research protocols, and the other trappings of evidence-based medicine, HIV clinics are good places to study legalism. As will become clear in what follows, the gap between rules on the books and rules in action is a real concern of clinic workers, particularly when rules are transported from rich countries to poorer ones and from legal to medical settings. In order to understand the effects of the migration of rules, the research was designed to include HIV clinics in countries where rules originated as well as those to which rules were transplanted. Generally, the receiving countries were also poorer, and clinics in these countries struggled to find the resources needed to comply with rules and to document that compliance. Beyond the shortage of resources, clinics also struggled with the differences among rules. Clinical guidelines and medical standard operating procedures (SOPs) seemed more intuitive to clinic workers, while rules emanating from research committees, administrative units, or states posed greater challenges. For this reason, we studied clinics engaged in both treatment and research and therefore subject to multiple regulatory regimes.

The ethnographic research was conducted in two HIV clinics in the United States and one each in South Africa, Thailand, and Uganda. All five clinics in the study were engaged in both treatment and research, though, as readers will see, the boundary between the two is blurry. All of the clinics had hospital and university affiliations. All but the Thai clinic received American government funds for treatment (as well as receiving funds from local sources), and all five clinics received some of their research funding (directly or indirectly) from the US National Institutes of Health (NIH), necessitating adherence to American government rules about the ethical conduct of research. Because some research results would be used in drug approval processes, the clinics were also attentive to the rules of the US FDA.

In each field site, one or two members of the team conducted the bulk of the research while others visited the site for brief periods.[1] The fieldwork in the American clinics was of longer duration (just short of two years in US1; thirteen months in US2) but was less intensive (we were not in the field every day). We spent four months doing intensive fieldwork in Thailand, Uganda, and South Africa, with multiple two-week visits before and after. We began fieldwork in US1 in September 2003 and last revisited our sites in Uganda, Thailand, and South Africa between June and August 2007.

We shadowed staff as they conducted the study visits of clinical trials; examined patients coming for treatment; made phone calls; went over records with research monitors, site visitors, and accreditors; and attended endless meetings. We gathered copies of forms (for recording data, reporting serious adverse events, referring patients, etc.) and policies used in clinic work (standard operating procedures, clinic guidelines, etc.). We talked with and observed staff in a variety of positions at all levels – physicians, principal investigators, nurses, administrators, social workers and counselors, receptionists, and data processors. The information we gathered allowed us to observe the operation of both official rules and rules in action and to see how the gap between the two varied from one setting and one kind of rule to another.

In addition to the ethnographic fieldwork and associated informal discussions, we conducted well over a hundred formal interviews with clinic workers and experts not directly affiliated with the clinics. Interviews were audio recorded and transcribed. Field notes and interview transcripts were coded using Atlas.ti.

III. CROSSING DISCIPLINARY BOUNDARIES

Both in the United States and in other parts of the world, health care is much more organized around rules than has been the case in the past. In recent decades, the number of bodies issuing rules about health care, the number of rules issued, and the number of activities governed by rules all have increased (Heimer, Petty, and Culyba 2005; Timmermans and Berg 2003). This is in part because successive forms of governance in health care join rather than supplant previous forms. Thus in American health care, professional, public, managerial, and market governance mechanisms are bewilderingly layered and interwoven (Scott, Ruef, Mendel, and Caronna 2000, 348–349). This has meant both a larger number of rules and a different mix of rules. Professional self-regulation has now been joined by mandates emanating from state bodies and third-party payers. The resulting formal law, official regulations, clinical guidelines, research protocols, rules of quasi-official regulatory bodies such as the Joint Commission, policies of insurers and other third-party payers, and organizational policies and standard operating procedures – different

[1] The fieldwork and associated interviews were conducted by Carol Heimer, JuLeigh Petty, Lynn Gazley, Rebecca Culyba, Enid Wamani, and Dusita Pheungsamran. Jaimie Morse conducted supplementary interviews in Geneva and coded field notes and interviews in Atlas.ti.

types of rules – are all authoritative statements intended to shape the activity of participants in health care settings. Moreover, in health care, as in other fields experiencing ramped-up pressures for accountability (Espeland and Vannebo 2007; Strathern 2000; Power 1997), new professions have arisen to write, revise, and track the rules; to monitor work and records to ensure adherence to rules; to assess the credentials and performance of staff members; to scrutinize bills and make decisions on payments; and to settle disputes.

In effect, the increasingly legalistic approach to health care amounts to an importation of law, legal actors, and legalistic, rule-driven approaches into health care settings. With some exceptions, though, the law transported across the boundary into health care is soft rather than hard law, gray-letter rather than black-letter law. The legalization that has occurred in the world of medicine thus can fruitfully be compared with soft legalization in international relations and international organization. "Highly legalized institutions," Abbott, Keohane, Moravcsik, Slaughter, and Snidal (2000) write, "are those in which rules are obligatory on parties through links to the established rules and principles of international law, in which rules are precise (or can be made precise through the exercise of delegated authority), and in which authority to interpret and apply the rules has been delegated to third parties acting under the constraint of rules" (Abbott et al. 2000, 43). The more "legalized" arrangements – hard law – are those in which parties are clearly and unconditionally obligated to follow the rules, the rules are precise with little room for interpretation, and provisions have been made both for delegated dispute resolution (by a courtlike entity) and for rule making and implementation (Abbott et al. 2000; Abbott and Snidal 2000). Less legalized arrangements can be softer on any or all of these dimensions; the three dimensions need not move in tandem.

In the world of medicine, legalization arises both from the efforts of formal legal systems and governments and from the legislative, interpretive, and oversight activities of other entities that govern subparts of medicine. The dimensions remain the same, but inevitably the mechanisms are somewhat modified when governance is carried out by nonstate actors. Almost inevitably, law in this realm is somewhat softer because its rules often are not fully articulated with the laws and regulations of the formal legal system. Yet there are many instances of well-developed mechanisms for monitoring and enforcement, a good deal of precision in the rules and routines themselves, instructions for how to figure out what to do when a situation is not covered by the rule, and bodies charged with settling disputes.

Some of the complexity of the system of governance in the world of health care arises because of its multi-cephalic character. In health care, there are many fiefdoms, each with its own "legislators," "executives," and "courts." But because what is being governed is not primarily a geographical area but instead semi-independent functions such as research, treatment, drug distribution, training of health care personnel, and payment for goods and services, these fiefdoms overlap in space and time, sometimes creating chaos rather than order.

To add to the complexity, some of these rules span national borders because, in contemporary medicine, research, training, and even some treatments draw funding and some personnel from distant places. Further, inequalities in HIV care and treatment are matters of governance, taken broadly to include providing, distributing, and regulating (Braithwaite, Coglianese, and Levi-Faur 2007). Much like governance of medicine generally, HIV treatment and research are regulated by national governments, but "soft governance" by nongovernmental bodies – gray-letter law rather than black-letter law – is equally important. Much of this soft governance is transnational and highly decentralized, with weak, indirect, or remote sites of enforcement that create typical principal–agent problems[2] at multiple layers in national- and clinic-level regulatory and health care delivery systems. The mechanisms of governance are sometimes rules of granting agencies and sometimes purportedly neutral standards established by international bodies. This chapter examines governance in the international world of HIV treatment and research to ask how mechanisms of governance – rules, standards, and other forms of soft law – travel across national borders and what the effects of these geographical boundary crossings might be. As we will show, all too often the burden of adjusting – both the rules and their associated practices – falls on clinic staff or other intermediaries who must make rules created at a geographical distance workable in new environments to which they are not always well suited.

But what, practically speaking, actually happens when law moves into HIV clinics, when the level of legal oversight increases, and when clinics themselves adopt more legalistic approaches? Our investigation of the encounter between law and legalistic/governance approaches, on the one hand, and medicine and medical/scientific approaches, on the other, suggests several points of tension. Some of these arise from struggles associated with shared jurisdiction and the embedding of medical work in organizations, while others arise from profession-based differences in approaches to rules. In practice, then, colonizing the clinic means entering a new organizational and professional space. As our examples will show, though, these tensions are likely to appear in messy, overlapping form in any particular real-world encounter between law and medicine.

We now turn to the responses to, and uses of, new rules in the HIV clinics we observed in Uganda, South Africa, and Thailand. We characterize these responses as entailing six analytically distinct processes: making preexisting routines legible to outsiders, adoption and compliance, adaptation, resistance, mutual influence, and mutual adjustment.

2 For a useful review of the literature on principal–agent relations, see Shapiro (2005).

IV. RESPONSES TO AND USES OF RULES IN HIV/AIDS CLINICS IN UGANDA, SOUTH AFRICA, AND THAILAND

Sociolegal scholars have long been interested in variations in the effectiveness of attempts to remold the world with legal and regulatory tools (Lempert and Sanders 1986; Nonet and Selznick 2001; Edelman, Uggen and Erlanger 1999; Heimer 1996, 1999; Dobbin 2011, to name only a few). Much of this scholarship has developed through studies of organizations and professions. HIV clinics are, after all, organizations made up of persons of particular professions and their associated disciplinary skills, expertise, and ways of approaching problems. However, organizations in the United States have been the central empirical sites that organization theorists (March 1994) and institutionalist scholars (DiMaggio and Powell 1983; Edelman et al. 2011; Dobbin 2011) have studied to generate much of the theory that is used to explain whether new laws and regulations achieve their intended outcomes in particular settings. The same is true of research that has looked specifically at how health care settings adapt to legal and regulatory mandates (Zussman 1992; Shapiro 2012; Fagerlin and Schneider 2004; Heimer 1996, 1999).

While this large body of work suggests important mechanisms of transfer and reasons for greater or lesser uptake of new rules once introduced in a variety of organizational settings, much of this theory has not yet been tested in empirical sites outside of the United States. Thus, tracing the processes and impacts of the globalization of law and its introduction into HIV clinics in low- and middle-income countries requires recentering empirical sites in the global South, marking laws and legal regimes developed in the global North as both particular and local in their origins, assumptions, and prescriptions, and also marking the theory used to explain outcomes of regulation as both particular and local as well.

Drawing on insights about mechanisms of transfer and reasons for varying degrees of uptake of transported rules that have been suggested by existing theory, we describe six analytically distinct ways that the clinics in Uganda, South Africa, and Thailand responded to new rules. Although many social processes occur in the shadow of the law (Mnookin and Kornhauser 1979), the effect of law is by no means uniform. Some of the variation is accounted for by how law is brought into and adjusted to new settings. Often these new settings are organizations, and often the actors who work out the details at the legal/substantive interface draw on organizational policies and their own professional training as well as the laws and regulations they are charged with implementing. Our purpose here is to ask what happens when law moves into the clinic. Note that "law moves into the clinic" means both that formal law enters the clinic and that clinics adopt more legalistic approaches.

But the geographical distance between *makers* and *implementers* of rules is just one feature of the transnational legal regulation of medicine. Another equally important feature is the geographical distance between the *enforcers* and *implementers* of rules. In some ways there are weaker pressures for harmonization and standardization in the transnational governance of medicine than in other domains of formal law (e.g., trade and bankruptcy). The degree of compliance, enforcement, and sanctions for noncompliance varies greatly – between regions, between countries, and even between particular hospitals and clinics in the same country. Relative access to resources matters greatly for being able to comply with standards created and enforced in the global North but implemented in the global South, such that higher-resource hospitals in lower-income countries – such as the clinics in this study – may have a significant advantage in being able to comply, but also in being able to resist, adapt, or obscure noncompliance – namely, in the ability to both create and guard the "dark corners" that we will discuss.

A. MAKING PREEXISTING ROUTINES LEGIBLE TO OUTSIDERS

When global rules, whether they be clinical guidelines, research protocols, SOPs for laboratories, or monitoring and evaluation systems, arrive along with the research and treatment dollars, there is typically already something there. As Bartley (2011) notes, those studying transnational governance tend to think of global governance and transnational standards as either transcendent or essentially technical. In either case, what gets overlooked, Bartley argues, is the very important fact that almost always there are already rules, standards, laws, codes of conduct, and so forth in place within a country, and the global rules are not just filling a vacuum but instead are being layered on top of whatever was already there. That makes for a much messier regulatory problem than has been imagined.

The outcomes of these realignment processes are consequential, not simply for managing and demonstrating compliance, but also for maintaining positive evaluations of reputation, competence, and perceived worthiness of continued investments and aid. Whatever standards seek to influence, these standards come to be not just "the way it's done" but also what is considered *good*. Particular ways of doing things become valorized, and others may be evaluated not as valid alternatives or next-best methods but rather as deviant, odd, subpar.

As a result, as Douglas (1986) observed, dark corners have their advantages, and that is certainly true in these matters of governance. Heimer (2012) discusses how some of these dark corners emerge, arguing that *regulatory forms* (literally the paperwork) often conceal as much as they reveal. And it is exactly because of the regulatory mismatches between global and local that clinic workers wish to protect their dark corners. In this way, much governance is indeed global in origin but superimposed on preexisting local regulatory systems that are then charged with doing the arduous work of adjusting.

In this section, we describe the work that clinic staff do to make preexisting routines legible to outsiders and, in so doing, make informal procedures and workflow logics appear more standardized. We observed countless instances where outsiders initially suspected noncompliance because they had not come to the site to see for themselves but were instead drawing conclusions from a distance, did not understand which records were stored in a hospital and which in the clinic, or were unaware that some records would be kept in a local language and others in English. We use two examples to elucidate these processes.

In Uganda, this concern with legibility pervaded clinic work. Overwhelmed clinic staff were deeply concerned about whether they could comply fully with the specifications of research protocols. The problem was not that they were doing their work haphazardly, but that because their routines were not always formalized or identical to those used in the United States, their work might *appear* haphazard to outsiders. The problem was solved when a research monitor helpfully informed the research team that although following clinic SOPs was mandatory, the rules permitted them to write their own SOPs. Once the clinic SOPs had been written, the Ugandan clinic could demonstrate that its staff members were working in an orderly, rule-governed way and the monitor could cite the SOPs as evidence in support of this claim. But the production of the full complement of SOPs that would make local work routines legible to outsiders was an exceedingly time-consuming process. As if this investment in legible SOPs were not enough, Ugandan clinic staff also undertook an extensive guideline-writing project to formalize and document their practices. Without this documentation, they worried that monitors and site visitors "could read variability [from rich-country practices] in treatment decisions as people really not knowing what they're doing." Regulatory affairs staff also carefully instructed counselors, who were responsible for securing consent of patients and research subjects, to provide a "clear trail" in their notes, with ample supplementary information "for people who may have little or no knowledge of the local situation."

Our second example illustrates what happens when local practices are judged inadequate because they are not legible to powerful outsiders. Scientists, including the HIV researchers we studied, are eager to disseminate their work and to publish it in high-prestige outlets. Generally speaking, general medical journals outrank specialty journals, and international journals outrank local ones. To publish in the highest-status outlets typically requires that researchers produce high-quality data on questions that are deemed to have global importance. Both elements have proven difficult for researchers in low- and middle-income countries, as Gazley (2011), drawing on data from this project, explains. Locally relevant research (on appropriate dosages for people with lower body weight in Thailand, or on inexpensive regimens to prevent mother-to-child transmission of HIV in Uganda, for example) might seem less vital to international audiences. In both treatment and research programs, the clinics of poorer countries have necessarily relied on a different balance between costly viral load tests and less expensive CD4 measurements than have clinics in richer countries.[3] As international journals changed their policies, insisting on viral load data when they had previously accepted less expensive CD4

[3] CD4 cells are a type of white blood cell that fights infection.

counts, the clinics of poorer countries found it hard to keep up. When the top journals of the global North dictate publication standards, research results from low- and middle-income countries do not get disseminated. Much local knowledge and expertise is therefore undervalued, not publicly available, and less likely to be used in crafting formal guidelines. And because publication is the coin that buys inclusion in scientific circles, marginalization of researchers from poorer countries tends to be self-perpetuating. However, as we will discuss, some principal investigators based in the United States recognized the experience and expertise of their Ugandan counterparts, particularly in the areas of preventing mother-to-child transmission (PMTCT) and treatment of children, topics that were understudied in the United States due to differences in the profile of the epidemic and much wider availability of treatment for pregnant women.

B. ADOPTION AND COMPLIANCE

Our observations in HIV clinics suggest that the effects of incursions of law into medical settings range from small, annoying "taxes" on nearly everyone, through more substantial modifications of work environments, to deeply distressing bottlenecks with the potential to cause serious harm. New rules often brought new accountability regimes to severely underresourced clinics and hospitals, necessitating the creation of new staff positions dedicated to monitoring and reporting duties and the diversion of precious resources and skilled personnel from routine care and treatment. Such reallocations underscore the very material effects of global inequities in AIDS governance. These inequities are directly tied to the relative power of clinic staff in agenda setting, rule making, and ultimately the opportunity for intellectual ownership of HIV treatment and research in the settings in which they work.

To be clear, clinic staff were not opposed to rules per se. But they did distinguish rules that "made sense" to them from rules that seemed arbitrary. Generally, the rules that clinic workers had learned as part of their professional training had come to seem "natural"; other rules felt "foreign" or "unnatural" – an intrusion into the medical world. In our field sites, those rules that felt imposed were marked linguistically as "what they want," whereas rules and procedures that seemed natural and did not feel like regulation were referenced by such phrases as "you always..." or "you must...." Because staff members felt that these regulations sometimes prevented them from paying attention to more important matters, they looked for shortcuts that would make compliance less costly. In US1, for instance, after the clinic was repeatedly "dinged" by the monitor for failing to specify whether weights were being recorded in kilos or pounds, staff members revised their forms so that units of measure were prespecified. With the revised forms, nurses no longer had to remember to specify that weights were in pounds and temperatures in Fahrenheit. Compliance with this particular rule became costless.

In the daily work of the clinics, staff members were obliged to attend to compliance with the mandates of a variety of outsiders. Records of patient visits had to be documented in a way that would satisfy payers, and service and patient counts had to be maintained for grants reporting. Other clinic records had to meet the exacting requirements of research protocols and stand up to inspection by research monitors.

Researchers compile data from the ordinary medical visits of their research subjects, as well as from regularly scheduled research appointments. Records that were adequate for caregiving sometimes proved inadequate for research. When a research subject visited a primary care physician because of a bout of diarrhea, for instance, the physician might not bother to assign a numerical grade to the patient's symptoms. But when patients are also research subjects, researchers need data about the severity of their symptoms. In such cases, research nurses contacted primary caregivers, asking them to assign numerical grades to these "adverse events" (symptoms) after the fact. Research monitors regularly checked records to see that adverse events were properly recorded and appropriately reported up the research chain. They also inspected consent forms, verified that research staff had administered medications and conducted tests on the schedule mandated by the protocol, checked that data entered into case report forms matched data from source documents, and confirmed that researchers were following standard operating procedures specifying exactly how data are to be gathered and recorded.

In some cases, though, ensuring compliance required much more than imposing a "tax" on everyone's attention. As the volume and complexity of rules increased and as monitoring of compliance became more common, clinics often found it necessary to assign this compliance work to specialists. Thus, all clinics assigned the work of managing research ethics reviews, interfacing with research monitors, and communicating with protocol teams to research coordinators or regulatory affairs specialists. To be absolutely certain that they are compliant, clinics may also create quality assurance teams or add positions for internal monitors. In Uganda, the previous experiences with skeptical regulators and concerns about whether their clinical trials data would stand up to FDA review led staff to create an elaborate, three-tiered quality assurance/quality control (QA/QC) program that even reached into hospital units that helped with clinic data collection. The Thai clinic's internal monitoring program began with scrutiny of two studies, but evolved into a clinic-wide program with extensive production of special forms to remind staff how to collect and present information to meet the exacting standards of regulators. The South African clinic invested heavily in its monitoring and evaluation (M&E) procedures to satisfy the requirements of funders. In all of the clinics, similar adjustments were made in clinical work, with nurse managers devoting considerable time to compliance work.

In an interesting twist, then, despite their objection to the volume and rigidity of rules, HIV clinics have typically not resisted the rules. Instead, they have looked for ways to protect the time and attention of clinical and research staff, creating a division of labor in which some workers attend to the technical core (research, treatment) while others take on the more peripheral but still highly consequential work of ensuring compliance. And even if other staff were not enthusiastic about the extra work, the compliance specialists were deeply invested in both compliance and the appearance of compliance. The latter could be especially challenging for clinics in poor and middle-income countries. As a member of the Thai staff explained, there was much to lose if work appeared shoddy: "If these [a box of blood samples] go out wrong, we look stupid."

Some of the difficulties with the transfer of rules are legacies of the discovery of HIV as a new disease in the United States and the patient protections that were put in place as a result of the stigma and discrimination surrounding the new disease. By the time HIV/AIDS was recognized as a new disease in 1981, and especially by the time the disease was being treated in specialty clinics some years later,[4] health care organizations and their staff members were becoming accustomed to new legalistic ways of doing things. Nevertheless, the challenges of managing HIV led to a series of new rules and an even greater presence of law and legal institutions in health care organizations. Concerns and confusion about the new disease initially brought proposals to quarantine those who were infected, to keep infected children out of school, and so on. After the worst paranoia surrounding the disease faded away, what remained was a residue of new rules shoring up patient rights, including rules about HIV testing (especially that it should be voluntary and preceded and followed by counseling) and confidentiality (results not to be shared with anyone but the person being tested or that person's guardian, and in particular not to be shared with employers, schools, insurers, etc.).

HIV also reshaped the practice of medicine with new medical guidelines designed to curb the spread of infectious diseases. Among these were provisions to ensure the safety of blood products and "universal precautions" (mandated use of gloves, safe disposal of sharps, etc.). In addition, the practice of HIV medicine has been especially strongly organized around guidelines, perhaps because of the institutionalization of standards and conventions about how to assess and grade scientific evidence and how to use such knowledge to formulate clinical guidelines. Thus, from the very early days, a wide variety of guideline-writing bodies disseminated guidelines for "staging" the disease, preventing and treating opportunistic infections, composing a regimen of antiretroviral drugs (ARVs) and initiating therapy, monitoring progress, treating side effects, watching for evidence of failure, composing alternative or "salvage" regimens, and so forth. Alongside the rules about treatment

4 The opening dates for the clinics we observed ranged from 1988 to 1996. The oldest of our sites is the private US clinic (US1). Researchers applied to have a research center in 1987 and have been conducting research and treating patients since 1988. The public US facility (US2) opened its doors in 1996. The Ugandan clinic began its research program in collaboration with an American university in 1988, but did not acquire its own facilities until 2000. The Thai clinic, which also began as a dedicated research facility, was founded in 1996. The South African clinic began its work in 1996.

were parallel rules for HIV research, including strict provisions for ethics review, requirements to report adverse events, and obligations to care for research subjects during (and sometimes after) clinical trials.

Rules guarding patient confidentiality pose particular difficulties in settings in which HIV is a generalized epidemic and significant numbers of family members, caregivers, and clinic staff may be at risk of unintentional transmission when caring for HIV-infected patients. Clinic staff in urban settings in South Africa (like the area where we observed) know that as many as a third of pregnant women are estimated to be living with HIV, making the risk of transmission via accidental needle-stick injuries a very serious and daily concern. South African law does allow for some exceptions to rules about patient confidentiality in the case of needle-stick injuries.[5] However, the procedures that must be followed to make such exceptions legally acceptable can be cumbersome and time-consuming, and often continue to require formal permission to bypass the usual consent routines. During the time it takes to complete the legal procedure, the HIV infection can easily be transmitted. Patients were sometimes too ill, embarrassed, or fearful to disclose their status or to consent to be tested, even when a clinic staff member's life could be in danger. Often clinic staff expressed their own very real fears of getting themselves or the clinic into trouble if they tested a patient without his or her consent. But they had equally real fears for the health and safety of innocent third parties. Because of their fears of acquiring HIV, staff had at times administered "silent tests" after needle-stick injuries to determine if the patient was infected with HIV and if staff needed to begin a course of postexposure prophylaxis (PEP) treatment immediately. When this informal practice was mentioned during an in-house training session, the counselors laughed nervously, unsure whether the hospital's routine fully conformed to the law.

C. ADAPTATION

The management of discretion varies by field. In medicine, discretion is local and is concentrated in doctors. In law, in contrast, discretion is concentrated at the appellate level rather than at the first encounter between case and law (Stinchcombe 2001; Llewellyn 1960). In any given medical institution, the right to interpret and adjust is in the hands of the doctors first encountering the case; interpretation and adjustment generally does not have to wait for the judgment of higher-ranking, specialist doctors. We should not overstate this point, though. Within medical institutions, occupations are partially ranked, with doctors having authority over nurses and so having a larger sphere of discretion than nurses. Within this system of ranked occupations, though, nurses and other professionals

[5] South African law also allows for exceptions for people endangered by a nondisclosing, HIV-infected sexual partner.

(phlebotomists, physical therapists, various technicians) do retain some control over their separate jurisdictions and some discretion within that special sphere despite the overall dominance of doctors. And within the sphere of doctors, there are of course some medical problems that require referral and some categories of doctors (interns, residents) who have less autonomy.

In addition to tailoring their actions to fit the cases they encounter, in many places doctors also can modify the rules that they work with so that these rules have a better fit with the stream of cases they typically encounter. To put it differently, the medical "law" that doctors work with can be adjusted in the place where this "law" encounters the cases. Clinical guidelines can be recrafted to be local documents.

As medicine has become more legalized, though, some of this local flexibility has disappeared. More of the work of doctors (and other medical workers) has come to be organized around clinical guidelines, and this has disciplined the dialogue between cases and medical knowledge by making it more often a dialogue that takes place in the context of medical "law," a particular summation of medical knowledge. At the same time, these guidelines have been adopted as standards of practice by governments, granting bodies, insurers, and clinics. As the soft law of medicine is hardened, doctors are more often required to justify their decisions to senior doctors or external review panels. Discretion is thus less local, more constrained by medical "law," and more subject to review.

Increasingly guidelines have *both* medical and legal content, so jurisdiction is now *shared*. This sharing of jurisdiction usefully diffuses guidelines to places they otherwise would not have reached and raises questions about the allocation of medical resources. The difficulty, of course, is that sometimes the rigidity that is introduced by an increasing emphasis on rules undermines the very important local adjustment that is the hallmark of medicine. For example, doctors in the South African clinic worried that joining the national rollout program would reduce their discretion and endanger some of their patients. In particular, they were concerned about the government's requirement to get permission before switching patients off the first-line antiretroviral regimen. The government regimen included d4T, which sometimes caused lactic acidosis, a life-threatening metabolic disorder, in patients with a high body mass index (BMI). The clinic itself was cautious about prescribing d4T for obese patients, and watched carefully for lactic acidosis if the drug was used. As it turned out, the government operationalized "getting permission" as informing officials of the switch after the fact, so practitioner discretion was preserved. Yet clinic staff were right to worry. In another infamous case, provincial health authorities in KwaZulu-Natal charged a physician with "acting beyond his authority" and "without prior permission of his superiors" in accepting donations for and implementing a dual-therapy program for pregnant women that provided better treatment than mandated by the provincial guidelines (press release, KwaZulu-Natal Department of Health, February 11, 2008; Dugger 2008).

We have looked at how the use of medical guidelines changes when those guidelines have a legal element. Because they lack expertise in legal matters, clinic staff are often quite uncomfortable with these legal interfaces. In long years of training, medical staff are taught to use guidelines flexibly. It is their responsibility to assess whether and how guidelines actually apply. Although clinical guidelines may allow physicians to stand on the shoulders of generations of other doctors and scientists, they are always aware that there will be exceptions. Their medical training thus equips them intellectually and morally to make the judgment calls about when and how guidelines should be put aside. But physicians do not routinely know when to put the law aside or how they can do that even if they should.

Although recommendations of expert and scientific advisory bodies influence the development of law and legal regimes in many domains of formal law, our interviews suggest that these types of forums are particularly influential in the promulgation of new rules and conventions in medicine. As a result, in the governance of medicine, expert and ad hoc scientific advisory bodies are just as influential as courts and government regulatory agencies in promulgating new rules and regulatory regimes, and sometimes even more so, making geographical distance from – and unequal access to – sites of expert consensus making that much more consequential. Not only do mechanisms of regulatory change and enforcement in the domain of medicine often operate outside formal institutions of law, but they may in fact circumvent national-level law and policy adoption altogether.

Another example of local adaptation is the development of procedures to operationalize the principle of voluntary and informed consent in research in these new settings. Although the principles of informed consent are strongly and universally endorsed in the major statements on medical and research ethics (e.g., the Nuremberg Code and the Declaration of Helsinki), many questions arise when the principles are translated into concrete rules. What does informed consent mean in cultures where wives are usually not empowered to make decisions for themselves? How should procedures adjust for the changing capacities and independence of children on the brink of adulthood? In fact, the universal acceptance of the principle may make implementation more difficult. Informed consent procedures are thoroughly institutionalized, especially in clinical research and in HIV testing, and deviations from standard forms often are viewed with skepticism. Yet informed consent is completely unworkable without some adaptation, as two examples from Uganda illustrate. In the two American clinics, the process of securing consent from research subjects was thoroughly routinized. Research subjects are often handed a consent form and given a few minutes alone to read it. The staff member "consenting the subject" (to use clinic language) returns to summarize the key points and offers to answer questions. In Uganda, where literacy cannot be assumed, the staff member typically reads the form aloud to the research subject and offers to answer questions. The research subject is not asked to sign the form until it has been read aloud a second time, often on a different day. Often research subjects are not permitted to sign the form until they have passed a test on the content. Other adjustments are made for signatures for those who cannot write and for verification of age when people lack standard identity cards.

Even more extensive adaptations were required when questions arose about consent for infants and children whose HIV+ mothers had died. The clinic was supposed to follow up with the children, but the consent expired with the death of the mother. Often the mother's family cared for the child after the mother died. But under Ugandan law, the child belongs to the father and his family. The clinic's forms used a neutral language of "legal guardian," but the staff believed that someone from the father's family had to be the legal guardian. When the mother had not disclosed her infection to the father, the clinic staff worried that, given the stigma attached to HIV, the father would abandon the child when he learned the truth. The clinic struggled over this issue with the institutional review board (IRB), and the IRB finally said, "Well, go to the legal system." So the clinic asked the attorney general for a legal opinion, hoping to find some way to avoid violating the mother's confidentiality and possibly destroying the fragile tie between father and child. After thoroughly examining the law, the attorney general concluded that under the statutes on children's rights, the primary caretaker (and a careful legal definition of this term was also required) could be the legal guardian. The clinic happily modified its procedures accordingly, and the IRB accepted the solution. But untangling the complex legal and social situation "took us like two, three years," with some temporary adjustments in the interim because "you can't drop and start patients."

D. RESISTANCE

Though costly, adjusting, adopting and complying, and adapting are ways of coping with the increased legalism of clinical and research activity that can be regarded as largely successful. For the most part, research and treatment continue uninterrupted. Yet as episodic disputes show, the culture of the clinic, whether it is involved in research or treatment, has not been completely transformed by the legal overlay. Real-world consequences from following the rules can be extremely serious, as a couple of examples show.

When they receive funding from American government sources, Ugandan clinical research projects are required to undergo both local ethics review and review by an American IRB. The same regulations that govern clinical research also require compliance with US rules regarding protection of human subjects (as part of US rules governing the ethical conduct of research), such that clinics and hospitals participating in transnational, multisite clinical drug trials must adopt the Federal Wide Assurance (FWA) mandates and demonstrate compliance with all named ethics protocols and their associated standard operating procedures. Because American IRBs do not consider antiretroviral drugs (ARVs) short-term therapy, they refuse to approve studies that do not guarantee research participants a lifetime supply of the study drug.

Although the principle is indeed admirable, rigid adherence to such a principle ignores competing values. In Uganda, where very few have access to a lifetime supply of ARVs, ARVs are in fact treated as short-term therapy and valued as such. In Uganda, then, insisting on lifetime supply was seen by some as an extreme, narrow, legalistic position that too little valued both the short-term therapy and the findings of the research. In another dispute, when a research protocol was adjusted at the last minute to take account of newly available research results, another round of ethics review was required. In the interim, as the principal investigator told us, a group of women were "left in the lurch." Because the study population was pregnant women, delay meant that research subjects who had already been enrolled in the project would receive no prophylaxis to prevent them from transmitting HIV to their infants. A temporary solution had to be devised for the women about to give birth; apparently it simply was not possible for the IRBs to speed up their process to adapt to the imperious timetable of pregnancy.

In both of these cases, researchers embedded in HIV clinics seemed much more closely attuned to the variety of interests that had to be balanced, while those enforcing the rules from outside seemed narrowly focused on adhering to a principle. One American conducting research in Uganda bemoaned the "overzealousness" of American IRBs who excessively worried about "moral compromise." As he pointed out, the requirement to satisfy multiple ethics review committees "unconscionably delays research" with "very real implications for whether people live or die." Human bodies in crisis simply do not wait for IRBs to render their decisions; HIV clinics have adjusted to the timetable of the body in ways that IRBs have not.

E. MUTUAL INFLUENCE

Although we focus on the arrival of new rules often conceived in the global North that are subsequently introduced into settings in the global South, we demonstrate that uptake involves processes of adoption, adaptation, and sometimes resistance that can both reshape local medical norms and practices but also in effect modify or repurpose the rules, norms, and structures that facilitated the entry of new rules in the first place. For example, although caregivers often must find ways to comply, they also shield themselves and patients from ill-conceived or ill-suited rules by honoring their own sense of ethics, sometimes craftily using new rules and their associated resources to achieve the outcomes they feel are most important, such as using or creating research studies to provide continuity of drugs and treatment to existing patients, not just to enroll new patients in newly funded studies (Heimer 2013b).

The intensive phase of our clinic observations in Uganda, South Africa, and Thailand occurred between 2004 and 2006, such that we, in effect, observed efforts to roll out rapid HIV treatment scale-up programs in Uganda, South Africa, and Thailand. These efforts to make HIV treatment accessible in low- and middle-income countries followed a watershed historical moment from 2000 to 2002 that marked the ascendance of the global access to medicines movement and its success in prompting a sea change in normative understandings of what a right to health in the context of HIV means (i.e., access to ARVs, regardless of cost or patent protections).[6] We began observations just two years later in 2004, after the normative framework facilitating access to medicines had been established, but only shortly after attempts to actually put large numbers of people living with HIV in sub-Saharan Africa on ARVs had begun. We thus caught many of these rollout programs shortly after they were established – and therefore during the messy phase of early implementation when practitioners at the clinics we studied had started to run up against long-standing limitations in health care capacity, infrastructure, and staffing in their country contexts, but amidst a new climate in which the moral imperative to treat had finally become the international norm in global discourse, if not yet fully in policy involving all relevant sectors: trade, health care, and pharmaceutical regulation, among others.

In this context, enrollment in research studies was effectively also access to treatment. In all five clinics, but particularly in Uganda and Thailand, staff members recognized this and found ways to use resources allocated to research for maintaining continuity of treatment for existing patients and even for initiating treatment for newly diagnosed patients. As they considered the wisdom of participating in some study, they discussed whether the study would ensure continuity in drug supply for a patient just completing a previous study, whether it would at least provide the laboratory tests needed to track the progress of HIV and adjust medications, whether enrolling patients who were failing in an adherence or drug resistance study might help clinicians determine what had gone wrong, and which drugs might preserve the patient's health.

In the long run, the practice of looking for ways to meet patients' needs once a study had ended became somewhat routinized. In the US clinics, though, this was primarily a matter of matching individual patients with studies, admittedly a somewhat different approach than the designers of research protocols had in mind. In Uganda and Thailand, though, researchers and caregivers took a much more entrepreneurial approach, creating entirely new lines of "research" to accommodate their patients. The Thai clinic created a follow-up observational study, though the inclusion criteria (only people who had already been in studies at this clinic)

6 See Klug (2005, 2008, 2012) and 't Hoen (2009) for a more comprehensive account of the global access to medicines movement and its successes in making HIV treatment available in low- and middle-income countries. Among the important events occurring during this period were the 2000 AIDS conference in Durban, the 2001 Doha Declaration, the establishment of the first WHO treatment guidelines for resource-constrained settings, and the creation of the Global Fund to Fight HIV, Tuberculosis, and Malaria. The enactment of PEPFAR followed shortly thereafter in 2003.

betrayed its dual purpose. In Uganda, concerns about patient welfare led to a significant shift in the clinic agenda. Initially created as a research organization, by the time of our study, the clinic was also deeply invested in treatment. In one meeting, the senior management team discussed how to balance "[care] programs" and research. "Our business is mainly research," one staff member asserted. The organization's leader retorted: "We can't do research unless we also have care." Discussing the deaths in one clinical trial, he added: "Those who died didn't die from the research but from the disease – because we didn't then have the capacity to treat them." Both the Thai and the Ugandan programs could be regarded as "creative compliance" (though without the overtone of duplicity that the term carried in McBarnet and Whelan's [1991] original usage) with the rules of medical research. It was always possible to describe (and sometimes fund) a treatment as an observational study, and in poor countries this may be the only way to give anything approximating the supplementary care that research subjects would receive in a richer country. Observational studies may therefore be one way to address the distressing dilemmas of ethical pluralism.

F. MUTUAL ADJUSTMENT

For the most part, we have emphasized the flow of rules from the global North to the global South and stressed that often the rules come as a package with the funding for research and treatment. Yet we have also pointed out that though they are often the weaker partners in an unequal exchange, the HIV clinics of poor countries exercise considerable agency in how they engage with clinical guidelines, rules about patient/caregiver relations, research protocols, rules about the ethical conduct of research, and the whole panoply of procedures for tracking and reporting in research and treatment programs. Rarely are rules simply adopted. Far more commonly, local procedures have to be recast so outsiders can see that they are consonant with the new rules, and rules have to be adapted to the particularities of local cultural, legal, and health contexts. Occasionally when the fit is particularly bad, clinics may resist the imposition of rules that might cause serious harm to locals (either patients or clinics themselves).

Although this process is somewhat harder to observe in the clinics themselves, actors from the global South do also shape the evolution of the rules. This counter-influence occurs in several ways. First, representatives of the funders of research and treatment programs act as transporters of rule adaptations and modifications, sharing them with other sites as best practices. Our South African site was a recipient of a grant from the US President's Emergency Plan for AIDS Relief (PEPFAR) administered by the Elizabeth Glazer Pediatric AIDS Foundation (EGPAF). Representatives from our clinic were invited to join other local grantees for a user group meeting convened by EGPAF, which we were invited to observe. Although American government agencies are famous for the detail and rigidity of their rules,

EGPAF exercised its oversight responsibility with a much lighter hand. Participants were urged to share their experiences and pass on tips about how to cope with medical, administrative, and regulatory challenges. Such local adjustments were far more likely to travel back to Washington with EGPAF than to be carried there by representatives of individual grant recipients.

PEPFAR, NIH, and other funders of treatment and research craft many of the rules that govern clinic life. However, it is guideline writers, such as the US Centers for Disease Control and Prevention (CDC), WHO, and national ministries of health, that devise the softer rules that shape core medical decisions. We noted earlier that research results from poorer countries and richer countries diffuse at different speeds because publication outlets have ratcheted up their evidentiary standards beyond a level practically achievable by many researchers in poor countries. Because guideline writers likewise have a preference for the better data produced by rich-country researchers,[7] the findings of researchers from poor and middle-income countries are also less likely to shape guidelines. In this case, though, poor country practitioners have a strong incentive to share information whether or not it meets publication standards and influences guidelines. One Ugandan physician explained to us that although pediatric HIV guidelines had not been available for some time, hospital staff members began to set up guidelines that they photocopied and distributed. Eventually a network of African practitioners launched a pediatric HIV handbook. As this doctor explained, "... documentation in Africa is limited. But we have a lot of experience. So this was an opportunity to get African pediatricians or people taking care of children in Africa to actually say what they're doing, using the guidelines but also saying 'Even though we don't have it documented, our experience is this.'" Guidelines put out by Columbia University had in fact made adjustments for resource-poor countries, we were told, because the programs to treat mothers and children are mostly in Africa and so "they kept asking what's useful for us." We might expect more rapid adjustment of guidelines in fields (such as pediatrics or PMTCT) where poor countries were vastly overrepresented in both research (whatever its quality) and treatment. But if the speed has been faster in these fields, it is also important to note that entities such as WHO have noted the need to adjust clinical guidelines for resource-constrained countries.

In contrast to this slow adjustment and reshaping of rules with the input of users, the evolution of regulation of the ethical conduct of research shows a deeper rethinking occasioned by explicit discussions of inequities and injustices. The principles that anchor the rules about ethical conduct are articulated in a handful

7 This preference is typically formalized in a rating scheme that categorizes recommendations according to both quality of evidence (I–III) and strength of the recommendation (A–C or sometimes A–E). An A-I rating would mean that writers strongly recommended the action suggested in the guideline and that their assessment was based on data from one or more randomized trials with clinical results. See Panel on Antiretroviral Guidelines for Adults and Adolescents (2008, 57) for an example and Petty (2008, 74–79) for an analysis of these rating practices.

of documents, including the Nuremberg Code, the Belmont Report, the Declaration of Helsinki (of the World Medical Association), and the International Ethical Guidelines for Biomedical Research Involving Human Subjects (put out by the Council of International Medical Societies and WHO). Importantly, the Helsinki Declaration is episodically revised and amended (most recently in 2013) and has explicitly commented on relations between rich and poor countries in a series of debates about such matters as the ethics of experimenting on groups who will mostly not benefit from the experiments, the appropriateness of placebo trials, and the acceptability of cross-country variations in treatments offered to control groups. Although ethical universalism and ethical pluralism have both been around for some time, the debates were reignited by concerns about HIV research (Lurie and Wolfe 1997; Rothman 2000; Benatar 2001). These principles have been translated into policy by governments and governmental agencies, health care organizations, and NGOs. Admittedly, American agencies like the National Institutes of Health (NIH) and the Office for Human Research Protections (OHRP), backed by US statutes, play central roles in establishing and enforcing the rules about how human subjects research is to be conducted. Thus the global debate is filtered through policy-making bodies that continue to be dominated by the global North.

V. CONCLUSION

It is by now common in the social sciences to think about cultural forms as tools and people and groups as relatively savvy users of tools. As neo-institutionalists could tell us, tools and tool kits wax and wane in popularity, with waves of adoption of institutionalized practices when the use of particular tools becomes imperative in the bid for legitimacy. For reasons that are not entirely clear to us, legal tools have often been the tools of choice, diffusing outward from strictly legal domains to areas of social life that have more often been governed in less formal ways. The propensity to employ legal or quasi-legal tools may arise in part from the confusion created by the multiplicity of entities claiming jurisdiction and an emerging belief that legalization facilitates negotiation and reduces the time to arrive at some consensus about how things should be done. In effect, although they complain about the rigidity of rules and the cost of demonstrating compliance, people seem to tacitly believe that legalistic ways of doing things will reduce transaction costs.

By looking at HIV/AIDS clinics as a legalized domain, we have problematized the transport of law from core legal domains to other sites that have not been dominated by legalized ways of doing things. By comparing HIV/AIDS clinics in the United States with clinics in Thailand, South Africa, and Uganda, we have problematized the transport of rules from the global North (and the United States in particular) to the poorer countries of the global South. Juxtaposing these two border crossings allows us to think about how much of what others have observed about the transport of rules from one site to another is about transport, export, and import as general phenomena and how much of it is instead about the nature of the boundary that is being crossed (geographical vs. substantive). Our tentative conclusion is that border crossings do have some common properties, in particular that import essentially always entails introducing new rules into an environment already well populated with rules, norms, customs, and standard practices. But a substantive boundary crossing is, nevertheless, rather different than a geographical one.

Our observations suggest that the challenges of substantive boundary crossings arise especially from entrenched, often occupationally based, ways of coordinating work. Occupations differ in how knowledge is created, distilled, and translated into decision rules. They also vary in how novices are trained and introduced into work settings and how work is shared among occupations working in the same settings with the same materials. This means, for instance, that the import of law and quasi-law into medical settings has brought confusion about the status of rules and the authority of medical workers. Which rules are obligatory? Which rules are merely guidelines? Who has the final say when medical practitioners propose actions that seem medically necessary but also seem to contravene the law? Which adjustments to local conditions are permissible and which would be considered violations? As our own and others' (Shilts 1987; Epstein 1996; Heimer 2013b) research suggests, these questions are especially pressing in HIV/AIDS treatment and research where strict compliance with rules by some can sometimes be a matter of life or death for others.

Our research also suggests that these questions would be answered differently by lawyers and other legally trained actors than by medical staff without legal training. The two groups are steeped in different traditions about how to use rules, and each (initially at least) believes strongly in its own approach. Others have looked at arenas newly penetrated by law and legalistic ways of doing things – for instance, when definitions are broadened so new issues come under the umbrella of existing law (e.g., understandings of human rights are broadened to include new rights), when new laws are created to govern areas previously governed with more general laws (e.g., new law addresses domestic violence or hate crimes), or when legal actors begin to enforce existing law that had been dormant (e.g., laws prohibiting workplace discrimination). But they have not theorized this as transport of law and so have not compared it with the transport of law across geographical boundaries. Introducing a more legalistic approach may, at first blush, seem to be merely adding legal force to existing rules so that they become the rules of two institutions rather than one, and are supported and enforced by both – the double institutionalization that Bohanan (1965) describes. Yet our research suggests that the introduction of legalistic approaches does much more because rules are treated so differently in different spheres.

In contrast, when laws, regulations, guidelines, and legalistic approaches cross geographical boundaries, a topic that has received a good deal more attention from other authors, they encounter cultural differences, resource constraints, and a myriad of local ties. Laws and legalistic approaches transported across geographical boundaries are very likely to require interpretation, adjustment, resistance, and so forth. But, we suggest, they are somewhat less likely to encounter fully formed alternative approaches to how to interact with rules. To overstate, the contrast might be summarized as an encounter between "law" and "not law" for substantive boundary crossings and an encounter between "existing law" and "imported law" for geographical boundary crossings.

Compared to what others describe, what we have observed is a more disjointed unfolding of a dialogue between local and cosmopolitan practices, between the legal system and health care organizations, and between researchers, caregivers, patients (who are also research subjects) and families, and regulators. At any point in time, participants are usually able to give a coherent account of what they do and how their actions take account of laws, rules, and regulations – "We file SAE reports within the short window specified in the regulations" or "The informed consent documents are stored in a locked cabinet in the locked office of the regulatory affairs specialist." But the surface coherence penetrates less deeply where adjustments are continually required. Bartley's layering, Merry's vernacularization, and Klug's hybridization seem to us to underestimate the incoherence and especially the unsettled nature of the governance of HIV/AIDS clinics. We do not wish to be misread here. We are by no means suggesting that the staffs of HIV/AIDS clinics either in the United States or in Thailand, South Africa, and Uganda are inattentive to or actively opposed to the laws, rules, regulations, and guidelines that have been created to govern treatment and care. Rather, our point is that the adjustment is an exceedingly complex and necessarily incomplete business, requiring endless tinkering as clinic workers weigh priorities, look for ways to do more with less, move among tasks, and shift their attention from one set of demands to another. The legal colonization of the clinic is thus an unfinished project. Because legal colonization masks gross inequalities among sites, resistance is probably not a bad thing.

REFERENCES

Abbott, Kenneth W., and Duncan Snidal. 2000. "Hard and Soft Law in International Governance." *International Organization* 54: 421–456.

Abbott, Kenneth W., Robert O. Keohane, Andrew Moravcsik, Anne-Marie Slaughter, and Duncan Snidal. 2000. "The Concept of Legalization." *International Organization* 54: 401–419.

Bartley, Tim. 2011. "Transnational Governance as the Layering of Rules: Intersections of Public and Private Standards." *Theoretical Inquiries in Law* 12: 517–542.

Benatar, Solomon R. 2001. "Commentary: Justice and Medical Research: A Global Perspective." *Bioethics* 15: 333–340.

Bohanan, Paul. 1965. "The Differing Realms of the Law." *American Anthropologist* 67: 33–42.

Braithwaite, John, Cary Coglianese, and David Levi-Faur. 2007. "Editors' Introduction: Can Regulation and Governance Make a Difference?" *Regulation and Governance* 1: 1–7.

Dezalay, Yves, and Bryant Garth. 1996. *Dealing in Virtue: International Commercial Arbitration and the Construction of a Transnational Legal Order*. Chicago: University of Chicago Press.

Dezalay, Yves, and Bryant Garth. 2002. *The Internationalization of Palace Wars: Lawyers, Economists, and the Contest to Transform Latin American States*. Chicago: University of Chicago Press.
Dezalay, Yves, and Bryant Garth. 2010. *Asian Legal Revivals: Lawyers in the Shadow of Empire*. Chicago: University of Chicago Press.
DiMaggio, Paul J., and Walter W. Powell. 1983. "The Iron Cage Revisited: Institutional Isomorphism and Collective Rationality in Organizational Fields." *American Sociological Review* 48: 147–160.
Dobbin, Frank. 2011. *Inventing Equal Opportunity*. Princeton, NJ: Princeton University Press.
Douglas, Mary. 1986. *How Institutions Think*. Syracuse, NY: Syracuse University Press.
Dugger, Celia W. 2008. "Rift over AIDS Treatment Lingers in South Africa." *New York Times*, March 9.
Edelman, Lauren B., Linda H. Krieger, Scott R. Eliason, Catherine R. Albiston, and Virginia Mellema. 2011. "When Organizations Rule: Judicial Deference to Institutionalized Employment Structures." *American Journal of Sociology* 117: 888–954.
Edelman, Lauren B., Christopher Uggen, and Howard S. Erlanger. 1999. "The Endogeneity of Legal Regulation: Grievance Procedures as Rational Myth." *American Journal of Sociology* 105: 406–454.
Epstein, Steven. 1996. *Impure Science: AIDS, Activism and the Politics of Knowledge*. Berkeley: University of California Press.
Espeland, Wendy N., and Berit I. Vannebo. 2007. "Accountability, Quantification, and Law." *Annual Review of Law and Social Science* 3: 21–43.
Fagerlin, Angela, and Carl E. Schneider. 2004. "Enough: The Failure of the Living Will," *Hastings Center Report* 34: 30–42.
Gazley, J. Lynn. 2011. "Our Particular Patients: Local Relevance in Clinical Research." PhD diss., Northwestern University.
Halliday, Terence C., and Bruce G. Carruthers. 2007. "The Recursivity of Law: Global Norm Making and National Lawmaking in the Globalization of Corporate Insolvency Regimes." *American Journal of Sociology* 112: 1135–1202.
Halliday, Terence C., and Pavel Osinsky. 2006. "Globalization and Law." *Annual Review of Sociology* 32: 447–470.
Heimer, Carol A. 1996. "Explaining Variation in the Impact of Law: Organizations, Institutions, and Professions." *Studies in Law, Politics and Society* 15: 29–59.
Heimer, Carol A. 1999. "Competing Institutions: Law, Medicine, and Family in Neonatal Intensive Care." *Law and Society Review* 33: 17–66.
Heimer, Carol A. 2012. "Inert Facts and the Illusion of Knowledge: Strategic Uses of Ignorance in HIV Clinics." *Economy and Society* 41: 17–41.
Heimer, Carol A. 2013a. "Resilience in the Middle: Contributions of Regulated Organizations to Regulatory Success." *Annals of the American Academy of Political and Social Science* 649: 139–156.
Heimer, Carol A. 2013b. "Wicked Ethics: Compliance Work and the Practice of Ethics in HIV Research." *Social Science and Medicine* 98: 371–378.
Heimer, Carol A., JuLeigh C. Petty, and Rebecca J. Culyba. 2005. "Risk and Rules: The 'Legalization' of Medicine." In *Organizational Encounters with Risk*, edited by Bridget Hutter and Michael Power, 92–113. Cambridge: Cambridge University Press.
Kay, Tamara. 2011. "Legal Transnationalism: The Relationship between Transnational Social Movement Building and International Law." *Law and Social Inquiry* 36: 419–454.
Klug, Heinz. 2000. *Constituting Democracy: Law, Globalization, and South Africa's Political Reconstruction*. New York: Cambridge University Press.

Klug, Heinz. 2002. "Hybrid(ity) Rules: Creating Local Law in a Globalized World." In *Global Prescriptions: The Production, Exportation, and Importation of a New Legal Orthodoxy*, edited by Yves Dezalay and Bryant G. Garth, 276–305. Ann Arbor: University of Michigan Press.

Klug, Heinz. 2005. "Campaigning for Life: Building a New Transnational Solidarity in the Face of HIV/AIDS and TRIPS." In *Law and Globalization from Below: Toward a Cosmopolitan Legality*, edited by Boaventura de Sousa Santos and César A. Rodríguez-Garavito, 118–139. Cambridge: Cambridge University Press.

Klug, Heinz. 2008. "Law, Politics, and Access to Essential Medicines in Developing Countries." *Politics and Society* 36: 207–246.

Klug, Heinz. 2012. "Access to Medicines and the Transformation of the South African State: Exploring the Interactions of Legal and Policy Changes in Health, Intellectual Property, Trade, and Competition Law in the Context of South Africa's HIV/AIDS Pandemic." *Law and Social Inquiry* 37: 297–329.

Lempert, Richard O., and Joseph Sanders. 1986. *An Invitation to Law and Social Science: Desert, Disputes, and Distribution*. Philadelphia, PA: University of Pennsylvania Press.

Llewellyn, Karl N. 1960. *The Common Law Tradition: Deciding Appeals*. Boston: Little, Brown and Company.

Lurie, Peter, and Sidney M. Wolfe. 1997. "Unethical Trials of Interventions to Reduce Perinatal Transmission of the Human Immunodeficiency Virus in Developing Countries." *New England Journal of Medicine* 337: 853–856.

March, James G. 1994. *A Primer on Decision Making: How Decisions Happen*. New York: Free Press.

McBarnet, Doreen, and Christopher Whelan. 1991. "The Elusive Spirit of the Law: Formalism and the Struggle for Legal Control." *Modern Law Review* 54: 848–873.

Merry, Sally Engle. 2006a. *Human Rights and Gender Violence: Translating International Law into Local Justice*. Chicago: University of Chicago Press.

Merry, Sally Engle. 2006b. "Transnational Human Rights and Local Activism: Mapping the Middle." *American Anthropologist* 108: 38–51.

Mnookin, Robert H., and Lewis Kornhauser. 1979. "Bargaining in the Shadow of the Law: The Case of Divorce." *Yale Law Journal* 88: 950–997.

Munger, Frank. 2008–2009. "Globalization, Investing in Law, and the Careers of Lawyers for Social Causes–Taking on Rights in Thailand." *New York Law Review* 53: 745–804.

Munger, Frank. 2012. "Globalization through the Lens of Palace Wars: What Elite Lawyers' Careers Can and Cannot Tell Us about Globalization of Law." *Law and Social Inquiry* 37: 476–499.

Nonet, Philippe, and Philip Selznick. 2001. *Law and Society in Transition: Toward Responsive Law*. New Brunswick, NJ: Transaction Publishers.

Panel on Antiretroviral Guidelines for Adults and Adolescents. 2008. *Guidelines for the Use of Antiretroviral Agents in HIV-1-infected Adults and Adolescents*. Washington, DC: Department of Health and Human Services.

Petty, JuLeigh. 2008. "Science in the Clinic: HIV Research in the Era of Evidence-Based Medicine." PhD diss., Northwestern University.

Power, Michael. 1997. *The Audit Society: Rituals of Verification*. New York: Oxford University Press.

Rothman, David J. 2000. "The Shame of Medical Research." *New York Review of Books*, November 30.

Santos, Boaventura de Sousa. 1995. *Toward a New Common Sense: Law, Science and Politics in the Paradigmatic Transition*. New York: Routledge.

Scott, W. Richard, Martin Ruef, Peter J. Mendel, and Carol A. Caronna. 2000. *Institutional Change and Healthcare Organizations: From Professional Dominance to Managed Care*. Chicago: University of Chicago Press.

Shaffer, Gregory. 2012. "Transnational Legal Process and State Change." *Law and Social Inquiry* 37: 229–264.

Shapiro, Susan P. 2005. "Agency Theory." *Annual Review of Sociology* 31: 263–284.

Shapiro, Susan P. 2012. "Advance Directives: The Elusive Goal of Having the Last Word." *NAELA Journal* 8: 205–232.

Shilts, Randy. 1987. *And the Band Played On: Politics, People, and the AIDS Epidemic*. New York: St. Martin's Press.

Silbey, Susan S. 1997. "Let Them Eat Cake: Globalization, Postmodern Colonialism, and the Possibilities of Justice." *Law and Society Review* 31: 207–236.

Silbey, Susan S. 2011. "The Sociological Citizen: Pragmatic and Relational Regulation in Law and Organizations." *Regulation and Governance* 5: 1–13.

Stinchcombe, Arthur L. 2001. *When Formality Works: Authority and Abstraction in Law and Organizations*. Chicago: University of Chicago Press.

Strathern, Marilyn, ed. 2000. *Audit Cultures: Anthropological Studies in Accountability, Ethics and the Academy*. London: Routledge.

Sturm, Susan. 2006. "The Architecture of Inclusion: Advancing Workplace Equity in Higher Education." *Harvard Journal of Law and Gender* 29: 247–334.

't Hoen, Ellen F. M. 2009. *The Global Politics of Pharmaceutical Monopoly Power: Drug Patents, Access, Innovation and the Application of the WTO Doha Declaration on TRIPS and Public Health*. Diemen: AMB Publishers.

Tilley, Helen. 2011. *Africa as a Living Laboratory: Empire, Development, and the Problem of Scientific Knowledge*, 1870–1950. Chicago: University of Chicago Press.

Timmermans, Stefan, and Marc Berg. 2003. *The Gold Standard: The Challenge of Evidence-Based Medicine and Standardization in Health Care*. Philadelphia: Temple University Press.

Zussman, Robert. 1992. *Intensive Care: Medical Ethics and the Medical Profession*. Chicago: University of Chicago Press.

6

The Politics of Islamic Law and Human Rights: Sudan's Rival Legal Systems

Mark Fathi Massoud[1]

I. INTRODUCTION

Shortly after the end of Sudan's twenty-three year civil war in 2005, I visited an encampment for displaced survivors in the desert near Khartoum, Sudan's capital. At the time I was traveling with a small group of lawyers from the United Nations (UN). A sultan (local customary leader) greeted us and asked whether we sought information from his community to conduct "a needs assessment," as he put it, or whether we sought to provide assistance. His people required resources like clean water, schools, and money, he said, but foreigners visit, ask questions, and do not return. A member of the UN delegation responded that, as lawyers, the team could provide legal resources. She asked the sultan whether his community needed lawyers. He responded that he did not think lawyers would be able to help.

So goes the experience of human rights law among those displaced by war, refracted by encounters with aid agencies offering legal solutions to the cycle of poverty. And, I argue, so also goes their experience of law under Sudan's successive military governments. Just as aid activists promote a universal and immutable interpretation of human rights law, the Sudan government, particularly since 1989 under President Omar al-Bashir, has promoted its own interpretation of an immutable law, rooted in Islam. Viewed from the perspective of marginalized persons displaced by civil war, then, human rights and Islamic law offer competing narratives of legal order, salvation, and protection. But they do so only when one submits to a system of institutions and ideas configured and dominated by elites and outsiders, while rejecting the competing system.

[1] Some elements of this chapter draw from or expand upon material found in Mark Fathi Massoud, *Law's Fragile State: Colonial, Authoritarian, and Humanitarian Legacies in Sudan* (Cambridge University Press). Thanks to Anthony Tirado Chase, Heinz Klug, Sally Engle Merry, Adam Millard-Ball, the four anonymous reviewers, and audiences at UC Santa Cruz and the International Studies Association for helpful feedback. The Institute on Global Conflict and Cooperation, a Fulbright-Hays fellowship, and a University of California, Santa Cruz, Faculty Research Grant provided financial support for research in Sudan. Arabic translations and transliterations are my own; simple apostrophes are used to represent diacritical marks from the *International Journal of Middle East Studies* system. This research would not have been possible without the kindness of many respondents in Sudan.

In Sudan, a parallelism exists between the unitary and top-down character of law in the state's uses of religious law and the international aid community's uses of human rights law. Citizens experience the force of an authoritarian government advancing Islamic law to preserve the state, and they interact with aid agencies advancing human rights law to liberate citizens from the state's harmful actions. This chapter offers an empirically grounded analysis of these two rival discourses as they are presented to the survivors of civil war. My analysis draws on fifteen months of research in Sudan and fifty-seven semistructured interviews with officials, lawyers, and activists, along with ethnographic observations from encampments for those displaced by war.[2] Adopting a "new legal realist" approach that emphasizes the empirical study of people's lived experiences of law, politics, and power, I investigate the tensions and contradictions inherent in how civil society activists and the displaced persons whom they represent experience Islamic law and human rights, particularly in political contexts marked by authoritarian rule. Depicting this parallelism in the discourses of human rights and Islamic law reveals a pattern in the functions of law in conflict settings and the importance of comparing transnational (here, Islamic) and international (here, human rights) legal orders that circulate within national boundaries. Such comparative inquiry also illuminates the challenges of promoting the rule of law in the world's troubled regions.

The case of Sudan offers a useful site in which to examine this unlikely juxtaposition between the discourses of human rights law and state-imposed Islamic law. The country has been at war with itself for all but ten years since gaining independence in 1956, most recently in the Darfur region after 2003 and the Nuba Mountains region after South Sudan's 2011 secession. Sudan's multicolonial legacy – Turco-Egyptians through most of the nineteenth century followed by the British in the first half of the twentieth century – forms the bedrock of the contemporary leadership's claims to Islamic authority. One of Sudan's many interconnected civil wars was Africa's longest (1983–2005), resulting in the world's largest number of internally displaced persons and the 2011 secession of South Sudan, now the world's newest country (Johnson 2003; Deng 1995). In this place riven by parallel wars of ideologies and identities, those displaced by civil war must confront two visions of legal modernity, one from state authorities and another from aid workers. Both interpretations are portrayed as universal, unchanging, and designed to stabilize the state and prevent it from descending deeper into chaos. Survivors of war are conscripted into these wars either as believers or as sidelined adversaries.

The following analysis proceeds in three parts. First, I uncover how Sudan's governing officials have sought to monopolize political and economic power by disguising state law under the mask of religion and the will of God, turning a blind eye to the blend of religious and nonreligious sources that makes up Sudanese law.

2 I conducted 205 interviews between 2005 and 2010 in Sudan, from which I draw on a sample of fifty-seven of the most relevant for this essay.

Second, I discuss how international human rights activists encourage the war-displaced poor to see human rights similarly, as a form of incontrovertible law that would replace the immutable law promoted by the government. Finally, I conclude with implications of the two contending visions of legal modernity for civil society and the poor in conflict settings and authoritarian states, and for sociolegal scholars and policy makers examining the local experience of transnational and international law.

II. THE STATE'S FLATTENING OF ISLAMIC LAW DISCOURSE

Political elites in Sudan have used Islamic law to build up the state and to undergird their rule in a variety of ways throughout Sudan's modern history. Turco-Egyptian occupiers (1821–1884) sought to centralize their authority by installing a singular administrative law rooted in the Hanafi school of Islamic law (Fluehr-Lobban 1987). In so doing, colonial occupiers constructed a statelike legal apparatus over diffuse localized customs that had been generally associated with Islamic law's Maliki school.

Sudan's first modern independent government (1884–1898) rose to power in 1884 and adopted a similar vision of a state-controlled Islamic law under the self-proclaimed Mahdi, or "the anointed one." The *Mahdiyya* (Mahdist period), while short-lived, cemented the foundation of the Sudanese state's claims to Islamic authority (Collins 2008).

The fall of the Sudanese Mahdist state in 1898 and the concomitant rise of a British-led colonial administration (the Anglo-Egyptian Condominium, 1898–1956) resulted in an extreme compartmentalization of *shari'a* (roughly translated as Islamic law). The British governed the Sudanese according to what the British called "principles of justice, equity, and good conscience" (Sudan Government 1901 and 1929 Civil Justice Ordinances). Such broad legal language effectively allowed British colonial administrators to import Western norms of governance and cultural sensibilities into Sudan's administrative and legal structures, while confining Islamic law to family-related disputes (e.g., divorce and inheritance) among Muslims. These efforts were the British administration's bid to provide some domestic legitimacy by accepting and incorporating local religious values into the government (Mustafa 1971). British colonial administrators divided the judiciary into two divisions – *shari'a*, which handled Islamic personal status disputes, and civil, which handled crimes, torts, and all other matters outside family law (Ibrahim 2008; Massoud 2013a; for comparative examples see Mallat and Connors 1991; El-Gawhary 1995; Fyzee 2009). One lawyer I met referred to the British project to integrate Islamic personal status law into the government as "wise" given the Sudanese context. "The [British] left personal matters to *shari'a*," he continued, "for the simple reason that they took over from a fundamentalist Islamic government – the *Mahdiyya* – and the people were very sensitive about . . . their religion."[3]

3 Interview with Abdul Moneim, lawyer, in Khartoum, Sudan (February 2007) (Author's File Reference Number 70). All names have been changed to preserve confidentiality.

Hostile to their colonial past, postindependence governments in Sudan have expanded the scope of Islamic law to govern matters beyond the family, including public law, crimes, and constitutionalism. Their efforts culminated in three pivotal moments that together exemplify how postcolonial Sudanese political leaderships have sought to rule by Islamic law.

First, in the mid-1970s, then-President Nimeiri – at the time, a military ruler with deep socialist leanings – launched what he called a national reconciliation with opposition parties, including the Muslim Brotherhood. When the more secular- and democratic-minded parties fell out of favor with Nimeiri's regime after the reconciliation's failure, a faction of the Muslim Brotherhood led by Hassan al-Turabi (a lawyer and renowned intellectual) grew closer to President Nimeiri (Burr and Collins 2003). As socialism's popularity began to wane, Nimeiri took steps to curry favor with an increasingly influential conservative Muslim elite. His government, for instance, completed the process of translating all laws from English (the language of Sudan's European colonizer) into Arabic (the language of much of Sudan's citizenry, particularly those who live in and around the capital city).

Second, in 1983, in President Nimeiri's final bid to hold on to political power following a set of disastrous economic policies and rapid inflation, Nimeiri extraordinarily declared himself a sheikh and adopted a radical and sweeping vision of Islamic criminal law. In what is now known as Sudan's notorious *qanoon September* (September law), courts were ordered to implement corporal punishment, including amputations, for Islamic *huduud* crimes such as theft (Massoud 2013a, 113–114).

Third, soon after seizing power in 1989, President Omar Hassan al-Bashir claimed Islamic law as the source of all law for Sudan, just as Nimeiri had attempted to do in 1983.[4] Bashir successfully consolidated his authority under Islam, in a way that Nimeiri did not, through a series of critical revisions to the legal codes in 1991. The personal status code for Muslims codified the personal affairs rules of the Hanafi school. And a revised criminal code for the first time included the death penalty for the *huduud* crime of apostasy, or criticizing Islam.[5] The criminalization of religious criticism meant that any statements or actions interpreted as threats to Bashir's rule were labeled as condemnations of Islam – a crime punishable by death.

Bashir's self-proclaimed "national salvation revolution" had the express goal of cementing an Islamization of the Sudanese state, or, in the words of one Sudanese civil society activist, "to modernize Sudan as a modern, civilized, Islamic nation."[6]

4 Sudan's short-lived democratic government between Nimeiri's 1985 ouster and Bashir's 1989 coup failed to abolish Nimeiri's laws in part because "Islamists had much support on the streets." Interview with Shadi, lawyer, in Khartoum, Sudan (April 2007) (Author's File Reference Number 135).

5 Mahmoud Mohamad Taha, an outspoken 70-year-old Muslim activist against the Nimeiri regime's September laws, was put to death for apostasy in January 1985. His death – later deemed unlawful by Sudan's High Court because apostasy was not a crime in 1985 – spurred mass revolutions that led to the toppling of the Nimeiri dictatorship in April 1985 (Massoud 2013a, 115–116).

6 Interview with Michael, NGO program director, in Khartoum, Sudan (June 2010) (Author's File Reference Number 154).

Today, all Sudanese laws – regardless of their Islamic, Western, or mixed ancestry – are now ostensibly Islamic. A telling example is Sudan's corporate code, which is essentially the British colonial administration's 1925 corporate code, only translated into Arabic to reconfigure it as Islamic law (Massoud 2013a, 84). The state's claim to rule according to divine also allows it to reject international human rights law as a constraint on state behavior and, thus, on divine law.

These three key events – Nimeiri's reconciliation with the Muslim Brotherhood in the mid-1970s, his self-declaration as a sheikh and ensuing *qanoon September* in 1983, and Bashir's criminal and civil code revisions in 1991 and the resulting political uses of religious law – together showcase the diverse and complex ways that postcolonial governments have sought to control the discourse of religious law. Capitalizing on the broad appeal of *shari'a*, they claimed political authority, demanded citizen compliance, and consolidated state rule under a single, top-down and Islamic legal order. In other words, to enhance domestic legitimacy, state authorities replaced Sudan's multicolonial legacy of legal pluralism with an image of legal power under the force of the religion to which the majority of Sudan's urban citizenry belonged. As one Sudanese lawyer put it, "After independence we developed what I call Sudanese law, borrowed from our own practice. Now they call it Islamic law, but I don't think it's Islamic as such. It has borrowed certain principles from Islam."[7]

As Sudan's history reveals, Islamic law has been a layered project and remains an ongoing political and legal process (see, e.g., Harding 2001). It has been made and remade by multiple hands and the protean tools they use – Maliki customs, Hanafi decrees, and even non-Islamic traditions entirely, imported by colonial and nonstate actors and then labeled "Islamic" by subsequent governments. During Sudan's colonial and early postcolonial administrations, state authorities offered, transcribed, used, and compartmentalized different aspects of Islamic law to suit their purposes and govern the people of Sudan. Regimes like those of Nimeiri and Bashir – in, for instance, labeling waywardness as anti-Islamic and punishing it by death – also turned to religious law as their unalterable and everlasting defense of the state and its leadership. In this way, legal plurality and fluidity are masked by *legal rigidity*, an inflexible and absolutist system of law manufactured by state authorities seeking to monopolize political and economic power. Summing up his experience as a human rights lawyer under the Bashir government, one Sudanese man said, "They want to control everything, this regime," including religion.[8] And speaking of his experience of the Bashir government, a prominent judge said simply, "They wanted *shari'a* to prevail in all aspects of the law."[9]

7 Interview with retired senior judicial official 1, in Khartoum, Sudan (February 2007) (Author's File Reference Number 64).

8 Interview with Omer, human rights lawyer, in Khartoum, Sudan (November 2006) (Author's File Reference Number 35).

9 Follow-up interview with Hassan, retired senior judicial official, in Khartoum, Sudan (April 2007) (Author's File Reference Number 88).

III. GRASSROOTS EXPERIENCES AND INTERPRETATIONS OF LAW

As in other Muslim-majority contexts, Islam is central to law and politics in Sudan and is felt throughout urban life, whether or not one adheres to the faith. The call to prayer from the local mosque, for instance, is audible multiple times per day; it can grind court proceedings to a halt, often in midsentence (Massoud 2012). The state's top-down imposition of religious law, however, contrasts remarkably with the diverse experiences and interpretations of law, particularly Islamic law, at the grassroots level.

Some Sudanese activists I met turn to *shari'a* to justify their disapproval of the government's political uses of religious law. For instance, one young lawyer commented that *shari'a* is "something between me and my God. I'm not going to show [off] my religion or how good a Muslim I am; it's not another person's business to tell me that."[10] She continued, "If someone protects my rights, I will respect him. It doesn't matter if . . . he believes in God. Also, I don't mind taking a case for [a client who is] Christian or Jewish."[11]

The state's practice of *shari'a* is also felt differently across the population, with the poor and non-Muslim minorities more likely to experience *shari'a* as a punitive force. One striking example is the criminalization of alcohol sales and possession, which disproportionately impacts war-displaced persons who are monitored by police, women who survive by brewing and selling alcohol, and non-Muslims (see Abusharaf 2009; Massoud 2006). During the 1990s, the Bashir government strengthened its power to criminalize by constructing hundreds of new courts. By the end of the civil war in 2005, almost half of all courts in Sudan were criminal courts, shaping people's contact with state legal institutions through the criminal law (Massoud 2013a, 148–149).

Other prominent examples highlight the ways that criminal courts impact the experience of state law, especially for women and minorities. In 2007 a British schoolteacher working in Khartoum was imprisoned and later expelled for allowing her students to name a teddy bear Mohammed – ostensibly after one of the popular students in her class, though some state and religious leaders labeled it an affront to the Prophet (BBC News 2007). Two years later in 2009, police arrested and imprisoned a woman for wearing trousers in public, and Internet videos circulated of another woman begging for mercy as she was being flogged outside a courthouse (*The New York Times* 2009). And in 2014, a pregnant woman who claimed to be Christian was arrested and imprisoned for apostasy for marrying a non-Muslim man (Al-Jazeera 2014).

While these cases illuminate the ways people experience the state's power through criminal and religious law, many Sudanese citizens continue to access

[10] Interview with Malika, lawyer, in Khartoum, Sudan (October 2006) (Author's File Reference Number 31).

[11] Ibid.

courts in a way that has little to do with crimes or even religion. Sudanese courts hear more than 150,000 civil and family-related cases each year (Massoud 2013a, 149–150) – women divorcing their husbands, disgruntled employees in the local labor court seeking remuneration for wrongful dismissal, students bringing suits against universities for scholarships promised but not received, and thousands who file claims of justice denied before Sudan's Public Grievances Board (for examples, see Massoud 2013a, 146–148). In these ways, Sudanese people are certainly turning to state courts and other government agencies to have their disputes resolved and their grievances redressed.

Lawyers I met in Sudan told me how, in these myriad cases, they cite any legal provisions that might help their clients, including English common law (part of Sudan's colonial heritage), Egyptian civil law (imported when Sudan's legal system flip-flopped from common law to civil law and back again in the 1970s), and Islamic law (Massoud 2012; Salman 1981). Islamic law, for these lawyers, becomes another overlapping layer in Sudan's radically plural legal system – it offers another package of arguments that may be made before the judge. Consistent with other countries in the region, Sudan's labor laws stemming from the late 1960s and early 1970s under Nimeiri's socialist administration deliberately eschewed Islamic law, and work-related claims using these socialist rules continue to arise in Sudan's courts. Cases related to the transfer or sale of real property similarly articulate rules of fairness consistent with but not specific to any religious prescription. In other words, from the perspective of litigants and judges, a great number of the thousands of disputes before Sudan's courts may have little to do overtly with the core content of Islamic law – making people's experiences and interpretations of law more diverse than the unitary and top-down character of the state's interpretation of law.

Local experiences of *shari'a* are more complex when one considers that religion and religious law are also tools of war, strategy, and survival. Some Sudanese claimed to me that, particularly during the most repressive periods of rule over southern Sudan during Sudan's north–south civil war, conversion to Islam correlated with increased access to state resources. "People who accepted Islam, [the government] would give them more," said one activist and civil war survivor.[12] Benefits that people contended were unavailable to non-Muslims included food rations, higher status, and travel permits during curfew (on the implications of religious conversion from a comparative perspective, see Gilsenan 2011). For this reason, South Sudanese I met spoke of Islam as part of a state project to change society (*mushroo'a al-hada'i al-ijtima'i*). "The issue is to link [conversion] to material benefits. If you have poverty and no choice, and something is placed before you, people will say even temporarily that they accept the Islamic faith."[13]

[12] Interview with Michael, NGO program director, in Khartoum, Sudan (June 2010) (Author's File Reference Number 154).

[13] Ibid.

Despite people's diverse experiences of law, the Bashir-led government portrays law as an unchanging, top-down system of religious legality justifying state authority. But contemporary law, including Islamic law, typically draws from multiple sources and offers competing schools and interpretations. In Sudan, Islamic law has mixed origins, including Islamic and non-Islamic principles sometimes labeled Islamic. In comments echoed by many of those whom I met, one political activist told me that Sudan's enduring conflict is not founded upon a division between religions; rather, it is the way in which the "government is using religion as a tool."[14]

IV. THE POLITICS OF HUMAN RIGHTS DISCOURSE

As Sudan's north–south civil war drew to a close in the early 2000s and particularly after the 2005 peace accords, foreign aid agencies and nongovernmental organizations (NGOs) converged on Sudan, setting up headquarters or field offices in the capital city, Khartoum. While the organizations and their efforts are certainly diverse, many have been funding local Sudanese NGOs to spread knowledge of human rights and build the rule of law. They are the Sudanese arm of a global effort to build knowledge and appreciation of the values associated with international human rights law. While the goals of these NGOs often run counter to those of the government regime, there are numerous parallels in how the state and NGOs use law. Just as the Bashir-led government portrays *shari'a* as an unchanging, top-down system of legality, international rights activists disguise the politics of human rights with rigidity, immutability, and universality. Meanwhile, local activists turn to human rights for a variety of reasons, including material gain.

A centerpiece of the aid community's efforts to promote human rights consists of workshops and training sessions for Sudanese citizens, from judges and lawmakers to displaced persons living in encampments or squatter settlements. While conducting research in Sudan, I attended human rights education workshops in the vast desert encampments where war-displaced families had fled after their homes and villages were burned. In these training programs, I witnessed how human rights law was portrayed as an ideology meant to transform people's experiences of pain and suffering into thoughts of liberation (Massoud 2011). Just as Sudanese law was oppressing the workshop attendees in their daily experiences – including arrests and floggings for alcohol possession – a belief in human rights was simultaneously encouraged as a necessary step toward raising them up from that poverty and oppression.

Following one workshop, I spoke with the facilitator, who reiterated her call for displaced persons, particularly women, to frame their grievances as undelivered human rights. Doing so allows "women to raise their awareness ... and work

[14] Interview with Rafiq, political opposition leader, in Khartoum, Sudan (April 2007) (Author's File Reference Number 132).

together . . . to come together."[15] The trainings also encouraged displaced persons to inform police, in the event of an arrest, of their right to consult a lawyer. While participants I met did not seek to mobilize their rights in Sudanese courts or vis-à-vis the police, they did speak of the significant material benefits they gained from the human rights model. Workshop attendees earned an education, a training on nonviolent dispute resolution, and a certificate of completion. They also openly discussed democratic principles, postwar freedoms, and the independence of South Sudan – taboo topics, particularly prior to South Sudan's 2011 secession (Massoud 2011).

The workshops I visited promised liberation through knowledge of international law in a way that fundamentally conflicted with the regime's approach to law and with people's experiences of state-imposed Islamic law. For example, when I spoke at one of these workshops with a non-Muslim woman displaced by the civil war, she mentioned the contrast between rights as she was being taught them by aid groups and rights as she was experiencing them under Bashir's government. "They apply all these Muslim laws to us Christians," she said. She understood, in the abstract, that aid workers were leading her to believe that "you have the right to be free." "But," she continued, "our right is not considered [by the government] because we are living here under Islamic law. So we are not free."[16]

Human rights itself has plural beginnings, as with any set of legal principles or discourses. Each international human rights treaty is the result of the relative power of states on the international playing field; their relationships with interest groups, citizens, and neighboring states; and the particular values they seek to espouse to themselves, their constituents, and their allies and enemies abroad (Merry 2006; Hathaway 2002; Goldsmith and Posner 2005). The political origins and evolution of human rights principles are also the cause of spirited debate (Lauren 2011; Moyn 2008; Mutua 2008).

While human rights principles are the complex result of much of this diversity, when taught to displaced persons (often by Sudanese activists working for foreign aid agencies), the diverse origins and politics of human rights are swept aside. Human rights are repackaged and taught as the universal foundation of modern legal systems – an abstract and timeless form of law – and, thus, more authoritative than Sudanese state law.

International aid agencies also teach displaced persons to see human rights as an apolitical logic emanating from specific written texts, including international treaties and declarations such as the Universal Declaration of Human Rights (UDHR), the International Covenant on Civil and Political Rights (ICCPR), the International Covenant on Economic, Social and Cultural Rights (ICESR), and the Convention

[15] Interview with Majda, women's rights activist, in Khartoum, Sudan (June 2005) (Author's File Reference Number 14). See also Massoud (2006, 9).

[16] Interview with Najwa, health awareness educator, in Mayo camp for displaced persons, in Khartoum, Sudan (June 2005) (Author's File Reference Number 18).

on the Elimination of All Forms of Discrimination against Women (CEDAW).[17] At human rights workshops I attended, participants were given Arabic versions of these documents to take home with them and study, along with copies of Sudan's Interim National Constitution, adopted in 2005 following the end of the north–south civil war.[18]

Efforts to promote human rights in Sudan are also singular in that they largely dismiss the potential for other discourses of modernity, particularly those rooted in religious belief. Two competing visions of modernity, rooted either in Islamic faith or in Western political liberalism, are often set out in opposition, despite the many commonalities between the two visions and substantial efforts by scholars, past and present, to link Islamic and human rights norms (Al-Mawdudi 1961; An-Na'im 1990, 2008; Baderin 2003; Mayer 2012).

According to those designing and implementing human rights education programs, their goal was to educate people to mobilize human rights ultimately to "help [Sudan] to have an independent judiciary."[19] Notably, while discussing the relationship between human rights and Islamic law, one NGO director dismissed the possibility of activism that builds upon rights-based frameworks from Islamic law, rather than from international law. Equating *shari'a* with the state's unchanging interpretation of it, he commented, "If you do *shari'a*-oriented development, you won't be able to work in other [areas] like community development; you won't be able to achieve" your goals.[20] For these persons, the character of human rights and, ultimately, the attainment of human dignity derive from a set of international treaties and other legal solutions to poverty. Religion and religious law become reframed as part of the problem that human rights resolves, just as the state reframes human rights as part of the problem that Islamic law resolves.

In these ways, human rights in practice appear strikingly similar to a religious ideology into which the marginalized are asked to put their faith, just as the Bashir government asks its citizens to put faith into its distinct vision of legal order and modernism. That is, displaced persons are encouraged to experience human rights much as they already experience state law – top-down and imposed by elites (authoritarian or humanitarian) who aim to ensure a governable society and prevent the onset of chaos. Certainly Bashir's government and international aid activists

[17] Although Sudan has not ratified CEDAW, it has ratified or acceded to a number of human rights treaties, which like CEDAW are taught in these workshops. These include the ICCPR, ICESCR, and the Convention on the Rights of the Child. See "Ratification of International Human Rights Treaties – Sudan," University of Minnesota Human Rights Library (n.d.). Available at http://www1.umn.edu/humanrts/research/ratification-sudan.html.

[18] National constitutions that authoritarian states effectuate may paradoxically consolidate state power and construct leaders' images as "just and pious" believers in the rule of law (Stilt 2013, 134; see also Albertus and Menaldo 2013).

[19] Interview with Sohir, NGO director, in Khartoum, Sudan (June 2005) (Author's File Reference Number 15). See also Massoud (2006, 8).

[20] Interview with Tofeeq, NGO founder and director, in Khartoum, Sudan (June 2005) (Author's File Reference Number 17).

have different goals, backgrounds, and ideas of how to create a stable and functioning society, but both believe ultimately in the power of law – whether under Islam or human rights – to shape behavior and sustain political power in conflict settings.

V. BENEFITS AND COSTS OF "LEGAL RIGIDITY"

Despite the diverse origins of Sudanese law, state leaders use a singular version of Islamic law to promote their authority and build state institutions. Aid workers also portray human rights in a manner that befits secular development goals. Likewise, some citizens use human rights discourse strategically. That is, just as an Islamic conversion has yielded material benefits to some citizens, so too may a human rights conversion. For some, human rights is not only an abstract system of protections into which they put their faith but also an opportunity to gain donor funding, allowing their social-service programs to proceed. Human rights become a discursive resource critical to implementing social-service delivery programs and providing some relief from decades of war. In Sudan, for instance, I met with leaders of human rights networks, or umbrella groups representing a set of human rights NGOs. But many of these NGOs they represent had no offices or were managed by the same person, raising questions of their legitimacy (Massoud 2013a, 167–168). Activists told me privately that some of these groups are formed to siphon donor funds that come to Sudanese persons who speak the language of human rights, whether bona fide activists or NGOs affiliated with the ruling party (ibid.).

Civil society activists reported to me that their work in human rights has led to additional benefits, many of them material, including increased access to work and travel opportunities as they move into and out of positions with international NGOs and UN agencies. Despite these benefits, the disparity between compensation for local and expatriate staff creates a sense of relative deprivation. One Sudanese program director in an international NGO said, "Imagine, they [expatriates] earn US$12,000 [per month]. I earn less than US$1,800 per month. I am a program director!"[21]

For displaced persons and other intended beneficiaries, the benefits of adopting a human rights discourse are also uncertain (Massoud 2011; Englund 2004). Women's rights activists in particular told me of the tensions between human rights and religious law. For example, one of the difficulties they face in challenging laws permitting certain forms of female circumcision is the government's claims to authority arising from Islam.[22] The Quran is silent on women's circumcision, and the Hadith (teachings of Muslim scholars) offers a plurality of views, only some of which condone the controversial practice. But "once they [in the government] say

[21] Interview with Michael, NGO program director, in Khartoum, Sudan (June 2010) (Author's File Reference Number 154).

[22] Interview with Intisar, lawyer, in Khartoum, Sudan (December 2006) (Author's File Reference Number 52).

this law is based in religion, they cannot [overturn] this law because *shari'a* is the main source of legislation."[23] While some activists also try to use *shari'a* principles to advocate for outlawing all forms of female circumcision, they must confront a religious system that the government claims is the foundation of its authority and cannot be changed. One type of sweeping argument advanced by the government is that the rights of the Muslim society as a whole must take priority, and that women's rights fundamentally "contradict Sudanese family values" forged and enforced by Islamic law (Köndgen 2010, 222; see also Emon 2010 and Johansen 1999 on the enduring "rights of God").

Some people I met felt a tension between their personal religious beliefs and the outward expressions of those beliefs demanded by the regime. One woman lawyer said to me that "people . . . here in Sudan see me like [I am] not a good Muslim." She continued, "The way I dress maybe," as she gestured toward the head scarf that was draped around her shoulders and neck, but left her hair mostly uncovered.[24] Her experience of Islamic law was rooted in an institutional and hierarchical political structure seemingly incompatible with her promotion of human rights ideas in Sudan. Similarly, other women told me how the way a woman dressed provided an indication whether she supported or opposed Bashir's government. One women's rights activist told me she was often singled out for "not wearing the hijab." She continued that a police officer stopped her while she was driving and asked her to wear a veil, a legal obligation for Sudanese women since the 1990s. "I had to take [out] my marriage certificate. He said to take out my *tarha* (head scarf) from my bag. I told him that this bag has a *waraqa* (paper) not a *tarha* (head scarf)."[25]

The consequences of a regime of legal rigidity are faced in particular by displaced persons living in squatter encampments and those who attempt to serve them. According to Sudanese activists providing social services to these persons, "If you ask the people why [they] don't have these services, they wouldn't even answer you that the government didn't serve us. They just say to you, 'We don't know. It is God's fate,' things like that."[26] According to one displaced woman, the implementation of rights under the Sudanese state is at best incomplete: "Sometimes they give you a few rights, but they don't give you your full rights."[27] She suggested that the government should provide health treatments (*ihlajaat*) at no cost, but "everything costs money."[28]

[23] Ibid.

[24] Interview with Malika, lawyer, in Khartoum, Sudan (October 2006) (Author's File Reference Number 31).

[25] Interview with Najima, NGO founder, in Khartoum, Sudan (February 2007) (Author's File Reference Number 62).

[26] Interview with Nahda, women's rights activist, in Omdurman, Sudan (June 2005) (Author's File Reference Number 24).

[27] Interview with Nisreen, internally displaced person, in Haj Yoosef, Sudan (June 2005) (Author's File Reference Number 11).

[28] Ibid.

In addition to activists and lawyers, judges also experience benefits and costs associated with the regime's rigid imposition of law. Some judges resist strict interpretations of Islamic law, often to avoid imposing punishments like stoning or amputation. Part of the reason, legal professionals told me, is because local and foreign activists are watching.[29] Judges, however, must balance any acts of resistance with their need to earn a living. A senior lawyer told me, "If you don't pay allegiance to *al-mu'tamir al-watani* [the National Congress Party, led by President Bashir], you will not get anything."[30] The founder of an NGO echoed these comments; she had been dismissed alongside hundreds of judges and other public servants in the early 1990s during Bashir's self-proclaimed policy of *salah al-aam* (reforming the public interest). "When this government came to power, they retired all of them, not because they're not competent. It's because they were not supporters of this government."[31] Adhering to the government's ideology becomes a way to increase the likelihood of being protected (or at least ignored) by it.

VI. CONCLUSION

The discourses of human rights and Islamic law in Sudan are paradoxically quite similar. Both provide frameworks for interaction among people, for dealing with and resolving disputes, and for arranging sets of benefits to their adherents. Both require the teaching of and adherence to specific documents and texts as laws, proscribing certain behaviors under a threat of moral sanction. Both human rights and religious law are directive forces, claiming supremacy in their prescriptions and in the personal and social obligations they demand. Generally, Islamic law and human rights law are engaged in inculcating basic teachings or norms around how to interact with others and interpret facts, to guide and influence people's decision-making processes. But a political underclass is certainly maintained under each legal system as each is implemented in Sudan, constituted by those persons with little ability to access the norms, institutions, and funding that form those legal and ideological systems.

Fundamentally, this chapter has sought to reveal the parallel structure between how the state uses religion and how human rights activists use human rights charters and documents. Both the state and international aid agencies present a flattened and unchanging system of law as a means to increase their power and influence. Legal discourses, then – of Islamic law and of human rights – become the political tools of elite actors seeking to win the hearts and minds of the poor. But these tools are

[29] Interview with senior judicial official 3, in Khartoum, Sudan (January 2007) (Author's File Reference Number 58).

[30] Interview with Balima, human rights activist, in Khartoum, Sudan (March 2007) (Author's File Reference Number 73).

[31] Interview with Najima, NGO founder, in Khartoum, Sudan (February 2007) (Author's File Reference Number 62).

imperfect. Their power lies in the lure they provide to state and nonstate actors in war-torn contexts, and in the ways they change the behavior of elites in government and in civil society.

Just as Islamic law has plural roots, human rights comes not only through indigenous forms from local lawyers but also by way of international funding to those lawyers and NGOs seeking to promote rights-based approaches. In these ways legal norms built on a foundation of human rights principles are appearing through the interaction of local lawyers with international aid groups, just as Islamic legal norms in Sudan emerged through the interaction of local customs and practices with those introduced by foreigners. If both human rights and Islamic law are distinct but universal and unchanging – and need to call upon universalism to be effective tools of governance – then from the perspective of those subject to these legal systems, at least one of them cannot be universal, and must instead be fallible.

What do these interpretations of the discourses of human rights and state-imposed Islamic law mean for future studies of rights in countries that adopt narrow or strict interpretations of religious law, and for civil society groups and human rights promoters in these places? First, it means scholars cannot study the rise of modern forms of Islamic law without studying the relationship between religion and state politics, culture, or even economic development. (Recall that in 1983 at a time when Sudan's economy was crumbling, President Nimeiri sought to refocus the nation's attention on the law by declaring himself a sheikh and his government under Islam.)

Second, scholars, aid workers, and human rights activists must appreciate and contend with the similarities and tensions in how people experience both human rights and state-imposed Islamic law on the ground. While there is certainly rhetorical advantage to claiming the universality and immutability of religious law or of human rights, scholars and activists would be well suited to continue to investigate the local and contextual factors that enable deeper questioning of the grassroots experience of universalizing discourses.

Third, just as human rights cannot be disaggregated from the local polity in which those rights are promoted, those rights also cannot be disaggregated from people's experiences of religion and the state's uses of religion as a political tool. Studying law in settings divided by violence includes investigating how the promotion of human rights takes place in states that turn to religious law – as another layer of law, a separate system supplanting religious law, or something else – and investigating law from the perspective of those who experience it (Massoud 2013b). In these places, citizens may be conscripted to fight in a war of ideologies between religious law and human rights law, and between the state and activists calling for change. Future research in conflict settings and authoritarian states might also investigate the thorny questions of aid dependence and why some citizens adopt multiple or instrumental interpretations of religious law and human rights law, and whether the top-down, elite-controlled, and homogenized form of human rights promoted to war survivors is becoming a parallel kind of homogenizing authority.

This chapter is based on fieldwork in a specific context and during a specific time period, and the experience of Islamic law among those I studied in Sudan may not be the same for everyone in Sudan, or for citizens in other Muslim-majority contexts such as Saudi Arabia, Somalia, or Iran. A new legal realist approach to Islamic law and society demands a fine-grained, empirical understanding of the plurality within Islamic legal discourse and of the culture, politics, and economic practices shaping law and religion in each context in which Islamic law is used. Altogether, this inquiry invites scholars to analyze the layered construction of law in an interdisciplinary manner, involving politics, theology, economic development, culture, psychology, and society.

I conclude with three broad suggestions for scholars interested in law and society in conflict settings and authoritarian states, and in Islamic law and society. First, adopt an empirical or data-driven approach to understand the effects of how elites present distinct forms of secular and religious law to the marginalized. Second, investigate the ways in which state leaders mask legal pluralism under a disguise of legal rigidity. Finally, be mindful of the ways different legal orders and discourses – national, international, and transnational – are captured, experienced, and exported, and their similarities, tensions, and contradictions, particularly from the perspective of those whom they are most meant to support.

REFERENCES

Abusharaf, Rogaia Mustafa. 2009. *Transforming Displaced Women in Sudan: Politics and the Body in a Squatter Settlement*. Chicago: University of Chicago Press.

Al-Jazeera. 2014. "Sudan Apostasy Woman Given US Embassy Refuge." Last modified June 27. http://www.aljazeera.com/news/africa/2014/06/sudan-apostasy-woman-given-us-embassy-refuge-201462774531967564.html.

Al-Mawdudi, Sayyid Abu al-A'la. 1961. *Rights of Non-Muslims in an Islamic State*. Lahore, Pakistan: Islamic Publications.

An-Na'im, Abdullahi Ahmed. 1990. *Toward an Islamic Reformation: Civil Liberties, Human Rights, and International Law*. Syracuse: Syracuse University Press.

An-Na'im, Abdullahi Ahmed. 2008. *Islam and the Secular State: Negotiating the Future of Shari'a*. Cambridge, MA: Harvard University Press.

Albertus, Michael, and Victor Menaldo. 2013. "The Political Economy of Autocratic Constitutions." In *Constitutions in Authoritarian Regimes*, edited by Tom Ginsburg and Alberto Simpser, 53–82. Cambridge: Cambridge University Press.

Baderin, Mashood. 2003. *International Human Rights and Islamic Law*. Oxford: Oxford University Press.

BBC News. 2007. "'Muhammad' Teddy Teacher Arrested." November 26. http://news.bbc.co.uk/2/hi/africa/7112929.stm.

Burr, J. Millard, and Robert O. Collins. 2003. *Revolutionary Sudan: Hassan Al-Turabi and the Islamist State, 1989–2000*. Leiden: Brill.

Collins, Robert. 2008. *A History of Modern Sudan*. Cambridge: Cambridge University Press.

Deng, Francis. 1995. *War of Visions: Conflict of Identities in the Sudan*. New York: Brookings Institution Press.

El-Gawhary, Karim. 1995. "Shari'a of Civil Code? Egypt's Parallel Legal Systems." 25 *Middle East Report (MER197)*. http://ns2.merip.org/mer/mer197/sharia-civil-code-egypts-parallel-legal-systems.

Emon, Anver. 2010. *Islamic Natural Law Theories*. Oxford: Oxford University Press.

Englund, Harri. 2004. "Towards a Critique of Rights Talk in New Democracies: The Case of Legal Aid in Malawi." *Discourse & Society* 15(5): 527–551.

Fluehr-Lobban, Carolyn. 1987. *Islamic Law and Society in the Sudan*. London: Frank Cass.

Fyzee, Asaf A. A. 2009. *Outlines of Muhammadan Law*. 5th ed. Oxford: Oxford University Press.

Gilsenan, Michael. 2011. "Translating Colonial Fortunes: Dilemmas of Inheritance in Muslim and English Laws across a Nineteenth-Century Diaspora." *Comparative Studies of South Asia, Africa and the Middle East* 31(2): 355–371.

Goldsmith, Jack, and Eric Posner. 2005. *The Limits of International Law*. Oxford: Oxford University Press.

Harding, Andrew J. 2001. "Comparative Law and Legal Transplantation in South East Asia: Making Sense of the 'Nomic Din.'" In *Adapting Legal Cultures*, edited by David Nelken and Johannes Feest, 199–222. Oxford: Hart Publishing.

Hathaway, Oona A. 2002. "Do Human Rights Treaties Make a Difference?" *Yale Law Journal* 111: 1935–2042.

Ibrahim, Abdullahi Ali. 2008. *Manichaean Delirium: Decolonizing the Judiciary and Islamic Renewal in Sudan*, 1898–1985. Leiden: Brill.

Johansen, Baber. 1999. "Secular and Religious Elements in Hanafite Law: Function and Limits of the Absolute Character of Government Authority." In *Contingency in a Sacred Law: Legal and Ethical Norms in the Muslim Fiqh*, edited by Baber Johansen, 189–218. Leiden: Brill.

Johnson, Douglas. 2003. *The Root Causes of Sudan's Civil Wars*. Bloomington: University of Indiana Press.

Köndgen, Olaf. 2010. "Shari'a and National Law in the Sudan." In *Sharia Incorporated: A Comparative Overview of the Legal Systems of Twelve Muslim Countries in Past and Present*, edited by Jan Michiel Otto, 181–230. Leiden: Leiden University Press.

Lauren, Paul Gordon. 2011. *The Evolution of International Human Rights: Visions Seen*. Philadelphia: University of Pennsylvania Press.

Mallat, Chibli, and Jane Connors. 1991. *Islamic Family Law*. London: Graham and Trotman.

Massoud, Mark Fathi. 2006. "Rights in a Failed State: Internally Displaced Women in Sudan and Their Lawyers." *Berkeley Journal of Gender, Law & Justice* 21: 2–12.

Massoud, Mark Fathi. 2011. "Do Victims of War Need International Law? Human Rights Education Programs in Authoritarian Sudan." *Law & Society Review* 45: 1–32.

Massoud, Mark Fathi. 2012. "Lawyers and the Disintegration of the Legal Complex in Sudan." In *Fates of Political Liberalism in the British Post-Colony: The Politics of the Legal Complex*, edited by Terence C. Halliday, Lucien Karpik, and Malcolm M. Feeley, 193–218. New York: Cambridge University Press.

Massoud, Mark Fathi. 2013a. *Law's Fragile State: Colonial, Authoritarian, and Humanitarian Legacies in Sudan*. Cambridge: Cambridge University Press.

Massoud, Mark Fathi. 2013b. "Legal Poverty and the Rule of Law in Conflict Settings." *Whittier Law Review* 32(3): 1–15.

Mayer, Ann Elizabeth. 2012. *Islam and Human Rights: Tradition and Politics*. 5th ed. Boulder: Westview Press.

Merry, Sally Engle. 2006. *Human Rights and Gender Violence: Translating International Law into Local Justice*. Chicago: University of Chicago Press.

Moyn, Samuel. 2011. *The Last Utopia: Human Rights in History*. Cambridge, MA: Harvard University Press.

Mustafa, Zaki. 1971. *Common Law in the Sudan: An Account of the Justice, Equity and Good Conscience Provision*. Oxford: Oxford University Press.

Mutua, Makau. 2008. *Human Rights: A Political and Cultural Critique*. Philadelphia: University of Pennsylvania Press.

The New York Times. 2009. "Sudan Court Fines Woman for Wearing Trousers." September 7. http://www.nytimes.com/192009/09/08/world/africa/08sudan.html.

"Ratification of International Human Rights Treaties – Sudan." n.d. University of Minnesota Human Rights Library. http://www1.umn.edu/humanrts/research/ratification-sudan.html.

Salman, Salman. 1981. "Legal Profession in Sudan: A Study of Legal and Professional Pluralism." In *Lawyers in the Third World: Comparative and Developmental Perspectives*, edited by C. J. Dias, R. Luckman, D. O. Lynch, and J. C. N. Paul, 226–247. New York: International Center for Law and Development.

Stilt, Kristen. 2013. "Constitutions in Authoritarian Regimes: The Egyptian Constitution of 1971." In *Constitutions in Authoritarian Regimes*, edited by Tom Ginsburg and Alberto Simpser, 111–140. Cambridge: Cambridge University Press.

Sudan Government. 1901 and 1929. Civil Justice Ordinance.

7

Women Seeking Justice At the Intersection Between Vernacular and State Laws and Courts in Rural KwaZulu-Natal, South Africa

Sindiso Mnisi Weeks

I. INTRODUCTION

The Traditional Courts Bill (TCB)[1] is a piece of legislation drafted by the South African Department of Justice and Constitutional Development and introduced in 2008 to regulate customary courts and provide better access to justice for the 16 to 21 million South Africans living in rural areas (Claassens 2011; Mnisi Weeks 2012). Several problems have been raised with the legislation (Claassens 2011; Mnisi Weeks 2012). These include its having been drafted without consulting ordinary rural people, especially women, who make up 59 per cent of the rural population (Budlender, as cited in Claassens and Cousins 2008, 2n2, 168n22). Only traditional leaders and local government were properly consulted (Traditional Courts Bill, B15-2008 and later B1-2012, 'Memorandum to the Bill', clause 4).

The resultant substantive problems include a lack of adequate protections for women and their rights (Mnisi Weeks 2012n2). Two main examples are pertinent. Firstly, in the Bill, women are not guaranteed self-representation in traditional courts. Secondly, the Bill does not attempt to make women members of traditional courts or ensure their participation in decision making, and thus does not conceive of their participation beyond their being mere litigants. One argument would say that the constitutional right to gender equality (Constitution of South Africa,

[1] Initially introduced in the National Assembly in May 2008 as B18-2008, and then reintroduced in the National Council of Provinces in January 2012 as B1-2012. The Bill lapsed in February 2014 and was therefore not passed into law. The newly named Department of Justice and Correctional Services plans to introduce a revised version of the Bill in the next few months. It has promised that it will attempt to address the problems described in this chapter; however, in recent testimonies before the Portfolio Committee in the National Assembly, it has been pressured to speed up the process, which it has said it would do by curtailing its consultations. This would create the same fundamental problem with the process of developing the Bill exhibited by the 2008/2012 version. As described in this chapter, this failure to adequately consult affected people, especially women, is largely responsible for the severe failure of the Bill to address women's core needs. Moreover, unless the Bill is redrafted on the basis of an entirely different framework (the 2008/2012 version was based on the colonial and apartheid approaches to 'traditional' leaders, communities and courts) the revisions made to it cannot be expected to fully address the problems described in this chapter.

section 9(3)) would require that the Bill make these accommodations. This argument has been made repeatedly by opponents of the Bill.[2]

Aside from the Constitution, however, empirically-based lawmaking practice would also seem to demand that such provisions be included in the Bill. After all, among the problems put to the South African Law Reform Commission (SALRC), when it conducted its research and consultations in 1998–2003 (SALRC 2003), was the fact that in many rural areas women were not allowed to speak or represent themselves – they could only be represented by male relatives (18). This presented particular difficulties for women in mourning who, though they were also uniquely vulnerable to eviction by family members at this time, also faced restrictions on their ability to be seen in public and hence could not attend court hearings (Claassens and Ngubane 2008; Burman, Carmody, and Hoffman-Wanderer 2008; Claassens and Mnisi 2009; Mnisi Weeks 2011a, 2013). These women are required to be represented by male relatives who are, in some instances, the very ones seeking to dispossess them (ibid.). The Traditional Courts Bill enables the continuation of such discriminatory practices against women. It achieves this by providing that men can represent women, just as women can represent men 'in accordance with customary law' (what I refer to as vernacular law).[3] This may not be a problem if the Bill were not meant to operate in a cultural context in which men are never to be represented by women and women are required to be represented by men, often to their disadvantage.[4]

Another key problem in practice presented to the SALRC, which it appears the Department neglected to take into account, is that traditional courts are made up of mostly old men. It has been proven that these courts, so constituted, are often biased in favor of men, especially in family disputes (Claassens and Ngubane 2008; Curren and Bonthuys 2005; Higgins, Fenrich, and Tanzer 2007, 1700–1703). Curren and Bonthuys (2005) draw attention to the severe impact of this male bias in domestic violence cases, concluding that taking domestic violence cases to traditional courts is typically unbeneficial to women. The same has been said to be true in property disputes – particularly land disputes – where men typically win over women (Claassens and Ngubane 2008).

Suggesting a close connection (if not causation) between the fact that ordinary people were not consulted in the drafting of the Bill and traditional leaders were consulted almost exclusively, the Bill goes a long way towards strengthening the role of traditional leaders while providing ordinary people with few protections. For instance, the Bill centralizes the role of senior traditional leaders (formerly known as chiefs) (TCB, clauses 1 and 4(4)) and writes other officials, such as headmen and the

[2] See www.cls.uct.ac.za/research/focus/tcb/ for a number of submissions made in response to the Bill.

[3] TCB, clause 9(3)(b). As will be defined in this chapter, I choose to use the term 'vernacular law' instead of 'customary law', though they may be loosely understood to refer to the same reality.

[4] A telling example is Curren and Bonthuys's (2005) discussion of domestic violence in 'traditional courts'. See also Higgins, Fenrich, and Tanzer (2007).

'community-in-council',[5] out of the process, whereas these have a central role under vernacular law.[6] These other participants play a particularly significant role in holding the traditional leader accountable. Through their participation, they shape the interpretation of vernacular law given effect in the dispute resolution process.

The Bill gives senior traditional leaders extensive powers such as the ability to sanction people in their area by depriving them of customary benefits (TCB, clause 10(2)(i)), which may include community membership and land rights, in civil cases (TCB, clause 10(1)(b)). It also permits the sanction of forced labour.[7] Some decisions such as prohibition (the equivalent of an interdict), 'community service', and 'any other order that the presiding officer may deem fit' are unappealable (TCB, clause 13(1)). Further shoring up the position of traditional leaders, the Bill does not allow people to choose to go to state courts if they prefer not to have their disputes resolved under 'customary law'. This is while the rights to choose to live under custom and elect to perpetuate a customary system are given to individuals in the Constitution (sections 30 and 31).

Some argue, with the lofty Preamble to the Bill, that the Bill is simply reinforcing 'customary law' dispute resolution by capturing it in the legislation, and varies with vernacular law only insofar as this system of law is in irresolvable tension with the Constitution. Such people also often raise the concern that, despite its claims to the contrary, the Constitution itself is inconsistent with respect for 'customary law'.[8] However, this chapter argues that the Bill shuts out the expressions of vernacular law dispute management that work well in practice – or are key to its value to the people

5 A term coined by Hilda Kuper to describe how the community gathers and sits as a council in order to hear and resolve disputes locally. This distinguishes 'traditional courts' from state courts, especially in South Africa, where juries are not used.

6 See Mnisi Weeks (2012, 143–146). In this section, 'customary law' and vernacular law are used interchangeably; however, 'customary law' is placed in inverted commas to signify its contested status and the fact that it is not the term of choice in this chapter. Further explanation is provided for this in the next section.

7 TCB, clause 10(2)(g), states that the 'presiding officer' (who is defined as the senior traditional leader) may issue 'an order that one of the parties to the dispute, both parties or any other person performs some form of service without remuneration for the benefit of the community under the supervision or control of a specified person or group of persons identified by the traditional court'.

8 Principal among these proponents is the Advocate and Senior Traditional Leader, Patekile Holomisa, who was the leader of the Congress of Traditional Leaders of South Africa for 23 years, ending in November 2013. John and Jean Comaroff (2009, 6) describe the organization as having the "ultimate objective [of] a nation-state that accords to traditional leaders sovereign autonomy over their realms, a nation-state that puts the dictates of culture at least on a par with, if not above, universal rights of citizens." Until recently, Inkosi (Chief) Holomisa was also a member of parliament (representing the ruling party, the African National Congress) and sat on the Portfolio Committee on Justice and Constitutional Development, which is the legislative house that had to determine whether the Traditional Courts Bill would pass into law – subject only to the President's signature. In May 2014, Holomisa was appointed to the position of Deputy Minister of Labor. He remains vocal on traditional leadership affairs. An example statement by Chief Holomisa may be found at: www.politicsweb.co.za/politicsweb/view/politicsweb/en/page72308?oid=306586&sn=Marketingweb+detail&pid=90389: "The Abuse of Traditional Leaders Must Come to an End".

who rely on it – while it also fails to protect central constitutional rights. The chapter goes further to argue that, even where there are effective compromises to be reached by adopting the principle of 'passive development of customary law' (Lehnert 2005, 256, 270) that the Constitutional Court has embraced,[9] the Bill passes up these opportunities. Instead, the Bill elects to reinforce the rather conservative and patriarchal – indeed, stereotypical – notions of 'customary law' that developed during colonialism and apartheid.

The argument here is that the Bill fails to engage with vernacular dispute management in practice and to grapple effectively with the regulatory needs and challenges that practice raises. As a consequence, the Bill undermines some elements that are responsible for vernacular dispute management working in practice (to the extent that it does in fact work). In other words, it does not adequately consider the reasons why people continue to subscribe to vernacular dispute management forums. At the same time, it fails to remedy the problems with social and legal vernacular practices that might cause people to avoid the dispute management forums if and when they can. With regard to the needs of women, the Bill fails to address the particular problems they face in their social context and vernacular forums – issues pertaining to which thought and debate should be had. This is an important area for discussion about how state regulation can best respond to maximise the positive dimensions of the vernacular system while minimising the negatives.

Unlike the Bill, this chapter sets out to reason from the ground up. It draws on empirical research conducted over eleven months (from March 2011 to January 2012) in the deep rural area of Msinga, in KwaZulu-Natal – in two formally recognised traditional communities, in three wards (subcommunities) in each community. These are Zulu-speaking communities that are troubled by high levels of interpersonal violence and personal insecurity. They simultaneously face an ever-latent threat of political instability from long-standing tensions with their neighbouring communities (including each other), against whom they continue to contest territorial boundaries. The chapter's primary institutional focus is on the headmen's and chiefs' courts. However, the interplay between these forums and the many others that surround them is an important part of the portrait. They include family courts, neighbourhood courts, tribal policemen's courts, specialized vernacular forums, and magistrates' courts. These formal and informal forums compete with, complement, support, or undermine the headmen's and chiefs' courts, both locally and beyond the boundaries of the community.

Women attempt to negotiate justice and security in this terrain. They do so subject to different forms of vulnerability and strength, and with varying degrees of success. The power they hold and the success they achieve must be understood within the social relationships, values, politics, and economics that form the fabric of

9 *Shilubana and Others v. Nwamitwa* [2008] ZACC 9 (SACC); *Gumede v. President of the Republic of South Africa and Others* [2008] ZACC 2003 (SACC).

their context and inform their decisions (Mnisi Weeks 2011b, 2013). Also, accommodating diverse dispute management goals is important for a fuller grasp of what these women are seeking through dispute management, and thus whether they are successful in achieving these outcomes. The findings of the empirical data from this study raise uneasy questions for the quest for justice and security by rural women in Msinga amidst legal and institutional pluralism. They also bring up difficulties concerning the role that legislation like the Traditional Courts Bill can hope to play within vernacular groupings.

II. DEFINITIONS AND CONTEXT

In the following section, I explain the terminology that I have selected for use in this chapter and the reasons for choosing it. I then describe the institutional context of the chapter's discussion, which is the structure and processes followed by the 'traditional courts' in Msinga.

A. *Terminology*

In this chapter, I have elected to replace the conventionally used term 'customary law' with 'vernacular law'. The main reason is simple: 'customary law' carries too much baggage from the colonial era when, as Martin Chanock has argued, the very thing was invented (Chanock 2001, 295). Colonisers purported to refer to indigenous systems of norms. However, by naming, codifying, and distorting them through indirect rule, repugnancy clauses, and other means they created a system of law that more closely represented the colonisers' conceptions of the law and indigenous culture than those of the indigenous people themselves (2001). Now, 'customary law' carries with it negative connotations of a staid system of law that has been deeply tainted by colonialism and apartheid and is liable to be changed by the courts – even benevolent ones like the Constitutional Court.

'Vernacular law' more clearly captures the fact that the normative order being discussed here is one that has been developed by the local people through their use. 'Vernacular law' incorporates influences from other orders that have been imposed or electively embraced. Thus, as with vernacular language, 'vernacular' – when used with law and disputing mechanisms – describes a normative order that is not static but evolving even as the people evolve their legal needs and adapt the law and disputing mechanisms to their use. Moreover, 'vernacular law' expresses this chapter's emic approach to discussion of the normative orders of the people of Msinga.

In keeping with this use of the term 'vernacular' to describe law, I refer to what are now known (and described in the recent legislation) as 'traditional communities' as 'vernacular groupings'. This emphasises that the people who make up the grouping determine – with flexibility – what scale of association and organization is important to them at any one time. I reject the legislation's emphasis on tribal boundaries initially created by apartheid legislation.[10] Instead, I adopt the sphere of jurisdiction to which the grouping's self-identified members grant distinction at any one stage of the dispute management process. In this, I accept that their own self-identities are nested, layered (Cousins 2008, 129), and in flux. Thus, their groupings' boundaries are similarly constituted and will fluctuate according to circumstance.

I have also chosen to avoid the term 'dispute resolution'. Instead, I refer to what is being described here as 'dispute management'.[11] Such a paradigm allows for the recognition of a different social context in which disputes occur from that which state courts assume. The rural context considered here is one in which people's lives are profoundly entwined as they depend upon one another for security and survival, and relationships are so deep and contact so regular that conflict is sure to arise repeatedly at scales ranging from minor to major.

In such a bounded, relatively closed society, dealings with disputes represent management more than resolution, especially as relationships, proximity, and tensions mostly continue after the disputes have been 'decided'.[12] This is a need proven and partly met by the evolution of multiple forums varying in the formality of their existence and constitution. People living in such close socioeconomic proximity are able to air their problems and have them heard, mediated, or even arbitrated in these various forums both promptly and without an excessive amount of social upheaval (Merry 1979, 894–895). Yet, simultaneously with this regularity of conflict, given the intimacy of connections, problems are 'resolved' without too much finality. Indeed, disputes requiring such management are often even transformations and escalations of a single contestation or repeated and new expressions of a long-standing dispute over identifiable (though not always articulated) core differences.[13]

Within such a paradigm, one seeking 'resolution' must be able to avoid expenditure of the tremendous resources demanded by the state system in terms of emotion, involvement/activism, time, and costs (Felstiner, Abel, and Sarat 1980, 654). State courts might often dismiss the most minor of matters that are dealt with by vernacular forums as being trivial, and some matters (such as witchcraft) as not even legal matters. However, this does not mean that Msinga residents' trivial matters are not of great significance for continuation of life in their settings and, hence, in dire need of 'resolution' or simply management. Of course, the time and money it takes to try to get matters resolved in state forums is also often too great for most ordinary rural

[10] Section 28(3) of Traditional Leadership and Governance Framework Act 41 of 2003.

[11] This is not an unfamiliar term. It is used, for instance, by Merry (1979).

[12] This is similar to what is described by Merry (1979, 899–900). This can be contrasted with the situation in the United States where "there is no anticipated future relationship" described by Galanter (1983, 24–25). As will be seen, this expectation of continued relationships of some mutual dependency is part of the reason why cases do not often go to the state courts, which are viewed as more disruptive of such continuing relations (see Merry 1979, 894–895; Miller and Sarat 1980, 526).

[13] Felstiner, Abel, and Sarat (1980, 639) argue that this is the case with all dispute processes, even those that make it to and result in a decision by a state court.

people, 72 per cent or more of whom are living on $37 or less a month (Statistics South Africa).

Furthermore, the 'satisfaction' that the state courts might see fit to grant in both trivial and much less trivial cases, such as rape and murder, may sometimes also fail to be in keeping with what the parties expect, coming from their own sociolegal context. Hence, even when state courts are appealed to, often the matter is not finalised by the relief they give. Instead, the disputes may continue in a different iteration – accompanied by the search for perhaps different but related relief – in vernacular forums. Here, one sees that there is much benefit to be obtained from following the 'extended case method' employed by legal anthropologists, which requires that the dispute be tracked from its inception in its social context of origin through all the forums (formal and informal, legal and social) in which it is given expression. This method yields a rich picture of the transformation of disputes that demands that we describe what is happening as 'management' rather than 'resolution', since the latter artificially ascribes finality to a single outcome – usually one from a formal forum (Felstiner, Abel, and Sarat 1980, 639).

Most important, the paradigm of dispute management permits me to take account of a wide range of objectives motivating people to bring their cases (Felstiner, Abel, and Sarat 1980, 642–643) – or bring other external intervention into their long-standing disputes – not necessarily the often fetishized objective of a single, final decision that is delivered by the highest forum to render a judgement.[14] This means that different kinds of satisfaction can be pursued by means of activating the vernacular dispute management process – not just a guilty/not guilty finding, restoration of property, or damages and costs. Hence, people can seek publicity about a wrong they have suffered, acknowledgement of the wrong, or an apology. They can issue a warning to another, shame the other into doing what they will the other to do, prevent fighting/violence, be proven or affirmed to be right, have the other take financial responsibility, be reunified with another, or have their ability to continue living together with another reestablished. Another thing people can obtain is the simple rearticulation and reaffirmation of purportedly essential and shared values as being, indeed, essential and shared by their vernacular social grouping, at whatever scale they identify it. These are the range of motives often underlying the initiative people take in bringing a case and the judgement of an interdict, restoration of property, compensation, or damages that people request. This multiplicity of objectives also relates to the motivations for one's performing an offence in the first place.

[14] Galanter (1983, 26) writes of American disputing patterns: 'Many cases are withdrawn or abandoned because the mere invocation of the court served the initiator's purpose of harassment, warning or delay. . . . The invocation of official adjudicatory institutions does not necessarily express either a preference or an intention to pursue the dispute in official forums, to secure the application of official rules, or to obtain an adjudicated outcome. The official system may be invoked, or invocation may be threatened, in order to punish or harass, to demonstrate prowess, to force an opponent to settle, or to secure compliance with the decision of another forum.'

Vernacular dispute management forums are important in especially remote rural areas primarily because of their accessibility in terms of proximity, relative cost, speed, form, and language or discourse. There is also much scholarly ambivalence about their benefits and risks for women (Whitehead and Tsikata 2003, 104; Nyamu Musembi 2002, 126–150). As suggested earlier, the context in which these forums operate is one in which their key function is to enable members of the vernacular groupings they serve to live together well (again) as those depending on one another for security and often survival. In such a context, justice may sometimes look different from how it does in the state court context. However, an important caveat is that sometimes people need and want the kind of justice that the state courts provide, and therefore prize being able to move between local forums and state courts at will, if they can.

B. Vernacular Dispute Management Forums in Msinga

The structure of the mainstream vernacular dispute management system in both Msinga 'traditional communities' (formerly known as tribes) represented in this study is made up of a hierarchy of courts, often referred to as councils (*amabandla*), as follows. At the lowest level of social organization there are family councils, constituted by either a single family's elders sitting to discuss an internal family dispute or two families' elders meeting to resolve perhaps a marital or paternity dispute. At a similar level are neighbourhood councils, which are made up of people living in close proximity to one another who would gather relatively informally to resolve a conflict between a few of their own. An example is if one neighbour insulted or stole from another.

Neighbourhoods form part of subwards (*imihlathi*), which each have a council (*ibandla*) that is typically headed up by a tribal policeman known as *iphoyisa lenduna* (literally, the headman's policeman) or simply *iphoyisa* (the policeman). Subward councils are sometimes convened and chaired by a chairman who is a locally appointed or elected leader. Subwards form part of wards (*izigodi*), and each ward has a council headed up by a headman (*induna*) who oversees the area. The headman's council is known as *ibandla lenduna. Izinduna* (the various headmen) make up the core of the village or tribal council otherwise known as the chief's council (*ibandla lenkosi*). I refer to all these courts/councils as 'vernacular dispute management forums' or 'vernacular forums'.

Amabandla are made up of only adult men who live in the vernacular grouping at issue. These men are mostly, but not exclusively, married but must be postadolescence. All such men are welcome to attend and participate in the questioning, discussion, and deliberations that contribute to the final outcome of a dispute. Hilda Kuper has called this the 'community-in-council'.[15] Along with their dispute

[15] Kuper (1947); Hammond-Tooke (1989). I adapt this term to 'vernacular grouping-in-council'.

management function, all of these councils also play somewhat of a legislative and administrative role. In the case of the family council, *ibandla* gives some edicts on how family members should conduct themselves and makes resource distribution decisions concerning family assets, for instance, on the death of a family head responsible for one of the 'houses' (sublineages). The subward and headman's councils possibly make the least legislative and administrative decisions, as this role is largely played by the headman as an individual, and directives are filtered down to the subward through *iphoyisa*. At the village level (*isizwe*), the legislative and administrative council comprises the headmen and other chief-appointed and local officials publicly elected in terms of legislation.[16]

III. FRAMING THEORY

To ensure readers have full access to the empirical information in this chapter, it will help if they are familiar with theories of disputing. I have briefly introduced disputing theory and the 'transformations studies approach' to disputes. This section elaborates both theories and how they apply in a context like Msinga. It also explicitly engages with new legal realism as a theory. It argues that applying this theory could help the South African government begin to address the problems with its attempt to provide access to justice and regulate vernacular dispute management forums and groupings through the Traditional Courts Bill.

A. *Disputing Theory*

Disputes typically come into being by following a process of perception of an experience by the relevant party, the party's naming it as an injurious act, the party's blaming someone else for the injury, and then the party's claiming a remedy from the person thought responsible for the wrong (Felstiner, Abel, and Sarat 1980, 635–636). The first two steps are jointly referred to as constituting a perceived injurious experience (PIE) as such (1980). Key to whether a person externally claims a remedy is the party to whom the person attributes the wrong: if to self, the person is unlikely to blame another, express a sense of injury, and seek any external redress. But the person's initial attribution can change with time, discussions with or counsel from others, and how an institution to which the grievance is brought for settlement responds to or treats it. The ideology of the person and the scope of conflict that the forum will consider also affect the transformation of the PIE from one stage to another (Felstiner, Abel, and Sarat 1980, 641).

This transformation is sometimes referred to as the escalation of a dispute from a grievance to a claim to a full-blown dispute (Miller and Sarat 1980, 527). 'A dispute

16 Traditional Leadership and Governance Framework Act 41 of 2003, section 3. The Act requires that at least one-third of the councilors be women.

exists when a claim based on a grievance is rejected either in whole or in part' (527). As Miller and Sarat show, nonescalation of PIEs is most common. For instance, often in family situations, people may prefer to avoid confrontation and rather 'keep the problem quiet' (531). Numerous studies have shown that there are a variety of means that people use to address their grievances and obtain redress.[17, 18] The first and most common is self-help, where the individual finds one's own solution, which may include avoidance of the other party (Merry 1979, 894) or '"endurance," the threat of violence, and actual violence' (Miller and Sarat 1980, 531). Among self-help solutions, one might even include sorcery or witchcraft (Prinsloo 1999, 19). Second is negotiation, where the person feeling wronged might confront the other party and try to obtain what the person thinks is owed. Negotiation takes place where a dispute is in existence. Such negotiation may result in a compromise offer, which is in fact a partial rejection of the original claim and thus a dispute, no matter how brief (Miller and Sarat 1980, 527). Further escalation of the matter may follow.

Third is mediation or arbitration, wherein a third party is brought in either to facilitate discussions between the parties leading to a compromise (mediation) or to decide on a winner and a loser with the decision being binding on both parties and enforceable (arbitration). A last resort and a step rarely reached is a case – that is, judicial adjudication in court. In this chapter, the higher-level councils constituting the vernacular dispute management system are considered equal to courts and thus the ultimate forum. This makes sense since they are locally considered to be courts of a sort and, by and large, permanently exist to resolve disputes with the power to punish and hand down decisions that at least have the veneer of finality and allow for enforcement.

However, it is important to note that sometimes these forums sit in a mediatory, rather than an adjudicatory, role. Members of the vernacular groupings thus draw a distinction between a case and an instance where the parties are just being reconciled. Yet, note that the standard form of mediation in Msinga is a hybrid between mediation and arbitration in which the headman or chief uses his authoritative status to press for agreement between the parties. Sometimes mediation is conducted by the vernacular grouping-in-council alone, without the participation of the headman. Sometimes dispute management is performed by the single male headman of a locality or by him and a pair or handful of local men hearing a dispute between two parties at those parties' precise request (and in relative privacy), hence prompting me to consider it arbitration with mediatory overtones. These variations will be indicated when apposite.

17 Nader (2002, 150); Prinsloo (1999, 19–20); Merry (1979, 894); Norgren and Nanda (1996, 285): '[P]luralism expresses itself not only in the different issues brought to courts for resolution, but also in decisions not to use courts at all. Even when courts are called upon in dispute resolution situations, it may not be for their traditional, and legitimate dispute resolution functions. Courts do cast a shadow; but it is often distorted. . . . they may serve . . . as institutions to be manipulated in intracommunity and interpersonal struggles.'

18 Also see Merry (1979, 903), where she helpfully distinguishes avoidance and endurance.

B. New Legal Realism

In keeping with New Legal Realism, this chapter constitutes direct engagement with the policy matters that the Traditional Courts Bill seeks to address. It does so drawing on a bottom-up view of law as a means of questioning such policy development, with the hope of informing it in future (Erlanger, Garth, Larson, Mertz, Nourse, and Wilkins 2005).

> [A] bottom-up approach requires that assertions about the impact of law be supported by research at 'ground' level. This in turn requires that we rely on (or actually undertake ourselves) empirical research rather than using projections based simply on our theories or individual experiences. A bottom-up approach takes an expansive and open-minded view of the impact of law, and also includes within its purview a wide range of socio-economic classes and interests. (Erlanger et al. 2005, 339)

This approach demands in-depth understanding of the everyday experiences of ordinary people, particularly the disenfranchised. This is exceptionally important when concerned with a legal system like vernacular law, which is largely developed and enforced at local level (Comaroff and Roberts 1981), outside of the stereotypical hallways of justice.

Furthermore, bottom-up scholarship requires recognition of the differences in power that various people and institutions at different levels of social and legal hierarchies hold (Erlanger et al. 2005, 340). That is why I consider the exclusion of diverse socioeconomic groups and people with diverse interests a critical failure in the research and lawmaking that is embodied in the Traditional Courts Bill. Only senior traditional leaders were really consulted in that process, and the Bill therefore represents the interests of this elite group of public officeholders.[19] Because of how systemic power asymmetries and lack of resources tend to render poor and disempowered people silent, extra effort should be made to include them in such policy-making and lawmaking processes. The inclusion of vulnerable persons, in particular, is vital. This is why the consideration of women's and children's positions – and their exclusion from the process surrounding the drafting of the Bill – is of particular relevance. This chapter, therefore, seeks to accomplish consistency with the New Legal Realism approach by 'both remaining cognizant of hierarchies of power and the paradoxes they create for law, and also asking what can be done to work toward justice within the existing structures' (345).

'One essential task of [New Legal Realism] is . . . to see law in relation to other modes of authority and approaches to reform' (Erlanger et al. 2005, 344). This research approach requires extending one's gaze beyond formal legal institutions and their processes to look at other forums and means of normativity, regulation, and ensuring order. This applies all the more in South Africa, where a conflict between

[19] Traditional leaders earn a steady income as public officeholders in terms of the Remuneration of Public Office Bearers Act 20 of 1998, sections 1 and 5.

vernacular law and state law is very much alive. In Gordon Woodman's words, 'those who are said to weaken the rule of state law are contributing to the rule of customary law' (Woodman 1996, 160).

This chapter represents research methodologies selected as guided by the problem being investigated 'so that disciplinary orthodoxies do not wind up setting limits on [the] investigations' into the subject (Erlanger et al. 2005, 356). These methodologies include some legal and policy analysis of the Bill and Constitution but are primarily grounded in ethnographic methods for documenting disputes. They include interviews with disputants and officials about the disputes – after they have been mediated, arbitrated, or adjudicated. Such interviews are used to better understand the disputes, their contextual significance, and the consequences of the dispute management processes employed. Some historical knowledge is incorporated in the representation of the vernacular forums and officials, as well as the wider politics in which the Bill is situated, to which it contributes in turn.

The New Legal Realism approach has been duly related to pragmatism.

> The question that a pragmatist asks ... is not whether law succeeds or fails according to some end posited as good by the theorist-investigator. Like a good social scientist, it suspends judgment to understand better, that which goes on between the means and the ends (the 'betweenness' problem). It seeks a qualitative theory of the translation costs, if you will, of *law's movement from institution to institution*. ... Because rules, according to a pragmatist, are *always contextual*, the object is to use methods – including the methods of social science – that will bring us closer toward understanding *the particular ways in which institutions translate and create law*. (Erlanger et al. 2005, 358, emphasis added)

With respect to the Traditional Courts Bill, the hypothesis is that there is a dissonance between what the Bill intends to regulate and achieve by its regulation, on one hand, and, on the other hand, the realities in and norms according to which the subjects who are meant to be regulated and assisted live. This chapter puts that hypothesis to the test. The chapter also puts to the test the goal that the law sets for itself: improving access to justice for rural people by achieving compliance with vernacular law and the constitution. The chapter interrogates whether the goal can be achieved by such means as the law employs.

In turn, viewing vernacular law from an emic perspective, the chapter looks keenly at the ways in which dispute management works both institutionally and contextually. It observes the movement of disputes and the law in terms of which they are managed 'from institution to institution'. It studies the rules in their context to understand what purposes they are meant to serve and what function they actually perform. And it tries to make sense of how the exercise of creating law and translating it from one sociolegal context to another takes place, as well as how it is helped and hindered.

The chapter partially adopts the 'transformations studies approach' articulated by Felstiner, Abel, and Sarat, which 'approaches disputing through individual perceptions, behavior, and decision making' (Felstiner, Abel, and Sarat 1980, 649). Unlike the transformations studies approach in its fullness, however, this chapter does not discuss perception, naming, blaming, and claiming that do not result in an institutionalized dispute, though it limits itself to disputes that are 'institutionalized' in vernacular forums. Yet, it does discuss the factors that have enabled those particular claims studied to gain articulation in the local institutions and their processes. It is also able to say something about the viability of transformation of some of the claims by movement from the most local, vernacular institutions to the most removed, and from vernacular institutions to state courts. This is while it also discusses the transformations of the disputes from stage to stage, as discussed in the previous section – namely, the transformation of the nature and scope of the primary grievance or claim and the parties involved.

To the extent that the primary objective of the Traditional Courts Bill is to enhance access to justice – which I take seriously as a worthy goal – or, at least, to reduce obstacles to justice, this chapter makes a basic assumption concerning what is necessary for this. It is expanded from Nicola Lacey's assertion that strategies to realise rights for women in diverse situations must be sensitised to those women's peculiar circumstances and needs. She argues that, in order to ensure rights access for all, we must take into account 'the contextual factors which shape the *capacities* of differently situated subjects to *take up and realise their rights*'. She continues by inviting that we 'think of rights not just in formal but equally substantial terms: if the underlying value of rights lies in *human equality*, we have to think about the content and *enforcement of rights* in terms of their *equal value to differently situated subjects*' (2004, 29–31, emphasis added). My argument in this chapter is that the same applies to access to justice. A serious attempt to ensure equitable access to justice for women in remote rural areas must take seriously their socioeconomic and legal context and capacities to mobilise effective dispute management strategies and mechanisms.[20]

IV. THE CASES

The analysis in this section is based on nine cases selected from approximately seventy-three disputes (of well more than two hundred PIEs and claims) collected over the eleven-month period during which disputes were documented in the six wards selected for study. These cases include women in a central role and represent an array of issues that come before the vernacular forums. These are also cases on which follow-up interviews with the parties who agreed to speak to us were completed after the cases were documented (see Figure 1).

[20] See Nyamu Musembi's (2002) argument about the limits and possibilities for this for rural women living under 'customary law'. Also see Armstrong (1995) and Curren and Bonthuys (2005, 635).

Case No.	Disputed Issues	Forums Engaged	Institutional Outcome
Case 1	Attempted murder, defamation re: attempted murder, (failure to report) killing of goats	Tribal policeman's council; skipped headman's council by referral; chief's council	Undecided; potential fine of victim of shooting Witness fined for non-disclosure of suspect
Case 2	Defamation re: virginity	Headman's council; virginity testing; chief's council	Damages and fine
Case 3	Assault (grievous bodily harm)	Claim to other party headman's council	Damages
Case 4	Defamation re: witchcraft; previous, now underlying, issue of stolen phone	Previously, chief's council Present, mediation by headman and council	In chief's council: damages In mediation: apology, cleansing with goat
Case 5	Attempted assault (GBH), domestic violence	Mediation by neighbourhood council	Reprimand
Case 6	Defamation re: theft of identity and money	Headman's council	Damages
Case 7	Paternity dispute, damages, maintenance	Headman's council	DNA-based paternity test ordered
Case 8	Defamation re: witchcraft	Claim to other party's parents; neighbourhood council; headman's council	Cleansing by incense
Case 9	Theft of pipes	Tribal policeman; headman's council	Mutual forgiveness; investigation of real offender; potential appeal to chief's council

FIGURE 1 Table of cases – issues, forums, and outcomes

Case 1 initially began with an attempted murder that was reported to the local *iphoyisa* but not resolved because the perpetrator could not be identified. This attempted murder was then used in an insult (with the use of alcohol being involved), where a distant nephew of the woman who had been shot accused his drinking buddy of being hired by 'women' to kill 'people'. This statement evolved into a defamation claim by the husbands of the women in the accused young man's household – neighbours of the shooting victim – on the basis that they understood it to be their wives who were being accused of 'hiring' him and thus implicated in the murder attempt. The husbands said that they needed the matter cleared up publicly because, if the accusation were allowed to stand, their families ran the risk of members of the vernacular grouping hurting them in a form of vigilante justice. The case was brought directly to the subward council, which is chaired by *iphoyisa*.

Yet, it was escalated to *ibandla lenduna* as *iphoyisa* found that he could not resolve it. In the course of hearing the matter, *iphoyisa* had called the woman who had been shot to testify on who she believed had made an attempt on her life, but she had said she did not know. *Iphoyisa* had accepted her answer and not asked her to further testify before the council, for which the chief's council later chastised him.

Induna, to whom the matter was escalated, felt that this was a delicate (even dangerous) matter that ought to go directly to *ibandla lenkosi*, and so it did. The woman on whom the murder attempt had been made was called as a witness in the hearing of the defamation case in *ibandla lenkosi*, where she had to be represented by her older brother. However, in the proceedings, the matter evolved into a case against the woman who had been shot. This was, first, because of her failure to report the fact that between seven and eleven of her neighbours' goats had died on her property – in this pastoral context, an event socially regarded as being of seriousness almost equal to the death of a human being. Cited as the second reason was her failure to report that she had heard that people suspected her of killing their goats, even as she insisted that she had no explanation for the four goats' deaths of which she said she knew. Her failure to report the deaths to neighbours and ward authorities, additionally, was taken to suggest that she had indeed killed them. She told me that her silence had been because she is a Christian and believes silence breeds peace. Thirdly, the shooting victim had failed to report that a gun shot had been fired over her home a year prior to her shooting and that a woman with whom she worked in the irrigation scheme gardens had informed her of the rumour that this was related to people's anger about their goats' being murdered by her. The case was not concluded, as the irrigation scheme gardens coworker who had shared the rumour refused to reveal the possible avengers when testifying before the chief's council. In the last hearing, the coworker was fined, and the suggestion was made that the shooting victim should also be fined, though this was never realised.

Case 2 was a more straightforward defamation/insult case. A young woman whose brothers were generally regarded as a criminal nuisance within the ward accused another young woman whose mother was a councillor in the chief's legislative-administrative council of not being a virgin. The case was initiated by the second girl's father before the local *induna*. However, it had to be escalated to the chief's council when the defendant failed to bring her relatives (namely, her brothers who were young men not in good standing in the community) to two court dates though she had been advised that they were required for the hearing to take place. Additionally, the defendant had insulted the women who conducted the virginity test on the plaintiff's daughter, who had found her to be a virgin. The defendant also resisted all attempts to 'reason with' her by asking her to embrace the then-modest punishment in the form of damages to be paid to the plaintiff. She was required to pay substantial damages and fined the large sum of a cow in the chief's court, for all her wrongs combined – including her failure to appear before the chief's court accompanied by her family. Part of the discussion before the chief's council pertained to jurisdiction: the women in charge of virginity testing observed that the headman had erred in not immediately referring the matter to them once it had been reported to him.

Case 3 involved a teenage girl who was assaulted with rocks by a young man who it seems was a rejected suitor. As a result, she lost her front teeth and her face was seriously scarred. Her mother (acting on behalf of her father, who was working in Johannesburg) brought the matter to the attention of the boy's mother, attempting to solicit an apology and offer of payment for the harm suffered by the girl – at least for her medical treatment. The mother of the girl was met with resistance and a denial of the claim as well as a counterclaim that the boy was first to be attacked by the injured girl and her sister with whom she had been walking at the time. The injured girl's mother therefore asked her brothers to bring a case before *induna*. The matter was heard by *ibandla lenduna* and damages granted with the boy's family asking for, and being granted, a reduction after the council also pleaded on the fined family's behalf. After the matter was settled and damages paid to the girl's family via the medium of *induna*, the boy's uncle approached *induna* to say that he wanted the matter reopened because he thought it had been wrongly settled. *Induna* told him that such is not done. The injured girl's mother was not entirely satisfied with the resolution of the matter either, and, in a subsequent interview, she shared her belief that the headman can be bribed with alcohol.

Case 4 was another instance of defamation/insult, but it was billed as a mediation where the parties were just 'being corrected' by *induna* and his *ibandla*. In this case, a woman was accused of being a witch by her neighbour's daughter when she was standing by the neighbour's house at dawn, speaking to another neighbour. This instance came after an earlier occasion on which a similar accusation by the neighbour had been litigated right through to *ibandla lenkosi*, where the insulted woman had been found innocent and the neighbour ordered to pay damages to her. The first accusation of witchcraft (and subsequent litigation) had come after the woman's children had been accused of stealing the neighbour's cell phone, which cell phone was not found in her house when she granted permission for her neighbours to search it. The outcome of the present dispute was that *induna* and his *ibandla* asked that the neighbour's family – having again wrongly accused the woman of witchcraft – cleanse her name and home by slaughtering a goat. This way, according to *induna*, they would be able to forgive each other and 'return to living alongside each other as neighbours as before'.

Case 5 was part of a series of disputes involving the same protagonist, who seemed to terrorise the neighbourhood with his drunken violence and wielding of his firearm as a threat against others. In the presently relevant case, he had attempted to injure his wife with his firearm – not for the first time. As often before, his wife had run to find safety at one of the neighbours' homes. The relevant neighbour who had sheltered his wife had asked the vernacular grouping-in-council to reconcile him and the perpetrator, who had insulted him and shot at his house (calling him out so he could shoot *him*) for harbouring his wife. *Induna* was not present for the discussion.

As mentioned, this was a situation of ongoing domestic violence where the husband used an illegally possessed firearm to terrorise his wife. The wife had once before called the police, in the hope that they might arrest him for a short period of time and thereby give him enough of a fright that he would stop abusing her. The police had come and left him a warning in his absence, but had never returned. A core part of the dispute was the wife's awareness of her husband having an extramarital affair. In fact, she claimed that he had increased his terrorising of her and her daughter because he wanted to chase her away so that he could live in their home with his mistress. She, however, refused to leave the marital property on the grounds that she had worked for it and was not going to let it go to another woman. She accepted that the only way he might get her out of the house was by killing her.

In the mediation conducted by the neighbourhood *ibandla*, the husband acknowledged the differences between himself and his wife over his mistress. *Ibandla* asked why he had not reported to or called the (joint) family *ibandla* to help resolve their differences. He provided no real reason. The idea was floated by one of the councillors of the husband's moving his wife out of the home – returning her to her birth family if he no longer wanted her – rather than threatening or shooting at her. The husband was ultimately chastised for harassing his neighbour and entreated to stop terrorising his wife, even while his wife was instructed to respect him and be patient with his affair.

Case 6 concerned a girl whose mother brought the matter as a defamation case before *ibandla lenduna* on the basis of an insult that had been issued by a local man who was quite a bit older against her daughter. He had come to their home – according to him, intoxicated at the time – and accused her of having stolen his government-issued identity document and then used it to steal his employment benefits. She had worked for the census project almost a decade prior and had documented his identity number then. She said she had gotten rid of his details promptly after her census responsibilities ended and counterclaimed that he had spent his employment benefits with his (girl)friend who was an older woman. She speculated that his reason for accusing her was as revenge for her having vehemently rejected his recent overtures towards her. He claimed that he had just been drunk and, after successfully negotiating a reduction on the grounds that he was unemployed, he accepted the amount of damages claimed by her mother and ordered by *ibandla*. In a subsequent interview, the daughter shared that she had not wished her mother to collect damages from the man, just for the (public) record to be set straight.

Case 7 was a case brought by a girl's family against her boyfriend's family for the acceptance of paternity of the baby she had recently had, concomitant payment of damages for impregnating her outside of marriage, and maintenance costs (child support). The boy accepted that the child was his and testified to that effect before *ibandla lenduna*, but his mother refused to accept this and asserted that the child was not his. She claimed that the girl was duping her son, claiming another man's child as his. *Ibandla* ordered the parties to go to the clinic to have a DNA-based paternity test done. The boy, however, refused because he said he was sure that the baby was his. He was willing to support the baby but did not have the means and thus relied on his family for such support.

Case 8 involved a female member of the chief's legislative-administrative council (who lives with her four daughters while her husband spends most of his time working in Johannesburg) being accused of witchcraft by the neighbour's son, who was 30-odd years old. He was intoxicated at the time. She had invited his parents to discuss this with the intent of asking them to request that their son publicly withdraw his slanderous claim, shouted at night for the whole neighbourhood to hear. The failure of his parents to come to discuss the matter with her or to come and apologise to her on behalf of their son – if not ask their son to apologise publicly – prompted her to escalate the matter. Initially heard by the neighbourhood council at the insulted woman's request, the matter was not satisfactorily settled and was escalated further to *ibandla lenduna* when her husband returned home. The young man admitted to the neighbourhood council that he had never caught her conducting witchcraft, yet he refused to withdraw his accusation. His parents also did not insist on his doing so and did not offer to make amends. At *ibandla lenduna*, the decision was handed down that the young man had wronged the woman and should pay damages. When asked what damages she sought, she insisted that she did not want any damages – only R10 ($0.80), which would be put towards purchasing incense that would be burned over her wronged home to cleanse it. Her priority was that her tarnished name be cleansed, especially since she said she was a believing woman (a Christian) and was also concerned for her reputation as a member of the chief's council.

Case 9 pertains to a woman who rented a small garden from a wealthier man for three winters. After the woman had ceased to use the garden, his irrigation pipes (which he said had been placed on the side of the garden plot) disappeared from his property. Because of the timing, the man accused the woman of doing this. After a report to *iphoyisa*, followed by *iphoyisa*'s confronting the woman and searching the home of a man to whom she had taken some pipes she had borrowed from him, the owner of the garden brought a case against the woman before *ibandla lenduna*. At the hearing, the woman (assisted by her husband) denied that it had been she who had stolen his pipes. She said she had not found any pipes when she started gardening and had thus borrowed and used someone else's pipes. She continued that she had later returned the borrowed pipes after finishing her harvesting. The owner of the garden suggested that they go to a seer with a 'mirror' in Swaziland to find out who had stolen the pipes. However, this was rejected by *ibandla* because of the expense – replacing the pipes would be cheaper. In the absence of evidence that the woman had stolen them (and the suspicion having been raised that the old man might be a little senile), *induna* and his *ibandla* finally instructed the two to forgive each other. They told them to assume that someone else (who wanted to sow discord between them and saw this as an opportunity) had done this. The headman suggested that the old man 'ask God to replace your pipes' and that the parties 'seek out the third party who is sowing dissension between you' in the meantime so that they could heal. The owner of the garden was not satisfied with the outcome, saying that he could 'forgive' but his 'heart had not forgiven'. He said he wanted to appeal to the chief's council but had so far held off from doing so.

V. EVALUATING THE CASES

What emerges from the cases is a series of issues of profound complexity and tension, primarily within the vernacular dispute management system at issue, and secondarily with the regulatory framework proposed. The first pertains to the role of the vernacular grouping. The second concerns the volatility and insecurity of the context in which disputes arise, cases are heard, and some sort of outcome is to be delivered by the institutional forums. The third has to do with how the state's resources are engaged by parties and authorities. And the fourth relates to the flexibility of the process. All of these ultimately point to the challenges of codification, which will be discussed in the Conclusion.

1. *Role of Vernacular Grouping*

The first thing that stands out from many of these cases is the fact that the vernacular grouping is a crucial actor – often as a spectator or witness (Cases 1, 5, and 8), sometimes as judge (Cases 5 and 8), and sometimes as scapegoat (Case 9). And it is the vernacular grouping at the most local level that is the main player. Because the vernacular grouping is always watching and may act to enact vigilante justice, accusations of attempted or actual murder (Case 1) and witchcraft (Cases 4 and 8) cannot be allowed to stand. The same is true of less serious cases concerning deflowering (Case 2), paternity (Case 7), and theft (Case 6). And where the problem might not be resolved in any other way, 'someone' in the vernacular grouping can be said to clearly want to sow dissension (Case 9).

The vernacular grouping is also primarily responsible for providing security. In Case 1 the failure to report a serious wrong to neighbours and local authorities leads to suspicion of malicious damage to property. Essentially, the first and second institutional transformations in the case from murder to defamation then failure to report the goats' deaths are about the sanctity of the value of being a member of the vernacular grouping. The second transformation highlights the centrality of revealing publicly and preemptively what is happening in one's domain so as not to fall under suspicion and be vulnerable to harm. In this sense, the case is about the value of full participation in membership of the vernacular grouping as a means of security. The first transformation to the incrimination of those potentially rumoured to be responsible for the shooting (as seen in Cases 4 and 8, too) highlights the importance of people preemptively ensuring that they are known to be innocent. This is a means of safeguarding their own lives by attempting to guarantee that they will not be punished by the same vernacular grouping that provides them with security.

The reason the woman who was shot in Case 1 gives for not reporting the deaths of the goats is interesting. She says that she is a Christian and therefore believes that 'silence yields peace and talk yields more talk/gossip' and thus trouble. However, the ultimate transformation in the institutional case is a means of demonstrating or reasserting that this is not an option in a society in which security is so mutually dependent on others. It may also express some social reproach and punishment of those who refuse to abide by the shared assumptions and rules. The rest of the study shows that going directly to the state courts and ignoring the local forums as the first port of call can attract similar reproach.

2. *Context Insecurity and Volatility*

The extent of insecurity and volatility of conditions under which these women live is striking. However, it is not only the women who are subject to these uncertainties of circumstance; even the authorities themselves are at risk. While the headmen do strive to keep order, they are also fearful to act sometimes because they are concerned about the harm that may come upon them. Local headmen have been killed in the past. This has implications for their ability to ensure justice. As the girl's mother in Case 3 shared, she believes the headman to be susceptible to bribery and manipulation. The headman himself has intimated his own fear of criminals in his area of jurisdiction.

We see this fear and its implications for the enforcement of justice, particularly in Case 1 where the headman (a different one from the one in Case 3) passes the matter up to the chief's council due to its delicacy and danger. It is also expressed in Case 5 where the neighbourhood council seems unable to effectively reproach the man who intimidates his wife and neighbourhood. In the latter regard, it is worth observing that local authorities in Msinga give the fact that the state law bars them from banishing people who are a problem in the vernacular grouping as an additional challenge for local enforcement of justice. Hence, the authorities' ability, as well as the vernacular grouping's ability, to ensure people's security is weak. But that is not to say that the authorities' and vernacular groupings' authority is not important, at least as a first port of call – before people decide that the matter must be escalated to higher levels. And, as we see with Cases 3 and 6, some matters can be quite quickly resolved.

Women's position is particularly unstable. Cases 3 and 6 display the depth of the patriarchy that exists in the area where men are socially encouraged and thus feel entitled to proposition girls, and this can culminate in violence. Studies have been conducted about the intimate relationship in Zulu culture between romantic language and overtures on one hand, and violence against women on the other (Sathiparsad 2007, 181, 189; Campbell 1992, 617, 624–625, 627).

The vulnerability of the woman in Case 5 to a substantial amount of gender-based violence stands out alongside the relative helplessness the surrounding vernacular grouping seems to experience in the face of the recalcitrant member. One sees her exercising some choice in the matter, deciding that holding on to the marital property is important enough to die for. This is so, even as one of the councillors proposes that, if her husband doesn't want her anymore, he should take her back to her family, rather than terrorise her with the gun. She adopts numerous strategies – endurance, calling the police to scare her husband, and speaking to the council about the problem. Indeed, she is looking for resolution in the form of the violence ceasing and her being able to hold on to her home; but she also has a strong social objective in the form of her husband leaving the other woman and being good to her.

Case 1 is similarly indicative of the extent of physical violence, the threat and reality of which people – and especially women – live under. The sad outcome of both Cases 1 and 5 is that both women are not assured of safety. It cannot be said to be an accident that the women accused of witchcraft as in Cases 4 and 8, or killing goats by some unexplained means, maybe including poison, as in Case 1, are older women living (mostly) alone with their children or grandchildren. Studies show that older women are the most likely to be suspected of witchcraft, and most often by younger men as in Case 8 (Redding 2004, 524–525, 531, 535; Stadler 1996, 88; Harnischfeger 2003, 50; Hammond-Tooke 1989, 73).

While the outcome of every person's case is at least partially dependent on how the community perceives that person and his or her kin, women are particularly vulnerable to this fate. For instance, the highly gendered need for a virginity test to prove the innocence of the young woman accused in Case 2[21] as, well as the dependence of the outcomes on having relations of certain genders, age or status, both demonstrate this. In Cases 2 and 8 we see how the status of the women (especially the two female councillors) and the manner in which their kin are regarded by the vernacular grouping (clearly portrayed by the disputing young women in Case 2) shapes the attitudes of the vernacular forums towards them. This even explicitly affects the severity of the sanction – given in the form of damages and a fine – imposed at the end of Case 2.

This is connected also to the fact that women are generally required to be represented by or appear alongside their male relatives in dispute management forums (see Cases 2, 3, 7, 8, and 9; even in Case 1, the shot woman had to be represented by her brother). The failure to do this can have dire consequences and, in fact, disadvantaged the young woman in the earlier stages of Case 2. But, as is seen

[21] Though it is interesting also that it is a girl accusing a girl – an occurrence explained in the (witchcraft) literature in terms of jealousies between women, especially co-wives and mothers and their daughters-in-law. See Standler (1996) and Hammond-Tooke (1989).

in the initial stages of Cases 3, 6, and 8, this rule can sometimes be softened. As is particularly seen in Cases 1, 3, 6, and 7, when a wrong is done to a woman, the family claims the wrong. Therefore, the damages, usually in terms of financial damages, are attributed to the father; in Case 6, the mother collected damages against her daughter's wishes. While not shown in any of the cited cases, this can be true in the instance of rape, too. Some women draw some comfort from this symbol of 'restoration of honour', but others intimate that they think it is unfair that the family should benefit from the harm suffered by the victim while she who suffered gets nothing as compensation.

3. *Mobilisation of State Resources*

The importance of being able to draw on the state system's resources, especially the police, at any time – by both ordinary people and officials – is evident. For the ordinary people, this is true whether they have already been to the state courts before and are appealing to the vernacular forums for supplementary justice or are coming to the vernacular forums first. The police are often used as a pawn for other objectives. The headmen use them in order to assert some control where they have limited physical means for doing so. On seeing that they were unable to discipline or get rid of the abusive man in Case 5, it could just as easily have been the councillors or headman who called the police, as opposed to the woman involved. This is seen in other disputes in my data set. In Case 5, however, it was the abused wife who called the police. And she called them not so much for protection as to try to force her husband into submission, to continue as her husband under vernacular law and thus enable her to retain the property on which she had a tenuous hold under vernacular law.

For headmen, there is a strong sense of lacking effective partnership with the state system. The headmen feel insufficiently acknowledged and respected, and feel a sense of competition with the state, too. For ordinary people, especially women, there is incomplete knowledge of how to secure the state's assistance effectively. For instance, while the abused woman in Case 5 sought to use the police creatively, she was not sure of how to secure what she ultimately wanted, which was material security and to hold on to her home to which she had contributed significantly. More than that, there was the obstacle presented for her by the incomplete reliability of the state resources. When called to the rescue, the police came only once, issued a warning, and did no subsequent follow-up, which was discouraging for the woman. Other women with whom I have engaged have had similar experiences. Many local people also have the sense that, once you get the state system ball rolling, you cannot stop it, and that the punishments under that system are too extreme (see notes 12 and 14). This is sometimes off-putting for people and at times leads to negotiated settlements at home between families, or as mediated by local authorities, such as in Case 3. This is true even in rape cases or in instances of harm resulting in death.

4. *Flexibility of Process*

The flexibility of vernacular dispute management processes accommodates the complexity of the cases themselves – namely, presenting with multiple issues and actors, in the context of lengthy histories, as well as occurring between close and intimate relationships that will generally continue (see note 12). Such complexity is illustrated by the transformations already observed in Case 1, where the core issue of the dispute evolved to something completely different from what first presented. Such complexity can also be seen in Case 4, where the dispute continued despite an ultimate judgement being handed down previously, because the core issue which persisted was a grudge over a stolen phone. A number of the disputes arise in relationships with a long history and therefore form part of a chain of interactions that involve grievances that are not revealed at first (or at all) or directly addressed by the mediation or adjudication.

There is a system in place (as seen in Cases 1–4, 8, and 9), though cases do not always escalate to the highest possible level. However, often enough, cases follow a nonlinear progression, thus creating further complexity. Sometimes people skip stages of the process such as negotiation and mediation, rather going straight to adjudication, such as in Cases 2, 6, and 9. At other times new forums appear in the dispute management hierarchy and even disagree between them about their respective jurisdictions. This was demonstrated in Case 2 where the women who do the virginity testing argued that the headman should not have heard the case in the first place but should have immediately directed it to them to hear. It can also happen that, as in Case 1, the headman refuses to hear a matter because it is too sensitive and thus ought to go directly to the chief's court. In Case 4, we observe that a supposedly settled matter can be reopened by a new incident followed by fresh proceedings. Yet, the attempt to reopen a matter on the claim of new evidence fails in Case 3.

Part of the flexibility has to do with what kinds of solutions are feasible in vernacular forums. In Case 9, the order that they go to a seer is floated, though it is ultimately abandoned due to cost. Such remedies are not possible in a state court, despite the fact that the parties may believe in their legitimacy. Furthermore, rulings such as 'ask God to replace your pipes' – stated earnestly – are unlikely under state law. Yet, in vernacular forums, conclusions like 'forgive each other' (Cases 4 and 9), 'cleanse the home and name' so that the parties can be reconciled (Cases 4 and 8), and 'find the third party who is sowing dissension between you' (Case 9) are fair game. It is trite to say that restoring harmony is a high priority for vernacular forums, but harmonising people is indeed key. Yet, all the cases cast real doubt as to whether true harmony is in fact achieved – or, if so, for very long.

Damages and fines are often negotiated in vernacular forum proceedings. For instance, in Case 3, the boy's family asks for a reduction from what is asked from them, and the council asks the girl's family to be merciful and grant it, which they do. Likewise, in Case 6, the man conceding guilt pleads for a reduction on the grounds that he is unemployed and this request is also granted. As a demonstration of the fact that her objectives in bringing the case were simply to cleanse her name and make sure that others were not left believing the publicly made allegation, the female councillor in Case 8 rejected substantial damages and asked for only R10 for incense to be smoked over her home to cleanse it. Expensive fines and non-negotiable outcomes would make it difficult, for example, for the disagreeing mother and son in Case 7 to air their differences about the girl – expressed through the paternity dispute – in a public forum in order to be potentially reconciled.

VI. CONCLUSION

This chapter has argued from a new legal realism standpoint that vernacular dispute management forums are not courts in the manner that state courts are, but they play an indispensable role in ensuring access to some form of justice. It has only vaguely emerged, as yet, what the justice the forums dispense really is. It is at least evident that it is often meaningfully different from the state version and seems to be a combination of public airing of disagreements and basic counselling, yet accompanied by a need and a desire for more security.

All the same, the empirical findings just recounted leave open the gaping question of translation – precisely, translation from a flexible system to a rather rigid one, through a blunt instrument such as legislation. How do we translate these empirical findings into legally intelligible (juristic) 'facts' that can be appropriately accommodated in state lawmaking and enforcement? And hence, 'what can be done to work toward justice within the existing structures'? It seems clear that, at the very least, we are required to found the envisioned regulation for traditional courts on what we know of what people do in practice, and their experiences of law on the ground. This 'implies a rejection of theory-driven orthodoxies that do not take account of people's lived experience of the law in particular settings' (Erlanger et al. 2005, 345).

If we take seriously what the empirical findings tell us about actual practice, the following problems are highlighted in the Traditional Courts Bill. To start, the failure to recognise vernacular groupings as crucial actors in dispute management – and as being primarily responsible for providing security (and simultaneously constituting a threat) – is a gap. An institutional focus on only the most macro level of social organization, and only the most institutionalized forum at that level, seems another grave oversight.

Another suggestion from the data is that, without considering the full picture of the socioeconomic circumstances and threats that rural people like those in Msinga live under, the Bill makes naïve assumptions about what it can accomplish to ensure them security and justice. It makes similarly naïve assumptions about the impartiality of the authorities. Yet, the Bill also does not take necessary steps to shore up the ability of the authorities to enforce safety and security, for which they clearly play – but also struggle to play – a meaningful role. It also does not consider the needs of women like those in Case 5, for whom effective solutions to domestic violence and material insecurity would be needed, and Case 1 and less so Cases 4 and 8, for whom effectual interventions around women's vulnerability to 'witch killings' are necessary. This is not to mention the risks younger women face of violence from rejected suitors (Case 3, and nominally Case 6).

Women's legal representation by men is left virtually untouched by the Bill and, similarly, matters such as who receives compensation are ignored. In Case 3, given that the Bill bars the resolution of assault with intent to do grievous bodily harm in vernacular forums, what is to stop vernacular groupings from negotiating settlements at home as they often already do in rape and even culpable homicide cases at present? It is not considered that the state courts need to be reformed to provide sufficient incentive for their use in such cases and/or that the way in which vernacular forums deal with women's physical, social, and material interests in such disputes is in need of reform. Hence, how are women who wish to be the direct recipients of financial redress to be accommodated? The Bill's conceptualisation of access to justice in the face of such issues is thus deficient.

The failure of the Bill to consider the relationships among the vernacular groupings, their dispute management forums, and the police (as opposed to just the magistrates' courts) is a gross oversight. Moreover, the Bill's provision for the relationship between the magistrates' courts and the vernacular forums seems inadequate. For instance, the Bill has strictly dictated that legislation and, in terms thereof, the vernacular forum or magistrate's court will determine when parties can go to one or the other forum. Such a formulation fails to take into account the vast array of reasons for which the prospects of obtaining justice through the vernacular system are aided or improved by people's ability to turn to the state courts at strategically appropriate times. This is because the Bill fails to appreciate that people do not necessarily use dispute management forums as avenues for predetermined purposes set by the legislation or dispute management institutions.

In this respect, a strict separation of vernacular dispute management from that by state courts disregards the fact that vernacular law is a complexly mixed normative order that both is influenced by and sometimes resists the dictates of state lawmaking. Vernacular law can draw inspiration from state law, such as when one of the local chiefs' legislative-administrative councils elected to allow women to obtain independent sites for building their homes. In some instances, people draw from or use the state system in order to protect themselves from the vernacular law, as in a maintenance claim made by one woman through the magistrate's court when a vernacular forum was purporting to give custody of her children to her customary husband. In others, they use vernacular law to supplement the state system, especially when it comes to compensation for severe interpersonal crimes.

The flexibility of disputing processes under vernacular law presents both advantages and disadvantages. Sophisticated research and analysis are required to discern what constitutes and yields effective benefits for people and what produces unexpected and undesired outcomes. The Traditional Courts Bill unfortunately does not attain the necessary level of sophistication. Rather, it assumes clichéd portrayals of 'customary law' – either from archaic legislation[22] or from romanticized notions vehemently defended by senior traditional leaders in political rhetoric (see note 8) – to be true.

For instance, concerning decisions around sanctions, while the Bill assumes that a 'presiding officer' in the chief's court (namely, the senior traditional leader) makes this decision, this is not the case in Msinga. Firstly, there is a multiplicity of vernacular dispute management forums and forums *other than* the chief's council which actually bear a lot of dispute management responsibility. Secondly, the decision regarding sanction is largely made by the vernacular grouping-in-council, in discussion with the parties.

Hence, in determining how to regulate vernacular forums – especially how to do so in a manner consistent with both vernacular law and women's constitutional rights – we should reason from actual practice. Actual practice shows us that access to justice for women in vernacular settings is usually fraught and requires that wider socioeconomic reforms be simultaneously effected by the state. It also helps us to understand what women need from these forums to be able to access justice through them and other forums. Thus, reasoning from practice seems to raise two prior questions to that of regulation: whether what is being provided by vernacular forums is appropriately termed 'justice' and whether these forums are effectual. Yet, who gets to decide the answers to these very questions?

I would suggest that it should at least partly be the people – including women – who rely on the forums. As an example, the goal of ensuring access to justice demands that we investigate more deeply whether such conclusions as 'forgive each other' are satisfactory for vernacular forum users. This is instead of simply transferring such 'sanctions' from the stereotypical 'harmony' model of 'customary law' into a formalistic 'dispute resolution' framework (TCB, clause 10(2)(d)). We should do more than speculate on when they are effective and when they lead to social and legal atrophy that defies the achievement of harmony and an effective solution to the existing social tensions.

Reasoning from the ground up to formulate regulations for vernacular forums is ideal. However, a consideration – and serious challenge – is that state law finds it very difficult to accommodate this kind of flexibility. The legislature has yet to crack the code on how to regulate vernacular forms of law in ways that do not stifle them but allow them to flourish while bringing them under the positive influence and effective direction of universal human rights. The primary difficulty lies in the relative inflexibility of state law when compared to practice – as a matter of form. Moreover, codification more often tends towards petrification of conservative

[22] For instance, the Black Administration Act 38 of 1927 and Black Authorities Act 68 of 1952.

'normative ideals' (often what people say) at the expense of 'softening' nuances that can often be found in people's practice.

As such, vernacular law in Msinga holds to the 'normative ideal' that women should be represented by male relatives in cases, but vernacular forums often adapt to allow women and mothers in particular to be actively involved in cases and to represent themselves and their children in some instances. This is so particularly in the absence of migrant fathers, where the women are single and older, or in lower-level forums.[23] Putting the gender equality precepts of the Constitution aside for a moment,[24] one regulatory attempt to accommodate this flexibility in legislation might be to say women can be represented by men and men by women, 'in accordance with customary law' (as does the Bill) (TCB, clause 9(3)(b)). Yet, people are more inclined to say that the normative ideal constitutes 'customary law'. A clause so phrased would therefore most likely be used to deny women the right to represent themselves or represent men. Hence, might it not be said that such a formulation in the Bill more likely encourages or reinforces defaulting to the conservative 'normative ideal' rather than progressive, practical developments in the vernacular law in practice?

A less emotive example is that the amount to be fined as damages or compensation is usually said to be scripted and even legislated from the chief's legislative-administrative council. But, as already shown, it is actually negotiable and reducible in the case, and it is often the councils that help plead for a reduction. The matter is settled relationally: vernacular forums take into account the relevant person's remorse (or lack thereof) and financial circumstances. Therefore, might there be a need for the

[23] For instance, the definition of marriage provided in the Recognition of Customary Marriages Act 120 of 1998, sections 1 and 3(1)(b), is 'a marriage concluded in accordance with customary law' and 'negotiated and entered into or celebrated in accordance with customary law'. This is very flexible. But the Act then provides more strictly for the registration (section 4) and material consequences of marriage, especially polygamy (sections 6 and 7). The Act's definition of marriage has been criticised as being *too* vague and open to manipulation by Home Affairs officers (who are responsible for registering the marriages) and by state courts in the case of disputes. Courts have interpreted it in varying ways that are often conservative, show patriarchal bias, and do not comport with vernacular law in practice. (See, for instance, *Motsoatsoa v. Roro and Others*, Unreported Case No. 4631/09, South Gauteng High Court, Johannesburg.) Women therefore end up being disadvantaged. The Act – with its best intentions of ensuring that polygynous wives have equitable access to the marital property as overseen by the High Court – is also criticized for making registration of polygynous marriages virtually unattainable for the mostly poor women and men who would need to rely on the provision. Thus, the Act has had the opposite effect of making it very difficult to ensure protection of both monogamous and polygynous wives' access to the matrimonial property, because polygynous marriages most often remain unregistered. The most recent Constitutional Court decision in *Mayelane v. Ngwenyama and Another* 2013 (4) SA 415 (CC) declared it a requirement for the validity of a second marriage that the first wife have given consent before her husband takes his subsequent wife. While this decision strengthens the material position of the first wife, it has been criticised because the subsequent wife is left with little protection. Even if her marriage is entered into in good faith, if it is entered into without the first wife's consent, her marriage is out of community of property, and she may not inherit from the deceased husband's intestate estate.

[24] These are articulated in section 9(3) of the Constitution.

negotiability of the remedy – especially taking into account that sometimes people do not want monetary rewards but just want acknowledgement of the wrong or admission of the falsehood of their accusation?

However, taking into account the pressures and risks that officials serving in the vernacular system are under and the consequent reality of corruption and partiality in some case, mentioned earlier, wording like 'or any other order that the traditional court may deem appropriate' (TCB, clause 10(2)(l)) is questionable. This is so particularly considering that, at least in Msinga, those who decide – and, in fact, negotiate – the remedy are the vernacular grouping-in-council (with the parties) where the council members are, in their own way, vulnerable to partiality and social or physical risk.

It is indeed important to acknowledge the inherent difficulty of codification – even partial codification as South Africa has generally opted for. However, it would seem to me that the best chance of making trustworthy estimations of the extent to which legislatures should employ a combination of flexible and stringent formulations, and how these should be worded, remains to be found in robust, empirically grounded research.

As demonstrated, reasoning from practice helps us understand the prerequisites for access to justice through vernacular and other forums as women perceive them or determine that they need them. And, if the function of law is to secure justice – particularly for the protection of the most vulnerable – recognition should surely be given to the realities of those most vulnerable. Recognition and a targeted response to the power politics and asymmetries of the legislative process that yields legislation like the Bill are equally necessary. Following a bottom-up method of lawmaking, we can have honest discussions about what, in vernacular disputing, can and should be kept or dispensed with. We must acknowledge that sometimes access to justice for women is an uncertain exercise of piecing information and options together into an often-undirected strategy of 'hitting or missing' to have their core, underlying needs met. This element needs review and, ideally, effective reform by the state – socially and legally. However, unlike what has been the case with the Traditional Courts Bill, women should be part of that discussion.

REFERENCES

Armstrong, Alice. 1995. "Rethinking Customary Law in Southern Africa. What Relevance for Action?" *Women and Law in Southern Africa Research Project Newsletter* 7(1).

Burman, Sandra, Louise Carmody, and Yonina Hoffman-Wanderer. 2008. "Protecting the Vulnerable from 'Property Grabbing': The Reality of Administering Small Estates." *South African Law Journal* 125(1): 134–156.

Campbell, Catherine. 1992. "Learning to Kill? Masculinity, the Family and Violence in Natal." *Journal of Southern African Studies* 18(3): 614–628.

Chanock, Martin. 2001. *The Making of South African Legal Culture, 1902–1936: Fear, Favour and Prejudice.* Cambridge: Cambridge University Press.

Claassens, Aninka. 2011. "Resurgence of Tribal Levies: Double Taxation for the Rural Poor." *South African Crime Quarterly* 35: 11–16.

Claassens, Aninka, and Ben Cousins, eds. 2008. *Land, Power and Custom: Controversies Generated by South Africa's Communal Land Rights Act*. Cape Town: Juta Publishing.

Claassens, Aninka, and Sindiso Mnisi. 2009. "Rural Women Redefining Land Rights in the Context of Living Customary Law." *South African Journal on Human Rights* 25(3): 491–516.

Claassens, Aninka, and Sizani Ngubane. 2008. "Women, Land, and Power: The Impact of the Communal Land Rights Act." In *Land, Power and Custom: Controversies Generated by South Africa's Communal Land Rights Act*, edited by Aninka Claassens and Ben Cousins, 154–183. Cape Town: Juta Publishing.

Comaroff, John L., and Jean Comaroff. 2009. *Ethnicity, Inc.* Chicago: University of Chicago Press.

Comaroff, John L., and Simon Roberts. 1981. *Rules and Processes: The Cultural Logic of Dispute in an African Context*. Chicago: University of Chicago Press.

Cousins, Ben. 2008. "Characterising 'Communal' Tenure: Nested Systems and Flexible Boundaries." In *Land, Power and Custom: Controversies Generated by South Africa's Communal Land Rights Act*, edited by Aninka Claassens and Ben Cousins, 109–137. Cape Town: Juta Publishing.

Curren, Ericka, and Elsje Bonthuys. 2005. "Customary Law and Domestic Violence in Rural South African Communities: Notes and Comments." *South African Journal on Human Rights* 21(4): 607–635.

Erlanger, Howard S., Bryant Garth, Jane E. Larson, Elizabeth Mertz, Victoria Nourse, and David B. Wilkins. 2005. "Is It Time for a New Legal Realism?" *Wisconsin Law Review* 2: 335–363.

Felstiner, William L. F., Richard L. Abel, and Austin Sarat. 1980. "The Emergence and Transformation of Disputes: Naming, Blaming, Claiming . . . " *Law and Society Review* 15: 631–654.

Galanter, Marc. 1983. "Reading the Landscape of Disputes: What We Know and Don't Know (and Think We Know) about Our Allegedly Contentious and Litigious Society." *UCLA Law Review* 31(4): 4–71.

Hammond-Tooke, W. David. 1989. *Rituals and Medicines: Indigenous Healing in South Africa*. Johannesburg: Ad. Donker.

Harnischfeger, Johannes. 2003. "Witchcraft and the State in South Africa." In *Witchcraft Violence and the Law in South Africa*, edited by John Hund, 40–72. Pretoria: Protea Boekhuis.

Higgins, Tracy, Jeanmarie Fenrich, and Ziona Tanzer. 2007. "Gender Equality and Customary Marriage: Bargaining in the Shadow of Post-Apartheid Legal Pluralism." *Fordham International Law Journal* 30(6): 1653–1708.

Kuper, Hilda. 1947. *An African Aristocracy: Rank among the Swazi of Bechuanaland*. London and New York: International African Institute, Oxford University Press.

Lacey, Nicola. 2004. "Feminist Legal Theory and the Rights of Women" (Florence Lectures, Yale University). Accessed September 1, 2011. http://www.yale.edu/wff/cbg/pdf/LaceyPaperFeministLegalTheory.pdf.

Lehnert, Wieland. 2005. "The Role of the Courts in the Conflict between African Customary Law and Human Rights." *South African Journal on Human Rights* 21(2): 241–277.

Merry, Sally Engle. 1979. "Going to Court: Strategies of Dispute Management in an American Urban Neighborhood." *Law and Society Review* 13(4): 891–925.

Miller, Richard, and Austin Sarat. 1980. "Grievances, Claims, and Disputes: Assessing the Adversary Culture." *Law and Society Review* 15(3–4): 525–566.

Mnisi Weeks, Sindiso. 2011a. "Securing Women's Property Inheritance in the Context of Plurality: Negotiations of Law and Authority in Mbuzini Customary Courts and Beyond." In *Acta Juridica: Pluralism and Development: Studies in Access to Property in Africa*, edited by Hanri Mostert and Thomas Bennett, 140–173. Claremont [Cape Town]: Juta.

Mnisi Weeks, Sindiso. 2011b. "'Take Your Rights Then and Sleep Outside, on the Street': Rights, Fora and the Significance of Rural South African Women's Choices." *Wisconsin International Law Journal* 29(2): 288–318.

Mnisi Weeks, Sindiso. 2012. "Regulating Vernacular Dispute Resolution Forums: Controversy Concerning the Process, Substance and Implications of South Africa's Traditional Courts Bill." *Oxford University Commonwealth Law Journal* 12(1): 133–155.

Mnisi Weeks, Sindiso. 2013. "Women's Eviction in Msinga: The Uncertainties of Seeking Justice." In *Acta Juridica: Marriage, Land and Custom*, edited by Aninka Claassens and Dee Smythe, 118–142. Claremont [Cape Town]: Juta.

Nader, Laura. 2002. *The Life of the Law: Anthropological Projects*. Berkeley and Los Angeles: University of California Press.

Norgren, Jill, and Serena Nanda. 1996. *American Cultural Pluralism and Law*. Westport, CT: Greenwood Publishing Group.

Nyamu Musembi, Celestine. 2002. "Are Local Norms and Practices Fences or Pathways? The Example of Women's Property Rights." In *Cultural Transformation and Human Rights in Africa*, edited by Abdullahi Ana-Na'im, 126–150. London: Zed Books.

Prinsloo, Johan. 1999. "Conflict Resolution amongst Traditionally African Cultures." In *Models of Conflict Resolution*, edited by Irene Sagel-Grande and M. V. Polak, 15–38. Antwerpen-Apeldoorn: Maklu.

Redding, Sean. 2004. "Deaths in the Family: Domestic Violence, Witchcraft Accusations and Political Militancy in Transkei, South Africa, 1904–1965." *Journal of Southern African Studies* 30 (3): 519–538.

Sathiparsad, Reshma. 2007. "Masculinities in the Era of HIV/AIDS: The Perspective of Rural Zulu Youth." In *From Boys to Men: Social Constructions of Masculinity in Contemporary Society*, edited by Tamara Shefer, Kopano Ratele, Anna Strebel, Nokuthla Shabalala, and Rosemarie Buikema, 181–194. Lansdowne: Juta and Company.

South African Law Reform Commission. 2003. *Customary Law: Report on Traditional Courts and the Judicial Function of Traditional Leaders*. South African Law Reform Commission.

Stadler, Jonathan. 1996. "Witches and Witch-Hunters: Witchcraft, Generational Relations and the Life Cycle in a Lowveld Village." African Studies 55(1): 87–110.

Whitehead, Ann, and Dzodzi Tsikata. 2003. "Policy Discourses on Women's Land Rights in Sub-Saharan Africa: The Implications of the Return to the Customary." *Journal of Agrarian Change* 3(1–2): 67–112.

Woodman, Gordon R. 1996. "Legal Pluralism and the Search for Justice." *Journal of African Law* 40(2): 152–167.

SECTION III

Global Institutions and the Changing Roles of Judges and Lawyers

8

New Legal Realism and International Law

Gregory Shaffer[1]

To tap the spirit of a new legal realist approach to international law, let us begin with two quotations from two nonlegal sources that capture two defining aspects of a new legal realism. The first is from a letter written by Anton Chekhov (1977, 627) to Alexey Suvorin in 1892: "Let her first say what is, and only then I will listen to what one can and must do." Those words parallel a famous statement of Karl Llewellyn (1931, 1236), a leader of the original American Legal Realism, who maintained: "The argument is simply that no judgement of what Ought to be done in the future with respect to any part of law can be intelligently made without knowing objectively, as far as possible, what that part of law is now doing." Llewellyn thus called for "the temporary divorce of Is and Ought for purposes of study." The statement of Chekhov, a doctor, is particularly to a field – that of law and legal scholarship, and particularly international law and international legal scholarship – which is dedicated to prescriptions, yet spends far too little time on diagnoses. Let us call the Chekhovian approach the empirical strand of new legal realism.

The second complementary slant comes from the writer James Baldwin, who, disillusioned with American racism, left the United States in 1948 for France, where he lived much of his remaining life as a cosmopolitan outsider seeing things anew. Baldwin is quoted as saying: "The purpose of art is to lay bare the questions which have been hidden by the answers."[2] Let us paraphrase that statement to reflect a central, pragmatist tenet of new legal realism: a purpose of engaging in research in a new legal realist vein is to uncover issues and possibilities to which otherwise we are ignorant, to which otherwise we are blind because we are caught in a single way of

[1] My thanks to Mary Rumsey for her research assistance. This chapter is adapted from my inaugural Melvin C. Steen chair lecture at the University of Minnesota Law School.

[2] Or as the artist Paul Klee (1920 [1913]) wrote, "Art does not reproduce the visible; it makes visible." I read the quotation attributed to Baldwin and was taken by it, but upon further research discovered that it turns out that, though widely used, the quotation has not been found in anything Baldwin ever published. Baldwin (1962) did once write, analogously, that we "must drive to the heart of every answer and expose the question the answer hides." Ironically, the frequent use of the quotation supports the point attributed to it – the need to probe behind received thinking to unpack questions, information, and conventional perspectives.

viewing a situation. That is the creative aspect of a new legal realism, and it is uncovered through a critical, experimental approach to learning. Let us call the Baldwinian component the Deweyan pragmatist strand of new legal realism.

The purpose of engaging in research in a new legal realist vein is to uncover new vantages and perspectives through empirical engagement, permitting our incoming predispositions (inevitable no matter how neutral we aim to be) to be challenged and potentially transformed (Nourse and Shaffer 2014). This approach is particularly important for the analysis of international law in a world characterized by constituencies with differing priorities, perspectives, and opportunities to be heard in which the most read and influential international law scholarship tends to be written by those from particular backgrounds working in a particular language, English. This chapter first situates new legal realism in relation to the original Legal Realist movement in the United States and the current transnational context. It then discusses four key attributes of new legal realism: empiricism, critical pragmatism, institutionalism, and a problem-centred approach. It provides a number of research examples of what a new legal realist approach offers.

I. NEW LEGAL REALISM, OLD LEGAL REALISM, AND INTERNATIONAL RELATIONS REALISM

Legal realism rose and gained prominence at the time of social ferment in the 1930s, a time where progressives pushed for social legislation to address the hardships and inequalities of the Great Depression following the Roaring Twenties and the earlier Gilded Age.[3] It responded to what it viewed as formalist legal scholarship and the conservative social policies that legal formalism tended to support. It responded to the legitimization of inequalities that formal law gave with its constitutional doctrines of liberty of contract and its restraints on federal and state legislation to address them. It critiqued formalism for its failure to consider the operation of power in the private marketplace, and thus the law in action and the consequences of the legal doctrines and interpretive methods legal formalists used. It addressed, for example, issues of the workplace, so that legal doctrines would no longer block legislation on child labor, maximum hours, and collective bargaining.

Legal realists argued, among other matters, for the need to study the context in which law is made, operates, and has effects before making any proposition about what a law means or should do. For a legal realist, the focus (in terms of Chekhov's "is") lies in the social context in which law operates, and not only in the formal assessment of what the law says in the law books. Legal realists thus called for empirical study of the contexts in which law operates (our Chekhovian strand)

[3] For overviews of legal realism, see Leiter (2005); Fisher, Horwitz, and Reed (1993, including classic texts of legal realists and their antecedents); Singer (1988) (reviewing Laura Kalman, *Legal Realism at Yale:* 1927–1960, 1986); Schlegel (1995); Tamanaha (1999); Ewick, Kagan, and Sarat (1999); and de Been (2008).

and pragmatist learning to address the challenges society faced (our Baldwinian strand). Legal realism gained ascendancy with the political victories of Franklin Delano Roosevelt, his policies in the New Deal, and the rise of the administrative state in which many legal realists served. Given the dire domestic economic straits and inward-looking focus of the time, the original legal realism had no interest in international law. It was a US domestic law movement focused on domestic law in a domestic context and was unengaged with the broader international and transnational challenges of the interwar period.

What is new in a new legal realism for purposes of the study of international law is primarily, on the one hand, the shift in temperament within the legal academy toward empirical work and the development of empirical methods in the social sciences more generally, and, on the other hand, the shift in social relations so that international law today has greater implications across substantive areas, including the areas of business, regulatory, and human rights law.

First, what is "new" in new legal realism is arguably most importantly the empirical turn in legal scholarship and developments in empirical methods. While the legal realists called for greater empirical work, so that the practice (and thus the meaning) of law would be better understood in context, they were less accomplished in practicing what they preached.[4] They were less accomplished, in part, because the social sciences themselves were much less developed. New legal realists engage in empirical work, unlike many of their old legal realist predecessors.

Second, today we live in a different global context, one characterized by greater transnational social connectedness where policy makers across legal domains increasingly view problems in transnational and global terms. Accordingly, the legal academy and the social science disciplines, including economics, political science, sociology, and anthropology, increasingly recognize international law's significance (Shaffer and Ginsburg 2012). The old legal realists wrote at a time of national autarchy and retrenchment. The new legal realists write at a time of economic and cultural globalization in which the ambit of international law covers most substantive domains of law (Halliday and Shaffer 2015).

The greater recognition of international law's role today also reflects a shift in views from the time of the Cold War in which another form of realism dominated, that of international relations (IR) realism. Legal realism is not IR realism and should not be confused with it. IR realism views international law as epiphenomenal because state power, and not law, determines international relations outcomes.[5] If

4 Macaulay (2005, 375) ("The classic realists talked about doing empirical research, but relatively little was accomplished"); Leiter (2005, 51) ("For most of the Realists, however, the commitment to 'science' and 'scientific method' was more a matter of rhetoric and metaphor, than actual scholarly practice"). On the empirical component of the old legal realism, see Schlegel (1995); Kritzer (2010).

5 See, for example, Morgenthau (1963, 278) (calling international law "a primitive type of law primarily because it is almost completely decentralized law"), and Kennan (1951) (critiquing legalistic approaches to international relations as based on false assumptions). For a more contemporary variant, see Posner (2009).

international law is epiphenomenal, then there is little reason for social scientists to study it other than to prove it is epiphenomenal. International relations realism rose in the 1950s and 1960s to critique the legal liberalism of those who elided issues of power and interest in negotiating and relying on international law agreements, particularly those affecting a country's national security. IR realism did not focus on international economic law that it viewed as an issue of low politics, but when it did, it addressed the role of self-interest and balance of power, and remained wary of strong international institutions. Many of its adherents were political conservatives concerned with the spread and expansion of the Soviet bloc and, more generally, communist ideology.

Legal realism has parallels with IR realism in that both respond to formal idealist views of law, whether formalism (for legal realism) or international law liberalism (for IR realists). They both attempt in different ways to get underneath what shapes international law and how it operates in practice. In doing so, both are interested in the interaction of power and interest with law. But there the resemblance ends, in part because legal realism and IR realism arose in different moments in response to different contexts.

Legal realism differs from IR realism in two ways. First, it arises within the legal academy, and thus law, and not power, is its central unit of analysis. Second, it is interested in the prospect of international law in shaping outcomes, including through doctrine, legal institutions, and legal professionals. It is not idealist in that it calls for conditional theorizing of international law's role, and incorporates both the study of power and legal reasoning in its analysis. But it aims to study when and how law matters.

Like the old legal realism, new legal realism aims to build bridges with the social science disciplines. Those bridges, however, are to facilitate a two-way learning and not the mere adoption of lessons from the social sciences, such as international relations for international lawyers. New legal realists both incorporate social science findings in their study of international law and pay close attention to such traditional international law matters as doctrine, institutions, and professions to assess the ways in which international law can shape social understandings and practices in different domains.[6] New legal realism thus does not subsume law under the language of another discipline, such as power in international relations.

Although one sometimes hears within the legal academy that "we are all legal realists now" (Leiter 1999, 261), that is far from the case. On the one hand, legal formalism without attention to empirical context and processes arguably remains predominant in much of the legal academy, including as applied to the study and

[6] On the role of legal professionals in international and transnational contexts, see Flood (2007, 45–46) ("In many respects the Cold War was a golden era for international law firms. The West was out to ensure the world adhered to ideas of liberal democracy and free market economics – the Washington consensus – and not be seduced by irrational notions of socialist state-centered economic planning"); and Trubek, Dezalay, Buchanan, and Davis (1994).

teaching of international law. On the other hand, even those scholars who aim to move beyond legal doctrine often pay little heed to the empirical study of international law.

The gap between the focus of international law scholars and that of the social sciences, for example, is reflected in their different treatment of the concept of method. In the social sciences, the term "method" refers to different approaches to empirical study, such as quantitative, qualitative, and experimental methods. But in international law, the term "method" traditionally refers either to techniques for locating legal sources or to an analytical or theoretical method. For example, in 1999, the *American Journal of International Law* aimed to break new ground by publishing a "Symposium on Method." The symposium's introduction first noted the conventional definition of "methodology of legal research" as the "ways to identify and locate primary and secondary sources" (Ratner and Slaughter 1999, 292, citing Rosenne 1984). Such use of the term focuses on the formal sources used to determine what the applicable law is. Such empiricism is entirely internal and self-referential to law, looking only to legal pedigree and thus only to law books.[7] The introduction then noted how the legal academy has moved beyond such a formalist conception to include a heterodox range of different analytic and theoretical frameworks as "methods." The subsequent articles separately presented these analytic methods, and respectively covered Positivism, Law and Economics, New Legal Process, Critical Legal Studies, Rational International Relations Theory, Feminist Methods, and the Yale School of Policy-Oriented Jurisprudence.[8] The issue concluded with an essay entitled "The Method Is the Message" (Slaughter and Ratner 1999). It was an ironic title for a concluding essay, because neither the conclusion nor any of the articles in the special issue addressed method in the way that the social sciences do – which in itself was a message.

II. FOUR ATTRIBUTES OF A NEW LEGAL REALISM

New Legal Realism as applied to international law, in my view, should include four key attributes: empiricism, critical pragmatism, institutionalism, and a problem-centered approach. First (and most important), it should call for and engage in empirical work to understand how international law obtains meaning, operates, and develops over time. Second, and complementarily, it should take seriously critical concerns about the biases inherent in methods, and thus engage with critical analysis in a self-reflective manner to question incoming biases that a researcher

7 As Richard Posner (1990, 15) writes, "the formalists had conceived law as an inductive science. . . . The reports of appellate decisions were the data from which the principles of the common law could be inferred – principles."

8 The Yale School came out of legal realism but infrequently engaged with method in a social science sense, and was largely focused on advancing US goals in the context of the Cold War. Cf. Leiter (2005, 61) ("it had far more to do with rationalizing American imperialism than it did with science").

brings, but without losing sight of the importance of empirical inquiry. Empirical work should have a critical, reflexive, pragmatist edge so that results of inquiry are treated as provisional and probative, and the researcher remains open for fresh analytics to emerge. Third, it should stress the role of institutions in mediating the pursuit of any social goal, so that normative analysis must be grounded in institutional analysis in which no single institutional choice is prioritized and all institutions are subject to interaction giving rise to the potential for recursive learning. Fourth, it should be catalyzed by normative concerns in light of power asymmetries and distributive conflict. It should provide its empirical analysis for purposes of addressing social problems that both transcend and permeate the nation-state.

These attributes have much in common with the old legal realists, which is the reason for the common label, one that we adapt to capture ongoing struggles within the legal academy and the broader social sciences. The old realists, too, were concerned with inequality and the biases masked by the formal legal doctrines of their time that were used by lawyers and courts to attempt to limit progressive and New Deal reforms. They, too, responded to these normative concerns in their particular historical-political context. They, too, called for empirical work and the bridging of the disciplines. They, too, wished to translate their endeavors in practical terms within that context, engaging with institutional development and reform at a time of ferment.

Just as there was great diversity among the old legal realists, there is great diversity today among those adopting the new legal realist mantle. Thomas Miles and Cass Sunstein have written of new legal realism in terms of the study of legal and extralegal influences on judicial decision making. Daniel Farber has written of new legal realism in terms of behavioral economics. Elizabeth Mertz and Stewart Macaulay have written on new legal realism from a law and society perspective. Victoria Nourse and I have added an institutionalist vantage.[9]

In my view, what these approaches all should have in common is a call for empirical questioning of assumptions through engaging with empirics that is problem-centric and open to the emergence of new analytics. There is an increasing amount of international law scholarship that takes an empirical approach to the study of international law (Shaffer and Ginsburg 2012). For me, a pioneering figure in my field of international trade law was Robert Hudec of the University of Minnesota. Hudec understood law in a broader political and economic context, and he bridged research disciplines. He frequently went to Geneva to obtain a better understanding of what lay beneath the surface of trade disputes and litigation. He gave both law and political economy their due, and was highly respected by economists, political scientists, diplomats, and international civil servants. Hudec's

[9] These different approaches are reviewed in Nourse and Shaffer (2009). See also Miles and Sunstein (2008); Farber (2001) (reviewing Cass R. Sunstein, ed., *Behavioral Law and Economics*, 2000); Erlanger, Garth, Larson, Mertz, Nourse, and Wilkins (2005); Mertz and Suchman (2010); Nourse and Shaffer (2009); Shaffer (2013a).

databases and studies of General Agreement on Tariffs and Trade (GATT) dispute settlement formed the groundwork for analysis of international trade diplomacy and litigation across disciplines (Hudec 1993; Trubek 2008). He provided an example of the value of cross-disciplinary collaboration, building bridges between the law school, the broader academy, and practice. Today, empirical work on international law has become a common and flourishing enterprise.

Second, and complementarily, a new legal realism should be self-reflective in terms of its critical inquiry in order to support experimentation and learning in a pragmatist vein. It should address how context and frameworks of inquiry shape what we see, but without forsaking empirical inquiry. It should include, where possible in light of the research question posed, some form of open-ended attention to actors presenting their views in their own terms so that the researcher does not simply impose the researcher's particular frame in a way that predisposes research outcomes.

Empirical work is conventionally divided into quantitative and qualitative methods, each of which has its attributes and deficiencies, involving trade-offs. Yet while theorists of knowledge, from Karl Popper and Imre Lakatos to Thomas Kuhn and William Quine, disagree on some basic issues as to how we understand the world, they agree that theory ultimately must be tested against observation and experience. Quine, who was completely skeptical of any "truth" of perception that is independent from cultural context, also was a committed empiricist, but one who recognized the impact of the social environment in which empiricism takes place. He wrote, "As an empiricist I continue to think of the conceptual scheme of science as a tool, ultimately, for predicting future experience in the light of past experience.... But in point of epistemological footing, the physical objects and the gods differ only in degree and not in kind. Both sorts of entities enter our conceptions only as cultural posits."[10]

Taking from the work of Quine and others, we need to be aware of how presentations of "fact" reflect, to varying extents, a subjective, normative element that is socially constructed, even in the very framing of the questions posed. We need to be aware that these presentations, in turn, play into social dynamics with their dimensions of hierarchy and power.[11] What we need is an interactive process between the analytic framework used and critical empirical inquiry. A new legal realist approach should permit us to challenge the presuppositions that scholars unavoidably bring to their work.

New legal realism nonetheless is better positioned to show how all presentations of law and fact are not equal. The researcher aiming to approach a subject in an

[10] Quine (1980, 20); see also (Quine 1969, 69) (maintaining that our very thinking is constructed within a context from which it cannot be completely free).

[11] Those scholars engaged in work involving race and gender often have been at the forefront of exposing questions and data that were assumed away in conventional legal thinking and the prescriptions derived from it. See, e.g., Lawrence (1987, 317–388); Matsuda (1989); Alfieri (1999).

open and objective manner is almost always surprised by how wrong his or her initial assumptions were. The new legal realist approach calls into question ideological presumption. This is a key methodological point. Leaving one's office and venturing into the field can transform one's core assumptions regarding one's subject of study. As Mertz (2005, 483) writes, "the power of social science methodology [is] to push us beyond our personal politics or situations, to enforce a form of humility in which we must listen to voices other than our own." While social science is never entirely correct, it is the best way for us to proceed toward a better understanding of the world in which law operates. If we are to participate in an endeavor to make international law more legitimate, and thus more sustainable, our power lies in uncovering, from a bottom-up perspective, the processes that construct and develop it.

Third, a new legal realism should foreground the role of institutions that engage with law. New legal realism should examine how abstract law is translated in different institutional environments in which law is made, interpreted, and applied, aware that all institutional alternatives are imperfect and thus the pursuit of goals will always be mediated in different ways through different institutional processes. In particular, because all decision-making processes are characterized by unequal participation, a key question for new legal realists should be how affected constituencies participate, or otherwise are represented, directly or indirectly, in an institutional context in comparison with alternative nonidealized institutional settings (Komesar 1994; Shaffer 2005b).

Fourth, and complementarily, a new legal realism in international law should be grounded in addressing social problems that are transnational in scope, and, in doing so, engage with normative values. It should be committed to communicating its empirical findings for contributing to the advance of social welfare and distributive justice in a world characterized by power asymmetries and inequality, including unequal opportunities to be heard. New legal realism's empirical commitment thus must necessarily be linked to normative questions.

Since there are tensions among stakeholders' perspectives and priorities in a culturally diverse and changing world that raise questions regarding any universalist claims, a new legal realism should adopt a pragmatist conception of values that develops from experience and learning. Empirical study, building from experience, should catalyze a dynamic and revisable understanding of the ends in view that we pursue and the means through which we pursue them. Participation and reciprocal learning should be key values in the construction, practice, and development of international law.

III. SOME EXAMPLES OF A NEW LEGAL REALISM APPLIED

Let me give some examples from my own work in terms of the potential for learning and discovery in a new legal realist vein that implicates normative pursuits in the area of international trade law. As a beginning academic, I obtained a National

Science Foundation grant to examine the law and politics of international trade and environment issues and went to Geneva with a conventional conception that the World Trade Organization (WTO) was trade-biased and needed to balance competing environmental norms and objectives.[12] What happened next was that my interviews turned into lectures from individuals from developing country governments and nongovernmental organizations (NGOs) about how my questions reflected an American frame. I learned about how environmental issues, and thus the trade-environment debate, were constructed (and being constructed) by US and European academics, representatives, and nongovernmental organizations compared to their developing country counterparts. I learned of the advantages of the resources and status that US and European universities bring, of US and European scholars' greater access to Western media and learned journals, and their advantages with English being the international language used to diffuse their framings of the issues. I learned how the term "environment" has vastly different meanings to stakeholders in developing countries, where it is much more difficult to separate the concept from that of "development" because people's livelihoods are more intimately connected on a day-to-day basis with the environment.

I then tested what I learned from interviews by reviewing the minutes of WTO trade and environment committee meetings and noting who spoke at such meetings on which issues. I aggregated the data, and, in this way, I showed how environmental issues were framed in the WTO context, and how differently representatives from northern and southern countries understood trade-environment issues, and how NGOs from the north and south tended to reflect these frames. In this way, I addressed how legal scholarship in the United States reflected a particular national framing of trade-environment issues, and how the solutions sought and the answers given by liberal-minded US scholars imposed all the costs of adaptation on the poor, on those without voice.

In short, my assumptions and expectations were upset by the experience of weeks of interviewing and discussing the issues with people coming from a much broader range of experience and priorities than I could meet on Westlaw or at US academic conferences. That experience had a transformative impact on my scholarship. Whether it has been through interviewing regulators, parliamentarians and their staffers, technical assistance providers and recipients, private and government trade lawyers, civil society advocates, or international organization secretariat members, my incoming predispositions (inevitable no matter how neutral and unassuming I try to be) have always been challenged and transformed.

To give a second example, the key to the launching of the Doha Development Round was the creation of a fund for technical assistance and capacity building for developing countries. The first focus for this program was technical assistance provided by the WTO and the World Intellectual Property Organization (WIPO)

[12] This research was published in Shaffer (2001).

for developing country implementation of intellectual property protections, even though economists have shown how such intellectual property protections result in net wealth transfers from developing countries to the United States and Europe.[13] The lesson is that if we talk about foreign aid and capacity building, we also must ask about who defines the objectives and programs, who selects the experts, and how are they received. One discovers these processes only in a bottom-up way through interviews and archival research.

To turn to a third example, most WTO legal scholarship starts with WTO rules, then examines how they are interpreted, and concludes regarding why such interpretation is right or wrong from a legal positivist or a normative perspective (such as, in Ronald Dworkin's terms, making the law the best it can be) (Dworkin 1986, 411). A new legal realist project often reverses the telescope, starting with analysis of why certain WTO members and certain of their constituents use (or fail to use) WTO law and thereby give (or fail to give) WTO law meaning (Shaffer 2009). Only then does one turn to examine whether WTO procedures, the approach of WTO case law, the WTO's rules on remedies, and individual WTO member strategies could be modified in order to facilitate a more cost-effective representation of weaker parties.

From a top-down perspective, the WTO legal regime and its dispute settlement system seem to be based on consensus and neutrality. Dispute settlement under the WTO has been described as a system where law prevails over power politics, where "*right* perseveres over *might*" (Lacarte-Muro and Gappah 2000). Yet such optimistic declarations prompt a series of questions about how the WTO legal system actually operates in practice. Who predominantly uses this legal system, and who prevails? Can the legal system work for smaller players, such as small developing countries? To what extent has legal capacity – the ability to mobilize legal resources to prepare and litigate a WTO case – replaced the premium provided by market power? These are the questions, and implicit within them the challenges, that a new legal realist approach poses.

To show how international trade law actually works in practice, one can use a combination of quantitative and qualitative methods to assess the role of legal capacity in the use of WTO law, both in actual dispute settlement and in the shadow of the legal system. In an empirical study with political scientists Marc Busch and Eric Reinhardt (Busch, Reinhardt, and Shaffer 2008, 2009), we used original surveys combined with semi-structured interviews to show how WTO members with more legal capacity are more likely to challenge before the WTO and are less likely, up front, to have antidumping duties imposed on their products in the first place. We found that legal capacity mattered at least as much as, if not more than, raw market power, in affecting patterns of dispute initiation and protection.

A new legal realist also needs to assess how empirical findings can be translated pragmatically for policy. Here are two examples, one involving systemic reform and

[13] This research was published in Shaffer (2005a).

the other involving the development of practical tools for actors. The International Centre for Trade and Sustainable Development (ICTSD) created a program to solicit empirical work to assess ways in which the dispute settlement system could facilitate greater developing country participation. In a publication with a Swedish trade economist, we showed how the WTO dispute settlement system discriminates against those with small claims, particularly affecting small developing countries. We then put forward a proposal for a "small claims" procedure for such claims (Shaffer and Nordstrom 2008). This work, in turn, has helped bolster calls for supporting subsidized legal support for developing countries through the Geneva-based Advisory Centre on WTO Law (ACWL).

In addition, the empirical work can help countries and their constituencies address what can be done outside of WTO institutional reform so that WTO law can be used effectively by a wider variety of actors. Two Brazilian academics and I published a study that showed how Brazil's effort to use the WTO legal system has had a broader impact both within Brazil and on the WTO (Shaffer, Ratton-Sanchez, and Rosenberg 2008). Within Brazil, this effort has had an impact on legal education, government–business relations, and even the organization of the state itself, building more transparent government processes and developing new competitions for trade expertise. In the process, Brazil dramatically engaged the WTO system in challenging US and European agricultural subsidies. In that project, we linked the national and the global settings. We showed how developing country actors, wanting to promote different agendas to make international law reflect their priorities, can use international legal tools to their own advantage, including through reforming their own domestic systems. The study complemented others regarding developing countries' experiences with WTO dispute settlement as part of a series of workshops in Africa, Asia, and South America that contributed to the sharing of practices and policy learning (Shaffer and Meléndez-Ortiz 2011).

IV. CONCLUSION

A new legal realist approach both shows a healthy skepticism toward international law and takes international law seriously. Unlike internationalist idealists, a new legal realist perspective questions what constitutes international law. It questions whose voices are heard and not heard when one focuses on international society with a presumption that international law is there to serve common interests.[14] To adapt from Ed Rubin (1996, 1428), new legal realism attends to "all the social forces, inequalities, and ideological [factors that law-promoting theories have] ignored." Unlike international relations realists, however, a new legal realism takes

[14] That is, who constitutes the international law "community" and "international society," or, to paraphrase the great human rights scholar Oscar Schachter (1977, 217), "the invisible college" of international lawyers.

international law and legal reasoning seriously and thus also turns to examine the opportunities that international law can provide, building from empirical inquiry.

New legal realism is thus not opposed to traditional doctrinal, theoretical, and normative work. Rather, it complements them. New legal realism takes account of legal doctrine in that it examines the potential for law's normativity to shape social ordering. It aims to build conditional theory regarding international law's development, practice, and effects, which can inform the normative evaluation and potential transformation of international law.

Engaging in empirical work and translating empirical work for legal and other policy actors remains a critical challenge for the study of international law in a world characterized by constituencies with differing priorities, perspectives, and opportunities to be heard. The translation is not a simple one, and the success of a new legal realism will depend in large part on it. Those writing from the United States or Europe need to be particularly careful before they advance prescriptions based on a presumption that their perspectives are universal and not shaped and colored by their position and experience. Given that academics in the United States, in particular, are well placed to participate in international policy debates because they write from the center of global power (economically, militarily, linguistically, and socially, including in terms of the relative status of US universities), it is incumbent on them to question their own proclivities. Undertaking empirical work, and doing so with a critical gaze through engagement with the perspectives of those from other jurisdictions, should be a central goal of a new realist approach to international law.

If we are to fashion a more just, sustainable, and credible international legal order, we will need to do more than assume that international law is legitimate and to struggle for its respect. From a Baldwinian perspective, we must turn a critical gaze on our presumptions so that new learning and new ways of seeing may arise. From a Chekhovian one, we must not prescribe without first assessing what is, and only then listen to what one can and must do. Only then will learning arise that is grounded in experience and that attends to new and ongoing problems in a changing world.

REFERENCES

Alfieri, Anthony V. 1999. "Prosecuting Race." *Duke Law Journal* 48(6): 1157–1264.

Baldwin, James. 1962. "The Creative Process." In *Creative America*, 17–21. New York: Ridge Press.

Busch, Marc, Eric Reinhardt, and Gregory Shaffer. 2008. *Does Legal Capacity Matter? Explaining Patterns of Protectionism in the Shadow of WTO Litigation*. Geneva: International Centre for Trade and Sustainable Development.

Busch, Marc, Eric Reinhardt, and Gregory Shaffer. 2009. "Does Legal Capacity Matter? A Survey of WTO Members." *World Trade Review* 8(4): 559–577.

Chekhov, Anton. 1977. "Anton Chekhov to Alexey Suvorin, December 3, 1892." In *The Portable Chekhov*, edited by Avrahm Yarmolinsky, 626–627. New York: Penguin Books.

de Been, Wouter. 2008. *Legal Realism Regained: Saving Realism from Critical Acclaim*. Stanford, CA: Stanford University Press.

Dworkin, Ronald. 1986. *Law's Empire*. Cambridge, MA: Belknap Press of Harvard University Press.

Erlanger, Howard S., Bryant Garth, Jane E. Larson, Elizabeth Mertz, Victoria Nourse, and David B. Wilkins. 2005. "Is It Time for a New Legal Realism?" *Wisconsin Law Review* 2: 335–363.

Ewick, Patricia, Robert Kagan, and Austin Sarat. 1999. "Introduction: Legacies of Legal Realism: Social Science, Social Policy and the Law." In *Social Science, Social Policy and the Law*, edited by Patricia Ewick, Robert Kagan, and Austin Sarat, 1–38. New York: Russell Sage Foundation.

Farber, Daniel A. 2001. "Toward a New Legal Realism." *Chicago Law Review* 68: 279–303.

Fisher, William, Morton Horwitz, and Thomas Reed, eds. 1993. *American Legal Realism*. New York: Oxford University Press.

Flood, John. 2007. "Lawyers as Sanctifiers: The Role of Elite Law Firms in International Business Transactions." *Indiana Journal of Global Legal Studies* 14(1): 35–66.

Halliday, Terence, and Gregory Shaffer, eds. 2015. *Transnational Legal Orders*. New York: Cambridge University Press.

Hudec, Robert E. 1993. *Enforcing International Trade Law: The Evolution of the Modern GATT Legal System*. Salem: Butterworth Legal Publishers.

Kennan, George. 1951. *American Diplomacy*. Chicago: University of Chicago Press.

Klee, Paul. 1920 [2013]. "Creative Confession [Schöpferische Konfession]." In *Creative Confession and Other Writings*, edited by Matthew Gale, 7. n.p.: Tate Publishing.

Komesar, Neil K. 1994. *Imperfect Alternatives: Choosing Institutions in Law, Economics, and Public Policy*. Chicago: University of Chicago Press.

Kritzer, Herbert M. 2010. "The (Nearly) Forgotten Early Empirical Legal Research." In *The Oxford Handbook of Empirical Legal Research*, edited by Peter Cane and Herbert Kritzer, 875–896. New York: Oxford University Press.

Lacarte-Muro, Julio, and Petina Gappah. 2000. "Developing Countries and the WTO Legal and Dispute Settlement System: A View from the Bench." *Journal of International Economic Law* 3(1): 395–401.

Lawrence, Charles L. 1987. "The Id, the Ego, and Equal Protection: Reckoning with Unconscious Racism." *Stanford Law Review* 39(2): 317–388.

Leiter, Brian. 1999. "Legal Realism." In *A Companion to Philosophy of Law and Legal Theory*, edited by Dennis Patterson and William A. Edmundson, 261–279. Malden, MA: Blackwell.

Leiter, Brian. 2005. "American Legal Realism". In *The Blackwell Guide to the Philosophy of Law and Legal Theory*, edited by Martin P. Golding and William A. Edmundson, 50–67. Malden, MA: Blackwell.

Llewellyn, Karl. 1931. "Some Realism about Realism: Responding to Dean Pound." *Harvard Law Review* 44(8): 1222–1264.

Macaulay, Stewart. 2005. "The New versus the Old Legal Realism: 'Things Ain't What They Used to Be.'" *Wisconsin Law Review* 2005(2): 365–454.

Matsuda, Mari J. 1989. "When the First Quail Calls: Multiple Consciousness as Jurisprudential Method." *Women's Rights Law Reporter* 11(7): 7–10.

Mertz, Elizabeth. 2005. "Challenging Translations: New Legal Realist Methods." *Wisconsin Law Review* 2005(2): 482–489.

Miles, Thomas J., and Cass R. Sunstein. 2008. "The New Legal Realism." *Chicago Law Review* 75(1): 831–851.

Morgenthau, Hans J., and Kenneth W. Thompson. 1963 [2006]. *Politics among Nations: The Struggle for Power and Peace.* Rev./expanded ed. Boston: McGraw-Hill Higher Education.

Nourse, Victoria, and Gregory Shaffer. 2009. "Varieties of New Legal Realism: Can a New World Order Spur a New Scholarly Agenda?" *Cornell Law Review* 95: 61–137.

Nourse, Victoria, and Gregory Shaffer. 2014. "A New Legal Realism: Empiricism, Experimentalism, and Conditional Theory." *Southern Methodist University Law Review* 14: 101–142.

Posner, Eric A. 2009. *The Perils of Global Legalism.* Chicago: University of Chicago Press.

Posner, Richard A. 1990. *The Problems of Jurisprudence.* Cambridge, MA: Harvard University Press.

Quine, W. V. 1969. *Epistemology Naturalized from Ontological Relativity, and Other Essays.* New York: Columbia University Press.

Quine, W. V. 1980. "Two Dogmas of Empiricism." In *A Logical Point of View, 2nd ed., rev.*, 20–46. Cambridge, MA: Harvard University Press.

Ratner, Steven, and Anne-Marie Slaughter, eds. 1999. "Symposium on Method in International Law: A Special Issue of the *American Journal of International Law*." *American Journal of International Law* 93: 291–301.

Rosenne, Shabtai. 1984. *Practice and Methods of International Law.* London: Oceana Publications.

Rubin, Edward. 1996. "The New Legal Process, the Synthesis of Discourse, and the Microanalysis of Institutions." *Harvard Law Review* 109(6): 1393–1438.

Schachter, Oscar. 1977. "The Invisible College of International Lawyers." *Northwestern University Law Review* 72(2): 217–226.

Schlegel, John Henry. 1995. *American Legal Realism and Empirical Social Science.* Chapel Hill: University of North Carolina Press.

Shaffer, Gregory. 2001. "The World Trade Organization under Challenge: Democracy and the Law and Politics of the WTO's Treatment of the Trade and Environment Matters." *Harvard Environmental Law Review* 25(1): 1–93.

Shaffer, Gregory. 2005a. "Can WTO Technical Assistance and Capacity Building Serve Developing Countries?" *Wisconsin International Law Journal* 23(4): 643–686.

Shaffer, Gregory. 2005b. "Power, Governance, and the WTO: A Comparative Institutional Approach." In *Power in Global Governance*, edited by Michael Barnett and Bud Duvall, 130–160. New York: Cambridge University Press.

Shaffer, Gregory. 2009. "Developing Country Use of the WTO Dispute Settlement System: Why It Matters, the Barriers Posed." In *Frontiers of Economics and Globalization, Vol. 6: Trade Disputes and the Dispute Settlement Understanding of the WTO: An Interdisciplinary Assessment*, edited by James C. Hartigan, 167–190. Bingley, UK: Emerald Group Publishing.

Shaffer, Gregory. 2013a. "Comparative Institutional Analysis and a New Legal Realism." *Wisconsin Law Review* 2013(2): 607–628.

Shaffer, Gregory. 2013b. *Transnational Legal Ordering and State Change.* New York: Cambridge University Press.

Shaffer, Gregory, and Tom Ginsburg. 2012. "The Empirical Turn in International Legal Scholarship." *American Journal of International Law* 106(1): 1–46.

Shaffer, Gregory, and Ricardo Meléndez-Ortiz, eds. 2011. *WTO: The Developing Country Experience.* New York: Cambridge University Press.

Shaffer, Gregory, and Hakan Nordstrom. 2008. "Access to Justice in the World Trade Organization: The Case for a Small Claims Procedure?" *World Trade Review* 7(4): 587–640.

Shaffer, Gregory, Michelle Ratton-Sanchez, and Barbara Rosenberg. 2008. "The Trials of Winning at the WTO: What Lies behind Brazil's Success?" *Cornell International Law Journal* 41(2): 383–501.

Singer, Joseph William. 1988. "Legal Realism Now." *California Law Review* 76(2): 465–544.

Slaughter, Anne-Marie, and Steven Ratner. 1999. "The Method Is the Message." *American Journal of International Law* 93: 410–451.

Suchman, Mark C, and Elizabeth Mertz. 2010. "Toward a New Legal Empiricism: Empirical Legal Studies and New Legal Realism." *Annual Review of Law and Social Science* 6: 555–579.

Tamanaha, Brian Z. 1999. *Realistic Socio-Legal Theory: Pragmatism and a Social Theory of Law*. New York: Oxford University Press.

Trubek, David M. 2008. "Transcending the Ostensible: Some Reflections on Bob Hudec as Friend and Scholar." *Minnesota Journal of International Law* 17(1): 1–6.

Trubek, David M., Yves Dezalay, Ruth Buchanan, and John R. Davis. 1994. "Global Restructuring and the Law: Studies of the Internationalization of Legal Fields and the Creation of Transnational Arenas." *Case Western Reserve Law Review* 44(2): 407–498.

9

The Deconstruction of Offshore

Sol Picciotto

I. BLOWING THE WHISTLE ON BANK SECRECY

Rudolf Elmer ruefully remarks that of his twenty-eight encounters with the courts, twenty-seven decisions have gone against him. He has served two terms of imprisonment in Switzerland, one of 30 days and one of 187 days, both under that country's archaic laws that allow extended terms of prison for interrogation purposes.[1] His conviction by a lower court in January 2011, and the suspended sentence it gave him of 240 days in jail, are under appeal, a higher court in November 2011 having ordered further investigation and a possible amendment of the charges. The actions that led to these prosecutions, which he admits, were that he revealed details of transactions of global clients of the Cayman Islands affiliate of the Julius Baer Bank Group (JBB), for which he worked as chief operating officer. These revelations were made to the Swiss federal tax authorities, and subsequently to the public and press as well as the US and UK authorities, his aim being to expose widespread evasion and avoidance of laws in Switzerland and other countries. His case involves tangled interactions of national and international laws, as well as of law and morality.

Elmer is a key figure in the recent international battles to combat bank secrecy which has long sheltered not only tax evasion and avoidance, but also laundering of money from corruption, crime, and terrorism. His story also casts fascinating light into the 'offshore' system, constructed by lawyers and other professionals, which has been central to the emergence of transnational corporate capitalism as well as its complex system of networked multilevel governance.[2]

A. *Which Bank, Whose Secrecy?*

The main legal charge against Elmer has been that he breached Article 47 of Switzerland's Law on Banks. This makes it a criminal offence to reveal secrets

1 The account of Rudolf Elmer's story is based on personal conversations with him; to that extent the personal portrait is inevitably sympathetic, but I have tried to keep the exposition as factual as possible, and facts have been checked against documentary and other evidence, most of which is publicly available.

2 For a fuller exposition, see Picciotto (2011).

obtained by a person as an employee or official of a bank. The main plank of his defense is that the information he revealed came to him as chief operating officer of the Julius Baer Bank and Trust Company – Cayman Islands (JBBTC-CI), a separate legal entity from its parent Julius Baer Bank in Switzerland, and therefore not governed by the Swiss Law on Banks. As the cantonal High Court in Zurich accepted, the Law on Banks applies to enterprises which carry on in or from Switzerland regular activities subject to supervision under that Law.[3] For this main reason, the High Court overturned Elmer's conviction by the lower court, but left the case open for further investigation and possible revised charges. The case is still continuing, and is now entering its tenth year.

Elmer's defence involves turning the legal tables against his accusers. His whistle-blowing resulted from concerns that transactions were being attributed to the JBBTC-CI fictitiously, to facilitate evasion or avoidance of taxes and perhaps other laws, in Switzerland and elsewhere. The information he handed over showed that the real decisions regarding those transactions were taken elsewhere, and that records were constructed or doctored to make it seem that they took place in the Cayman Islands.

B. *High Finance and Low Taxes*

A major part of the business of the JBBTC-CI is to provide management services for hedge funds, as well as private equity companies such as the Carlyle Group. Indeed, by the time of the great financial crash in 2008, Cayman was the world's biggest centre for hedge funds, with over US$1.5 trillion estimated to be under management there, at least on paper (CIMA 2010). The money to be invested in hedge funds managed by the Baer group would be deposited in accounts with the JBB mostly in Zurich but also in London and New York, as safe places for money. The decisions on the investment of the funds would be taken by analysts and traders in New York or London. But the funds' profits, and most importantly the performance fees of 15 to 20 per cent, would be treated as earned in Cayman, which of course has no income or profits tax. Repatriating those profits to Switzerland did not even lead to taxable income in Switzerland since its parent company, Julius Baer in Zurich, could take advantage of its status as a holding company under Swiss law, which means profits from its subsidiaries are tax-free income. Hence, not only are the profits of funds attributed to JBBTC-CI untaxed in Cayman, but they are not taxed anywhere in the world.

In addition, this also means that dividend payments to the investors in the fund are not subject to any withholding tax at source, so the investors also receive these payments tax free. If they are liable to tax in their country of residence on such

[3] Obergericht des Kantons Zurich, Bericht vom 17 November 2011 in Sachen Rudolf Matthias Elmer gegen Staatsanwaltschaft Winterthur/Unterland, para. 4.1.5 (available at http://www.swisswhistleblower.com/).

foreign-source income, they should of course declare it to the tax authorities there. But should they omit to do so, they would be very unlikely to be found out, since Cayman, at least until very recently, prohibited the disclosure of such information. Indeed, its Confidential Relationships (Preservation) Law was enacted in 1976 specifically in response to attempts by the US authorities to try to obtain such information, and to ensure that such requests could be blocked.[4]

The hedge fund's analysts in London or New York are paid a fee based on the market rate for their 'advice' by the fund's 'managers' in Cayman, and of course JBB in Zurich, London, and New York earns the normal banking rates for managing the clients' accounts. This arrangement ensures not only that the funds pay no tax, but also that the JBBCT-CI has accounted for the lion's share of the worldwide profits of the Julius Baer group. Yet it employs only some 25 people, compared to about 800 in the Swiss parent company, 100 analysts in London, and 150 in New York. The operation in Cayman, once headed by Elmer, involves only formally booking the transactions 'recommended' by the analysts onshore. This legal structuring of hedge funds is well known to the tax authorities in the United Kingdom and the United States, who could in principle have decided to disregard it and treat the analysts in London or New York as the real investment managers, so that the funds' profits, particularly the performance fee, could be taxed there (Sullivan and Sheppard 2008). However, the UK and US tax authorities fear that this would run the risk that those operations would be moved elsewhere, perhaps Zurich or Singapore. The same pattern is found in the private equity business of Julius Baer, for instance, for the Carlyle Group, for which JBBCT-CI also acts as a booking centre.

This is the essence of 'offshore'. It is a system which exploits the legal fiction that corporations are individual and separate legal persons, even if they are owned and centrally controlled within a corporate group. It also plays with interpretations of the abstract legal concepts of corporate residence and definitions of the location of decisions and transactions. Crucially, it also rests firmly on the guarantees by countries such as Cayman and Switzerland of strong legal protections of banking, corporate, and commercial secrecy, and noncooperation with the public or governmental authorities in its home country but more importantly those of other countries.

The issue goes far beyond tax avoidance and evasion, serious as they are. Elmer's concerns about the sleight-of-hand involved in the Cayman–London–New York–Zurich nexus grew during the very period of the unprecedented financial boom, which some have termed 'financialization'. It has been estimated by the Tax Justice Network that by 2010 some US$21 to US$31 trillion of the world's financial wealth was invested by these virtually tax-free methods through the offshore system, US$12.1 trillion of which was under management by the top fifty private banks, amongst

4 Picciotto (1992, 269–270); although the US authorities, backed by the courts, subsequently found ways to override that law (Hudson 1998b).

which Julius Baer ranked seventeenth (Henry 2012, 5, 8, 63). These enormous sources of low-taxed and therefore low-cost money drove a wave of trading and speculation which fuelled a bubble that finally burst in the great financial crash of 2007–2009.

C. *Law and Legitimacy*

Yet in recent years, and especially since the great financial crisis, this edifice has begun to crumble. Elmer's story reveals in microcosm both the power of the system and its flaws. The main attraction of the Baer Bank, for those who choose to place large sums of money with it, is its reputation for security and probity, reinforced by its location in Switzerland. Elmer himself personifies those Swiss values, which stayed with him while he trained in accounting and auditing in Zurich with Credit Suisse and KPMG, and then joined the JBB. Indeed, when he arrived in Cayman in 1994 he was regarded as the 'Swiss spy from head office' by the other employees there, as well as the CEO of Baer's New York affiliate. Since this was a main source of clients, Elmer's probity became a focus for conflict. It was Elmer's personal morals as well as his professional training that led him increasingly to balk at some of the activities in which he was expected to assist or connive, especially the approval of false accounts or documents. Yet when he reported his knowledge of suspicious transactions and concerns about illegality to clients, to his Swiss bank superiors, and even to Swiss government authorities, they all provided no support. Instead he found that he was subjected to intimidation and threats in Cayman, and then to dismissal at the end of 2002.

Returning to Switzerland, he found another job in financial services; but the harassment and intimidation continued, affecting not only him and his wife but especially his young daughter. Nevertheless, he felt he could not let matters rest. Yet his attempts to get protection as a citizen against the stalking and harassment of his family, as well as the numerous complaints he filed against the bank with state and federal authorities, were turned down with little or no investigation. He had not begun as a tax justice campaigner, but just an employee trying to do a professional job. The frustration and resentment he felt about his treatment by his employers, and the lack of protection from the justice system, led him to seek wider support.

Eventually, in March 2005 he decided to hand over information in his possession to the Swiss federal and cantonal tax authorities. However, the Swiss prohibition against disclosure of bank secrets makes no exception for government agencies. The Swiss tax authorities were not able to make use of this information to investigate possible breaches of Swiss law, nor even to protect him as a whistle-blower. Switzerland as of today still has no protection for whistle-blowers in the private sector, as is characteristic for a secrecy jurisdiction. Instead, the Zurich prosecutors ordered a police search of his house, confiscated his laptop and other items, and took him into custody for interrogation for thirty days.

Elmer decided to get a new job and leave Switzerland, taking his family to Mauritius. From there, he concluded that he had to seek support from outside Switzerland. Early in 2008, he sent some of the information in his possession to WikiLeaks, which was published on its website. The Baer Bank applied to the US federal district court in San Francisco and obtained a temporary restraining order, *ex parte*, to stop the publication. This move backfired, as the case became publicized. WikiLeaks received wide support, including from lawyers acting pro bono, and at the *inter partes* hearing the court order was quickly revoked, inter alia on First Amendment grounds (*Baer v. WikiLeaks* 2008).

Almost five years after his detention and interrogation by the Zurich prosecutors, an indictment was issued against him in June 2010. Two days before the date of his trial, on the 17th of January 2011, he travelled to London, and appeared at a press conference in the Frontline Club to publicize his case, together with his US legal adviser and experienced investigator Jack Blum, and John Christensen of the Tax Justice Network.[5] The event included the handing over of a CD-ROM to Julian Assange of WikiLeaks, but this was a symbolic act, as on the advice of Jack Blum it contained no data. On the 19th of January 2011 the Zurich trial court found him guilty of violating Swiss bank secrecy based on his Swiss employment contract, as well as of other charges of making threats and coercion, and imposed a suspended sentence and a fine. On leaving court he was rearrested, once again for violation of bank secrecy, including for the Frontline Club action. This time he was kept in detention until the 25th of July. On the 17th of November the Zurich High Court overturned the lower court's decision, but remanded the case to the prosecutors for further investigation and possible amendment of the charges. At the time of writing he therefore still has two possible cases pending against him for violation of Swiss bank secrecy.

In the meantime, however, the international climate towards bank and financial secrecy had begun to change, a shift to which Elmer's actions had contributed. This will be discussed further later in this chapter. First, we should step back a little and consider the dynamics of development of the offshore system and its wider ramifications.

II. THE CONSTRUCTION OF OFFSHORE

A. *Regulatory Interactions*

The phenomenon of 'offshore' originated early in the twentieth century, was quietly nurtured from the 1950s, and grew to full maturity from the 1980s. It is generally thought of in terms of 'havens', usually imagined as palm-fringed tropical islands, and the Cayman Islands certainly fit this image. Havens are jurisdictions of

[5] Available on video at http://www.youtube.com/watch?v=JIdWl5KMSGo.

convenience with laws specially designed to facilitate avoidance or evasion of other countries' laws. Many are small countries, but by no means are all of them islands – Liechtenstein, and indeed Switzerland, are landlocked. Such havens are key nodes, but 'offshore' is better thought of as a networked system of regulatory interactions.

Different jurisdictions can offer varied advantages. The absence of any income or profits tax, plus its strong secrecy laws and other regulations, make Cayman a convenient place to accumulate profits and hold especially financial assets, so it may be described as a base haven, or a classic tax haven. However, another important node in tax avoidance strategies is the Netherlands, because it has a large number of tax treaties, which generally reduce taxation at source of payments such as interest, dividends, fees, and royalties. It is therefore a convenient jurisdiction for the formation of conduit companies to route such payments, an arrangement referred to as the 'Dutch sandwich' (McGauran 2013), and recently publicized as being widely used by digital economy companies such as Google (Drucker 2010; Sandell 2012; Bergin 2013). Mauritius offers similar conduit facilities, especially due to its treaty with India, which enables avoidance of capital gains tax there. As the Indian authorities have become stricter, Mauritius is hoping to benefit from its treaties with African countries such as Kenya and Zambia.

Facilities for easy company formation behind a cloak of anonymity are provided in countries such as the British Virgin Islands, which have made them a very popular jurisdiction for forming shell companies. However, following the strengthening of laws against money laundering, savvy operators prefer to seek greater respectability in countries such as the United States. States such as Delaware, Nevada, and Wyoming offer opacity of corporate ownership, and it seems that corporate service providers there are willing to create companies while turning a blind eye to the purposes, even if manifestly dubious (Sharman 2010; Findley, Nielson, and Sharman 2013). This is why it is important to understand that tax havens such as Cayman are only part of a wider network.[6] In many ways it is the main global financial centres such as London, New York, and Zurich that are at the centre of this network, since the main financial and legal services activities driving it take place there, as the account in the first section of this chapter explains. Indeed, the major factors which led to the emergence of Cayman as an offshore centre were its proximity to Miami, and hence to New York, and the links to London of British-educated lawyers, such as William S. Walker and John Maples. Indeed, it was London-based Milton Grundy who devised the Cayman Islands Trusts Act of 1967, causing great concerns to the UK Inland Revenue.[7] Hence, it is more

[6] This is made clear in the methodology adopted for the Financial Secrecy Index, which aims to map the offshore secrecy system and rank its various nodes; see http://www.financialsecrecyindex.com/. This networked nature of the offshore secrecy system seems inadequately understood even by some otherwise knowledgeable researchers (e.g., Findley et al. 2013, 23).

[7] UK Public Record Office file T295-892.

appropriate to use an ethnographic methodology to map the contours of the offshore system (see, e.g., Roberts 1995; Hudson 1998a; Huxley 2000; Rawlings 2004), rather than a state-based perspective derived from standard political science or international relations.

The offshore system has centred on the avoidance of tax, although this has been linked with and has spread to avoidance of other types of regulation, especially of financial regulation. International regulatory avoidance strategies essentially entail choosing a convenient jurisdiction in which to create a legal entity, such as a corporation, partnership, or trust, which can be used as a vehicle to own assets or through which to channel transactions. This is in a sense a type of forum shopping, since the aim generally is to relocate activities (at least nominally) to a jurisdiction which not only offers more favourable rules but, more importantly, can provide a shelter from the regulations of other jurisdictions. This type of shelter, which originated with the desire to avoid taxation, is generally referred to as a haven.[8]

Tax avoidance, in various forms, has no doubt existed as long as taxation. In the mercantile period, when states relied heavily on customs duties, it took the form of smuggling, and this still continues where high-value items such as cigarettes are subject to different levels of duty by different states. However, the modern tax haven was born after the First World War, when an increasing number of states had come to depend on taxation of income or profits, sometimes applied at very high rates on higher income. This led some wealthy families and firms with international investments or business to try to find ways of reducing their tax liability, if possible legitimately. They began to exploit the fiction of legal personality, and to use legal creativity to manoeuver within the space allowed by abstract legal concepts, in particular 'income', which is in many ways an arbitrary one (Prebble 1998), and residence.

The basic principles of tax avoidance through a haven are relatively straightforward. It simply consists of establishing one or more legal entities (company, trust, or partnership) in convenient jurisdictions, through which to channel an income flow derived from international investment or business activities. Routing income through a network of intermediary companies or other legal entities can reduce or eliminate taxation both at source and in the jurisdiction where the intermediary is resident, while insulating the ultimate beneficiary from tax liability (Picciotto 1992, 135–141; 2011, ch. 6.3.2). Such low-taxed income can either be reinvested or be used to benefit the ultimate owners, for example by acquiring assets (houses, yachts, aeroplanes) for their use, or dispensing funds to them or to family members in ways that might attract little or no taxation. It is certainly possible for states whose regulations are being avoided in this way to counteract such strategies. However, the development of antiavoidance measures may be greatly hindered, especially by

[8] This is a relatively neutral term, although sometimes regarded as pejorative. It also has positive connotations (a refuge from storms); the French term '*paradis fiscal*' is unequivocally favorable, and the English equivalent 'heaven' is sometimes substituted for the more normal 'haven'.

the tax authority's lack of information due to the use of complex structures and the protection of secrecy by havens.

Other kinds of activities, especially those which could easily be delocalized, particularly by taking advantage of new communications technologies, have also made use of the 'offshore' phenomenon. Commercial radio stations mushroomed in Europe in the 1960s aiming at breaking the monopoly of state broadcasting. They were described as 'pirates', since some of them actually broadcast from ships on the high seas, and this analogy was perhaps the source of the term 'offshore' (Palan 2003, 22). As with tax havens, cross-border radio had originated in the 1930s, in jurisdictions such as Monte Carlo (Monaco).

Similarly, 'flags of convenience' (FoC) in international shipping began to boom, especially after the Second World War, growing from under 4 per cent of world tonnage in 1948 to 26 per cent in 1970 and 34 per cent in 1990 (Kassoulides 1993, 83). This also had a longer history: in the 1920s the US authorities encouraged registration of US-owned ships in Panama, to reduce costs while ensuring availability of the ships in wartime.[9] They were joined by others, notably the Greek Aristotle Onassis and Erling Naess, a Norwegian who had set up a whaling company in London in 1928. He found that by reregistering his ships in Panama and moving the residence of his company to Paris, the company's shipping profits would be tax free (Naess 1972, 2–3). After the Second World War, another group of US lawyer-diplomats developed Liberia as a flag state, with the added advantage that its shipping (and later corporate) registry business was subcontracted to a US corporation based near Washington, DC.[10] Thus, the FoC system could combine avoidance of tax and

9 Panama had seceded from Colombia in 1903, with US support, to facilitate construction of the Canal. William Cromwell, of the New York law firm Sullivan and Cromwell, having drafted some of the documents for Panama's independence, became that country's representative in the United States, and also acted for the shipowners; he was succeeded in this role by John Foster Dulles, the future secretary of state (Carlisle 1981, 16).

10 The Liberian International Ship and Corporate Registry is run from Vienna, Virginia, USA. This is a continuation of an arrangement originally devised by a group including former US State Department officials, headed by Edward R. Stettinius, who, after working in the corporate sector at General Motors and as chairman of US Steel, had been Roosevelt's secretary of state. In 1947 he formed Stettinius Associates with other former State Department staff, and established a number of development projects in Liberia on a profit-sharing basis with the government, of which the ship registry became the longest-lasting; indeed, it became the leading flag of convenience in 1955. The Stettinius group drafted Liberia's Maritime Code (with contributions from Esso and State Department lawyers), aiming to take over the flags of convenience business from Panama, one of its advantages (from the perspective of shipowners) being that the administration of the ship registry was subcontracted to a private company based in the United States (Carlisle 1981). During the 1990–1996 civil war, its contribution to the Liberian government budget increased from 10–15 per cent to 90 per cent. However, in 1996 Charles Taylor, who had launched a rebellion in 1989 and was at that time a member of a six-person Council of State, initiated challenges to International Registries Inc. of Virginia, which was running the registry and from which Taylor had been unable to obtain funds during the civil war. Legal proceedings were begun in the US courts alleging that International Registries was diverting shipowners from Liberia to the Marshall Islands registry, and was failing to account properly to Liberia for its receipts. Taylor worked with a US lawyer, Lester Hyman, and on Taylor becoming president of Liberia the Liberian government signed an agreement with Hyman for

other regulations, including vessel safety rules and labor laws (Murphy 2004, ch. 2). By the 1990s, the growth of the Internet opened up new possibilities for 'offshore', such as online gambling, which also was a development of the earlier phenomenon of casinos being located in favourable jurisdictions (once again, Monte Carlo).

B. Sovereignty for Sale

'Offshore' became a generalized phenomenon by the 1970s, and acted as a catalyst for a dual process of national deregulation and international reregulation. The term 'offshore' has generally been used to refer to jurisdictions, often small countries, offering regulatory advantages, usually for nonresidents. In particular, some jurisdictions built on their advantages as tax havens to develop offshore financial centres (OFCs; see Picciotto 2011, ch. 6.3.5). Consequently, states with generally strict levels of regulation often reacted by carving out special regulatory regimes to attract such business back 'onshore'. Thus, 'offshore' became a system or process of deregulation, with the result that controls over economic activity based on direct state command over national firms often had to be abandoned. However, in many cases new forms of international regulation gradually emerged, based on networks.

In some cases, states decided that the only way to compete with offshore jurisdictions was to imitate them, by creating onshore enclaves, in the hope of reestablishing some degree of control. For example, the US Federal Reserve created an International Banking Facility in New York in 1981, yielding to domestic pressures and in response to the rebirth of London as an international finance centre. The intention of the US authorities was to pressure the Bank of England to agree to reserve requirements for international banking (Hawley 1984). They did not succeed until 1988, but gradually the central banks, acting mainly through the Basel Committee on Banking Supervision (BCBS), did evolve coordinated arrangements for prudential supervision of banking and finance, although this has been a painful process marked by dramatic failures, not least the great financial crash of 2007–2009 (see Picciotto 2011, chs. 6.3 and 7.2.1).

Similarly, a number of developed states reacted to the growth of flags of convenience for international shipping by introducing special 'captive' registries of their own for nationally owned vessels, offering tax breaks and allowing employment of foreign seafarers.[11] This followed the failure of attempts to bring shipping back under national state control through an international agreement requiring a genuine

the establishment of a new company, the Liberian International Shipping and Corporate Registry, which took over the business in 2000 (UN Security Council 2001). It continues to provide a significant proportion of Liberian government revenue, although competition for the ship registry business, as well as the costs of ensuring adequate safety standards for the ships it registers, mean that the Registry makes profits mainly from the corporate registry side of the business (UN Security Council 2001; interview information), which essentially facilitates tax avoidance.

[11] Some of these are through offshore dependencies, such as the Isle of Man, Madeira, the Netherlands Antilles, or the French Kerguelen Islands, while others (such as Denmark, Germany, Luxembourg,

connection with the flag state.[12] States have also introduced internal special regimes or zones to attract investment, sometimes at the expense of other states. Japan followed the US example and created special banking facilities in Tokyo in 1986, by allowing freedom from interest rate controls, bank reserve requirements, and tax regulations for yen transactions outside Japan (Adam 1992, ch. 20). Other countries aimed to combine financial deregulation with fiscal benefits linked to specific industrial strategies, such as Singapore's facilities for regional headquarters and research and development centres. Another example is Ireland's combination of tax incentives for foreign investors with its launching of an International Financial Services Centre in Dublin in 1987, taking advantage of its participation in the European Union's liberalized market for financial services to attract offshore business such as captive insurance. The dangers of deregulation were shown by the Asian financial crisis of 1997–1998, which stimulated an attempt to improve coordination of international financial regulation. However, the limits, and indeed dangers, of this regulatory system were starkly revealed by the eruption of the global financial crisis of 2007–2009.

Other countries went further, and aimed to stimulate investment in manufacturing by establishing Export Processing Zones (EPZs), such as Mexico's duty-free *maquiladora* zone, or, in other countries, Special Economic Zones (SEZs) or Enterprise Zones. Building on the older concept of free ports, which allowed duty-free importation of goods in transit, the EPZs aimed to facilitate the establishment of industries based on assembly or processing of imported inputs for reexport. However, they often went further and created enclaves in which other measures were relaxed or waived, especially employment protection regulations, turning EPZs into sweatshop zones. The concept was also expanded from that of a geographical enclave to single-industry zones (jewellery in Thailand, leather in Turkey, or coffee in Zimbabwe), while in some countries individual factories could apply for special status, becoming essentially a type of discretionary industry-support scheme. While such zones have helped some countries develop new industries and boost exports, the investments they attract often have few links with the local economy and are highly mobile, leading to continual turnover of firms and sometimes a swift decline if better opportunities arise elsewhere (ILO 2003). For example, garment

and Norway) are special facilities, sometimes established in cooperation with other states (Luxembourg, which is landlocked, established its registry as a facility for Belgium).

[12] A requirement of a genuine link between a ship and its flag state was included, at the instigation of the Netherlands, in the 1958 Geneva Convention on the High Seas, and repeated in identical terms in Article 91 of the 1982 UNCLOS. However, 'genuine link' was not defined, and the article explicitly states that 'each state shall fix the conditions for the grant of nationality to ships'. Article 94 of UNCLOS requires flag states to administer their fleets and take measures to ensure safety at sea, but only in general terms. Attempts through UNCTAD to negotiate an agreement defining the 'genuine link' produced a 1986 UN Convention which was a weak compromise, effectively legitimizing the FoC (Kassoulides 1993, 83): it specifies that there must be 'appropriate' participation in the ownership of ships by nationals of the flag state, or a 'satisfactory' proportion of the crew must be its nationals. The convention received too few ratifications to enter into force.

factories were established in a variety of countries, such as Sri Lanka and Kenya, to take advantage of import quotas allocated by developed countries, but faced large-scale closures when the quota system was ended in January 2005. Countries are under competitive pressure to keep wages and other costs to investors low in their EPZs/SEZs, making it hard to use this type of inward investment as a basis for more general economic and social improvement.

C. *The Role of Creative Lawyering*

The offshore phenomenon is not just a matter of a few rogue jurisdictions, but the result of the mutual interactions of states more generally. The jurisdictional interaction inherent in the classical liberal system of interdependence could be exploited by the strategies of jurisdictional selection and regulatory avoidance designed by transnational lawyers and other specialists (see Picciotto 2011, ch. 2). As national regulation became more rigorous, techniques of avoidance became more sophisticated. As one such specialist put it, '[F]or the professional, "offshore" is now a structural tool in the efficient management of clients' affairs' (Cabral 1995, 24).

Operating at the interface between the private and the public, these specialists were active not only in creating regulatory avoidance devices for private clients, but also in designing favourable regulatory provisions by acting as advisers to governments. As part of attempts to restore confidence and credibility in the financial security of OFCs, some countries have had their laws designed by global professional firms acting as government consultants.[13] Although this role of double agent is a delicate one and therefore confined to a small elite in large developed countries such as the United States (Dezalay 1996, 66), small jurisdictions can be prone to the advice of a less scrupulous character.[14] Particularly radical advice was provided by a team of US lawyers in the early 1990s aiming to promote Nepal as an 'offshore' financial centre (though it is entirely landlocked, as is Liechtenstein). They suggested that, rather than developing its own regulatory system (even if based on foreign models), Nepal should directly incorporate the laws of other countries by allowing foreign firms registering in Nepal to choose the laws under which they and their transactions would be regulated. This astounding proposal was put forward by lawyers working at the interface of business, government, and the academy.[15]

13 For example, the report of Rodney Gallagher of the accounting firm Coopers & Lybrand for the British government (Gallagher 1990) on offshore finance sectors in Britain's Caribbean dependent territories included draft legislation.

14 Thus the Cayman Islands Trusts Act of 1967 resulted from advice from 'private interests' in the United Kingdom (actually, Milton Grundy), causing great concerns to the UK Inland Revenue (UK Public Record Office file T295-892).

15 Collins, Hutchinson, and Wekstein (1996) and Jackson (1998). The main attraction would be the India–Nepal tax treaty, which allows exemption from withholding taxes to residents of Nepal, like the India–Mauritius treaty, which led to a boom of incorporations of intermediary companies in Mauritius. Although Nepal did introduce some legislation with this aim, its attractiveness to investors

Although specially designed laws may be found everywhere, some states or statelets offer a more comprehensive package of arrangements specifically devised for avoidance purposes of one sort or another, so they may be considered designer jurisdictions. This phenomenon has been described as the 'commercialization of sovereignty' (Palan 2002, 2003, 59–62). They often create an extensive package of laws, aimed mainly at nonresidents, so that what Antoine describes as the 'offshore legal subculture' creates in effect a dual legal system (Antoine 1999). The competition among such jurisdictions makes it hard to take countermeasures against them, since if one is targeted another is likely to take its place. This competition also leads to differentiation.

Typically, states which established themselves early as leaders, such as Liberia for shipping, Switzerland for private banking, or the Cayman Islands for offshore bank accounts, are more willing to try to safeguard their reputations (and hence their market share) by ensuring high standards in some aspects of regulation, such as maritime safety or prudential regulation of banks. However, they have generally drawn the line at cooperation in tax enforcement. Their later competitors entering the market are likely to be less scrupulous and more willing to relax standards, for example in regulating corporate service providers or banks. These bad apples are therefore more likely to become the targets of intensified international scrutiny. This has occurred, notably, with the development of a stronger program for international monitoring of financial centres established by the Financial Stability Forum following the Asian financial crisis of 1997–1998. This involves a system of peer review, coordinated mainly by the International Monetary Fund (IMF), under a program known as the Review of Standards and Codes (ROSC). The leading well-established offshore centres have taken pains to ensure they achieve a high level of compliance with financial security standards to safeguard their reputations, while continuing to resist measures to combat tax evasion or avoidance.

Generally, the exploitation of jurisdictions of convenience relies on taking advantage of fictions such as corporate personality, and the indeterminacy of abstract legal concepts such as income and residence. It is not usually, as is sometimes asserted, a matter of the greater international mobility of capital, since this type of avoidance normally involves little or no genuine economic activity in the haven jurisdiction. Thus, ships registered under a flag of convenience have little contact with their state of registry; offshore radio stations will generally broadcast programs recorded elsewhere; companies formed in tax havens to receive tax-avoiding income are usually no more than 'brass plate' entities to which assets have been notionally transferred; and financial transactions or activities attributed to entities in offshore centres are generally directed from elsewhere. Thus, a distinction can in principle be made between a legitimate jurisdictional choice, for example if a person chooses to be a tax

was marred by political instability, notably the massacre of the royal family by the Crown Prince in 2001, and a resurgence of Maoist guerrilla activity, which eventually led to the demise of the monarchy.

exile by deciding to live in a low-tax state, in contrast to avoiding tax in their country of residence by accumulating foreign earned income in a trust or company formed in a haven. However, the distinction can be very hard to maintain, especially for financial services (e.g., insurance, portfolio investment), and these are therefore the main users of the offshore system.

Combating the use of havens is certainly possible, but requires closer international coordination among regulatory authorities, to establish feasible and optimal regulatory standards, and cooperation in their enforcement. However, in many cases, havens have been developed with the tacit or overt encouragement of at least some of the government departments or public bodies of the states whose regulations they were helping business firms to avoid.[16] The often ambivalent positions of these latter states have meant that the countermeasures have generally been at best halfhearted. Although often neglected or treated as interesting but marginal, the offshore system is very important for key economic sectors (international transport, and industries such as oil and clothing) and thus central to the world economy.

Above all, the centrality of 'offshore' to finance and taxation makes it crucial to the international state system. Following the great financial crisis, it is now widely accepted that restoring effective internationally coordinated regulation of finance is essential to future economic security and stability. The fiscal crises in many states due to the enormous costs of bank bailouts, and the ensuing cutbacks and austerity policies, have also generated enormous political pressures on governments, and have led to increased support for the rapidly growing tax justice movements.

III. REINING IN OFFSHORE

A. *Politics and Technocracy of International Tax*

In the past two decades, in parallel with Rudolf Elmer's personal travails with the Baer Bank, the problem of offshore has increasingly become an issue of public concern. This has included the issue of tax avoidance and evasion, leading to two major international initiatives. Both have been taken up through summit meetings of world leaders, first the G7 and more recently the G20. They, however, have handed the task of devising a solution to the Committee on Fiscal Affairs (CFA) of

[16] Notably, in the UK, attempts to develop a coherent policy towards moves by UK dependent territories to become tax havens from the late 1960s failed, with divergence of views between the Inland Revenue (wanting to combat tax avoidance), the Foreign Office (concerned both to reduce the territories' dependence on aid and to comply with the United Kingdom's international obligations), the Bank of England (interested in boosting the business brought to the City of London by the Eurodollar and other forms of international finance), and the Treasury (treading a fine line between all of these considerations): see exchange of letters between White (Foreign Office) and Ward (Treasury), May 1977, in UK Inland Revenue (1967–1977).

the Organization for Economic Cooperation and Development (OECD), which now has the main institutional responsibility for the international tax system.[17]

The CFA consists of national tax and finance ministry officials, with a secretariat largely made up of people with a similar background. They are of course unelected, and work with no real political accountability, due to the technical nature of the field. Indeed, over the past three decades they have elaborated increasingly complex rules, expressed in specialized concepts and language. They do issue proposals for public comment and organize consultations, but again, due to the specialist nature of the issues, responses are overwhelmingly from business representatives and tax advisers. Many of these are themselves former CFA officials or members, who are often hired by large accounting and law firms. Together with a sprinkling of academics, they form a closed community, speaking the same language and reinforced by frequent contacts and participation in professional meetings and bodies, such as the International Fiscal Association.

This is symptomatic of the typical gap in contemporary global governance between the politicians, generally in national governments, and the technocrats who are in practice responsible for both the design and the operation of regulatory regimes (Picciotto 2011, esp. 22–24, 463–468). In recent years, this gap has begun to be filled to some extent by activists and campaigners, who have been able in many cases to combine expertise with campaigning skills. A number of organizations began to campaign on tax justice issues from around 2000, stimulated especially by the Tax Justice Network, formed in 2003.

B. *First Steps to Stronger International Cooperation*

It was somewhat earlier, in 1996, that political concerns about international tax avoidance resulted in the first formal political initiative, through the G7 world

[17] International coordination of taxation was initiated early in the previous century, when states realized that taxation especially of business income or profits involved mutual interactions. The issue was taken up through the League of Nations in 1922, which organized a conference in 1928 and then established a Fiscal Committee. The 1928 meeting agreed on the texts for model conventions, to be used as a basis for negotiation of bilateral tax treaties. The League of Nations' work was taken up by the United Nations under a Financial and Fiscal Commission, but it quickly became deadlocked by east-west and north-south splits, and ceased to meet after 1954. In 1956 a Fiscal Committee was set up under the Organization for European Economic Cooperation, which in 1961 became the OECD. The Committee on Fiscal Affairs is now part of the OECD's broader tax work, and consists of member state representatives, serviced by a very large number of staff. Subsequently, in 1967, the UN established an Ad Hoc Committee of Experts, which was slightly upgraded in 2004 to become the Committee of Experts on International Cooperation in Tax Matters. However, it remains dominated by OECD members, and is very underresourced (only one full-time professional staff person), so is only able to play a minor role. The IMF has a strong Tax Policy Division, mainly engaged in research; although both it and the World Bank carry out advisory work and capacity building, especially with developing countries, they have left tax policy issues to the OECD.

leaders, meeting in Lyon.[18] This resulted in the OECD's report in 1998 on *Harmful Tax Competition: An Emerging Issue*. However, this project was effectively derailed by a change in US policy, when the new Bush administration accepted arguments that the initiative, as first formulated, entailed dictating tax policy to other states.[19]

The project then refocused on obtaining information from tax havens. Although the OECD began with a model for a multilateral treaty for exchange of tax information, it quickly shifted to negotiation of bilateral tax information exchange agreements (TIEAs), aimed at the classical tax havens. The havens not unreasonably complained at being singled out, and pointed to the limitations of information exchange arrangements even among OECD states in their tax treaties. Switzerland, of course, had only ever agreed to supply information in cases of outright tax fraud (defined very narrowly). However, others also, including the United Kingdom, had no powers to obtain information to help other states enforce their taxes.[20] Also, since 1984, the United Kingdom and the United States have allowed payment of interest to nonresidents free of withholding tax, and they turn a blind eye to evasion of other countries' taxes on such payments, since they collect no information which could help them to identify the avoiders.[21] Even while a US Senate Committee was denouncing the use of 'shell companies' in havens such as Cayman for avoiding US taxes (US Senate 2006), other agencies documented the facilities for such companies offered by the United States itself (US GAO 2006; Spencer 2007). Thus, leading states such as the United States and the United Kingdom could be accused by campaigners of being among the main secrecy jurisdictions.

Ironically, the OECD was forced to adopt a more global approach by the demands of the targeted havens for a level playing field. This led to the formation

18 Russia was at that time an aspirant member of what then became the G8; following the great financial crisis of 2008 a wider group was also created, the G20. The G7 communiqué of June 1996 concluded: 'Finally, globalization is creating new challenges in the field of tax policy. Tax schemes aimed at attracting financial and other geographically mobile activities can create harmful tax competition between States, carrying risks of distorting trade and investment and could lead to the erosion of national tax bases. We strongly urge the OECD to vigorously pursue its work in this field, aimed at establishing a multilateral approach under which countries could operate individually and collectively to limit the extent of these practices. We will follow closely the progress on work by the OECD, which is due to produce a report by 1998. We will also follow closely the OECD's continuation of its important work on transfer pricing, where we warmly endorse the significant progress that the OECD has already achieved.'

19 See Statement of Paul H. O'Neill before the Senate Committee on Governmental Affairs Permanent Subcommittee on Investigations on July 18, 2001. The change was symbolized by the replacement of the term 'competition' by 'practices', signalling that tax competition cannot be harmful. The last substantive report on preferential tax regimes was in 2004, with an Update in 2006. Among the many commentaries on the initiative, one may single out the somewhat divergent evaluations by Sharman (2006) and Avi-Yonah (2009).

20 This power was introduced in the Finance Act 2000, s. 146.

21 Under the 'qualifying intermediary' regime in the United States, paying agents can certify that the recipients are not US taxpayers. Attempts to reform the regulations have been blocked by Treasury concerns of a potential outflow of portfolio investment; the United States in particular is dependent on large foreign deposits to maintain the strength of the dollar.

of the Global Forum on Taxation, renamed the Global Forum on Transparency and Exchange of Information for Tax Purposes in 2009, with a self-standing secretariat (based at the OECD) and a budget financed by all its members. Its work focused on encouraging the negotiation of bilateral TIEAs and evaluating levels of compliance through peer review. These efforts to attain tax transparency were greatly weakened by being limited to information on request and by shelving the initial idea of a multilateral treaty. However, a more comprehensive approach was adopted within the European Union for automatic provision of information on payments to non-residents, in a Savings Directive, although limited to individual interest income.

In this changing climate, Elmer was not the only source of revelations of dubious banking practices. Tax authorities have also used unorthodox methods to obtain information, such as purchasing data of client accounts from disaffected bank employees.[22] Following up such information, the US Internal Revenue Service (IRS) in 2009 issued a 'John Doe' summons against the Swiss bank UBS, seeking information regarding a large number of its US clients suspected of evading taxes based on advice provided to them by UBS staff, for which UBS was charged with defrauding the US government. This resulted in a settlement between the IRS and UBS (which admitted the charges and paid $780 million), as well as an intergovernmental agreement (Switzerland–USA 2009) establishing a procedure under the bilateral tax treaty for examining US requests for information relating to some 4,500 accounts. This followed the revelations of systematic tax evasion through Liechtenstein banks after raids by German police acting on evidence obtained by the purchase of a data disk from a disgruntled employee (Weiner 2009).

The resulting public outrage fuelled renewed attempts to overcome the obstacles that bank secrecy poses for cooperation in tax enforcement. In 2009 the United States introduced the Foreign Account Tax Compliance Act (FATCA). This was targeted at banks, requiring them to establish rigorous checks on all clients to verify the individual recipients of interest payments. It also adopted an extraordinary scope, applying to any banking institution doing business in the United States or with US clients. To resolve jurisdictional conflicts, implementation required negotiation of intergovernmental agreements; and, not surprisingly, other countries demanded reciprocity. Thus, the cooperation efforts gradually became more extensive and increasingly multilateral.

Finally, at the 2013 G8 summit meeting, world leaders agreed to establish a new global standard of multilateral and automatic exchange of tax information, as well as transparency of beneficial ownership, confirmed by the G20 in St. Petersburg in September 2013.[23] The design and implementation of this standard was added to the

[22] Bradley Birkenfeld, a former banker with UBS, was controversially paid $104 million by the US IRS for providing information that ultimately helped it to collect more than $5 billion in unpaid taxes from banks and individuals. In contrast, Rudolf Elmer rejected offers of hush money from Baer, and received no payments for any disclosures.

[23] See 2013 Lough Erne Leaders' Communiqué: 'We commit to establish the automatic exchange of information between tax authorities as the new global standard, and will work with the Organization

work of the Global Forum on Transparency and Exchange of Information for Tax Purposes. Now more than sixty states, including Switzerland, have signed the OECD–Council of Europe Multilateral Convention on Mutual Administrative Assistance in Tax Matters.[24] Although it had taken fifteen years to establish this global transparency standard as a target, achieving it will inevitably take still further time. Time will tell whether the political will is strong enough to secure effective outcomes.

C. *A Bigger Goal: International Tax Reform*

Elmer's revelations in fact raised an issue which is more fundamental than outright tax evasion. They pointed to the ways in which the offshore system had fomented systematic avoidance of tax, especially by transnational corporations (TNCs). This results from a deep structural flaw in the international tax system: the failure to treat TNCs according to the economic reality of their activity as integrated firms (Picciotto 2013a). Instead, a principle has become gradually entrenched that they should be taxed as if they were separate enterprises in each country dealing independently with each other. This not merely allows but encourages TNCs to organize their affairs by forming entities in suitable jurisdictions to reduce their overall effective tax rate, by a variety of means. Many of these were increasingly publicized in the climate of increased concern about tax justice since 2008. It also became clear that the problem does not result solely from the immoral and sometimes illegal activities of companies: it is governments which are responsible for the rules, and should therefore ensure that they are thoroughly reformed.

This led to a new initiative by world leaders, this time through the G20 group, again requesting action through the OECD and its CFA. Responding to a request from the G20 in June 2012, the OECD-CFA launched a project on Base Erosion and Profit Shifting (BEPS), which produced an Action Plan in August 2013, approved by the G20 in September. It is extremely ambitious by the normal standards of OECD work on international tax, aiming to produce proposals by December 2015. However, these will also take some time to implement. They have also been criticized both by tax specialists and campaigners as being limited to

for Economic Cooperation and Development (OECD) to develop rapidly a multilateral model which will make it easier for Governments to find and punish tax evaders. . . . We agree to publish national Action Plans to make information on who really owns and profits from companies and trusts available to tax collection and law enforcement agencies, for example through central registries of company beneficial ownership.' https://www.gov.uk/government/uploads/system/uploads/attachment_data/file/207771/Lough_Erne_2013_G8_Leaders_Communique.pdf.

[24] However, only some two-thirds of these have ratified; also, activation of the provisions for automatic information exchange depends on supplementary agreements to establish modalities, which the OECD is tasked with expediting. This Multilateral Convention was first agreed in 1988, but had only a handful of participating states for its first 20 years: see http://www.oecd.org/tax/exchange-of-taxinformation/Status_of_convention.pdf.

patching up the existing system, when a wider reform is both necessary and possible (Sheppard 2013, Picciotto 2013b).[25]

IV. CONCLUSION

The role of an individual such as Rudolf Elmer should neither be idealized nor be overstated. Far from setting out to reform the offshore system, he found himself caught up in its tentacles. In somewhat desperately fighting to cut himself free, he landed some blows which helped to weaken it, at a time when the creature's environment was anyway becoming less supportive.

At this time of writing, Elmer's struggles with Swiss law are still to be resolved. Even more questions remain open about the future of the offshore system and the prospects for international tax reform. But perhaps tracing out both his personal odyssey and its much wider systemic context can give us a feel for the interplay of agency and structure in the dynamics of the development of legal and social institutions.

REFERENCES

Adam, Nigel. 1992. *Regulating Global Financial Markets*. London: Economist Intelligence Unit.

Antoine, Rose-Marie Belle. 1999. *Commonwealth Caribbean Law and Legal Systems*. London: Cavendish.

Avi-Yonah, Reuven. 2009. "The OECD Harmful Tax Competition Report: A Retrospective after a Decade." *Brooklyn Journal of International Law* 34(3): 783–795.

Baer v. WikiLeaks. 2008. *Bank Julius Baer & Co. Ltd and Julius Baer Bank and Trust Co. Ltd v. WikiLeaks.org, Dynadot LLC et al.* In 535 *F. Supp.* 2d 980; 2008 *U.S. Dist. LEXIS* 18809: U.S.D.C. N.Ca.

Bergin, Tom. 2013. "Special Report: How Big Tech Stays Offline on Tax." *Reuters*, July 23.

Cabral, Warren. 1995. "Bermuda." In *Comparative Law Yearbook of International Business* (Special Issue on Offshore Trusts), edited by Dennis Campbell and Susan Cotter, 23–73. London and Boston: Kluwer Law International.

Carlisle, Rodney. 1981. *Sovereignty for Sale*. Annapolis: Naval Institute Press.

Cayman Islands Monetary Authority (CIMA). 2010. "Investments Statistical Digest." Cayman Islands: CIMA.

Collins, Joseph H., Donald S. Hutchinson, and Walter D. Wekstein. 1996. *A Financial Future for Nepal*. Boston: Collins & Associates.

Dezalay, Yves. 1996. "Between the State, Law, and the Market: The Social and Professional Stakes in the Construction and Definition of a Regulatory Arena." In *International Regulatory Competition and Coordination*, edited by William Bratton, Joseph McCahery, Sol Picciotto, and Colin Scott, 59–87. Oxford: Clarendon Press.

Drucker, Jesse. 2010. "Google 2.4% Rate Shows How $60 Billion Lost to Tax Loopholes." *Bloomberg*, October 21.

[25] For detailed comments on the Action Plan proposals, see the reports of the BEPS Monitoring Group, http://bepsmonitoringgroup.wordpress.com/.

Findley, Michael, Daniel Nielson, and Jason Sharman. 2013. "Global Shell Games: Testing Money Launderers' and Terrorist Financiers' Access to Shell Companies." http://www.griffith.edu.au/business-government/centre-governance-public-policy/research-publications/?a=454625.

Gallagher, Rodney. 1990. *Report of Mr Rodney Gallagher of Coopers and Lybrand on the Survey of Offshore Finance Sectors in the Caribbean Dependent Territories*. London: House of Commons.

Hawley, James P. 1984. "Protecting Capital from Itself: US Attempts to Regulate the Eurocurrency System." *International Organization* 38(1): 131–165.

Henry, James S. 2012. "The Price of Offshore Revisited." Tax Justice Network. http://www.taxjustice.net/cms/front_content.php?idcat=148.

Hudson, A. C. 1998a. "Placing Trust, Trusting Place: On the Social Construction of Offshore Financial Centres." *Political Geography* 17(8): 915–937.

Hudson, A. C. 1998b. "Reshaping the Regulatory Landscape: Border Skirmishes around the Bahamas and Cayman Offshore Financial Centres." *Review of International Political Economy* 5(3): 534–564.

Huxley, Andrew. 2000. "Rhodes, Arakan, Grand Cayman: Three Versions of Offshore." In *Comparative Law in Global Perspective: Essays in Celebration of the Fiftieth Anniversary of the Founding of the SOAS Law Department*, edited by Ian Edge, 145–170. Ardsley, NY: Transnational Publishers.

International Labour Office (ILO). 2003. *Employment and Social Policy in Respect of Export Processing Zones (EPZs)*. Geneva: International Labour Office.

Jackson, Howell E. 1998. "The Selective Incorporation of Foreign Legal Systems to Promote Nepal as an International Financial Services Centre." In *Regulation and Deregulation – Policy and Practice in the Utilities and Financial Services Industries*, edited by Christopher McCrudden, 367–408. Oxford: Clarendon Press.

Kassoulides, George C. 1993. *Port State Control and Jurisdiction: The Evolution of the Port State Regime*. Dordrecht: Nijhoff.

McGauran, Katrin. 2013. "Should the Netherlands Sign Double Tax Treaties with Developing Countries?" Amsterdam: SOMO.

Murphy, Dale D. 2004. *The Structure of Regulatory Competition: Corporations and Public Policies in a Global Economy*. Oxford: Oxford University Press.

Naess, Erling D. 1972. *The Great Panlibhon Controversy: The Fight over the Flags of Shipping*. London: Gower Press.

Palan, Ronen. 2002. "Tax Havens and the Commercialization of State Sovereignty." *International Organization* 56(1): 151–176.

Palan, Ronen. 2003. *The Offshore World: Sovereign Markets, Virtual Places, and Nomad Millionaires*. Ithaca and London: Cornell University Press.

Picciotto, Sol. 1992. *International Business Taxation, Law in Context*. London: Weidenfeld & Nicolson. Electronic version available at http://taxjustice.blogspot.be/2013/06/international-business-taxation.html.

Picciotto, Sol. 2011. *Regulating Global Corporate Capitalism*. Cambridge: Cambridge University Press.

Picciotto, Sol. 2013a. "Can the OECD Mend the International Tax System?" *Tax Notes International* 71(12): 1105–1115.

Picciotto, Sol. 2013b. "Is the International Tax System Fit for Purpose, Especially for Developing Countries?" ICTD Working Paper 13.

Prebble, J. 1998. "Should Tax Legislation Be Written from a Principles and Purpose Point of View or a Precise and Detailed Point of View?" *British Tax Review* 2: 112–123.

Rawlings, Gregory. 2004. "Laws, Liquidity and Eurobonds: The Making of the Vanuatu Tax Haven." *Journal of Pacific History* 39(3): 325–341.
Roberts, Susan M. 1995. "Small Place, Big Money: The Cayman Islands and the International Financial System." *Economic Geography* 71(3): 237–256.
Sandell, John. 2012. "The Double Irish and the Dutch Sandwich: How Some U.S. Companies Are Flummoxing the Tax Code." *Tax Notes International* 67(9): 867–878.
Sharman, Jason C. 2006. *Havens in a Storm: The Struggle for Global Tax Regulation*. Ithaca: Cornell University Press.
Sharman, Jason C. 2010. "Shopping for Anonymous Shell Companies: An Audit Study of Anonymity and Crime in the International Financial System." *Journal of Economic Perspectives* 24(4): 127–140.
Sheppard, Lee A. 2013. "Will U.S. Hypocrisy on Information Sharing Continue?" *Worldwide Tax Daily*, January 22.
Spencer, David. 2007. "International Tax Evasion." *Journal of International Taxation* (April & May): 3–34, 44–52.
Sullivan, Martin A., and Lee A. Sheppard. 2008. "Offshore Explorations: Caribbean Hedge Funds." *Tax Notes*, January 7 and 14.
Switzerland–USA. 2009. "Agreement between the Swiss Confederation and the USA on the Request from the Internal Revenue Service for Information Regarding UBS AG, a Corporation Established under the Law of the Swiss Confederation." www.ejpd.admin.ch/.
UK Inland Revenue. 1967–1977. *Review of Tax Havens* 2. Public Records Office File IR40/16744. London.
United Nations Security Council. 2001. *Report of the Panel of Experts Pursuant to Security Council Resolution* 1343 (2001), paragraph 19, concerning Liberia. New York.
US Government Accountability Office (GAO). 2006. "Company Formations: Minimal Ownership Information Is Collected and Available." Washington, DC: Government Accountability Office.
US Senate. 2006. "Tax Haven Abuses: The Enablers, the Tools and Secrecy." Washington, DC: Permanent Subcommittee on Investigations of the Committee on Homeland and Security Affairs.
Weiner, Joann M. 2009. "Is Switzerland a Tax Haven?" *Tax Notes International* 54 (May 4): 356–360.

10

The Changing Roles of Lawyers in China: State Bureaucrats, Market Brokers, and Political Activists

Sida Liu

The contemporary Chinese legal profession has been built on the ruins of the Cultural Revolution (1966–1976). When the economic reform began in the late 1970s, the traditional social structure of the country had been bulldozed, and most state and market institutions had to be rebuilt from scratch. Reflections on the social and political turmoil during the Cultural Revolution made the Chinese leadership reconsider the importance of law and legal institutions in maintaining social order and promoting economic development. This generated the most comprehensive state-led legal reform in Chinese history, which has lasted until the present day.

The three decades of rapid reform have changed the landscape of the Chinese legal system in fundamental ways. In legislation, more than 10,000 laws, regulations, ministerial regulations, judicial interpretations, and local regulations have been promulgated and many revised more than once in less than thirty years (Cai 1999; Zhu 2007; Liu and Halliday 2009). In the judicial system, army veterans have been gradually replaced by law graduates, while Chinese courts and procuracies have become complex organizations with an internal bureaucratic structure (Woo 1991, 1999; Zhang 2003; Liu 2006a; Liebman 2007; He 2012). In legal education, more than 600 law schools have been reestablished or newly inaugurated (Zhu 2007: 520), and the knowledge basis of Chinese legal research and education has become Westernized and increasingly technical (Liu 2011b). In appearance, we seem to have witnessed a classic Weberian rationalization of law in the Middle Kingdom (Weber 1978).

Yet the legal system never operates in a vacuum – it always evolves through interactions with its market and political environments. As Chinese law develops into a complex and self-sustaining formal system (Luhmann 2004), its distance from ordinary social life is also substantially increased. The massive appropriation of foreign legal codes and institutions has resulted in the decoupling of formal law from law in action in almost every aspect of the Chinese legal system. Most important, the construction of the legal system is accompanied by rapid structural changes in both the Chinese state and the market economy it seeks to develop. This peculiar juxtaposition of law, state, and market has produced a highly fragmented market for Chinese lawyers in the reform period.

Understanding the legal services market in today's China is like wandering in a big rain forest. As you walk into the jungle, you find a bewildering array of occupational species adhering to different licensing requirements but competing for similar work. In ordinary litigation, lawyers (*lüshi*) face strong competition from a parallel occupation called "basic-level legal workers" (*jiceng falü gongzuozhe*), from many types of legal advisory agencies (*falü zixun jigou*), and from a large number of unauthorized "black lawyers" (*hei lüshi*) and "barefoot lawyers" (*chijiao lüshi*) (Alford 1995; Fu 2006; Wang 2006; Ying 2007; Liu 2011a). In the corporate law market, foreign lawyers, enterprise legal advisors (*qiye falü guwen*), patent agents, and trademark agents are all separately licensed from Chinese lawyers, and they often compete with lawyers in business transactions (Liu 2006b, 2008, 2012; Li and Liu 2012). Even in criminal defense, where lawyers have a monopoly according to the law, the unfriendly attitudes and practices of the judiciary and law enforcement agencies make lawyers' work difficult and sometimes dangerous (Yu 2002; Lu and Miethe 2002; Michelson 2006, 2007; Liu and Halliday 2011).

Chinese lawyers' weak market position is accompanied by an even weaker political position. The Ministry of Justice (MOJ), the official state agency for regulating lawyers, faces strong and persistent pressures from several other administrative agencies, often more powerful than itself, in professional regulation (Liu 2011a, 2012). Meanwhile, it also struggles to cooperate with the judiciary and law enforcement agencies in protecting lawyers' professional interests (Liu and Halliday 2011). Furthermore, unlike lawyers in many other countries who play important roles in national and local politics (Halliday 1987; Halliday and Karpik 1997; Dezalay and Garth 2002, 2010), Chinese lawyers have extremely limited capacities for political participation, especially after the privatization of the legal profession and its separation from the state in the 1990s (Michelson 2007; Michelson and Liu 2010).

This chapter traces the changing roles of Chinese lawyers in both the legal services market and the state by analyzing three periods of China's legal reform: (1) the 1980s: when lawyers and other legal service providers worked in state-administered institutions and mainly served in the role of *state bureaucrats*; (2) the 1990s–2000s: when lawyers were gradually privatized from the state and adapted to their new role as *market brokers* between clients and the state; (3) the mid-2000s to the present: when lawyers were entrenched in a fragmented market for legal services but began to mobilize collectively and to challenge the state as *political activists*. These three changing roles of Chinese lawyers are not exclusive or mutually replaceable, but together they characterize the emergence and transformation of a modernizing legal profession between market and state.

I. LAWYERS AS STATE BUREAUCRATS: THE 1980S

Lawyers as a profession were formally revived in China in 1980. Two significant events happened in that year. On August 26, the Standing Committee of the National People's Congress promulgated the Interim Regulation on Lawyers, which reestablished the profession of lawyers, following a twenty-three-year vacuum, after lawyers were purged during the Anti-Rightist Campaign in 1957. This "interim" regulation remained in place for fifteen years from 1982, until China's first Lawyers Law came into effect in 1997. The Regulation defined the nature of lawyers as "legal workers of the state" (Article 1) and used legal advisory divisions (*falü guwenchu*) as the primary work institution for lawyers' practice (Article 13). The legal advisory division was a public service unit (*shiye danwei*) affiliated with different levels of the justice bureau and other relevant state agencies, and its main task was to provide legal services to state agencies and enterprises at the same administrative level, as well as to individuals affiliated with these work units.

A more notable lawyer-related event in 1980 was the trial of the major criminals of the Cultural Revolution, including Lin Biao's associates and the Gang of Four (Ma 2007). The trial opened on November 20, 1980, and lasted for more than two months. In the trial process, ten lawyers appointed by the Chinese government appeared in the special tribunal as the defense for those major criminals. The significance of this trial to the revival of the Chinese legal profession cannot be exaggerated. It had an important symbolic meaning – namely, to show the nation and the world that even the despicable criminals most responsible for the Cultural Revolution had the right to counsel under China's new legal procedures. However, as this trial was the first time that Chinese lawyers appeared on television in front of millions of Chinese viewers and they were defending major criminals of the Cultural Revolution, it might have aggravated the negative public image of lawyers (Michelson 2003, 16). It was in the unique political moment of this "special defense" (Ma 2007) that the Chinese legal profession was revived.

Not surprisingly, the first question after the revival was where lawyers would come from. As most old-generation lawyers experienced traumatic persecutions during the Anti-Rightist Campaign in the late 1950s and during the Cultural Revolution, few of them were willing to return to the profession. Legal education in China had also stagnated during the Cultural Revolution, with only two remaining departments of law, at Peking University and Jilin University. Although the five Institutes of Political Science and Law (*zhengfa xueyuan*) and a number of major law departments were soon reestablished after the higher education system had been resumed in 1978, the total number of legal professionals that these schools produced in the early reform period remained small, and most law graduates became judges and procurators instead of lawyers. By 1987, therefore, the total number of Chinese lawyers was still small, a mere 27,280 (*China Law Yearbook* 1988) in a country with a population of more than one billion.

In July 1983, Shekou District Law Firm was founded in Shenzhen. It became the first legal service agency with the title "law firm" (*lüshi shiwusuo*) following China's legal reform. A year later, in August 1984, the MOJ made a decision at its national work conference to change the official title of "legal advisory division" to "law firm" across the country. Meanwhile, the national bar examination began to be held biannually from 1986, and from 1993 it was held every year until it was replaced in 2001 by the unified judicial examination applying to lawyers, judges, and procurators. Nonetheless, until the late 1980s all Chinese law firms remained state-owned, usually numbered in their titles (e.g., "Beijing No. 3 Law Firm"), and the daily work of most lawyers focused on criminal defense, divorce, and inheritance, plus limited legal counsel work for state-owned and collective enterprises.

As the economic reform made progress in the mid-1980s, particularly after the "law dissemination" (*pu fa*) campaigns began in 1986 (Gallagher 2006), demand for legal services in Chinese society increased rapidly. Consequently, many new areas of work emerged in the growing legal services market, but there were not enough lawyers to occupy them. It was precisely in these vacant areas that alternative legal professions were created. To accommodate the rising demands for legal services, starting in the mid-1980s several state ministries began to set up law-related professional groups. Like lawyers, most of these groups were incorporated into the state apparatus in their early years.

In urban streets and rural townships, a grassroots profession affiliated with local justice agencies (*sifa suo*) and providing legal services to local communities gradually emerged. In 1987, the MOJ promulgated a regulation formalizing this profession with the name "township legal workers" (*xiangzhen falü gongzuozhe*). The number of township legal workers rapidly increased to 81,520 in 1988, more than twice the number of lawyers (31,410) in that year (*China Law Yearbook* 1989). Despite their lower educational and licensing requirements (i.e., high school diploma and certain legal knowledge), township legal workers occupied large proportions of the legal services market in both urban and rural China. Meanwhile, legal advisory companies (*falü zixun gongsi*) also emerged in urban areas in the late 1980s under the wing of the State Administration of Industry and Commerce. These agencies mainly specialized in legal consulting, but the scope of their services could be as wide as drafting legal documents, court representation, and enforcing judicial decisions.

In the corporate sector, the State Economic Commission (SEC) started in the early 1980s to train legal experts in state-owned enterprises, mainly following the Soviet model. This model distinguished "enterprise legal work" from "social legal work" and set up "enterprise legal advisors" (*qiye falü guwen*) as a separate legal profession from lawyers, with its own licensing and official status within the enterprise (Liu 2012). Still, due to the general shortage in legal personnel, few state-owned enterprises in China were able to establish their own internal legal advisory offices until the mid-1980s. When they needed legal services, enterprises usually sought help from lawyers working in legal advisory divisions in the same city or county.

At the high end of the corporate sector, before the 1990s no Chinese law firm could independently handle foreign-related business transactions such as foreign direct investments (FDIs) or mergers and acquisitions (M&As). However, as early as 1978–1979, a few American law firms had begun to represent globalizing American companies in foreign investment negotiations with Chinese enterprises. Not surprisingly, none of the foreign law firms entering China was allowed to establish an office, and the number of foreign lawyers retained by Chinese government agencies or work units was limited. Nevertheless, because of the nonexistence of local corporate lawyers and the urgency of attracting foreign investment, a small number of foreign lawyers played an important role in China's corporate transactions in the 1980s (Liu 2008; Li and Liu 2012).

Finally, in the area of intellectual property (IP), the State Council appointed the State Science and Technology Commission as early as 1978, to develop a patent system to accommodate the demands for scientific and technological learning and innovation. By the mid-1980s, both patent and trademark regimes had been formally established. Like the legal system, the original systems of patent and trademark also followed the Soviet model; that is, all patent and trademark agencies were affiliated with patent and trademark bureaus and other relevant administrative agencies. The two regimes were developed by two separate state agencies – namely, the China Patent Bureau and the State Administration of Industry and Commerce (Mertha 2005). The division of labor between these agencies was relatively clear in the 1980s, and the number of patent and trademark agents remained small.

The decade of the 1980s, therefore, was a time when lawyers and other legal service providers were all created inside the Chinese state and dominated by the socialist bureaucratic system. They were qualitatively different from the self-regulating professions in Anglo-American countries, because all of them were also state bureaucrats with administrative ranks. Most law practitioners in this period lacked professional training because they were either army veterans or transferred cadres, with a limited number of graduates from newly revived law departments (Liu 2006a). It was not until the 1990s that these state bureaucrats began their march into the market.

II. LAWYERS AS MARKET BROKERS: THE 1990S–2000S

In the 1990s, Chinese lawyers experienced a massive, rapid process of privatization. This decade-long process began with the creation of "cooperative law firms" (*hezuo suo*) in 1988 and culminated in the "unhooking and restructuring" (*tuogou gaizhi*) campaign around 2000–2001, when law firms and other professional service providers were mandatorily detached from their state regulatory agencies (Michelson 2003). The initial pressure for the privatization of Chinese law firms came mainly from abroad. With the increase in foreign trade and international cooperation in the 1980s, state-owned law firms became unfit to meet the demands of China's economic reform. Most important, few foreign investors would trust a Chinese law firm directly administered by the government (Liu 2006b, 2008). Accordingly, the primary objective of law firms' privatization was to gain global legitimacy – that is, to signal to foreign governments and investors that China has a modern legal profession that is relatively autonomous from the Party-state. Underneath this symbolic meaning, however, connections between law practitioners and state officials have persisted and been transformed into a complex relationship, which I have referred to in earlier work as "symbiotic exchange" (Liu 2011a).

The privatization of Chinese law firms took two steps. In 1988–1989, a transitional organizational form called "cooperative law firms" was created in a few major cities such as Beijing and Shenzhen. Then, from the mid-1990s, these cooperative firms and many state-owned law firms were gradually reorganized into partnerships. A large number of new partnership law firms were also founded in this period. As the profession of lawyers was privatized from the state in the 1990s, many new types of corporate legal work, such as finance and securities, real estate, FDIs, M&As, commercial arbitration, and IP work, emerged. Meanwhile, labor, contracts, consumer rights, and administrative litigation were all added to the list of lawyers' litigation work. By the turn of the millennium, the majority of law firms in China had become partnership law firms, most of which were generalists in the orientation of their practice (Michelson 2003).

The privatization of Chinese law firms coincided with the entrance of foreign law firms into China. In 1992, the MOJ made the Interim Regulation on the Establishment of Foreign Law Offices in China, which permitted foreign law firms to set up offices in mainland China. Because Chinese corporate law firms were still at the embryonic stage of development, the MOJ Interim Regulation adopted a highly restrictive rule on the jurisdictional boundary of foreign law offices; that is, they were forbidden to "represent Chinese legal affairs," to "interpret Chinese law," or to "employ Chinese lawyers" (Article 16). In practice, however, foreign law offices often drafted legal opinions by themselves and then let their Chinese collaborators sign the documents for a small fee. In other words, Chinese law firms were used as rubber stamps for their foreign collaborators, and a gray area of corporate legal practice was constituted at the boundary of global–local interaction (Liu 2008).

By the late 1990s, the nature of the global–local collaboration had become more substantive. A few major local corporate law firms recruited many new partners with training and work experience abroad or in foreign law offices. These new partners were generally fluent in English and had relevant experiences in complex corporate transactions, which significantly increased the expertise of local firms in FDI and M&A projects. In the meantime, some foreign law offices in China also began to outsource the low-end work, such as due diligence, to local firms to reduce cost, minimize risks, and satisfy their clients. A relatively stable symbiotic relationship was formed between them (Liu 2008; Li and Liu 2012).

But the privatization of the Chinese legal profession had far wider and deeper consequences than those that impacted the corporate sector. It changed the dynamics of interaction in the entire legal services market. The most notable change was the rapid increase in the total number of lawyers. In 2000, the total number of lawyers in China reached 117,260, approaching the total number of township legal workers (121,904) in the same year (*China Law Yearbook* 2001). The educational background of lawyers was also improved; although only a junior college degree was required to sit for the bar examination and most lawyers had prior careers before entry into practice, the vast majority of them at least received a law degree of some kind (Michelson 2003, 149–188). A more significant consequence was that lawyers as a group lost their status as state bureaucrats and thus most lawyers could no longer rely on the state for business. Instead, they had to find work from every corner of Chinese society to accommodate their basic survival needs. Consequently, these developments greatly intensified the market competition between lawyers and other legal service providers, particularly township legal workers.

The market competition between lawyers and township legal workers fully demonstrates the transition of the Chinese legal professionals from state bureaucrats to market brokers in the process of privatization. Despite lawyers' advantages in terms of education and social status, township legal workers were often more successful in the market. In fact, the decade of the 1990s was a golden age for the profession of township legal workers. In most provinces across the country, their number far exceeded the number of lawyers. And because township legal service firms were generally smaller than law firms, the difference in the number of firms was even more salient. In 1989, there were 30,920 legal service firms in comparison to 3,653 law firms (*China Law Yearbook* 1990). In 2000, there were 34,219 legal service firms in comparison to 9,541 law firms (*China Law Yearbook* 2001). By 2006, after the nationwide shrinkage of basic-level legal services, there were still 21,835 legal service firms in comparison to 13,096 law firms (*China Law Yearbook* 2007).

To a large extent, the proliferation of township legal service firms was due to the active support of local justice bureaus. In this period, the justice bureaus created a variety of symbolic and organizational forms for township legal service firms that closely resembled law firms in order to strengthen the market position of township legal workers (see Liu 2011a for details). The primary reason for justice bureaus' strong support for township legal service firms was the emergence of a symbiotic exchange relationship between them in the 1990s. While law firms were gradually privatized into partnerships, township legal service firms were only partially privatized. Most firms in urban streets and rural townships remained "one team, two titles" (*yitao renma, liangkuai paizi*) with the grassroots justice agency and the firm director remaining a staff member in that agency. Other practitioners in the firm often had no administrative position, but many of them were transferred personnel from either the local justice bureaus or the local judicial agencies. These former state officials were brokers (Burt 1992, 2005) between the state and the legal services market – they were able to use the formal and informal connections with different levels of courts, procuracies, police bureaus, and other state agencies to attract clients and solve problems in legal practice. Besides exchange of personnel with local justice agencies, township legal service firms also paid an annual "management fee" (*guanli fei*) to justice bureaus, used their revenue to support the operation of local justice agencies, and assisted justice agencies in their daily work. In return, justice bureaus often provided office space for and referred cases to township legal service firms.

The symbiotic exchange of power, resources, and personnel between justice bureaus and township legal service firms significantly influenced the market competition between lawyers and township legal workers. According to Michelson's (2003, 163) survey in 2000, only about a quarter of Chinese lawyers had previous work experience in government bureaus or judicial agencies, and the privatization of law firms sharply reduced the direct personnel exchange between law firms and justice bureaus. As a result, despite their advantages in education and legal training, lawyers often felt disadvantaged when competing with township legal workers in the market. In public discourse, lawyers often actively accused township legal workers of being unqualified or unethical practitioners and emphasized their own advantages in education, training, and legitimacy. But it was to no avail; in the workplace they had no effective means to counterbalance the market brokerage by township legal workers. Many township legal service workers even printed the word "lawyer" on their name cards, wore the lawyer's gown in court, or asked some familiar judges to address them as lawyers in court proceedings (Liu 2011a).

Symbiotic exchange between legal practitioners and state officials was not the sole privilege of township legal workers, but is also observed in the practice of many lawyers and in other sectors of the Chinese legal services market. Michelson's 2000 survey of Chinese lawyers shows that "political embeddedness," or the "diverse portfolio of direct and indirect, individual and organizational ties to the state" on which lawyers rely in their everyday work (Michelson 2007, 353), is the most effective means for reducing lawyers' professional difficulties in litigation. Similar dynamics were also found in the Chinese corporate law market. The MOJ's ambiguous regulatory policies on foreign and local law firms created a gray area of corporate law practice. Both types of law firms actively develop and utilize symbiotic exchange with the MOJ and other central state agencies in order to gain market advantages (Liu 2008).

Therefore, as the state continued to hold the most vital resources for China's socialist market economy, the privatization of various legal service providers did not "unhook" them from the state, but transformed them into brokers between the strong state and the nascent market economy. Another good example of this transformation is IP work. At roughly the same time when partnership law firms were permitted in the mid-1990s, market-oriented patent and trademark agencies also started to emerge in major Chinese cities. The first sixteen patent agencies were all certified by the China Patent Bureau and staffed with former patent bureau employees (Mertha 2005). Similarly to township legal service firms, these patent agencies also shared their revenues with local patent bureaus. Because of their monopoly over the lucrative patent services market, in the late 1990s the combined revenues of the four most profitable patent agencies were comparable to the total billings of all law firms in Beijing (Liu 2008). Nevertheless, as the main regulatory agency for legal services, the MOJ was completely excluded from the licensing and regulation of patent and trademark agents. The China Patent Bureau and the State Administration of Industry and Commerce firmly held their turfs in the regulatory structure and enjoyed benefits from the symbiotic exchange with patent and trademark agencies.

The exclusion of the MOJ from the professional regulatory regime was also observed in enterprise legal services, which had been a more contested area than IP work since the late 1980s. From 1987 to 1992, several central ministries promulgated regulations on enterprise legal advisors in their own industries (Liu 2012, 553–554). Officially, however, the regulatory power for this profession belonged to the State Economic Restructuring Commission, and the MOJ played only a complementary role. In 1994, the State Council authorized the newly established State Economic and Trade Commission (SETC), a powerful state agency that controlled the pace of China's market reform in the late 1990s, to regulate state-owned enterprises and their legal advisors. In 1997, the SETC promulgated the Enterprise Legal Advisors Regulatory Method, which introduced formal licensing, examination, and registration to this rapidly developing profession. By 2001, the total number of legal staff in state-owned enterprises was approximately 90,000, of which more than 23,000 were licensed enterprise legal advisors (Zhang 2001).

In 2001, the path of entry into the Chinese bar experienced a major reform. Administered since 1986, the bar examination was replaced by the national judicial examination as the uniform qualification standard for lawyers, judges, and procurators. The educational requirement for taking the unified judicial examination was raised from junior college to a college degree, though legal training was still not required. This new examination system has facilitated the collegiality and mobility among the three professions, which, in the long run, might reduce lawyers' difficulties and risks in law practice, especially in criminal defense work (Michelson 2006, 2007; Liu and Halliday 2011). It is also an effective way to produce occupational closure (Larson 1977; Abel 1988, 1989) – that is, consolidating lawyers' professional licensing, and constraining the development of alternative legal service providers.

Along with the MOJ's leadership change, its attitude and policies toward township legal service began to change dramatically. In 2000, the MOJ made two regulations and changed the official name of township legal workers to "basic-level legal service workers" (*jiceng falü fuwu gongzuozhe*), a long and awkward name. In a national work conference held in Shanghai in August 2002, the MOJ proposed to gradually move basic-level legal service firms in large and medium-size cities out of litigation work in three to five years. Although this radical policy was not fully implemented, it led to a major reorganization of the profession of basic-level legal workers. All basic-level legal service firms were required to be affiliated with the streets or townships in which they were located and to use the names of the streets or townships as their firm names. Furthermore, basic-level legal service firms were permitted to represent cases only within the locality, and they were expected to be unhooked from the local justice agencies as state-owned law firms had been unhooked a few years before (Michelson 2003; Liu 2011a). These regulatory measures had a significant negative impact on the development of basic-level legal service. From 2000 to 2006, the total number of basic-level legal workers declined from 121,904 (*China Law Yearbook* 2001) to less than 80,000, a sharp reduction of more than one-third.

The privatization of the profession of basic-level legal workers, as well as the earlier privatization of the profession of lawyers, weakened the formal regulatory relationship between these legal professions and justice bureaus, but also increased the importance of symbiotic exchange between them. To a large extent, personal networks replaced institutional connections to become the structural basis for the profession–state exchange (Liu 2011a). Maintaining a personal relationship with judges and other state officials often requires long-term investments of money, resources, trust, and emotional attachment rather than one-time monetary transactions. In ordinary litigation, most law practitioners, including lawyers, use creative methods to nurture their relationships with judges, such as playing "business mahjongg" (*yewu majiang*) and intentionally losing money to judges, sending birthday cakes to the children of judges, or even renting apartments in the court's residential community and becoming neighbors of judges (Liu 2011a). The goal of these activities is not to gain advantage in a specific case, but to establish trust and reciprocity with judges in order to get case referrals and favored judicial decisions in their general practices.

Symbiotic exchange and personal networks are equally important in the corporate sector, though the state agencies and officials involved in the exchange are not judges or justice bureau officials, but officials in more powerful central state agencies such as the Ministry of Commerce (MOFCOM) or the State Development and Reform Commission (SDRC). After China joined the World Trade Organization (WTO) in 2001, more than a hundred new foreign law offices were established in Beijing and Shanghai, which significantly intensified the competition in the corporate law market. While elite Chinese corporate law firms grew into megafirms with hundreds or even thousands of lawyers, foreign law offices also localized by employing Chinese lawyers and developing localized expertise on practicing Chinese law (Liu 2008). Because both foreign and local corporate law firms had strong and frequent exchanges with powerful central state agencies such as the MOFCOM or the SDRC, the MOJ kept the blurred boundary between them on purpose to leave enough flexibility for adapting to changes in the market environment and in the policies of other ministries. Although in theory foreign law offices in

China are still forbidden to handle "Chinese legal affairs" in their work, the MOJ has rarely taken any substantive actions against the aggressive market behavior of some foreign law firms.

Overall, since the privatization of law firms in the 1990s, Chinese lawyers have been practicing in a highly fragmented legal services market. As this market grew more complex, exchanges of power, resources, and personnel between legal professions and state agencies also became stronger and led to the formation of symbiotic relations in all sectors of the market. This new pattern of symbiotic exchange is formed and maintained by the similar educational and career backgrounds and complementary power and resources of law practitioners and state officials, at both individual and institutional levels. While the state channeled a large amount of resources and personnel to the legal professions as part of its downsizing efforts, the rapid growth of the legal services market also economically and politically enriched the state agencies through their rent seeking and protection of professional monopoly (Liu 2011a). As a result, Chinese lawyers and other legal service providers have been transformed from state bureaucrats to market brokers – structurally separated from the state but closely connected to it in their law practices.

III. LAWYERS AS POLITICAL ACTIVISTS: THE MID-2000S TO THE PRESENT

Across the world, lawyers always exist between market and politics. No legal profession can merely perform its economic functions without the pursuit of political ideals, even in countries where lawyers have limited professional autonomy (Halliday and Karpik 1997; Halliday, Karpik, and Feeley 2007, 2012; Dezalay and Garth 2002, 2010). In the short history of the contemporary Chinese legal profession, however, lawyers' political mobilization has until recently been rarely observed. Regardless of their roles as state bureaucrats or market brokers in different periods, Chinese lawyers have been tightly regulated by the MOJ and other state agencies, and, consequently, the profession has a very low capacity for collective action outside the state apparatus.

Nevertheless, with the total number of lawyers reaching 232,384 by the end of 2012 (ACLA 2013), as well as the rise of the Internet and new social media in recent years, we have witnessed Chinese lawyers' political mobilization in certain legal cases and political causes. Based on the core issues involved, these collective activities can be categorized into four types: (1) collective action against bar associations and justice bureaus concerning professional self-regulation; (2) collective action against the judicial and law enforcement agencies concerning judicial justice and independence; (3) collective action concerning nonprofessional causes, such as women's rights, labor rights, and environmental protection; and (4) collective action concerning politically sensitive human rights cases.

Bar associations became a prime target for lawyers' political mobilization for two reasons. First, bar associations in China are not self-regulated professional associations, but semi-administrative work units closely controlled by the justice bureaus. The main function of the work units in practice is not only to provide services to lawyers, but also to act as a proxy of justice bureaus for rent seeking from the legal profession and repressing politically active lawyers. Since the 1990s, every Chinese lawyer must pay an annual fee to renew his or her practice license, usually ranging from several hundred to a few thousand yuan, depending on the locations of practice. This fee used to be collected directly by the local justice bureau, but after the promulgation of the Administrative License Law in 2003 it was changed into the membership fee of the local bar association. A large proportion of this fund was informally converted to cover the administrative expenses of the local justice bureau. In cities with a large number of lawyers, such as Beijing, Shanghai, and Shenzhen, the total amount of membership fees for the bar associations has reached tens of million yuan annually (Liu 2013).

As the amount of membership fees accumulated, bar associations in major Chinese cities have begun to make innovative uses of them. A controversial practice that emerged in the mid-2000s was to use the fees to purchase office space for the bar association staff, which generated the first wave of collective action in the Chinese legal profession. As in China's economic reform, Shenzhen became the avant-garde for this movement. In 2004, more than sixty Shenzhen lawyers filed an "impeachment" of the president of Shenzhen Lawyers Association on the ground that the bar association purchased a floor of office space in a luxurious downtown office building without the approval of its lawyer members. At the time, the Shenzhen Lawyers Association had only fourteen staff members, but the office space was 1,600 square meters and cost more than 30 million yuan. Although the impeachment turned out to be unsuccessful, it drew great media attention and the president resigned within a year in the face of public pressure.

In 2008, a similar but even more political incident occurred in Beijing. On August 26, thirty-five lawyers wrote an open letter to the Beijing Lawyers Association and circulated it on the Internet. In the letter, the lawyers criticized the exorbitant amount of membership fees that the bar association accumulated over the years and called for direct voting in the incoming election of bar association leaders. On September 5, the Beijing Lawyers Association responded to this letter with a harsh announcement, accusing the thirty-five lawyers of "intending to break away from the regulation of the justice bureau and the bar association, to deny the current lawyer regulatory system, judicial system, and political system" (Zhou 2008). The lawyers were not intimidated by this announcement and continued to spread their claims to the media and other lawyer colleagues over the next several months. Eventually, several leaders of this movement were disbarred or forced to leave their firms, but the Beijing Lawyers Association also reduced the amount of its annual membership fees from 2,500 yuan to 2,000 yuan in 2010. Although the results of both the Shenzhen and Beijing movements did not meet the expectations of the lawyers involved, they still led to some positive effects in the struggle for professional self-regulation.

The second wave of Chinese lawyers' collective action was a response to the populist judicial policies and widespread procedural problems in Chinese courts and law enforcement agencies. Since the leadership change of the Supreme People's Court in 2008, talk of a "turn against law" (Minzner 2011) had become a popular discourse both in China's legal community and among foreign observers. Slogans such as "judiciary for the people" (*sifa weimin*) and "proactive judiciary" (*nengdong sifa*) suggested a notable change in judicial ideology, which embodies the populism of the socialist period that dates back to the judicial practice in Communist areas in the 1940s. This populist approach clashed with orientations toward legal professionalism increasingly displayed by Chinese lawyers and legal scholars, which led to several notable cases of political mobilization.

A milestone in this recent wave of collective action against the judicial and law enforcement agencies was the Li Zhuang case in 2009–2011, in which a criminal defense lawyer from Beijing was charged with perjury twice in the city of Chongqing under the rule of Bo Xilai, a populist Chinese politician who initiated a large-scale campaign against organized crime as part of his striving for a top leadership position but who eventually fell due to corruption charges. During the dramatic unfolding of this high-profile case, a number of elite lawyers from all over China mobilized voluntarily to defend Li Zhuang, and thousands of ordinary law practitioners closely followed the legal process and showed their support on the Internet (see Liu, Liang, and Halliday 2014 for details). To many lawyers involved, the Li Zhuang case was not only about rescuing an individual lawyer, but collective defense for the basic procedural rights of the entire Chinese legal profession against socialist populist justice.

The Li Zhuang case represents a new pattern of professional mobilization through social media, particularly the Twitter-like micro-blogs. In several more recent cases, this new pattern has become an effective means for lawyers to gain public attention and expose the judicial agencies' procedural problems (Liu 2013). These lawyers communicate with one another using the micro-blogs and then form "lawyer groups" (*lüshi tuan*) across China to handle specific cases. When procedural or substantive injustices occur in court, members of these "lawyer groups" were not only able to collectively challenge them in court, but also able to use the media and the Internet to expose them in the public domain and generate greater social impact. In fact, since the rise of the bulletin board system (BBS) in China in the early 2000s, lawyers all over China have used the Internet to criticize and fight against problems in judicial practice and have even formed some virtual cross-regional professional communities (Halliday and Liu 2007). The rise of "lawyer groups" suggests that Chinese lawyers' collective action against state power has shifted from virtual and abstract Internet forums to real and specific judicial practice. The future development of this new type of mobilization depends on both the collegiality among members of these nascent groups and the tolerance of the state toward them.

In addition to professional and political causes, the scope of Chinese lawyers' collective action also includes public interest litigation, which resembles "cause lawyering" in the United States and other countries (Sarat and Scheingold 1998, 2001). The causes of public interest litigation in China vary from railway fares to highway tolls, from gender and educational inequality to consumer rights (Xu 2008). Although the topics of some of those cases seem trivial, all of them are concerned with the basic legal rights of citizens. Compared to criminal defense and other politically sensitive cases, public interest litigation has lower risks, higher chances of being heard in court, and sometimes more exposure in the mainstream Chinese media. Accordingly, it has generated interest among many lawyers and other legal service providers. Even some "amateurs of law" who have no professional qualification have joined the practice of public interest litigation using the "citizen representation" (*gongmin daili*) system in Chinese law. These practitioners of public interest litigation do not challenge China's political system in fundamental ways, but they seek to take advantage of the loopholes in the state bureaucracy to push for social reforms incrementally.

Finally, a small number of human rights lawyers have emerged over the past decade to take on the most controversial and even dangerous cases across China, such as defending believers of Falun Gong, tortured prisoners, or parents of poisoned children (Pils 2005; Fu and Cullen 2008, 2011). These lawyers are located principally in Beijing, but they practice throughout the country. Their names are rarely known to the Chinese public, but often appear in the international media. They take great risks and live with the consequences in fraught circumstances where they can lose their livelihoods and practices, and periodically suffer from surveillance, detention, torture, and imprisonment. As Fu and Cullen (2008, 2011) argue, Chinese human rights lawyers are differentiated into three categories (i.e., moderate, critical, and radical) and constitute a pyramid in which a radicalizing process often occurs and defines their motivation and behavior. They persist in their unique style of lawyering not only because their political and sometimes religious beliefs inspire them to sacrifice for a reformed legal and political system in China, but also because they obtain vital and sustaining support from social networks inside and outside China.

In sum, although Chinese lawyers continue to practice in a highly fragmented market for legal services and many still struggle to make ends meet, in the past decade an increasing number of lawyers have mobilized, in cyberspace and in real cases, to challenge state power and fight for professional autonomy, legal proceduralism, human rights, and other public interest causes. These recent developments might signal the "birth of a liberal moment" (Halliday and Liu 2007) in the short history of the Chinese legal profession, but its future prospects depend much more on the reforms in the judicial system and broader political reform in China. Given the unfavorable structural position of lawyers in China's legal and political system, it would be unrealistic to expect lawyers to realize their political ideals by acting alone.

IV. CONCLUSION

Since the Chinese legal profession was revived in 1980, it has experienced rapid, fundamental changes. In this process, the primary role of lawyers in Chinese society has been transformed from state bureaucrats to market brokers, with a symbiotic exchange relationship forming between law practitioners and state officials. In recent years, a new political role has emerged with some progressive lawyers mobilizing individually or collectively to challenge state power. Although the Chinese state has overwhelmingly emphasized lawyers' market function and marginalized their political function through its laws and regulatory policies, in practice the pursuit of basic legal rights and professionalism has become increasingly important for the legal profession in China. Meanwhile, even after the large-scale privatization in the 1990s, many Chinese lawyers still perform the functional role of state bureaucrats by "bringing knowledge to the service of power" (Carr-Saunders and Wilson 1937; Halliday 1987) in their everyday work. These three roles, as state bureaucrats, market brokers, and political activists, are likely to persist, and their interactions will characterize much of the future transformation of the Chinese legal profession.

REFERENCES

Abel, Richard L. 1988. *The Legal Profession in England and Wales*. Oxford and New York: Blackwell.

Abel, Richard L. 1989. *American Lawyers*. New York and Oxford: Oxford University Press.

Alford, William P. 1995. "Tasselled Loafers for Barefoot Lawyers: Transformations and Tensions in the World of Chinese Lawyers." *China Quarterly* 141: 22–38.

All China Lawyers Association (ACLA). 2013. "Zhongguo Lüshi Hangye Shehui Zeren Baogao [Report on the Professional Social Responsibilities of Chinese Lawyers]." Accessed September 10, 2013. http://www.acla.org.cn/html/xinwen/1920130827/11102.html.

Burt, Ronald S. 1992. *Structural Holes: The Social Structure of Competition*. Cambridge, MA: Harvard University Press.

Burt, Ronald S. 2005. *Brokerage and Closure: An Introduction to Social Capital*. New York: Oxford University Press.

Cai, Dingjian. 1999. *Lishi yu Biange: Xin Zhongguo Fazhi Jianshe de Licheng* [*History and Change: The Process of the Construction of Legal System in New China*]. Beijing: China University of Political Science and Law Press.

Carr-Saunders, Alexander M., and P. A. Wilson. 1933. *The Professions*. Oxford: Oxford University Press.

China Law Yearbook. 1987–2007. Beijing: China Law Yearbook Editorial Committee.

Dezalay, Yves, and Bryant Garth. 2002. *The Internationalization of Palace Wars: Lawyers, Economists and the Transformation of Latin-American States*. Chicago: University of Chicago Press.
Dezalay, Yves, and Bryant Garth. 2010. *Asian Legal Revivals: Lawyers in the Shadow of Empire*. Chicago: University of Chicago Press.
Fu, Hualing, and Richard Cullen. 2008. "*Weiquan* (Right Protection) Lawyers in an Authoritarian State: Building a Culture of Public Interest Lawyering." *China Journal* 59: 111–127.
Fu, Hualing, and Richard Cullen. 2011. "Climbing the *Weiquan* Ladder: A Radicalizing Process for Rights-Protection Lawyers." *China Quarterly* 205: 40–59.
Fu, Yulin. 2006. *Nongcun Jiceng Falü Fuwu Yanjiu [Research on Rural Basic-Level Legal Services]*. Beijing: China University of Political Science and Law Press.
Gallagher, Mary E. 2006. "Mobilizing the Law in China: 'Informed Disenchantment' and the Development of Legal Consciousness." *Law & Society Review* 40: 783–816.
Halliday, Terence C. 1987. *Beyond Monopoly: Lawyers, State Crises, and Professional Empowerment*. Chicago: University of Chicago Press.
Halliday, Terence C., and Lucien Karpik, eds. 1997. *Lawyers and the Rise of Western Political Liberalism: Europe and North America from the Eighteenth to Twentieth Centuries*. Oxford: Clarendon Press.
Halliday, Terence C., Lucien Karpik, and Malcolm M. Feeley, eds. 2007. *Fighting for Political Freedom: Comparative Studies of the Legal Complex and Political Liberalism*. Oxford: Hart Publishing.
Halliday, Terence C., Lucien Karpik, and Malcolm M. Feeley, eds. 2012. *Fates of Political Liberalism in the British Post-Colony*. Cambridge and New York: Cambridge University Press.
Halliday, Terence C., and Sida Liu. 2007. "Birth of a Liberal Moment? Looking through a One-Way Mirror at Lawyers' Defense of Criminal Defendants in China." In *Fighting for Political Freedom: Comparative Studies of the Legal Complex and Political Liberalism*, edited by Terence C. Halliday, Lucien Karpik, and Malcolm M. Feeley, 65–107. Oxford: Hart Publishing.
He, Xin. 2012. "Black Hole of Responsibility: The Adjudication Committee's Role in a Chinese Court." *Law & Society Review* 46: 681–712.
Larson, Magali S. 1977. *The Rise of Professionalism: A Sociological Analysis*. Berkeley: University of California Press.
Li, Xueyao, and Sida Liu. 2012. "The Learning Process of Globalization: How Chinese Law Firms Survived the Financial Crisis." *Fordham Law Review* 80: 2847–2866.
Liebman, Benjamin L. 2007. "China's Courts: Restricted Reform." *China Quarterly* 191: 620–638.
Liu, Sida. 2006a. "Beyond Global Convergence: Conflicts of Legitimacy in a Chinese Lower Court." *Law & Social Inquiry* 31: 75–106.
Liu, Sida. 2006b. "Client Influence and the Contingency of Professionalism: The Work of Elite Corporate Lawyers in China." *Law & Society Review* 40: 751–782.
Liu, Sida. 2008. "Globalization as Boundary-Blurring: International and Local Law Firms in China's Corporate Law Market." *Law & Society Review* 42: 771–804.
Liu, Sida. 2011a. "Lawyers, State Officials, and Significant Others: Symbiotic Exchange in the Chinese Legal Services Market." *China Quarterly* 206: 276–293.
Liu, Sida. 2011b. "With or Without the Law: The Changing Meaning of Ordinary Legal Work in China, 1979–2003." In *Chinese Justice: Civil Dispute Resolution in Contemporary China*, edited by Margaret Y. K. Woo and Mary E. Gallagher, 234–266. Cambridge and New York: Cambridge University Press.

Liu, Sida. 2012. "Palace Wars over Professional Regulation: In-House Counsel in Chinese State-Owned Enterprises." *Wisconsin Law Review* 2012: 549–571.

Liu, Sida. 2013. "Falü Zhiye de Zhengzhi Mingyun [The Political Fate of the Legal Profession]." Jiao Da Faxue [SJTU Law Review] 2013(1): 93–100.

Liu, Sida, and Terence C. Halliday. 2009. "Recursivity in Legal Change: Lawyers and Reforms of China's Criminal Procedure Law." *Law & Social Inquiry* 34: 911–950.

Liu, Sida, and Terence C. Halliday. 2011. "Political Liberalism and Political Embeddedness: Understanding Politics in the Work of Chinese Criminal Defense Lawyers." *Law & Society Review* 45: 831–865.

Liu, Sida, Lily Liang, and Terence C. Halliday. 2014. "The Trial of Li Zhuang: Chinese Lawyers' Collective Action against Populism." *Asian Journal of Law and Society* 1: 79–97.

Lu, Hong, and Terence D. Miethe. 2002. "Legal Representation and Criminal Processing in China." *British Journal of Criminology* 42: 267–280.

Luhmann, Niklas. 2004. *Law as a Social System*. Translated by Klaus A. Ziegert. New York: Oxford University Press.

Ma, Kechang. 2007. *Tebie Bianhu: Wei Lin Biao, Jiang Qing Fangeming Jituan An Zhufan Bianhu Jishi [Special Defense: Notes on the Defense for the Counter-Revolutionary Groups of Lin Biao and Jiang Qing]*. Beijing: Chang'an Press.

Mertha, Andrew C. 2005. *The Politics of Piracy: Intellectual Property in Contemporary China*. Ithaca, NY: Cornell University Press.

Michelson, Ethan. 2003. "Unhooking from the State: Chinese Lawyers in Transition." PhD diss., University of Chicago.

Michelson, Ethan. 2006. "The Practice of Law as an Obstacle to Justice: Chinese Lawyers at Work." *Law & Society Review* 40: 1–38.

Michelson, Ethan. 2007. "Lawyers, Political Embeddedness, and Institutional Continuity in China's Transition from Socialism." *American Journal of Sociology* 113: 352–414.

Michelson, Ethan, and Sida Liu. 2010. "What Do Chinese Lawyers Want? Political Values and Legal Practice." In *China's Emerging Middle Class: Beyond Economic Transformation*, edited by Cheng Li, 310–333. Washington, DC: Brookings Institution Press.

Minzner, Carl F. 2011. "China's Turn against Law." *American Journal of Comparative Law* 59: 935–984.

Pils, Eva. 2005. "Asking the Tiger for His Skin: Rights Activism in China." *Fordham International Law Journal* 30: 1209–1287.

Sarat, Austin, and Stuart A. Scheingold, eds. 1998. *Cause Lawyering: Political Commitments and Professional Responsibilities*. New York: Oxford University Press.

Sarat, Austin, and Stuart A. Scheingold. 2001. *Cause Lawyering and the State in a Global Era*. New York: Oxford University Press.

Wang, Yaxin. 2006. "Nongcun Falü Fuwu Wenti Shizheng Yanjiu (1) [Empirical Research on Rural Legal Service (1)]." *Fazhi yu Shehui Fazhan [Law and Social Development]* 2006(3): 3–34.

Weber, Max. 1978. *Economy and Society*. Edited by Guenther Roth and Claus Wittich. Berkeley: University of California Press.

Woo, Margaret Y. K. 1991. "Adjudication Supervision and Judicial Independence in the P. R. C." *American Journal of Comparative Law* 39: 95–119.

Woo, Margaret Y. K. 1999. "Law and Discretion in the Contemporary Chinese Courts." *Pacific Rim Law & Policy Journal* 8: 581–615.

Xu, Hui. 2008. *Tongxiang Shehui Zhengyi zhi Lu: Gongyi Susong Lilun Yanjiu [The Road to Social Justice: Theoretical Studies of Public Interest Litigation]*. Beijing: Law Press.

Ying, Xing. 2007. "'Yingfa Ruxiang' yu 'Jiejin Zhengyi': Dui Zhongguo Xiangcun 'Chijiao Lüshi' de Ge'an Yanjiu ['Welcoming Law into the Countryside' and 'Access to Justice': A Case Study on 'Barefoot Lawyers' in Rural China]." *Zhenfa Luntan* [*Tribune of Political Science and Law*] 25(1): 79–94.
Yu, Ping. 2002. "Glittery Promise vs. Dismal Reality: The Role of a Criminal Lawyer in the People's Republic of China after the 1996 Revision of the Criminal Procedure Law." *Vanderbilt Journal of Transnational Law* 35: 827–865.
Zhang, Delin. 2001. "Qiye Falü Guwen: Qiye Gaige Fazhan de Baohushen [Enterprise Legal Advisors: The Patron Saint for the Reform and Development of Enterprises]." Accessed April 28, 2009. http://www.sasac.gov.cn/n1180/n1566/n11183/n11214/1803815.html.
Zhang Qianfan. 2003. "The People's Court in Transition: The Prospects of the Chinese Judicial Reform." *Journal of Contemporary China* 12(34): 69–101.
Zhou, Hua. 2008. "Beijing Lüshi Xiehui Zhixuan Fengbo [The Direct Election Incident of the Beijing Lawyers Association]." *Nan Feng Chuang* [*Southern Reviews*], October 14. Accessed September 10, 2013. http://www.nfcmag.com/article/1116.html.
Zhu, Jingwen, ed. 2007. *Zhongguo Falü Fazhan Baogao: Shujuku he Zhibiao Tixi* [*Report on China Law Development: Database and Indicators*]. Beijing: Renmin University of China Press.

SECTION IV

Global Justice

11

The Irreconcilable Goals of Transitional Justice

Bronwyn Leebaw

I. INTRODUCTION

In 1994, Madeleine Albright, then Ambassador to the United Nations, gave a speech that made the case for establishing the International Criminal Tribunal for the Former Yugoslavia (ICTY). Albright addressed potential critics of the court by arguing that "establishing the truth about what happened in Bosnia is *essential to* – not an obstacle to – national reconciliation" (Bass 2000, 263). Although this was once a controversial claim, the idea that a durable peace requires countries to address past violence is now widely held and promoted by influential leaders and institutions under the broad heading of "transitional justice."[1] The United Nations Department of Peacekeeping renamed its Justice and Security Sector Reform Team the "Security Sector Reform and Transitional Justice Unit" (UNDP 2003). A number of specialized organizations, institutes, and research networks now sponsor comparative research or training in transitional justice.[2] In recent decades, numerous transitional justice institutions, most notably truth commissions and war crimes tribunals, have been established around the world.

Transitional justice has been associated with an array of goals, including the pursuit of justice and repair in response to past wrongs, the goal of advancing progress in the institutionalization of human rights, the goal of establishing rule of law, and the pursuit of democratizing political reform. The promotion of transitional justice institutions as a basis for advancing political *reconciliation* might appear puzzling, however. Truth commissions and war crimes tribunals investigate divisive and violent histories. As a result, they are routinely accused of *threatening*

[1] Ruti Teitel has defined transitional justice as "the conception of justice in periods of political transition" (2000, 3). Teitel sees transitional justice as encompassing *legal* responses to wrongdoings of successor regimes. For Jon Elster, the definition is somewhat broader, encompassing private forms of retribution such as the chopping off of hair as a penalty for consorting with German occupation forces (2004).

[2] See, for example, the International Center for Transitional Justice in New York, the Harvard Project for Justice in Times of Transition, the Transitional Justice Project at Notre Dame School of Law, the War Crimes Study Center at the University of California at Berkeley, the Transitional Justice Institute at the University of Ulster, the Institute for Justice and Reconciliation in Cape Town, and Oxford Transitional Justice Research.

political reconciliation by "opening old wounds," generating political instability, or interfering with forward-looking political change. In the post–Cold War context, debates on transitional justice centered on dilemmas and tensions associated with efforts to reckon with systematic abuse, which were commonly framed as tensions between the goals of "justice" and "reconciliation." How did these goals, once thought to be deeply at odds with each other, come to be seen as mutually reinforcing and complementary? Is it possible, and is it desirable, to overcome the tensions and dilemmas that have been associated with transitional justice?

Albright's claims regarding the role of the ICTY echoed a general shift in thinking about transitional justice that occurred as a number of scholars and policy makers began to assert that dilemmas once associated with transitional justice were illusory. Some argued, persuasively, that many such dilemmas had been rooted in reductive and misleading ways of defining basic conceptual goals (Méndez 2001; Roht-Arriaza and Mariezcurrena 2006; Philpott 2012). Others suggested such dilemmas might be resolved or overcome through the elaboration of more sophisticated, holistic, hybrid, or international approaches to transitional justice policy. For critical theorists and other skeptics, on the other hand, the shifting claims associated with transitional justice are better understood as evidence of an agenda that increasingly has more to do with legitimating state and global power configurations than it has to do with justice (Meister 2002, 2012; Nagy 2008; Wilson 2001).

This chapter argues that the goals associated with transitional justice remain irreconcilable. Transitional justice contains profound internal tensions, which are obscured by debates that focus on abstract ideals and technical policies, but which come into sharper view when transitional justice is examined as a political intervention and practice. My analysis is informed by the work of legal scholars and political theorists who have drawn attention to the dual role of law in relation to violence. While law can be a tool for regulating violence and exposing abuses of power, law is also utilized to obfuscate and legitimate abuses of power (Brown and Halley 2002; Jochnik and Normand 1994; Sarat 2001). I suggest that this insight is particularly salient in evaluating transitional justice interventions due to the nature of the abuses that these projects aim to address.

Of course, as transitional justice institutions proliferate, they have investigated a range of very different forms of abuse, including genocide, "ethnic cleansing," mass rape, torture, and other systematic violations of human rights and humanitarian norms. Transitional justice practices have emerged in many forms in diverse political contexts. As Naomi Roht-Arriaza has observed, the term "transition" has always been slippery in transitional justice debates, which have never clearly articulated "what the state is transitioning *to*" (2006, 2). However, all transitional justice projects do have one thing in common, which is that they all aim to investigate forms of abuse and violence that were politically authorized – that is, abuses that were, in some fashion, rationalized, normalized, legalized, legitimized, or even institutionalized, under a prior political authority. Thus, although scholars have tended to identify the distinctiveness of transitional justice with the specific context of formal regime change, I would suggest that what lends coherence to contemporary debates on transitional justice has to do with the unique challenges associated with efforts to reckon with forms of abuse that are systematic and politically authorized. These are abuses that generally involve widespread complicity or acquiescence, which means that efforts to reckon with such abuses must first involve a process of naming as abuse, criminalizing, or otherwise condemning acts that were once carried out as a matter of course or in the name of duty. Whether or not a formal regime change is underway, *some* kind of political reform or transition is implied by such an exercise.

Tensions between the goal of preserving order and the goal of facilitating change over time are present in any legal system, but the tensions between these goals are sharpened in the context of transitional justice. As an effort to reckon with widespread and systematic forms of abuse, transitional justice implies systemic, and therefore radical, critique of past practices. At the same time, transitional justice practices aspire to establish and legitimate a new order (Teitel 2000). These goals may both be desirable, but they are inevitably in tension with each other. Transitional justice institutions aim to expose, remember, understand, or remedy politically authorized abuse, which is an inherently political task and one that is always met with some degree of backlash. At the same time, transitional justice institutions aim to establish their own legitimacy and the legitimacy of a new order. This means that the long-term aspirations associated with transitional justice institutions are likely to be in tension with their short-term strategic considerations: In the short term, transitional justice institutions engage with inherited traditions and centers of power in order to maintain a degree of stability and legitimacy. However, transitional justice institutions also aspire to challenge and transform inherited values and political relationships over the long term. Understanding how transitional justice institutions navigate the tensions between these competing goals, I suggest, is critical to any effort to evaluate their moral and political role as responses to systematic abuse.

The following section examines changing ideas about the relationship between transitional justice and reconciliation. The contemporary view that transitional justice goals are mutually reinforcing and complementary is a departure from the debates of the 1980s and early 1990s, which focused on tensions, trade-offs, and dilemmas associated with transitional justice. This shift is often interpreted as evidence that a new generation of approaches to transitional justice is capable of transcending or overcoming dilemmas associated with previous eras. I suggest that new approaches have not entirely overcome such dilemmas, but rather made them more difficult to evaluate to the extent that they have reconceptualized the goals of transitional justice in apolitical terms. The third section surveys a range of scholarship on transitional justice institutions, focusing on truth commissions and war crimes tribunals, to demonstrate how attention to the conflicting aspirations of transitional justice is important in evaluating assumptions associated with three major justifications for transitional justice institutions: (1) to counter denial and promote accountability, (2) to expand dialogue and open political space to previously marginalized or silenced people, and (3) to alleviate volatile emotions associated with trauma and the desire for revenge. A concluding section discusses how the analysis sheds light on problematic assumptions and unacknowledged trade-offs associated with transitional justice policy, as well as the general significance of transitional justice advocacy.

II. THE SHIFTING CLAIMS OF TRANSITIONAL JUSTICE ADVOCACY

A. *Transitional Justice and Democratization: Dichotomies and Dilemmas*

Contemporary transitional justice debates were greatly influenced by World War II–era responses to Nazism. In that context, it was assumed that retribution for Nazi atrocities was appropriate, and major debates focused on the appropriate role for international law in framing retribution (Bass 2000). In addition to the Trial of the Major War Criminals before the International Military Tribunal, Nuremberg, the Allied forces had prosecuted thousands and executed several hundred Nazis under Allied Control Council Law 10. This period also involved wide-ranging private forms of retribution and reprisal (Elster 2004). However, comparative scholarship on transitional justice did not really begin to develop until the period of "third wave" transitions to democracy in Latin America and Eastern Europe, as leaders and scholars examined the question of how new leaders should address systematic political violence committed under a prior regime.

In the 1980s and early 1990s, transitional justice debates focused on the role of trials and administrative purges for past abuses in democratizing transitions. In the context of Argentina's 1984 transition and Chile's transition in 1990, successor regimes debated the question of whether to "punish or pardon" human rights violations committed under a prior regime. Argentina's efforts to prosecute abuses committed during the "Dirty War" ended when military protests threatened to destabilize the transition (Malamud-Goti 1990; Nino 1996; Osiel 1997; Pion-Berlin 1993; Zalaquett 1992). Truth commissions were developed in both Argentina and Chile as alternative forms of accountability. Although they did not satisfy what some human rights advocates had identified as an "international duty to prosecute" human rights violations committed under a prior regime, truth commissions would investigate and condemn violations of human rights as outlined in evolving international legal standards. In Eastern Europe, purge laws were passed in a number of countries emerging from Soviet rule, though widespread purges occurred only in the Czech Republic and Germany (González-Enríquez 2001, 219). A number of highly publicized trials took place in these countries, with the prosecution of East German border guards receiving perhaps the most widespread attention. "Truth-telling" was also adopted as a prominent mechanism for dealing with

Soviet-era repression. East European countries did not develop official truth commissions to pursue state-sponsored official histories, but rather opted for procedures to open secret police files (Cohen 1995; Huyse 1995; McAdams 1997).

In 1992, the New York–based Charter 77 Foundation hosted a conference to focus on the question of whether and how Eastern European leaders might learn from the experience of the Latin American transitions of the previous decade. Present at this conference, held in Salzburg, Austria, were fifty participants from twenty-one countries, who had all been involved in projects to address the legacy of past brutalities. The conference was also attended by Neil Kritz. Kritz was then directing the Rule of Law Program of the US Institute of Peace and in that capacity had embarked upon what would become a three-volume comparative and theoretical study of transitional justice projects over the past five decades (Kritz 1995). This conference and others like it would set the stage for the development of comparative transitional justice analysis and the expansion of networking.

Despite the wide variation in context, design, and implementation of transitional justice institutions, the expanding field of comparative transitional justice scholarship identified a unique set of dilemmas that distinguished transitional justice from "ordinary" justice. First, the widespread and systematic character of political violence gives rise to a tension between procedural and substantive justice. There is a conflict between "the desire to demarcate oneself from the earlier regime and the desire to punish that regime as severely as it deserves" (Elster 2004, 237). Procedural standards, such as the prohibition of retroactive punishment, maintain the integrity of the law in stable systems of justice. Yet transitions imply paradigm shifts in broad conceptions of justice (Teitel 2000, 6).

Second, scholars observed that transitional justice projects face basic practical or policy challenges stemming from the sheer number of those implicated in past abuses, which would generally overwhelm even a well-functioning judicial system. Yet in most cases, successor regimes are also engaged in rebuilding political and judicial institutions and are in no position to process the volume of cases associated with past abuses.

Third, transitional justice efforts confronted a basic political challenge. The criminalization of political violence is likely to be controversial and potentially destabilizing, whether this takes the form of prosecution and punishment or the acceptance of state responsibility through official acknowledgment, apology, or reparations. It is a process that condemns as shameful certain actions that may previously have been championed or widely accepted. Justice is commonly evaluated in relation to community norms. Transitional justice institutions represent the aspiration to *transform* political communities. What constitutes justice in this context will be a matter of potentially volatile conflict, and transitional justice institutions generally make use of the law in accomplishing political goals (Sriram 2005; Teitel 2000).

In the debates on transitional justice that began in the 1980s and early 1990s, these and other related dilemmas were routinely framed as tensions between justice and reconciliation. In human rights advocacy, justice was closely identified with prosecutions in accordance with international law that would advance the precedents set by the Nuremberg trials. Yet prosecution and other forms of transitional justice were designed not only to promote retribution, but also to advance the broader goal of fundamental political reform. In debates associated with this era, "transition" generally implied a transition to democracy. The goal of reconciliation was commonly invoked as shorthand for compromises and bargains with the old regime that were perceived as necessary to stabilize newly democratizing governments, but were often opposed by human rights advocates. Truth commissions were seen as a compromise designed to advance reconciliation, while simultaneously pursuing some level of accountability for past abuse. In the Southern Cone, the appeal for reconciliation was invoked *in opposition to* calls for prosecution, and it was in the interest of promoting national reconciliation that the Alywin government in Chile opted against prosecution for Pinochet-era abuses (Zalaquett 1992). As a result, the rhetoric of "reconciliation" was viewed by many as catering to apologists (Hayner 2001, 160–161).

B. *Transitional Justice and Reconciliation*

In the mid-1990s, human rights advocates and scholars increasingly began to argue that many of the dilemmas once associated with transitional justice were based on false dichotomies and limited thinking about the range of forms that transitional justice might take (Sikkink and Walling 2007; Sriram 2004). Three developments arguably played an important role in shifting the terms of debate during this period: the expansion of international law and norms, the development of hybrid and complementary transitional justice practices, and changing ways of framing the goal of political reconciliation.

As international law and institutions expanded, international actors began to play a greater role in framing approaches to transitional justice (de Brito, González-Enríquez, and Aguilar 2001). Some argued that the political dilemmas of transitional justice could be alleviated through the development of clear international standards and stronger international institutions. In the aftermath of the Argentine junta trials, for example, it had been argued that an "international duty to prosecute" would remove the question of whether to "punish or pardon" from the volatile national context (Orentlicher 1991). As the role of international law and institutions in transitional justice expanded, references to "transition" were also less political. Instead of referring to transitions from authoritarian to democratic regimes, post–Cold War debates more typically invoke "transition" in ostensibly neutral terms to refer to a "post-conflict" situation that required resolution and the establishment of authority bound by rule of law (Teitel 2003; United Nations Security Council 2004).

More recent scholarship on the ad hoc international criminal tribunals for Rwanda and the former Yugoslavia (ICTR and ICTY) suggests that optimism regarding the role of international law in transcending transitional justice dilemmas rested on a problematic pair of assumptions. First, these arguments assumed that international laws and institutions would be widely accepted as legitimate and neutral. Second, these claims suggested that international institutions would easily establish independence from local elites. Yet international criminal courts continue to depend on state cooperation for access to archives, permission to conduct forensic investigations, permission to interview witnesses, and the ability to make arrests (Peskin 2000). The legitimacy of ICTY and ICTR was challenged in Rwanda and the former Yugoslavia (Drumbl 2005; Human Rights Center et al. 2000; Moghalu 2002; Peskin 2000; Snyder and Vinjamuri 2003/2004; Uvin and Mironko 2003). International tribunals may override national conflict over the question of whether to "punish or pardon," yet debates over "whether to cooperate or not to cooperate" may still undermine the goals of these institutions in important ways (Peskin and Boduszynski 2003; Subotic 2009).

At the same time, some of the perceived dichotomies or dilemmas associated with transitional justice were addressed through the development of hybrid and complementary institutions. Hybrid tribunals, developed in Sierra Leone and Cambodia, for example, combine local and international authority. Truth commissions are no longer seen as a second-rate alternative to trials, but came to be championed as an important complement to prosecution of systematic atrocity.

As such changes took place, a shift also occurred in the framing of policy debates on the relationship between justice and reconciliation. Several leaders associated with South Africa's Truth and Reconciliation Commission (TRC) argued that justice and reconciliation should be viewed as mutually reinforcing rather than conflicting aspirations. They developed this position to claim that truth commissions should no longer be viewed as "second best" alternatives to trials, but as forms of "restorative justice" (Boraine 2000; Tutu 1999; Villa Vicencio 1998). Restorative justice theory developed out of a range of alternative dispute resolution practices, including indigenous courts and juvenile justice programs around the world. It centers on the idea that justice must involve an effort to restore a lost balance and that prosecution is not the only, or the best, means to attain this balance (TRC of South Africa 1998; Zehr 1990).

Claims regarding the role of transitional war crimes trials also changed during this time. In his opening statements at the Nuremberg trials, Chief Prosecutor Robert Jackson observed, "One of the dangers ever present in this trial ... is that it may be protracted by details of particular wrongs and that we may become lost in a wilderness of single instances" (International Military Tribunal 1947, 7). He argued that the officials who were tried at Nuremberg should not be condemned as individuals alone, but as "living symbols" that represented "racial hatreds," "fierce nationalisms," and the "arrogance and cruelty of power" (ibid.). Contemporary advocates of international justice have advanced a very different rationale for individual guilt, arguing that it will serve to counteract collective blame and so advance reconciliation (Akhavan 1998). The International Criminal Court has incorporated a commitment to responsive justice with a view to enhancing domestic reconciliation (G. Bitti, personal communication, July 23, 2003).

More generally, claims regarding the relationship between human rights and reconciliation changed in the post–Cold War era. In the early 1990s, a number of prominent human rights advocates with significant moral authority, including José Zalaquett of Chile and Nelson Mandela and Desmond Tutu of South Africa, began to recast the relationship between human rights and reconciliation, arguing that reconciliation would be an important prerequisite for establishing a regime capable of protecting human rights. These claims were based in part on a view that pragmatic compromises made in the name of stability would be essential to establishing a human rights regime (Zalaquett 1992). Yet these concerns also coincided with changing views on the relationship between human rights and state power. In the aftermath of the Second World War, the human rights movement had been concerned primarily with challenging state-sponsored violence. Following the Cold War, prominent human rights advocates and scholars began to view the collapse of state authority as a central cause of political violence and to see the reconstruction of state authority as an important priority for human rights (Ignatieff 2001, 25).

As reconciliation became a concern of human rights and transitional justice advocacy, however, it was redefined to encompass not only the goals of stabilizing and legitimating state authority, but also the aspiration for political community based on consent and shared norms. The discourse of reconciliation had previously been associated with the imperative of compromise in the name of stability. Where transitional justice was deemed a threat to short-term *stability*, there it would also threaten reconciliation. As theoretical and policy debates on transitional justice developed in the late 1990s and early 2000s, reconciliation came to be associated with the long-term aspiration for political community based on consent and shared norms. Whereas minimalist conceptions of peace might refer to the "absence of large scale organized violence or war and the extremely low probability of the resumption of war" (Mendeloff 2004, 363), minimalist conceptions of reconciliation have been associated with the principle of democratic reciprocity among conflicting parties or between the governors and the governed (Hesse and Post 1999; Gutmann and Thompson 2000). More expansive conceptions of reconciliation typically incorporate a range of features associated with democracy, including tolerance of political and ethnic diversity and respect for human rights (Borer 2003; Gibson 2004; Wilson 2001).

With these developments, transitional justice became increasingly depoliticized. Earlier debates on transitional justice were framed in relation to dilemmas at the intersection of justice and politics, dilemmas associated with the goal of judging politically authorized abuses in a context of political transformation. Over time, transitional justice has become increasingly professionalized and less explicitly political. The dilemmas associated with transitional justice were not overcome in this period, but rather became more difficult to see as the goals associated with transitional justice institutions were framed in ways that conflated their long-term and short-term aspirations. Whereas the discourse of reconciliation once referred to the political compromises to stabilize a new regime, it now also encompasses the goals of political community and consensus. The conflation of these goals can be understood as a strategic confusion as well as a logical confusion. It may be strategically useful to confuse compromise and consensus as a way to legitimate compromises made in the name of a hoped-for political community. Yet it is a logical error to assume that compromises will result in consensus, let alone a transformed political community. In practice, the strategies developed by transitional justice institutions to judge and transform the basis of political community are often in tension with the strategies that transitional justice advocates have adopted to mitigate volatile conflict and legitimate transitional compromises.

III. EVALUATING TRANSITIONAL JUSTICE

This section takes a closer look at the conflicting goals of transitional justice by investigating three types of claims regarding the role of transitional justice institutions in promoting political reconciliation: claims about how they serve to counter denial and promote accountability, claims about how they function to expand dialogue, and claims about how they function to alleviate volatile emotions and advance healing processes. In so doing, one goal is to identify and examine internal tensions in the goals that have been associated with transitional justice. A second goal is to demonstrate what is at stake in recognizing these tensions by considering their implications in relation to the scope and design of transitional justice investigations.

A. *Countering Denial, Establishing Accountability, Writing Political Myth*

In his opening address to the Nuremberg tribunal, Justice Robert Jackson famously announced that the trials would aim to "establish incredible events by credible evidence" (International Military Tribunal 1947, 45). A primary justification for transitional justice institutions is that they establish a historical record of political violence. One reason for doing so is to counter denial about the extent and impact of systematic violence. Transitional justice institutions also aim to counter denial about responsibility for past violence. A unique contribution of truth commissions has been their efforts to analyze patterns of violence as a basis for facilitating political reform (Hayner 2001).[3] These goals align with what might be viewed as a Habermasian approach to confronting the past. In the context of the German

[3] See Chapman and Ball (2001) for a comparative analysis of the methodology used by truth commissions.

Historikerstreit, Habermas argued that confronting and remembering past abuses would reinforce a commitment to democratic values and reforms (Habermas 1997). Thomas McCarthy and Andrew Valls invoke a similar logic to argue that the general lack of awareness, among whites in the United States, of the extent and impact of slavery, segregation, and lynching undermines the quality of our democracy (McCarthy 2002; Valls 2003).

By establishing a historical record of abuses that are denied, transitional justice institutions seek to challenge conventional understandings of the past. In several cases, transitional justice investigations seem to have played an important role in generating awareness of abuses that were previously hidden or denied. Historian Jeffrey Herf writes that following the Nuremberg trials, "no major national political figure in either of the two parties questioned the factual occurrence of [Nazi] crimes" (Herf 1997, 373). In Argentina, installments of truth commission reports sold an average of 200,000 copies per week (de Brito et al. 2001, 156). South Africa's truth commission aired public hearings on a weekly television show. Based on a series of surveys, James Gibson reports that the vast majority of South Africans now accept the TRC's claim that apartheid was a "crime against humanity" (Gibson 2004, 115). The report of Guatemala's Historical Clarification Commission was criticized by the right wing, but neither the government nor the military openly disputed its findings (Sieder 2001, 117).

In other cases, however, the findings of transitional justice investigations have been ignored, rejected, or not even disseminated. Although confronting denial is ostensibly a major goal of transitional justice, officials associated with ad hoc tribunals have tended to frame their work for audiences of international lawyers rather than the affected local populations.[4] Where the legitimacy of transitional justice institutions is successfully challenged, this undermines their impact in addressing denial. In El Salvador, the military and the Supreme Court accused the truth commission of political bias, and the president condemned the report for failing to meet expectations for reconciliation. Five days later, an amnesty law was passed (Sieder 2001, 171). Although ICTY convened four trials focusing on a massacre in the village of Amhici, Stover and Weinstein report that even the testimony of a dozen Bosnian Croat defendants "has not transformed the way in which Croats in the village interpret what happened on that fateful day," and Amhici remains a divided village (Stover and Weinstein 2004, 332).

In response to this problem, transitional justice advocates have argued that truth commissions and criminal tribunals play an important role in conveying messages or lessons about past violence that serve as the basis of a shared history, even where people continue to dispute factual and causal claims. Despite variation in the context and extent of the violence addressed by transitional justice institutions,

[4] In a 2002 survey, 87.2 percent of Rwandan respondents claimed that they were either not well informed or not informed at all about the ICTR proceedings (Des Forges and Longman 2004, 56).

they commonly seek to teach a similar set of lessons about past violence. For example, many transitional justice institutions now seek to convey the message that regardless of what caused atrocities or abuses to occur, both or all parties to the conflict committed abuses.

Another message that many transitional justice institutions seek to convey is that individuals can and should be held responsible for systematic political violence. In contrast with the Habermasian goal of confronting and learning from the past, these historical lessons are framed in relation to the needs of the present: to legitimate transitional justice institutions and transitional regimes. Insofar as the historical lessons associated with transitional justice institutions function to avoid volatile conflict or contentious issues, they combine history and political myth in the spirit of Renan's claim that "the essence of a nation is that all individuals have many things in common and also that they have forgotten many things" (Renan 1990). At the same time, transitional justice institutions generally portray themselves as operating in the "aftermath" of abuse, thereby shifting attention away from ongoing abuses and continuities between past and present (Meister 2012).

James Gibson has argued that the most important truth promoted by the TRC was that "both sides in the struggle did horrible things" (Gibson 2004, 160). Through public opinion polling in South Africa, Gibson found evidence that acceptance of the TRC's messages was correlated with greater levels of interracial reconciliation among substantial proportions of the population.[5] However, South Africa's TRC was able to focus on political violence committed by parties on both sides of the struggle because its mandate was designed to investigate crimes committed *in excess* of apartheid, rather than the violence of apartheid (Mamdani 1996; Meister 2002). Thus, the pursuit of a common basis for understanding past violence was in tension with the goal of countering denial regarding the implications of apartheid per se. International courts have also made strategic decisions designed to convey the message that all parties to the conflict are culpable. As Osiel observes, in international courts, "defendant selection consistently seeks to broaden liability to kingpins of all culpable groups, irrespective of how small a group's contribution to the horrors" (Osiel 2005, 1814).

Another common argument for transitional justice is that "individualizing guilt" will minimize feelings of vengefulness, lessen stereotyping, and reinforce respect for the law. On the role of ICTY in the Balkans, Payam Akhavan writes: "By telling the truth of what transpired in the former Yugoslavia and ascribing individual guilt to those responsible for manipulating ethnic tensions, the ICTY can counter the campaign of collective demonization instigated by political elites" (Akhavan 1998, 764). The idea of individualizing guilt is appealing in theory because it shifts attention away from the controversial terrain of explaining and responding to widespread

[5] Gibson developed a measure of racial reconciliation using a series of indicators to evaluate levels of trust, comfort, and stereotyping of other racial groups.

involvement and participation in systematic violence. However, Akhavan's case for individualizing guilt rests on the premise that widespread participation in systematic political violence either is, or should be portrayed as, a product of elite manipulation of the masses. The question as to why large numbers of people became involved in systematic violence is avoided in this formulation. If criminal trials aimed to demonstrate how a large segment of society had participated in mass atrocities, writes Osiel, "then victims and the public at large would no longer be content to vent their rage on a small handful of now powerless individuals" (Osiel 2005, 1811). Thus, the goal of individualizing guilt is also in direct tension with the goal of countering denial regarding widespread complicity in systematic political violence. Fletcher and Weinstein take this point further, arguing that where individualizing guilt is successful, it offers leaders "the opportunity to rationalize or deny their own responsibility for crimes that were committed in their name" (Fletcher and Weinstein 2002, 601).

One of the most common arguments made on behalf of transitional justice institutions is that they will end impunity, not only by holding leaders accountable, but also by conveying a message to the broader public that in the new regime, no one will be above the law (Orentlicher 1991). However, transitional justice institutions are extraordinary, temporary responses to past abuses, which places them in tension with core principles associated with the rule of law.[6] The difficulty with arguments regarding the role of transitional justice in conveying a message about the dangers of impunity is that they tend to assume that the pragmatic compromises that narrow the scope and efficacy of transitional justice will not serve to undermine the intended symbolic message of their principled judgments. Yet lenient sentences, plea bargaining, and the refusal or inability to attain custody of key suspects can undermine the message that international tribunals will serve as vehicles for "ending impunity" (Drumbl 2005).

Finally, it is important to consider that the historical lessons favored by transitional justice institutions typically focus on local responsibility, with little attention to the role of external intervention. One worrisome implication of this is that the phenomenon of transitional justice may function to construct a revisionist history of Cold War–era repression that portrays it as an entirely local affair, thereby contributing to denial regarding the role of great power interventions in local conflicts. The proliferation of truth commissions in the developing world has led to some critical debate and reflection on US Cold War policies. Some commentators have called for truth commissions to investigate various US actions (Brody 2001; Valls 2003). However, as transitional justice institutions investigate atrocity and conflict in Central America, East Timor, and now Cambodia, there has been very little effort to consider US involvement in these conflicts.[7] Calls for truth commissions,

6 Political transition itself poses dilemmas for rule of law. For an argument about the unique role of transitional justice in mediating these dilemmas see Teitel (2000, 11–26).

7 An exception is the report of Guatemala's truth commission, which evaluates US responsibility in relation to atrocities dealt with in the investigation, stating that US military assistance "had significant

prosecutions, and reparations in response to abuses committed by the United States during recent counterterror wars have also been largely ignored (Leahy 2009).

Recent efforts to evaluate the impact of transitional justice institutions have tended to take for granted the premise that these institutions are designed to advance accountability and challenge denial regarding past wrongs, while measuring their impact in relation to a range of forward-looking goals. Yet the relationship between transitional justice and accountability is not that simple or straightforward. Transitional justice institutions and advocates have accommodated and advanced mythologies about the logic of abuse alongside their efforts to uncover evidence, establish facts, and challenge denial. Transitional justice projects have opened spaces for criticizing past practices, while simultaneously seeking legitimacy by accommodating compromises that limit the scope of their critique.

B. *Expanding Inclusive Dialogue, Transforming the Terms of Debate*

Transitional justice investigations have also been championed as a way to promote reconciliation by fostering dialogue across lines of political and social conflict (Osiel 1997). South Africa's TRC suggested that it came closest to fulfilling its goals by "listening carefully to the complex motives and perspectives of all those involved," and by trying to "provide an environment in which all possible views could be considered and weighed, one against the other" (TRC of South Africa 1998, 113). Gutmann and Thompson argue that truth commissions can foster deliberative democracy by encouraging "accommodation to conflicting views that fall within the range of reasonable disagreement" (Gutmann and Thompson 2000, 41). In their view, truth commissions can "express respect for differing points of view without either endorsing them as clearly correct or rejecting them as clearly incorrect," leaving it to the participants and observers to determine what constitutes the "range of reasonable disagreement." In this way, they suggest, truth commissions contribute to both democracy and reconciliation.

In theory, a nonjudgmental truth commission may be in a better position to foster dialogue, yet this approach is in tension with one of the central activities of these institutions, which is to criminalize past political violence by labeling acts once considered legally or politically appropriate as "human rights violations." Advocates of transitional justice as a basis for inclusive dialogue may be suggesting that under the right conditions, dialogue among those who once condoned abuse and those who suffered from it will generate a common disdain for that abuse. Whether or not this is the case, the uncritical display of varying perspectives on past violence is unlikely to function as a neutral listening exercise, and may function instead to

bearing on human rights violations during the armed confrontation," and that US anticommunism and the National Security Doctrine were expressed in Guatemala as "anti-reformist, then anti-democratic policies, culminating in criminal counterinsurgency" (Guatemalan Commission for Historical Clarification 1996).

legitimate the views of apologists for the old regime. Thus, the long-term goal of utilizing transitional justice institutions to shift the terms of debate on past abuse is often in tension with the goal of facilitating inclusive dialogue in the immediate aftermath of transition.

Others have argued that truth commissions and war crimes tribunals can foster a more inclusive democratic dialogue by providing official spaces for previously marginalized or silenced populations to share their stories. In assessing this claim, it is important to observe that focusing on the stories of official victims is a strategy for narrowing the scope of transitional justice inquiries and avoiding destabilizing challenges to transitional compromises. In South Africa, for example, those who did not view themselves as victims, but rather as unrepentant soldiers of a just struggle, did not view the TRC framework as appealing, and the historical record developed by the TRC did little to incorporate their stories (TRC of South Africa 1998). Truth commissions also define the very category of victimhood in ways that are designed to avoid destabilizing conflict. In South Africa, TRC investigations addressed only victims of "gross violations of human rights," which did not include abuses that were legal under apartheid, such as forced removals, but only extreme forms of physical abuse (TRC of South Africa 1998, 70–71). In Chile, truth commission investigations addressed only murdered victims and did not document the vast number of torture cases (Hayner 2001, 303). More generally, to the extent that transitional justice institutions frame dialogue as a conversation between victim and perpetrator populations, they diminish attention to questions of political agency and responsibility.

At the same time, victim and survivor groups, along with other civil society groups, have, in many cases, taken up political agency in response to transitional justice institutions and expanded the scope of debate about past wrongs. Rachel Sieder and Victoria Sanford have both argued that the Guatemalan Historical Clarification Process contributed to the political empowerment of marginalized groups (Sanford 2003; Sieder 2001). In Guatemala, where changes at the elite level have been minimal, a "grassroots memory politics" emerged around the official work of the truth commission. Activities such as the exhumation of mass graves and construction of monuments have, according to Sieder, contributed to the formation of transregional communities of survivors, and, "with the support of international observers, many rural Mayans have come to reject military domination and to demand their rights" (Sieder 2001, 187). For example, in South Africa, the Khulumani Support Group on Behalf of Victims and Survivors of Apartheid organized in response to the TRC and has been a vocal critic of the disappointing reparations process in South Africa. Lara Nettlefield contends that victim and survivor groups organizing in response to the ICTY succeeded in broadening the scope of debate about accountability in Bosnia and Herzegovina (Nettlefield 2010). Where previously marginalized people mobilize in response to transitional justice, they may expose the limitations of transitional compromises and exert pressure for further reform.

The idea that transitional justice institutions would advance reconciliation by opening up spaces for dialogue about past wrongs has always been based on a fairly optimistic assessment of the role of dialogue as a basis for furthering common ground. A closer look at the claims associated with the role of transitional justice in advancing dialogue sheds light on the internal tensions associated with this claim. Transitional justice institutions and advocacy *do* aspire to open spaces for dialogue between previously warring groups, but they also aspire to narrow the scope of legitimate debate on the past, to decisively reject rationales for past abuse, and to communicate clearly to those who committed or supported such abuses that they were in the wrong.

Transitional justice institutions have opened spaces for previously marginalized or silenced peoples to give testimony and to be heard. In doing so, they have also offered new frameworks and institutional spaces for analyzing past violence that may function as the basis for collective empowerment and political mobilization. However, transitional justice institutions also perform a kind of gatekeeping role in relation to the framing of debates on past wrongs. They elevate some forms of victimization as worthy of moral attention, while implying that other forms of violence and suffering are less salient. They generally showcase voices associated with particular experiences of victimization and criminal guilt. Attention to the voices and experiences of various kinds of resistance, of bystanders, or of beneficiaries tends to emerge only at the margins of the official dialogues associated with transitional justice inquiries.

C. *Establishing Closure, Committing to Remembrance*

It is commonly argued that transitional justice investigations promote reconciliation by addressing volatile emotions resulting from past violence. Antonio Cassesse, the first ICTY president, has argued that trials are the only "civilized alternative to revenge" and that without justice, "feelings of hatred and resentment seething below the surface will, sooner or later, erupt and lead to violence" (quoted in Williams and Scharf 2002, 21). G. Jonathan Bass argues that, "if the international community does not punish war crimes, then, in many cases, victims will be tempted to take justice into their own hands" (Bass 2000, 305). According to Kenneth Roth, executive director of Human Rights Watch, this has been a dominant cause of violence in Haiti. "Frustrated by their inability to bring persecutors before a court of law," he argues, "many Haitians took matters into their own hands" (Roth 1999, 95). Claims regarding the role of transitional justice in healing individuals, communities, and nations continue to serve as "articles of faith" for transitional justice policy (Ignatieff 1996).

In many cases, however, transitional prosecutions have been ineffective as a response to vengeful or volatile emotions. For example, substantial reprisal killings have taken place in Kosovo and Rwanda since the creation of ICTY and ICTR. One problem is that the goal of individual healing is often in tension with other transitional justice goals. The pursuit of individual accountability in the context of a criminal tribunal requires adherence to due process guarantees, which means that justice is slow and that those who are guilty may be released on a technicality. Yet as Jon Elster has observed, the demand for reprisals is historically strongest in the immediate aftermath of abuses, and it fades over time (Elster 2004, 223). The slow pace of criminal proceedings may inevitably limit their role in addressing cycles of revenge (Mendeloff 2004). Based on interviews with eighty-seven ICTY witnesses, Eric Stover finds that those who testified at the tribunal did not generally do so out of a desire for revenge, but the experience actually seemed to exacerbate painful or volatile emotions associated with past violence (Stover 2005). Victims and survivors have commonly perceived the sentences as too lenient, and they have been frustrated to see sentences overturned on appeal (Peskin 2000; Stover 2005).

Some have proposed that truth commissions may do better than trials at addressing trauma, anger, or fear (Minow 1998; Phelps 2004; Zalaquett 1992). Restorative justice has combined ideals associated with therapeutic healing and the traditional use of informal justice as a tool for mediating conflict. South Africa's TRC developed this therapeutic conception of its mission by hiring "briefers," who were specially trained in mental health, to provide assistance to victims who appeared at public hearings. Early enthusiasm for the healing potential of truth commissions was connected to the view that human rights advocates, in their drive to promote prosecution, had neglected the needs of those damaged by past abuses. The subsequent attention to the psychological dimension and the needs of affected populations is a welcome development (see, for example, Cobban 2002; Chayes and Minow 2003; Roht-Arriaza 1995; Stover and Weinstein 2004). However, a number of studies call into question the role of truth commissions in healing traumatized individuals. As in the case of criminal tribunals, the role of truth commissions in addressing individual trauma changes over time and cannot be divorced from the context of political and social conflict.

David Backer, who conducted a systematic survey of participant experiences at South Africa's TRC, found that victims in general were "reasonably satisfied" with their engagement with the truth commission, but that many had experienced the process as an "emotional roller coaster" with initial feelings of relief followed by anguish, confusion, and frustration (Backer 2004, 16). The role of truth commissions in contributing to individual healing can also conflict with their efforts to address community and social divisions. Backer reports that some victims felt stigmatized as a result of their exposure through the TRC process, and a few describe having been "shunned" by their communities after they appeared at public hearings (Backer 2004, 16). Rosalind Shaw's ethnographic study of local responses to Sierra Leone's TRC finds that the concept of healing through truth resonated in powerful ways with certain very vocal constituencies, but was starkly at odds with dominant local strategies for reintegrating ex-combatants through "social forgetting" (Shaw 2005).

Another study conducted in Sierra Leone concluded that the reconciliation rituals associated with the truth commission did have a powerful cathartic impact on communities, but this effect was not a result of success in getting at the truth. Rather, the process of confession functioned as an elaborate prelude for the closing ritual (Kelsall 2005).

Claims regarding aggregate individual responses to truth commissions do not translate into conclusions regarding the political implications of these institutions. However, transitional justice officials and advocates often explain the connection between individual healing and political reconciliation by way of metaphor, suggesting that by facilitating a public "working through" of the past, these institutions will contribute to a national "healing process" (Boraine and Levy 1995). As Vanessa Pupavac has argued, this analogy "promotes emotional adjustment for societies, rather than material advancement of their circumstances" (Pupavac 2004, 385). When individual healing is used as a metaphor for national healing, this implies a preexisting body politic or a single collective psyche with shared wounds and experiences (Ignatieff 1996; Leebaw 2001; Des Forges and Roth 2002). As a general way of framing the process of transitional justice, then, the concept of a "national healing process" is consistent with the goal of stabilizing transitional compromises, but in tension with the goal of countering denial and analyzing the legacy of political violence.

The focus on establishing closure at a national level is also in tension with the moral commitment to remembrance that has been associated with transitional justice. Theodor Adorno analyzed this tension in a 1959 speech entitled "What Does Coming to Terms with the Past Mean?" (Adorno [1959] 1986). In the speech, Adorno argued that the German process of "coming to terms" with the past was functioning as a way to guard against the moral implications of remembrance by treating painful memories as part of a "guilt complex." Adorno observed that talking about the past is not necessarily an indication that people are confronting issues of accountability and rather may serve the opposite purpose.

This insight remains vital in relation to the contemporary phenomenon of transitional justice. Transitional justice institutions insist on the importance of remembrance as an ongoing process. In their efforts to document and broadcast the voices of victims and survivors, transitional justice institutions aspire to prevent people from simply moving on, and to compel their audiences to confront the full horror of the abuses under investigation. Transitional justice institutions are championed and developed in the name of assuring that past wrongs will not simply be forgotten as people become increasingly focused on present-day imperatives. Yet transitional justice institutions and advocates have also increasingly identified the goal of reconciliation with an idea of therapeutic healing and closure that is affiliated with an emphasis on letting go of the volatile emotions connected to past wrongs and prioritizes adapting to their aftermath.

IV. CONCLUSION: THE POLITICAL DYNAMICS OF TRANSITIONAL JUSTICE

If the tensions associated with transitional justice are rooted in politics, a prominent response to such tensions has been to seek a basis for detaching transitional justice from arenas of political conflict and compromise. In policy and practice, transitional justice has been increasingly professionalized. As transitional justice became associated with promoting reconciliation, the goals of transitional justice were depoliticized and framed in relation to legalistic and therapeutic categories. Yet efforts to depoliticize transitional justice policy are, themselves, in tension with a defining aspiration of transitional justice, which is to reckon with violence and abuse that is systemic and political in character. Thus, the identification of justice and accountability with "individualizing guilt" is in some degree of tension with the aspiration associated with exposing and confronting "crimes against humanity," which are, by definition, widespread, systematic, and organized.

The development of transitional justice as an arena of professional expertise and policy, aimed at establishing what works and best practices, has yielded important comparative insights. At the same time, scholars recognize that the scope of accountability in transitional justice institutions has narrowed or widened in response to patterns of political mobilization and negotiation. A 2004 report by the Secretary General of the United Nations, entitled "The Rule of Law and Transitional Justice in Conflict and Post-Conflict Societies," also acknowledges this point, observing that transitional justice policies are essentially grounded in political questions, rather than merely technical decisions (United Nations Security Council 2004, 8).

Another general rationale for efforts to divorce transitional justice from political concerns is that such efforts are necessary to establish the critical role of transitional justice, and to insulate judgments regarding right and wrong from the pressures of power politics. When examined as abstract ideals, held at a remove from political and institutional context, the goals that have been associated with transitional justice are, indeed, mutually reinforcing and complementary. Scholarly and public debates on the concepts and ideals associated with transitional justice, such as justice and reconciliation, play an important critical and visionary role in efforts to reckon with systematic abuse. However, such efforts cannot overcome the tensions and dilemmas associated with transitional justice as *praxis*. And it is in the arena of praxis, I would suggest, that transitional justice remains particularly important – not only to countries undergoing formal transitions to democracy, but globally.

The central declared aspiration of transitional justice institutions and practices has been to reckon with the kind of widespread abuses that have been authorized and rationalized in the name of a political authority. As a response to organized, politically authorized violence, transitional justice embodies a conflicting set of aspirations. Transitional justice institutions aim not only to condemn past abuses, but also to transform the basis of political legitimacy by rejecting rationales for abuse that were once widely accepted. This entails efforts to investigate the relationship between individual acts and systemic context, to challenge mythologies that are still cherished by many, and to examine how present-day inequalities and suffering are linked to the past in ways that were previously unacknowledged. At the same time, transitional justice institutions seek to establish their own legitimacy in contexts marked by ongoing conflict and division over how to interpret past violence. Doing so has involved various efforts to narrow and soften their judgments, to conflate consensus and compromise, to shift the investigative frame away from divisive matters, and to emphasize vague generalities as a basis for establishing some form of common ground.

This chapter has argued that understanding the tension inherent in the politics of transitional justice helps to shed light on some of the problematic assumptions and unacknowledged trade-offs in the design of institutions and strategies. One problem with the "transition paradigm" adopted by the US government in the mid-1980s, according to Thomas Carothers, was the view that initial "breakthroughs" would lead to the progressive implementation of democracy (Carothers 2002, 7). Transitional justice institutions and advocates have sometimes adopted a similar logic in relation to the goal of reconciliation, formulating the goal of reconciliation in ways that conflate political compromise with political consensus, and political stability with political community. Failure to distinguish among these goals contributes to the assumption that the influence of transitional justice will be progressive and linear. This assumption has reinforced the questionable view that if transitional justice investigations are initially controversial or volatile, this will undermine the transition altogether.[8] Similarly, the assumption of a linear, progressive transitional path has informed the view that, if transitional justice institutions succeed in reinforcing approval of compromises and negotiations that frame political change, they will also contribute to the long-term goal of cultivating political community based on principles of human rights and the rule of law.

Instead, as Sriram has observed, "transitional situations are dynamic," and transitional compromises are better understood as serving interim purposes, rather than permanent goals (Sriram 2004, 203). Understanding transitional justice as dynamic also means thinking about how the short-term compromises associated with stability are in tension with the long-term aspirations that have been associated with reconciliation as community building. Where transitional justice institutions seek to avoid destabilizing compromise or to establish legitimating political myths, these achievements are often in tension with their efforts to challenge denial and expose the extent of complicity. Where reconciliation is identified with the goal of treating the symptoms of political violence and establishing closure, this has been in tension

8 In a study of eleven civil conflicts, Long and Brecke (2003) concluded that even where "truth-telling" processes could threaten stability in the short term by countering denial, they still contributed to long-term goals associated with reconciliation.

with the goals of analyzing cause, assigning responsibility, promoting ongoing political reform, and establishing a moral commitment to ongoing remembrance.

As scholars and political leaders evaluate the political role of transitional justice institutions, it will be important to consider how they negotiate these tensions in the short term. It will also be important to devote more attention to the way in which the role of transitional justice changes over time. Arguments about the role of truth commissions and war crimes tribunals are often based on the official actions and short-term impact of these institutions. This is especially common with regard to claims about their role in promoting healing. In thinking about the long-term role of transitional justice, more attention should be given to questions such as how people mobilize in response to these institutions, how historical records are made available to the public, and how the transitional justice process is revised over time.

Most important, this analysis suggests that transitional justice institutions function in ways that are more complex than either human rights advocates or their critics typically acknowledge. It is possible for transitional justice institutions to establish accountability, promote remembrance, and challenge denial, yet at the same time advance political myths that obfuscate responsibility, distort the legacy of political violence, and encourage people to forget potentially volatile issues. In other contexts, transitional justice institutions may function primarily as tools for legitimation of state power, yet also open avenues for widening accountability, dialogue, and ongoing political reform over the long term. Understanding the role of individual transitional justice institutions, as well as the significance of expanding transitional justice advocacy, means moving beyond the poles of earnest idealism and savvy cynicism that have traditionally divided branches of transitional justice scholarship to examine the political dynamics associated with their irreconcilable goals.

REFERENCES

Adorno, Theodor W. (1959) 1986. "What Does Coming to Terms with the Past Mean?" In *Bitburg in Moral and Political Perspective*, edited by Geoffrey Hartman, 114–129. Translated by Timothy Bahti and Geoffrey Hartman. Bloomington: Indiana University Press.

Akhavan, Payam. 1998. "Justice in the Hague, Peace in the Former Yugoslavia? A Commentary on the United Nations War Crimes Tribunal." *Human Rights Quarterly* 20: 737–816.

Backer, David. 2004. "Exit, Voice & Loyalty in Transitional Justice Processes: Evidence on Victims' Responses to South Africa's Truth and Reconciliation Commission." Paper presented at the annual meeting of the American Political Science Association, Chicago, IL, September 2.

Bass, Gary Jonathan. 2000. *Stay the Hand of Vengeance: The Politics of War Crimes Tribunals*. Princeton: Princeton University Press.

Boraine, Alex. 2000. *A Country Unmasked: Inside South Africa's Truth and Reconciliation Commission*. Oxford: Oxford University Press.

Boraine, Alex, and Janet Levy. 1995. *The Healing of a Nation?* Cape Town: Justice in Transition.

Borer, Tristan Anne. 2003. "A Taxonomy of Victims and Perpetrators: Human Rights and Reconciliation in South Africa." *Human Rights Quarterly* 25(4): 1088–1116.

Brody, Reed. 2001. "Justice: The First Casualty of Truth?" *The Nation*, April 30.

Brown, Wendy, and Janet Halley, eds. 2002. *Left Legalism/Left Critique*. Durham: Duke University Press.

Carothers, Thomas. 2002. "The End of the Transition Paradigm." *Journal of Democracy* 31(1): 5–21.

Chapman, Audrey, and Patrick Ball. 2001. "The Truth of Truth Commissions: Comparative Lessons from Haiti, South Africa, and Guatemala." *Human Rights Quarterly* 23: 1–43.

Chayes, Antonia, and Martha Minow, eds. 2003. *Imagine Coexistence: Restoring Humanity after Violent Ethnic Conflict*. San Francisco: Jossey-Bass.

Cobban, Helena. 2002. "The Legacies of Collective Violence." *Boston Review* 27(2): 4–15.

Cohen, Stanley. 1995. "State Crimes of Previous Regimes: Knowledge, Accountability, and the Policing of the Past." *Law and Social Inquiry* 20(1): 7–49.

de Brito, Alexandra Barahona, Carmen González-Enríquez, and Paloma Aguilar, eds. 2001. *The Politics of Memory: Transitional Justice in Democratizing Societies*. Oxford: Oxford University Press.

Des Forges, Alison, and Timothy Longman. 2004. "Legal Responses to the Genocide in Rwanda." In *My Neighbor, My Enemy: Justice and Community in the Aftermath of Mass Atrocity*, edited by Eric Stover and Harvey Weinstein, 49–68. Cambridge: Cambridge University Press.

Des Forges, Alison, and Kenneth Roth. 2002. "Justice or Therapy?" *Boston Review* 27: 3–4.

Drumbl, Mark. 2005. "Pluralizing International Criminal Justice." *Michigan Law Review*. http://papers.ssrn.com/sol3/papers.cfm?abstract_id=587430.

Elster, Jon. 2004. *Closing the Books: Transitional Justice in Historical Perspective*. Cambridge: Cambridge University Press.

Fletcher, Laurel E., and Harvey M. Weinstein. 2002. "Violence and Social Repair: Rethinking the Contribution of Justice to Reconciliation." *Human Rights Quarterly* 24: 573–639.

Gibson, James L. 2004. *Overcoming Apartheid: Can Truth Reconcile a Divided Nation?* New York: Russell Sage Foundation.

González-Enríquez, Carmen. 2001. "De-communization and Political Justice in Central and Eastern Europe." In *The Politics of Memory: Transitional Justice in Democratizing Societies*, edited by Alexandra Barahona de Brito, Carmen Gonzaléz-Enríquez, and Paloma Aguilar, 218–247. Oxford: Oxford University Press.

Guatemalan Commission for Historical Clarification. 1996. *Guatemala Memory of Silence: Report of the Commission for Historical Clarification*. http://shr.aaas.org/guatemala/ceh/report/english/toc.html.

Gutmann, Amy, and Dennis Thompson. 2000. "The Moral Foundations of Truth Commissions." In *Truth v. Justice*, edited by Robert I. Rotberg and Dennis Thompson, 22–44. Princeton and Oxford: Princeton University Press.

Habermas, Jurgen. 1997. *A Berlin Republic: Writings on Germany*. Translated by Steven Randall. Lincoln: University of Nebraska Press.

Hayner, Priscilla. 2001. *Unspeakable Truths: Confronting State Terror and Atrocity*. New York: Routledge.

Herf, Jeffrey. 1997. *Divided Memory: The Nazi Past in the Two Germanys*. Cambridge, MA: Harvard University Press.

Hesse, Carla, and Robert Post, eds. 1999. *Human Rights in Political Transitions: Gettysburg to Bosnia*. New York: Zone Books.

Human Rights Center, International Human Rights Law Clinic, University of California, and Centre for Human Rights, University of Sarajevo. 2000. *Justice, Accountability, and Social Reconstruction: An Interview Study of Bosnian Judges and Prosecutors.*

Huyse, Luc. 1995. "Justice after Transition: On the Choices Successor Elites Make in Dealing with the Past." *Law and Social Inquiry* 20(1): 51–77.

Ignatieff, Michael. 1996. "Articles of Faith." *Index on Censorship* 5: 110–122.

Ignatieff, Michael. 2001. *Human Rights as Politics and Idolatry*. Princeton: Princeton University Press.

International Military Tribunal. 1947. *Trial of the Major War Criminals before the International Military Tribunal.* http://avalon.law.yale.edu/subject_menus/imt.asp#proc.

Jochnik, Chris, and Roger Normand. 1994. "The Legitimation of Violence: A Critical History of the Laws of War." *Harvard International Law Journal* 35: 49–95.

Kelsall, Tim. 2005. "Truth, Lies, Ritual: Preliminary Reflections on the Truth and Reconciliation Commission in Sierra Leone." *Human Rights Quarterly* 27: 361–391.

Kritz, Neil, ed. 1995. *Transitional Justice: How Emerging Democracies Reckon with Former Regimes*. Washington, DC: US Institute of Peace.

Leahy, Patrick J., 2009. "Commission of Inquiry." Congressional Record S2461-2463, February 25, 2009 (Senate).

Leebaw, Bronwyn A., 2001. "Restorative Justice for Political Transitions: Lessons from the South African Truth and Reconciliation Commission," *Contemporary Justice Review* 4: 267–289.

Long, William J., and Peter Brecke. 2003. *War and Reconciliation: Reason and Emotion in Conflict Resolution*. Cambridge, MA: MIT Press.

Malamud-Goti, Jaime. 1990. "Transitional Governments in the Breach: Why Punish State Criminals?" *Human Rights Quarterly* 12(3): 1–46.

Mamdani, Mahmood. 1996. "Reconciliation without Justice." *Southern Review* 10(6): 22–25.

McAdams, A. James, ed. 1997. *Transitional Justice and the Rule of Law in New Democracies*. Notre Dame: University of Notre Dame Press.

McCarthy, Thomas. 2002. "Vergangenheitsbewältigung in the USA: On the Politics of Memory and Slavery." *Political Theory* 30: 623–648.

Meister, Robert. 2002. "Human Rights and the Politics of Victimhood." *Ethics and International Affairs* 16(2): 91–108.

Meister, Robert. 2012. *After Evil: A Politics of Human Rights*. New York: Columbia University Press.

Mendeloff, David. 2004. "Truth-Seeking, Truth-Telling, and Post-Conflict Peacebuilding: Curb the Enthusiasm?" *International Studies Review* 6: 355–380.

Méndez, Juan E. 2001. "National Reconciliation, Transnational Justice, and the International Criminal Court." *Ethics and International Affairs* 15: 25–44.

Minow, Martha. 1998. *Between Vengeance and Forgiveness: Facing History after Genocide and Mass Violence*. Boston: Beacon Press.

Moghalu, Kinglsey Chiedo. 2002. "Image and Reality of War Crimes Justice: External Perceptions of the International Criminal Tribunal for Rwanda." *Fletcher Forum of World Affairs* 26: 21–43.

Nagy, Rosemary. 2008. "Transitional Justice as Global Project: Critical Reflections." *Third World Quarterly* 28(2): 275–289.

Nettlefield, Lara J. 2010. "Research and Repercussions of Death Tolls: The Case of the Bosnian Book of Dead." In *Sex, Drugs, and Body Counts: The Politics of Numbers in Global Crime and Conflict*, edited by Peter Andreas and Kelly M. Greenhill, 159–187. Ithaca, NY: Cornell University Press.

Nino, Carlos. 1996. *Radical Evil on Trial*. New Haven: Yale University Press.
Orentlicher, Diane. 1991. "Settling Accounts: The Duty to Prosecute Human Rights Violations of a Prior Regime." *Yale Law Review* 100: 2539–2615.
Osiel, Mark. 1997. *Mass Atrocity, Collective Memory, and the Law*. New Brunswick: Transaction Press.
Osiel, Mark. 2005. "The Banality of Good: Aligning Incentives against Mass Atrocity." *Columbia Law Review* 105(6): 1751–1862.
Peskin, Victor. 2000. "International Justice and Domestic Rebuilding: An Analysis of the Role of the International Criminal Tribunal for Rwanda." *Journal of Humanitarian Assistance*. Accessed April 9, 2005. http://www.jha.ac/greatlakes/b003.htm.
Peskin, Victor, and Mieczylslaw P. Boduszynski. 2003. "International Justice and Domestic Politics: Post-Tudjman Croatia and the International Criminal Tribunal for the Former Yugoslavia." *Europe–Asia Studies* 55(7): 1117–1142.
Phelps, Teresa Godwin. 2004. *Shattered Voices: Language, Violence, and the Work of Truth Commissions*. Philadelphia: University of Pennsylvania Press.
Philpott, Daniel. 2012. *Just and Unjust Peace: An Ethic of Political Reconciliation*. New York: Oxford University Press.
Pion-Berlin, David. 1993. "To Prosecute or to Pardon? Human Rights Decisions in the Latin American Southern Cone." *Human Rights Quarterly* 16(1): 105–130.
Pupavac, Vanessa. 2004. "International Therapeutic Peace and Justice in Bosnia." *Social Legal Studies* 13: 377–401.
Renan, Ernst. 1990. "What Is a Nation?" Reprinted in *Nation and Narration*, translated by Martin Thom and edited by Homi Bhabha, 8–22. London: Routledge.
Roht-Arriaza, Naomi, ed. 1995. *Impunity and Human Rights in International Law and Practice*. New York and Oxford: Oxford University Press.
Roht-Arriaza, Naomi. 2006. "The New Landscape of Transitional Justice." In *Transitional Justice in the Twenty-First Century: Beyond Truth versus Justice*, edited by Naomi Roht-Arriaza and Javier Mariezcurrena, 1–16. New York: Cambridge University Press.
Roht-Arriaza, Naomi, and Javier Mariezcurrena, eds. 2006. *Transitional Justice in the Twenty-First Century: Beyond Truth versus Justice*. New York: Cambridge University Press.
Roth, Kenneth. 1999. "Human Rights in the Haitian Transition to Democracy." In *Human Rights in Political Transitions: Gettysburg to Bosnia*, edited by Carla Hesse and Robert Post, 93–134. New York: Zone Books.
Sanford, Victoria. 2003. *Buried Secrets: Truth and Human Rights in Guatemala*. New York: Palgrave.
Sarat, Austin, ed. 2001. *Law, Violence, and the Possibility of Justice*. Princeton: Princeton University Press.
Shaw, Rosalind. 2005. "Rethinking Truth and Reconciliation Commissions: Lessons from Sierra Leone." US Institute of Peace Special Report 130, February.
Sieder, Rachel. 2001. "War, Peace, and Memory Politics in Central America." In *The Politics of Memory: Transitional Justice in Democratizing Societies*, edited by Alexandra Barahona de Brito, Carmen González-Enríquez, and Paloma Aguilar, 161–189. Oxford: Oxford University Press.
Sikkink, Kathryn, and Carrie Booth Walling. 2007. "The Impact of Human Rights Trials in Latin America." *Journal of Peace Research* 44: 427–445.
Snyder, Jack, and Leslie Vinjamuri. 2003/2004. "Trials and Errors: Principle and Pragmatism in Strategies of International Justice." *International Security* 28: 5–44.
Sriram, Chandra Lekha. 2004. *Confronting Past Human Rights Violations*. London and New York: Frank Cass.

Sriram, Chandra Lekha. 2005. "Transitional Justice Comes of Age: Enduring Lessons and Challenges." *Berkeley Journal of International Law* 23(2): 101–118.

Stover, Eric. 2004. "Witnesses and the Promise of Justice in the Hague." In *My Neighbor, My Enemy: Justice and Community in the Aftermath of Mass Atrocity*, edited by Eric Stover and Harvey M. Weinstein, 104–120. Cambridge: Cambridge University Press.

Stover, Eric. 2005. *The Witnesses: War Crimes and the Promise of Justice in the Hague*. Philadelphia: University of Pennsylvania Press.

Stover, Eric, and Harvey M. Weinstein. 2004. "Conclusion: A Common Objective, a University of Alternatives." In *My Neighbor, My Enemy: Justice and Community in the Aftermath of Mass Atrocity*, edited by Eric Stover and Harvey M. Weinstein, 323–342. Cambridge: Cambridge University Press.

Subotic, Jelena. 2009. *Hijacked Justice: Dealing with the Past in the Balkans*. Ithaca, NY: Cornell University Press.

Teitel, Ruti G. 2000. *Transitional Justice*. New York: Oxford University Press.

Teitel, Ruti G. 2003. "Transitional Justice Genealogy." *Harvard Human Rights Journal* 16: 69–94.

Truth and Reconciliation Commission (TRC) of South Africa. 1998. *The TRC Report*, Vols. I–V. Available at http://www.justice.gov.za/trc/report/index.htm.

Tutu, Desmond Mpilo. 1999. *No Future without Forgiveness*. London: Rider Books.

United Nations Development Program (UNDP). 2003. "Oslo Conference on Justice and Security Sector Reform." http://www.undp.org/bcpr/pubinfo/transitions/2003_04/oslo confhtm.htm.

United Nations Security Council. 2004. "The Rule of Law and Transitional Justice in Conflict and Post-Conflict Societies: Report of the Secretary General." S/2004/616 (August 23). http://www.unrol.org/files/S_2011_634EN.pdf.

Uvin, Peter, and Charles Mironko. 2003. "Western and Local Approaches to Justice in Rwanda." *Global Governance* 9: 219–231.

Valls, Andrew. 2003. "A Truth Commission for the United States?" *Intertexts* 7(2): 157–170.

Villa Vicencio, Charles. 1998. "A Different Kind of Justice: The South African Truth and Reconciliation Commission." *Contemporary Justice Review* 1: 407–428.

Williams, Paul R., and Michael P. Scharf. 2002. *Peace with Justice? War Crimes and Accountability in the Former Yugoslavia*. Lanham, MD: Rowman and Littlefield.

Wilson, Richard A. 2001. *The Politics of Truth and Reconciliation in South Africa: Legitimizing the Post-Apartheid State*. Cambridge: Cambridge University Press.

Zalaquett, Jose. 1992. "Balancing Ethical Imperatives and Political Constraints: The Dilemma of New Democracies Confronting Past Human Rights Violations." *Hastings Law Journal* 43: 1425–1438.

Zehr, Howard. 1990. *Changing Lenses: A New Focus for Crime and Justice*. Scottdale, PA: Herald Press.

12

Pushing States to Prosecute Atrocity: The Inter-American Court and Positive Complementarity

Alexandra Huneeus

I. INTRODUCTION

A key issue regarding the future of the International Criminal Court (ICC) is the evolution of its complementarity regime. Under Article 17 of the Rome Statute, the ICC can take jurisdiction only if a state is "unable or unwilling" to prosecute for genocide, crimes against humanity, or war crimes. The doctrine of complementarity was originally designed as a way to respect sovereignty: states that wanted to avoid international prosecution could do so by initiating domestic prosecutions. But here is the rub: it is the ICC itself that holds the power to decide whether domestic proceedings pass muster, or whether they are flawed and show that the state is "unable or unwilling" to prosecute. Complementarity is thus understood by some as allowing the ICC to monitor the domestic criminal system's response to the crimes that could trigger ICC jurisdiction. Under this vision of "positive complementarity," the ICC has the potential to become not only a site of criminal adjudication but, perhaps more ambitiously, a new kind of global monitoring body that bolsters domestic judiciaries and fosters accountability for international crimes at the national level (Burke-White 2008).

In trying to imagine how such a positive complementarity regime might evolve, and, in particular, how it can be tailored to contribute to post-conflict settings, the experience of the human rights system of the Americas proves vital. Created by the Organization of American States (OAS) in 1959, the Inter-American System (IAS) was born into and shaped by a region in which regime change and state-sponsored violence against civilian populations abounded. The dockets of the Inter-American Court and Commission have been filled with human rights violations that also amount to crimes against humanity, war crimes, and genocide. Through the years, and in parallel to the emergence of a system of international criminal courts, the Court and Commission have quietly developed their own system of oversight of situations of state-sponsored crime and transitional justice. Both organs regularly instruct states to investigate and punish for acts that are international crimes (Huneeus 2013). They then closely monitor state compliance, issuing reports on the advance of national prosecutions and making suggestions for further progress. They also instruct states to compensate victims with material and symbolic reparations, and to provide society sites of remembrance and information about the underlying crimes.

This chapter analyzes the Inter-American Court's established practice of supervising transitional justice situations, highlighting two features that could inform the practice of complementarity under the Rome Statute. The chapter begins with a description of the Inter-American System's demands for transitional justice in the post-dictatorship era, and the organic emergence of something akin to what many hope the ICC's complementarity regime will become. It then highlights two of its distinctive features. The first is the use of experimentalist methods in legal processes. International courts are dependent on states for implementation of their orders, yet they have no top-down means of forcing states to comply. This has been as great a challenge for the international criminal courts (Peskin 2009; Lamont 2010) as it has been for the human rights courts (Hawkins and Jacoby 2010; Hillebrecht 2014). In scenarios in which there is not a clear hierarchical relationship, experimentalist methods of regulation, which "combine more flexible and provisional norms with procedures for ongoing stakeholder participation and measured accountability," can be more effective than top-down command (Sabel and Simon 2004, 1019). By using experimentalist methods, such as holding hearings in which all stakeholders participate in creating an implementation plan, the Inter-American Court has been able, at times, to overcome some of the structural barriers and state-actor resistance that impede prosecution and other transitional justice measures.

The second feature of IAS supervision that could prove relevant to proactive complementarity is the creative pairing of retributive with restorative justice measures, and, in particular, the ongoing participation of victims and other stakeholders in the international as well as domestic criminal proceedings. This participation, the Inter-American System's practice suggests, can be viewed as an act of procedural justice in itself, as it responds to and offsets the victims' systematic exclusion from justice systems in the past. The chapter closes by reflecting on the ways in which the Inter-American System's practice around questions of transitional justice could inform the positive complementarity regime of the International Criminal Court.

II. THE INTER-AMERICAN COURT'S "POSITIVE COMPLEMENTARITY" REGIME

The Inter-American System for Human Rights is one of the world's three major regional human rights systems. Its two main bodies are the Inter-American Commission and the Inter-American Court of Human Rights. While all thirty-five OAS member states are subject to the oversight of the Commission, only twenty are currently under the jurisdiction of the Inter-American Court.[1]

1 Of twenty-four American nations that have ratified the American Convention, twenty-two have also accepted the binding jurisdiction of the Court: Argentina, Barbados, Bolivia, Brazil, Chile, Colombia,

The Inter-American Commission began its work in 1959. Thus, it was a young institution when the era of military dictatorships began in Latin America. As the region's authoritarian regimes began to undertake campaigns of illegal state violence against dissidents in the 1960s and 1970s, the young Commission took on the role of publicizing state-sponsored torture, forced disappearances, and extrajudicial killings. Through field visits and well-documented reports, it was able to reveal the crimes the Southern Cone military dictatorships denied, and it soon forged a reputation for its autonomy and principled opposition (Padilla 1993). With the transitions to democracy in the 1990s, the Commission began to emphasize the individual petition system, moving to a more judicial form. Nonetheless, it remained involved in matters of state violence. Many of the individual petitions that it processed dealt with the unfinished business of the past: finding the disappeared and holding accountable those responsible for the dictatorship's atrocities.

Today the Commission receives roughly 2,000 complaints a year. Once it deems a petition admissible, it investigates the claims and guides the claimant and state toward a friendly settlement. If that fails, the Commission issues a report in which it advises the state to take certain actions. If the state does not comply, the Commission may refer the case to the Court. In 2013 it evaluated 2,061 petitions, issued nineteen reports on individual petitions (reports on the merits), and referred eleven cases to the Court.[2]

The Inter-American Court was created in 1979, and it first issued a judgment in a contentious case in 1988. It began its work, then, in the wake of the political transitions away from dictatorship, and toward the end of the internal conflicts in Central America. Nonetheless, its first cases, and the majority of cases on which it has ruled to this day, have focused on questions of how states contend with the aftermath of state-sponsored atrocity. The synchronicity with the Commission's emphasis is no coincidence. There is no direct petition to the Inter-American Court: it is the Commission that decides which of its individual petition cases to refer to the Court. Thus, through the individual petition system, the two organs have worked together (and at times in tension with one another) to develop legal doctrine and institutional working methods to help Latin American states contend with their violent pasts, and in particular to foster criminal accountability. The Court issues under twenty judgments per year.

Much has been written about the Inter-American System's creative role in developing the law on how states respond to state-sponsored atrocity, and to transitional justice more generally. The IAS has been key to the development of doctrines

Costa Rica, Dominican Republic, Ecuador, El Salvador, Guatemala, Haiti, Honduras, Mexico, Nicaragua, Panama, Paraguay, Peru, Suriname, Trinidad and Tobago, Uruguay, and Venezuela. However, Trinidad and Tobago denounced the Convention and withdrew from the Court's jurisdiction in 1999, and Venezuela denounced it in September 2012.

2 Rep. Inter-Am. Ct. H.R. 2013, available at http://www.oas.org/en/iachr/docs/annual/2013/docs-en/AnnualReport-Chap2A-B.pdf.

related to forced disappearance, the right to truth, the right to justice, and amnesty (including its outlawing of self-amnesties) (Binder 2011; Laplante 2009). But the Commission and the Court have also been concerned with making the rules they enunciate effective on the ground. The two organs have developed a regime of remedial measures that demand retributive and restorative justice in situations of transitional justice, and both organs undertake ongoing monitoring of state compliance to their orders and recommendations as a way to pressure states to take meaningful action.

Among the Inter-American Court's many remedies, the practice of ordering and supervising prosecutions of acts that amount to crimes against humanity is of particular relevance here. Early on in its tenure, the Court concluded that it was not enough to demand monetary compensation for the victims, particularly for the relatives of forced disappearance, who yearned only to learn what had happened to the disappeared and to see justice done. The Court accordingly began to focus its efforts on developing the doctrine of the state's duty to prosecute, demanding that the state undertake a judicial investigation of the underlying atrocities and punish accordingly. It is the only international court that typically orders investigation of criminal responsibility as an equitable remedy. Subsequently, the Court opens the supervisory stage of its process, monitoring the progress of the resulting domestic prosecutions. The Commission, the state, and the victims participate in the ongoing supervision of compliance by submitting reports to the Court and by attending compliance hearings. The Inter-American Court closely monitors criminal proceedings on the ground, engaging local justice systems and courts in particular, and pushing them to action. The Court is currently supervising the progress of domestic prosecutions in more than fifty cases in which the underlying human rights violations are also, on their face, tantamount to genocide, war crimes, or crimes against humanity.

The Court and Commission are not focused exclusively on retributive justice as a response to transitional justice dilemmas. They typically pair orders for retributive measures with restorative measures, tailoring a holistic response to the multifold harms caused by state-sponsored atrocity. In the past, for example, the Inter-American Court has issued orders that the state apologize in an official act, including high-level officers of the state; that the state name a school or street after the victims or construct a memorial for the victims; that the state translate the Court's ruling into local indigenous languages; that the state's police or other officials take classes on human rights (the courts will at times even specify particular human rights content that should be included in the lessons); or that the state create a DNA database to facilitate identification of the disappeared. As with the orders to prosecute, the Court then supervises compliance to these specific equitable orders, monitoring and guiding states toward their fruition through a system of closed hearings and public reports.

The reparatory orders and supervision, taken together, make up a unique and original transitional justice regime forged by the IAS in response to situations on the

Latin American continent. But it is potentially of relevance to the construction of a global complementarity regime of supervision of state response to atrocity. The next section examines in more detail two distinctive features of the IAS system for confronting post-conflict situations.

III. TWO INNOVATIONS FROM LATIN AMERICA

The Inter-American Court is overseeing compliance to fifty-one cases of international crimes in transitional justice situations in which it has ordered states to prosecute, and in which it has issued at least one compliance report.[3] For most of these cases, however, it has issued more than one compliance report: for the fifty-one cases together, it has issued over 160 compliance reports. These compliance reports, some of which are very detailed, provide a rich record of the evolution of the Court's supervision of domestic processes in response to transitional justice situations, and show how the Court has refined its method of ordering and supervising equitable remedies, sometimes in a single case. Analysis of the reports reveals two distinctive features of the Inter-American Court's transitional justice regime that merit further consideration: first, experimentalist methods of fostering domestic prosecution, including engagement of victims and civil society in legal processes; second, enhancing retributive measures with creative restorative measures.

A. *Experimentalism and Weak-Form Review*

The role of the Inter-American Court has expanded with time. Initially, the Court was engaged primarily with the traditional courtly tasks of adjudicating on the merits and ordering monetary compensation. Through the years, however, it began to emphasize equitable remedial orders. Further, it added to its work the supervision of compliance to its orders, as a method of pressuring states to comply. Thus, like the US federal courts described by Abram Chayes's seminal article on public law litigation (1976), the Court remains seized of its cases until the remedies have been fully implemented, supervising and guiding the responses of state bureaucracies, and of justice systems in particular, to its orders.

In striving to pressure states to prosecute though its supervisory jurisdiction, the Court has adopted a variety of experimentalist methods. In the early days of structural reform litigation, US courts used what Simon and Sabel call "command-and-control" tactics (2004). They took on a strong "directive role" for the court in creating the remedy, and issued detailed remedial decrees that attempted to anticipate all the different changes required for compliance. Compliance was understood to be conformity of the burdened party to the detailed decree.

[3] The figures account for the Court's caseload through December 2012. The Inter-American Court's rulings and compliance reports are available on the Court's website, http://www.corteidh.or.cr/.

However, US courts have changed tactics in recent years. As Simon and Sabel note, the more recent trend in public law litigation in the United States, as well as in other countries, is toward experimentalism, in which courts allow the parties and other stakeholders to participate in defining how, exactly, particular goals will be met:

> In the most distinctive cases, the governing norms are general standards that express the goals the parties are expected to achieve – that is, outputs rather than inputs. Typically, the regime leaves the parties with a substantial range of discretion as to how to achieve these goals. At the same time, it specifies both standards and procedures for the measurement of the institution's performance. (Sabel and Simon 2004, 1019)

Another key feature of experimentalist governance is that it is dialogic, meaning that the main stakeholders are empowered to participate in the elaboration of working processes. Scholars of constitutional review in the developing world have recently begun arguing for the importance of dialogic monitoring of compliance as key to the legitimacy and successful implementation of difficult court orders. In a recent discussion of the Colombian constitutional court's rulings, César Rodríguez-Garavito argues that "dialogic decisions tend to open a monitoring process that encourages discussion of policy alternatives" to solve the problem (Rodríguez-Garavito 2011, 1691). Where courts set deadlines, hold public hearings in which many actors participate, and issue follow-up compliance decisions that tailor expectations in response to the dialogue, they achieve higher compliance. Such a practice empowers stakeholders to participate in monitoring, and can "provoke and moderate" a dialogue among public authorities and civil society actors (Rodríguez-Garavito 2011, 1696). Through this ongoing dialogue, a court is able to stimulate deliberation and compromise between interested parties and adapt its own suggestions to realities on the ground, even as it keeps up the pressure and publicizes instances of ongoing noncompliance. The idea is that dialogic processes unlock stalled processes, and facilitate coordination among disparate agencies.

Like US courts and the Colombian constitutional court, the Inter-American Court has begun employing dialogic tools in its supervision phase. The Inter-American Court's remedial orders are detailed if measured against other international judgments. But compared to regulation, they are, as Sable and Simon state, "general standards that express goals" (2004, 1019). They specify the outputs. The inputs, in turn, are defined through an ongoing dialogue among the Court, the parties, and other stakeholders. Starting in 2008, the Court began holding closed supervision hearings to monitor the implementation of its orders. For these hearings, it calls different stakeholders – the state, including different substate actors; the claimants; and the Commission – to appear before it and discuss ways to move toward implementation. In the closed hearings, the judges act more as mediators than adjudicators, helping the parties develop accords and time lines in order to accomplish their goals. At times, the accords adjust or give more detailed content to the original court order demanded, in light of the interests of the parties and the realities of the situation on the ground.

In addition to adopting dialogic tools for its own supervisory process, the Court has ordered that states, in turn, create dialogic processes as they work toward implementation. A major obstacle to implementation of orders to prosecute is that they require concerted action by distinct and autonomous state actors in geographically disparate places. Traditionally, it is the executive, through diplomatic channels, that acts as the Court's interlocutor. But while the executive can single-handedly implement orders for monetary compensation, it cannot single-handedly implement orders to prosecute. These orders require the cooperation of the judiciary (or in federalized states, judiciaries) and the prosecutor, which in Latin American is often a distinct state entity autonomous from the executive. But these state institutions have less involvement with international matters, and may lack incentive to prosecute despite the Inter-American Court's order.[4] Some actors relevant to implementation may not even be aware of the Court's judgment. Through the recommendations that accompany its compliance reports, the Court asks states to create their own working methods for coordination of implementation of orders across the branches of government and different bureaucracies, and to create special working groups to implement its rulings.

In *Masacre Mapiripán v. Colombia*, for example, it ordered the state to create a mechanism for implementation of the ruling that would include participation by the victims, and would last for two years.[5] Colombia complied by putting together the Official Mechanism for Supervision (MOS Mapiripán). Participants included the victims, along with representatives of different state institutions, including the executive, the judiciary, and the national prosecutor. By 2009, the MOS had met twenty-four times to discuss the implementation of the Court's orders, and the victims and state agreed of their own accord to prolong its mandate.[6] The Court has fostered similar institutional innovation in cases against Guatemala, and in other cases against Colombia. In one case against Guatemala, the Court even went so far as to stipulate specific persons who should participate.[7] Note that through these temporary compliance mechanisms, actors beyond the executive learn about the Inter-American Court and come to view compliance to its rulings in a different way. Thus, even if, as in the MOS Mapiripán, they are created for one case only, they are staffed by local state officials, who may learn through the experience. The mechanisms thus educate those in the justice system about the international human rights system, and its emphasis on prosecution.

4 Ibid.

5 *Masacre Mapiripán v. Colombia*, Monitoring Compliance with Judgment, "Considering," para. 20 (Inter-Am. Ct. H.R. July 8, 2009), at http://www.corteidh.or.cr/docs/supervisiones/mapiripan_08_07_09_ing.pdf.

6 Ibid.

7 See *Molina-Theissen v. Guatemala*, Monitoring Compliance with Judgment (Inter-Am. Ct. H.R. Nov. 16, 2009) (designating specific actors to coordinate the implementation of the remedies), at http://www.corteidh.or.cr/docs/supervisiones/molina_16_11_09_ing.pdf.

The Inter-American Court's compliance reports also show that Guatemala, a state with one of the highest levels of impunity in the world, has undertaken many efforts to push forward prosecutions in cases that have come before the Inter-American Court. In a report on compliance with *Bámaca Velásquez v. Guatemala*, the Court notes that Guatemala created a Roundtable on Human Rights. Again, this was an instance for dialogue in which otherwise disparate actors such as the judiciary, the public ministry, and the national human rights institution came to the table to discuss issues of impunity.[8] The Roundtable aimed to uncover the anatomy of Guatemala's procedural impunity through analysis of selected cases, including *Bámaca*. In another case, the Court reports that Guatemala created special committees (*Comites de Impulso*), in which members of the judiciary, the public ministry, the executive, and other entities involved in the implementation of the Court orders could discuss and coordinate their actions toward implementation.[9]

Similarly, in a report on compliance in *Gutiérrez Soler v. Colombia* (2009), the Court reports that the state, in a meeting with the victims' representatives, had committed to:

> carry out a joint activity to raise the awareness of judges on the decisions of the Supreme Court of Justice, the Superior Council of the Judicature [*Consejo Superior de la Judicatura*] and the State Council [*Consejo de Estado*] regarding the protection of the victims of human rights violations, [in order to] prevent unfavorable decisions from lower judges who are not cognizant of the case law of [the Inter-American Court].[10]

In a report on compliance with *Castillo Páez v. Peru*, the Court writes that the Peruvian judiciary had, on its own initiative, "created the National Criminal Chamber, with jurisdiction to 'hear crimes against Humanity and crimes that constituted cases of violations to human rights.'"[11] Such a result reflects a reform, instigated by the judges of Peru, which lends visibility, transparency, and speed to the processing of such cases.

In its battle against impunity, then, the Court uses creative measures to achieve compliance, and at the same time encourages and empowers states to do so as well. It orders general "outputs" that the state should achieve, and then engages the parties in dialogic processes through which more specific methods of achieving those

[8] *Bámaca Velásquez v. Guatemala*, Monitoring Compliance with Judgment (Inter-Am. Ct. H.R. Nov. 18, 2010), at http://www.corteidh.or.cr/docs/supervisiones/bamaca_18_11_10_ing.pdf.

[9] *Villagrán Morales et al. v. Guatemala*, Monitoring Compliance with Judgment, Order of the Court (InterAm. Ct. H.R. Jan. 27, 2009), available at http://www.corteidh.or.cr/docs/supervisiones/villagran_27_01_09_ing.pdf.

[10] I/A Court H.R., Case of *Gutiérrez Soler v. Colombia*. Monitoring Compliance with Judgment, para. 28, Order of the Court (InterAm. Ct. H.R. June 30, 2009).

[11] *Castillo Páez v. Peru*, Monitoring Compliance with Judgment, "Declares," paras. 1, 2 (Inter-Am. Ct. H.R. Apr. 3, 2009), at http://www.corteidh.or.cr/docs/supervisiones/castillo_03_04_09_ing.pdf.

outputs are agreed upon. It then monitors the implementation over time, and, through ongoing hearings, allows the parties to revise the working plan if needed.

Some of these innovations are designed to respond to the ruling in one specific case. Even these case-by-case innovations, however, provide state actors with a firsthand lesson on prosecution of (and the problem of impunity for) human rights violations. Through these dialogic mechanisms, state officials working in distinct areas of government come together to learn about and coordinate their actions regarding the international crimes that are the subject of the case.

B. Restorative Justice and Participation by Victims and Civil Society

Transitional justice, "conceived, minimally, as the particular form of justice required by a society's move from a state where international crimes are committed to one where they are no longer" (Mégret 2010, 45), differs from the narrower retributive justice that is traditionally the domain of criminal law. While retributive justice is important, restorative justice measures can contribute greatly toward constructing a stable and peaceful society, and toward individual recovery. In recent years, scholars have argued that the international criminal tribunals should also be concerned with reparative measures, and some argue that for the ICC, ordering reparations "is no longer simply an issue of policy but one increasingly tainted with obligation" (Mégret 2010, 4). At a minimum, the Rome Statute regime acknowledges the importance of measures beyond retributive justice through the Victims Trust Fund and a still-developing reparations regime. Thus it is relevant to consider how the ICC can become involved in reparatory justice not only after a verdict has been reached in its own cases, and not only through the Victims Trust Fund "general assistance" mandate, but also through its complementarity regime.

The Inter-American Court has long interpreted its remedial powers to allow it to order a broad array of transitional justice measures. Indeed, the Inter-American Court is unique in the broad array of victim-focused remedies it orders states to undertake in the wake of atrocity. It orders a variety of reparative measures focused on making the victims whole, and on societal learning and reconciliation, including monetary compensation to victims; victim participation in the criminal proceeding; finding the disappeared; the construction of monuments, shrines, and museums; state apologies; and commemorative rituals. In this realm, moreover, the Court has received relatively high compliance. Three features of the Inter-American Court's reparatory practice merit further consideration in light of the complementarity regime.

The first refers to victim participation. The Inter-American Court – and the rights bodies more generally – afford individuals and civil society an important role throughout the legal process. Most notably, in the Inter-American System individuals work with nongovernmental organizations (NGOs) to initiate proceedings by filing a case before the Inter-American Commission. Thus, IAS involvement in a case is initially triggered by the individual victims: it is victims and civil society that shape the docket. The Commission then tries to resolve the case; if it cannot, it refers the case to the Inter-American Court. Throughout the proceedings before both organs, victims have an important participative role. This is significant because participation in the legal process can itself be a form of remedy, or alleviation of the wrong, and NGOs have played an important part in shaping IAS processes so that they are more responsive to victims' needs (Antkowiak 2011, 279–332). Indeed, the very mechanism here under examination – that of prosecution as a remedial order coupled with ongoing dialogic supervision – developed in light of the demands of victims and their advocates.

Perhaps because of civil society participation in shaping the caseload of the IAS, the IAS remedial and supervisory regimes emphasize, in turn, the role of the victim in the criminal proceeding. The reparations, including the Court's orders to investigate and punish, are formally conceived as focused on making victims whole. In other words, the state must prosecute as a *duty to the victim* (Basch 2007). Further, the Inter-American Court has prioritized victim participation in the judicial process, and, in cases of disappearances, has emphasized the importance of finding the missing. The Inter-American Court requires states to allow victims access to the criminal process (even in closed inquisitorial systems). While this request can violate procedural norms, some states have found creative ways to accommodate the Court's demands for transparency and participation. At least one state has allowed the executive to have access, in the name of the victim, to the initial, and usually secret, stages of the investigation. In response to Court orders, states have also made judicial proceedings more transparent so that victims can follow the prosecution as it progresses, or stalls.

A second feature of interest is the emphasis on the right to the truth. The Inter-American Court has found that victims and their relatives have a right to truth as well as justice (Groom 2011). Relatives of the disappeared in particular have a right to know how their loved ones died, and to know where their remains are buried. The Court thus orders states not only to seek criminal responsibility but also to seek the disappeared. In *Castillo Páez v. Peru*, for example, the Court found that Peru had fulfilled its duty to punish, as all those responsible for the underlying crime had been tried and were serving time. However, it had not fulfilled the duty to investigate, because the victims' bodies had not been found, and the Court held that there was still more the state needed to do to find them.[12] In that case, the duty to find the disappeared was read into the initial order to investigate and prosecute. In more recent cases, the Court issued a distinct remedial order to find the disappeared. In eight cases, states have reported some success in conducting exhumations and returning the remains of the victims to their loved ones, even where prosecutions faltered. One dilemma facing the Court is what to do in those cases where the state

[12] Ibid.

has conducted a verifiably exhaustive investigation, and yet the remains of the disappeared cannot be found. The Inter-American Court has never closed such a case, emphasizing, as some have argued, outcomes over procedure.

A third feature is the emphasis on rituals of memory. The Inter-American Court has been particularly creative in ordering states to conduct rituals of remembrance, such as the construction of shrines and memorials, and holding public ceremonies where the state officially apologizes to the victims. Pursuant to Court orders, states have held public ceremonies in which high-level officials have apologized to victims and their relatives. They have also named streets and schools after victims, and constructed memorials in their honor. The Court's intervention has not always been well received. In one well-known case, the Court ordered Peru to construct a memorial to the victims of the internal conflict and to include the names of *all* victims of the internal conflict, including those who had been members of the Shining Path insurgency. Peru complied, but the order caused a public outcry that the memorial "joined victims and perpetrators."[13] In this area of reparations, state compliance to the Court's orders has been roughly 45 percent, which is higher than compliance with most other forms of reparatory orders (Huneeus 2010; Hillebrecht 2014).

C. The Inter-American Court's Challenges

So far, this chapter has painted a rather rosy picture of the advantages of the Inter-American Court's innovations in transitional justice remedies and supervision. But the experience of the Inter-American System also serves to highlight the challenges and limits an international body faces in fostering national prosecutions.

Like the ICC, the Inter-American Court was created as an institution of adjudication. Through time, its role expanded to include oversight of the implementation of detailed, injunctive relief orders. Its founding instruments, however, have not been updated to reflect many of the evolutionary changes that it has undergone. In other words, the court's elaborate remedial regime and supervisory processes are a judicial creation, and, accordingly, those who oppose the innovations charge that they have no legal basis. A group of academics based in Argentina and Uruguay in particular have condemned the Inter-American Court as "activist," and as overstepping its mandate (Pastor 2005; Basch 2007; Malarino 2012). In particular, they argue that the Court is "neo-punitivist," overemphasizing punitive responses to human rights violations. Recall that the Inter-American Court is the only human rights body to issue binding orders to investigate and punish, and it has done so in a majority of its cases. The European Court of Human Rights (ECHR), by contrast, has repeatedly refused to issue orders to prosecute, despite repeated requests from litigants that it do so (Leach 2008). The opponents of the Inter-American Court, like the ECHR, are of the position that states are due greater deference in criminal matters.

[13] http://elcomercio.pe/politica/741749/noticia-martha-chavez-no-iria-jamas-ojo-que-llora.

Another criticism of human rights courts' work toward accountability is that their "capabilities are ill-suited to the task" (Ratner, Abrams, and Bischoff 2009). Through its supervision of domestic prosecutions, the Inter-American Court delves deeply into national criminal procedures and substantive law. The Latin American legal systems have many shared features, but they are also quite diverse, and seemingly similar institutions have evolved in varied ways. Considering that there are more than twenty criminal legal systems under the Court's jurisdiction, each with its own culture, procedural idiosyncrasies, and laws, one might wonder whether the Court's judges, most of whom are not criminal lawyers, can adequately understand and supervise such a diversity of jurisdictions. Were the ICC to take on the task of supervising domestic prosecutions across the globe and assessing their conformity with the demands of complementarity, it would face an even broader array of institutional cultures. At the same time, this task does not seem more difficult than the kind of learning that international and even national courts often have to undertake. The US Supreme Court is expected to review the work of more than fifty different jurisdictions' criminal procedures for constitutional adherence, and that is only a small piece of its caseload. Nor does it seem more difficult than the challenge of the ICC's work in investigations, during which it has to work with officials and procedures from the different states involved in the investigations it opens.

Perhaps the greatest challenge facing a court that attempts to foster reform of domestic bureaucratic processes is the slow pace of change, as the US federal courts have learned through their experiences with structural reform litigation. Of the fifty-one cases in which the Inter-American Court has issued orders to investigate and punish, it has found compliance in only one. Of the prosecutions that have followed, an average period of five years elapsed between the Court's order to prosecute and the finding that there had been a final judgment in the domestic case. Note that it usually takes seven to eight years for a case to even reach judgment in the Inter-American System, adding to the delay. In the interim, victims and witnesses age and pass away, evidence is lost, and the harm caused by the crimes continues unabated.

Perhaps, however, such slowness is inevitable. The international criminal system is similarly slow, in part because international prosecutions also rely on cooperation from domestic justice systems actors working in systems that have been deemed unable or unwilling to prosecute on their own (Whiting 2009). In considering whether the pace of institutional change is *too* slow, however, the baseline must be not the ideal of the speedy trial, but rather the pace of post-conflict prosecutions in the absence of pressure and intervention from international bodies.

D. The ICC and the Inter-American Experience

International criminal tribunals are created not to displace but to complement, supplement, guide, and otherwise coexist with domestic criminal systems. But fixing the contours of the relationship between the institutions of international criminal justice, on the one hand, and national justice systems, on the other, has posed a central challenge in the new era of international criminal law institutions that began with the ad hoc tribunals for Rwanda and the former Yugoslavia in the 1990s. What type of relationship should supranational courts hold to national criminal legal systems? Do they have a duty to improve national justice systems, and, if so, how? The Inter-American Court's system of supervision, through which it keeps open a dialogue with the state on the obstacles to compliance and how to overcome them, may provide insights as the ICC strives to help states overcome institutional and attitudinal obstacles to prosecution. It is a system that developed slowly over two decades as the Court was confronted with post-conflict situations throughout its hemisphere.

There are important differences between the international criminal and human rights systems, of course. Through restorative measures, the Inter-American Court seeks to accomplish transitional justice goals that are often said to be shared by the international criminal tribunals: societal reconciliation, compensation, and restoring the dignity of victims of mass atrocity. However, because the Inter-American Court does not exert criminal jurisdiction, but rather assigns remedies for a violation of the American Convention, it enjoys greater remedial flexibility than does a criminal court. Further, while the International Criminal Court has worked hard to increase the role of individuals and civil society, only state parties, the prosecutor, or the United Nations Security Council (UNSC) can trigger an international proceeding. Individuals cannot themselves initiate the legal procedure, as they can in the human rights individual petition system.

There are also differences in the contexts in which these two international bodies work. A skeptic might object that the experience of Latin America will not be relevant to the ICC, which has focused its attention on the African states. One difference might be that Latin American judicial systems are more institutionalized and autonomous than those in the states where the ICC is active in Africa. Indeed, some argue that human rights scholarship in general, and the transitional justice scholarship in particular, have overemphasized Latin American experiences in elaborating theories and models (Hafner-Burton and Ron 2013). At the same time, if we consider Latin America to be a leader in transitional justice matters, rather than a typical case, the uniqueness of the Inter-American System, and its long-term, creative involvement in transitional justice issues in the region, suggests itself all the more compellingly: perhaps the IAS is part of the reason for Latin America's leadership on the issue of accountability for state-sponsored crime. In any case, it seems that many of the innovations of the Inter-American Court in its remedial and supervisory regime could translate to other settings of state atrocity. At the least, the IAS experience should be of great relevance to the ICC as it reviews situations in Latin America, where it is in conversation with the very same state actors as the Inter-American Court.

The ICC's mandate is not explicit about how it should exercise complementarity. The ICC, and in particular the Office of the Prosecutor, have been left to forge their own path. Had the ICC chosen to limit complementarity to merely a yes/no decision on whether to open an investigation, its behavior would be clearly within the bounds of the Rome Statute, but it would arguably have wasted an opportunity for having a more diffuse and constructive impact. Instead, the ICC has chosen a path of greater intervention in domestic judicial processes. Through positive complementarity jurisdiction, the ICC casts itself in the role not only of formal adjudicator, but as an actor that supervises national proceedings, and pressures local justice systems toward investigation and punishment – much like the Inter-American Court in its supervisory jurisdiction.

In carrying out this broader mandate, it should borrow from the Inter-American System the spirit of experimentalism and of inclusion of a broad array of local actors in devising solutions to barriers to prosecution on the ground. Using soft power tools, for example, the ICC can emphasize the importance of enhancing victim and civil participation in domestic trials, and of observing the right of victims and their families to know the truth about what happened to those missing or killed. Further, it is possible that the ICC in proactive complementarity mode could monitor not only judicial responses, but other kinds of state undertakings in response to mass atrocity, such as holding truth commissions (Roche 2005; Totten 2009; Mégret 2010).

The terms of the currently unfolding Colombian peace process, over which both the Inter-American Court and the ICC will be called, at some point, to opine, provides an important test-case for complementarity. As part of the peace accord, Colombia has, after much debate, agreed with the FARC guerrilla on the creation of a special jurisdiction for investigating the crimes committed during the internal conflict. Some argue that the agreement allows those who commit the crimes under the jurisdiction of the ICC – especially war crimes and crimes against humanity – to escape too lightly, with alternative sentences. The Rome Statute is not specific about what level of sentencing would trigger or, alternatively, obviate an ICC prosecution, so the ICC arguably has a high degree of discretion on this matter. One reading of the Inter-American Court's legacy – that contained within its judgments –is that of what some call "neo-punitivism": the guilty should be punished at almost any cost. But when read through its supervision and ongoing collaborative work with state and non-state actors, the Inter-American Court's legacy can also be understood to emphasize symbolic reparations, truth-telling, and other societal processes around post-conflict scenarios. And its manner of working with state and non-state actors toward prosecution also shows that prosecutorial processes in the wake of atrocity or civil war do not happen overnight. They can be approximated over time through collaborative work towards overcoming the obstacles to impunity. Compliance to these orders is lower than to other remedial orders, but the compliance records reveal that the states do respond to orders, adjusting their working methods, advancing investigations as political spaces open, and at times even achieving justice (Huneeus 2013).

This more nuanced interpretation of the Inter-American Court's supervisory processes, as opposed to its judgments, might caution the ICC to approach certain complex post-conflict situations with a more deferential, collaborative long-term strategy. It is true, of course, that the ICC carries a bigger stick than the Inter-American Court. In the face of blatant noncompliance, the Inter-American Court simply continues to monitor, ever attempting to engage the state, no matter how unlikely that it will respond. The ICC, by contrast, can wield the strong incentive of opening prosecutions of their own, which carries a greater reputational cost to the state and directly threatens actors of political salience. Alternatively, the ICC also wields the positive incentive of closing a preliminary investigation. One might argue that in light of this greater power, the ICC should rely less on experimentalism, and more on the methods of top-down control. The advantage of involving national stakeholders in crafting progress toward the goals of prosecution and transitional justice, however, is that there is greater buy-in from local actors, and the goals developed are more realistic. These are advantages that most courts – and especially international courts – cannot afford to forgo. In any case, once the ICC does open its own investigation, it will again face the resistance of state justice system actors and other barriers to accountability as it seeks their cooperation in myriad prosecutorial tasks. In the end, all international courts rely on cooperation from states: scholars have shown, and international prosecutors well know, that without willing states, prosecutions are greatly hampered if not entirely impeded from carrying out their work (Peskin 2009).

V. CONCLUSION

In the early twentieth century, there was a scholarly movement that argued for the existence and importance of "Latin American international law," a regime of customary rights and obligations unique to the region (Obregón 2006). This chapter has argued that through the Inter-American System for human rights, Latin American states and civil society have constructed a twenty-first-century regional regime for responding to issues of transitional justice. While the jurisprudence of the Inter-American Court can be read to demand prosecution in every situation and at almost any cost, the Inter-American Court's remedial practice and supervisory regime read more broadly also suggest that prosecutions come slowly, and are only one important aspect of how states respond to atrocity in post-conflict situations. As the ICC continues to develop a global proactive complementarity regime, it should turn to this experience from the South, drawing lessons from the IAS's methods of ordering and supervising domestic prosecutions for international crimes, and of balancing retributive with restorative justice.

REFERENCES

Antkowiak, Thomas M. 2011. "An Emerging Mandate for International Courts: Victim-Centered Remedies and Restorative Justice." *Stanford Journal of International Law* 42: 279–332.

Basch, Fernando Felipe. 2007. "The Doctrine of the Inter-American Court of Human Rights Regarding States' Duty to Punish Human Rights Violations and Its Dangers." *American University International Law Review* 23: 195–229.

Binder, Christina. 2011. "The Prohibition of Amnesties by the Inter-American Court of Human Rights." *German Law Journal* 12: 1203–1230.

Burke-White, William W. 2008. "Implementing a Policy of Positive Complementarity in the Rome System of Justice." *Criminal Law Forum* 19: 59–85.

Chayes, Abram. 1976. "The Role of the Judge in Public Law Litigation." *Harvard Law Review* 89: 1281–1316.

Groom, Dermot. 2011. "The Right to Truth in the Fight against Impunity." *Berkeley Journal of International Law* 29: 175–199.

Hafner-Burton, Emily, and James Ron. 2013. "The Latin Bias: Regions, the Western Media and Human Rights Coverage, 1981–2000." *International Studies Quarterly* 57: 474–491.

Hawkins, Darren, and Wade Jacoby. 2010. "Partial Compliance: A Comparison of the European and Inter-American Courts of Human Rights." *Journal of International Law and International Relations* 6: 35–85.

Hillebrecht, Courtney. 2014. *Domestic Politics and International Human Rights Tribunals: The Problem of Compliance*. New York: Cambridge University Press.

Huneeus, Alexandra. 2010. "Courts Resisting Courts: Lessons from the Inter-American Court's Struggle to Enforce Human Rights." *Cornell International Law Journal* 44: 101–142.

Huneeus, Alexandra. 2013. "International Criminal Law by Other Means: The Quasi-Criminal Jurisdiction of the Human Rights Courts." *American Journal of International Law* 107: 1–44.

Lamont, Christopher K. 2010. *International Criminal Justice and the Politics of Compliance*. Burlington, VT: Ashgate Publishing Company.

Laplante, Lisa J. 2009. "Outlawing Amnesty: The Return of Criminal Justice in Transitional Justice Schemes." *Virginia Journal of International Law* 49: 915–984.

Leach, Phillip. 2008. "The Chechen Conflict: Analysing the Oversight of the European Court of Human Rights." *European Human Rights Law Review* 6: 732–761.

Malarino, Ezequiel. 2012. "Judicial Activism, Punitivism and Supranationalisation: Illiberal and Antidemocratic Tendencies of the Inter-American Court of Human Rights." *International Criminal Law Review* 12: 665–695.

Mégret, Frédéric. 2010. "Of Shrines, Memorials and Museums: Using the International Criminal Court's Victim Reparation and Assistance Regime to Promote Transitional Justice." *Buffalo Human Rights Law Review* 16: 1–56.

Obregón, Liliana. 2006. "Noted for Dissent: The International Life of Alejandra Álvarez." *Leiden Journal of International Law* 19: 983–1016.

Padilla, David J. 1993. "The Inter-American Commission on Human Rights of the Organization of American States: A Case Study." *American University International Law Review* 9: 95–115.

Pastor, Daniel R. 2005. "La Deriva Neopunitivista de Organismos y Activistas como Causa del Desprestigio Actual de los Derechos Humanos." *Nueva Doctrina Penal* 73(1): 73–114.

Peskin, Victor. 2009. *International Justice in Rwanda and the Balkans: Virtual Trials and the Struggle for State Cooperation*. New York: Cambridge University Press.

Ratner, Steven R., Jason S. Abrams, and James L. Bischoff. 2009. *Accountability for Human Rights Atrocities in International Law: Beyond the Nuremberg Legacy*. New York: Oxford University Press.

Roche, Declan. 2005. "Truth Commission Amnesties and the International Criminal Court." *British Journal of Criminology* 45: 565–581.

Rodríguez-Garavito, César. 2011. "Beyond the Courtroom: The Impact of Judicial Activism on Social and Economic Rights in Latin America." *Texas Law Review* 89: 1669–1698.

Sabel, Charles F., and William H. Simon. 2004."Destablization Rights: How Public Law Litigation Succeeds." *Harvard Law Review* 117: 1015–1101.

Totten, Christopher D. 2009. "The International Criminal Court and Truth Commissions: A Framework for Cross-Interaction in the Sudan and Beyond." *Northwestern Journal of International Human Rights* 7: 1–33.

Whiting, Alex. 2009. "In International Criminal Prosecutions, Justice Delayed Can Be Justice Delivered." *Harvard International Law Journal* 50: 323–364.

13

When Law and Social Science Diverge: Causation in the International Law of Incitement to Commit Genocide

Richard A. Wilson[1]

I. INTRODUCTION

Prior to the outbreak of the armed conflict, the SDS started waging a propaganda war which had a disastrous impact on the people of all ethnicities, creating mutual fear and hatred and particularly inciting the Bosnian Serb population against the other ethnicities. Within a short period of time, citizens who had previously lived together peacefully became enemies and many of them, in the present case mainly Bosnian Serbs, became killers, influenced by a media, which by that time, was already under the control of the Bosnian Serb leadership.

Brđanin Trial Chamber Judgment (2004, ¶80)[2]

Over the past decade, there has been an appreciable shift at international criminal tribunals and in domestic legal proceedings toward greater criminalization of propaganda and inflammatory speech acts during armed conflict and genocide.[3] During and after the 1994 genocide in Rwanda, observers emphasized the role of media propaganda in inciting ordinary Rwandans to participate in the extermination of 500,000 members of the Tutsi minority population, with one of the more influential accounts of the role of the media stating that the two main tools of the genocide were "the radio and the machete" (Chrétien, Dupaquier, Kabanda, and Ngarambe 1995, 191). As a steady stream of commentators referred to "radio genocide" and "death by radio" and "the soundtrack to genocide," a widespread

[1] Special thanks are due to Eleni Coundouriotis, Predrag Dojčinović, Jordan Kiper, and Nishith Prakash. Research assistants Janie Crocco and Ahmad Wais Wardak provided invaluable support.

[2] *Prosecutor v. Radoslav Brđanin* (Case No. IT-99–36) Trial Chamber Judgment, IT-99–36-T, September 1, 2004 ("*Brđanin* Trial Judgment").

[3] See Dojčinović (2011), Gordon (2008, 2010, 2012), Kearney (2007), and Timmermann (2005, 2006) on the growing criminalization of propaganda in international law. With regard to domestic jurisdictions, see *Mugesera v. Canada* (Minister of Citizenship and Immigration), [2005] 2 S.C.R. 100, 2005 SCC 40 (Can.), June 28, 2005, which issued a deportation order based on a speech made by the defendant in Rwanda in 1992 that the court deemed incitement to commit genocide. On *Mugesera*, see Schabas (1999) and Rikhof (2005). In the United Kingdom, the Racial and Religious Hatred Act (2006) makes it an offense to incite hatred against a person on the grounds of the individual's religion.

consensus emerged that key responsibility for the genocide lay with the Rwandan media.[4]

A direct connection between media broadcasts and widespread human rights violations was articulated in successive judgments of the International Criminal Tribunal for Rwanda (ICTR) that found the defendant guilty of genocide and/or direct and public incitement to commit genocide.[5] While the International Criminal Tribunal for the Former Yugoslavia (ICTY) never issued an indictment for direct and public incitement to commit genocide, defendants such as Radoslav Brđanin were charged with complicity to commit genocide, in part on the basis of their speeches. In a number of other ICTY trials, prosecutors have introduced evidence from speeches and propagandistic broadcasts as evidence of the defendant's participation in a joint criminal enterprise to commit crimes against humanity.[6] Propaganda became one of the ICTY's overarching explanations for why neighbors became killers in the 1991–1995 conflict in the former Yugoslavia, as illustrated in the opening quote from the *Brđanin* Trial Chamber Judgment.

This chapter examines the framework of criminal accountability for direct and public incitement to commit genocide (ICG) and evaluates the repeated claims made in ICTR Trial Chamber Judgments that there was a causal connection between speech acts and genocidal acts of violence. What is immediately curious and perplexing about the judgments at the ICTR (e.g., *Akayesu*, *Nahimana et al.*, *Ruggiu*) is that in international criminal law, direct and public incitement to commit genocide is an "inchoate" crime, meaning that only the intention of the speaker matters: there is no requirement that the crime of genocide occur.[7] Therefore no causal link between a speech act and subsequent genocidal acts need be shown: demonstrating that a speech, broadcast, or publication made a public and direct call to exterminate a protected group is sufficient to establish criminal responsibility for ICG.

4 See Kellow and Steeves (1998), La Mort (2009), Pavlakis (2008), Schabas (2000), and Thompson (2007). Straus (2007, 612) reviews numerous instances of the "genocide by radio" theory. A prosecution expert witness at the ICTR, Mathias Ruzindana (2011, 145), exemplifies this view when he writes, "In the case of the 1994 genocide in Rwanda, the effect of language was lethal . . . hate media played a key role in the instigation of genocide."

5 On incitement to commit genocide specifically, see Mendel (2006).

6 In addition to the Trial Chamber judgment against Radoslav Brđanin (¶80, 323–332), see the 2010 Trial Chamber judgment against Milan Gvero, Assistant Commander for Morale of the Bosnian Serb Army (*Popović et al.* Trial Chamber Judgment; on Gvero's propaganda role, see ¶¶1812–1821). See *Prosecutor v. Vojislav Šešelj*. Case No. IT-03–67, Third Amended Indictment, December 7, 2007, ¶¶5, 10b. See Oberschall (2010), expert witness for the prosecution in the trial of Vojislav Šešelj. See also *Prosecutor v. Radovan Karadžić*. Case No. IT-95–5/18-PT. Third Amended Indictment, February 27, 2009. ¶14c. "Disseminating, encouraging and/or facilitating the dissemination of propaganda to Bosnian Serbs intended to engender in Bosnian Serbs fear and hatred of Bosnian Muslims and Bosnian Croats or to otherwise win support for and participation in achieving the objective of the joint criminal enterprise." Surdukowski (2004) asks whether the poetry of Bosnian Serb President Radovan Karadžić might constitute the basis of a case against him for war crimes.

7 On inchoate crimes generally, see Cahill (2012). See Alexander and Kessler (1997) on inchoate crimes and mens rea.

Nonetheless, ICTR judges have advanced robust claims about the direct, causal relationship between inciting speeches and subsequent public violence in the context of the Rwandan genocide, and they have not only asserted that this constitutes factual proof of ICG, but have gone on to indicate that causation is a legal requirement for proving ICG. Introducing a causality requirement for incitement is a radical departure from two centuries of the criminal law of inchoate crimes. This chapter evaluates the developing jurisprudence on the role of speeches and propaganda in the light of social science studies of the concrete effects of propaganda in Rwanda in 1994, and concludes that the Tribunal's understanding of causality is neither clearly reasoned nor especially justified by the evidence.

The chapter also seeks to make a contribution to the wider theoretical question, why do courts make bad law? The answer, I argue, is not only to be found doctrinally (i.e., by reference to the internal logic of jurisprudence or judicial reasoning per se). In seeking to understand why an international criminal tribunal has handed down flawed judgments, the chapter proposes a legal realist explanation that refers to the concerns (and, indeed, anxieties) that prosecutors and judges shared regarding the threshold of special intent to commit genocide. In so doing, I hope to contribute to the growing literature on the internal organization and culture of international criminal law institutions.[8]

II. SPEECH ACTS AND CAUSATION IN INTERNATIONAL CRIMINAL LAW

> A person commits the crime of direct and public incitement to commit genocide if he directly and publicly incites the commission of genocide with the intent to directly and publicly incite others to commit genocide, which presupposes a genocidal intent. As an inchoate crime, public and direct incitement to commit genocide is punishable even if no act of genocide has resulted therefrom.
>
> Bikindi Trial Chamber Judgment (2008, ¶419)

US Constitutional law places well-known legal protections on freedom of speech, but there is also a fairly deep case law that limits violent speech and "fighting words" that "by their very utterance inflict injury."[9] The prevailing incitement case in US law is *Brandenburg v. Ohio* (1969), which involved a Ku Klux Klan leader in Ohio who was fined $1,000 and sentenced to 1 to 10 years' imprisonment for inciting violence against African-Americans and Jews at a public televised rally in 1964.[10] The US Supreme Court reversed Brandenburg's conviction, noting that while his speech was "derogatory," it merely advocated vague and abstract measures and did not represent incitement to likely law violation or "imminent lawless action."[11]

8 See also Nuijten and Anders (2009), Clarke (2009), Hagan (2003), and Kelsall (2009).

9 *Chaplinsky v. State of New Hampshire*, 315 U.S. 568 (1942).

10 *Brandenburg v. Ohio*, 395 U.S. 444 (1969).

11 Up until that point, the standard had been the "clear and present danger" test that first appeared in the *Schenck* decision (1919).

On its own, mere advocacy of force or violence is not prohibited in US law. In the "Brandenburg test," public speech does not warrant First Amendment protection when all three of the following conditions are met: (1) it is intended to incite violence or lawlessness, (2) it is likely to incite such action, and (3) such lawlessness is likely to occur imminently. There remain a number of unresolved issues, however, and Healy (2009, 660) notes that *Brandenburg* "does not tell us how likely it must be that speech will lead to unlawful conduct or how imminent that conduct must be."[12] US law warrants a mention here because elements of the judicial reasoning found in *Brandenburg*, and the gray areas surrounding likelihood and imminence, resurface repeatedly in the international criminal law of incitement.

In international law, criminal responsibility for propaganda and violent speech was first established in the Julius Streicher case at the Trial of the Major War Criminals before the International Military Tribunal (IMT) at Nuremberg in 1945–1946. Founder and publisher of *Der Stürmer*, a vicious anti-Semitic German weekly, Streicher was convicted on October 1, 1946, of "persecution on political and racial grounds in connection with war crimes" punishable as a crime against humanity under the IMT Charter. Streicher was the only defendant convicted and executed at Nuremberg solely for count four of crimes against humanity. Justifying its verdict, the Tribunal noted that the defendant had knowledge of Hitler's policy of extermination of the Jews and yet he continued to incite Germans "to murder and extermination at the time when Jews in the East were being killed under the most horrible conditions." In an interview some twenty years after the Nuremberg trials, British prosecutor Mervyn Griffith-Jones clarified that the prosecution's case rested on Streicher's involvement as an accessory to genocide – his incitement and encouragement of a policy of extermination of the Jews made him "a party to the crime" (quoted in Eastwood (2011, 220).

Nevertheless, the fleeting, almost cursory Streicher judgment failed to "specifically define the *mens rea* necessary for an act of incitement to genocide," according to Margaret Eastwood (2011, 220). In addition to leaving criminal intent indeterminate, the decision was also short on specifics regarding the mechanisms through which propaganda influenced historical events. Notably, it did not find a nexus between Streicher's speeches/publications and actual violent events, but rather asserted a link between his propaganda and the anti-Semitic mind-set of Germans: "In speeches and articles, week after week, month after month, he [Streicher] infected the German mind with the virus of anti-Semitism and incited the German people to active persecution."[13] The IMT judgment found evidence of a connection, not between the defendant's mind and subsequent genocidal acts, but between the defendant's mind and the minds of other Germans, through the metaphor of viral contagion.

[12] For a useful discussion of First Amendment and *Brandenburg* jurisprudence, see Gey (2010).

[13] Judgment of the International Military Tribunal for the Trial of the Major War Criminals. Streicher, "Crimes against Humanity." On the trial of Streicher, see Taylor (1992, 376–380).

In the aftermath of Nuremberg, on December 9, 1948, the United Nations General Assembly adopted the Convention on the Prevention and Punishment of the Crime of Genocide, Article III(c) of which declared "direct and public incitement to commit genocide" to be an international crime. Given the brevity of judicial commentary in *Streicher* and the dearth of incitement cases in international courts after 1948,[14] the International Criminal Tribunal for Rwanda (ICTR) established in 1994 had little international jurisprudence to guide its reasoning on the role of propaganda during the Rwandan genocide.[15] The Trial Chamber confronted this question head-on in its very first case, and in 1998 convicted the defendant, Jean-Paul Akayesu, of direct and public incitement to commit genocide under Article 2(3)(c) of the ICTR statute.[16]

The verdict in *Akayesu* contained two novel aspects that distinguished it from *Streicher* and from conventional domestic criminal laws of incitement more generally: its formulation of "direct," and its claims about the causal effects of speech. Whereas the IMT decision quoted Streicher's plain, self-evident calls for the extermination of the Jews, the ICTR in *Akayesu* adopted a broad view of incitement that encompassed implicit as well as explicit calls to exterminate a protected group. The Trial Chamber in *Akayesu* based its understanding of the nuances of Kinyarwanda and the cultural meaning of speeches on the report and testimony of Dr. Mathias Ruzindana, the prosecution's expert witness on Kinyarwanda linguistics (see Ruzindana 2011, 145–170). The judgment held that Akayesu's exhortations to fight "the Inkotanyi" to a crowd of 100 people at Gishyeshye in the early hours of April 19, 1994, "would be construed as a call to kill the Tutsi in general."[17] *Akayesu*'s generous interpretation of euphemistic calls to genocide created a resilient precedent, and the ICTR Trial Chamber would adopt an even more expansive reading in later cases such as *Ruggiu* (2000), where it stated that "the term *Inyenzi* (generally construed as 'cockroaches') became synonymous with the term 'Tutsi'" (*Ruggiu* Trial Chamber Judgment 2000, ¶44(iii)). With the passage of time, the expression "go to work" "came to mean 'go kill the Tutsis and Hutu political opponents of the interim government'" (*Ruggiu* Trial Judgment, ¶44(iv)). In my view, the Trial Chamber's repeated declarations of a causal relationship between a defendant's words and criminal deeds were made in order to justify including euphemistic speech within the boundaries of the directness criterion of the crime of ICG.

[14] In the years between 1948 and 1998, the International Law Commission issued a Draft Code of Crimes against the Peace and Security of Mankind (1996), which contains incitement to a variety of crimes such as genocide, war crimes, the crime of aggression, and crimes against humanity. Article 2.3(f) states that liability is established only where the accused "directly and publicly incites another individual to commit such a crime which in fact occurs." http://untreaty.un.org/ilc/texts/instruments/English/draft%20articles/7_4_1996.pdf.

[15] The ICTR was established on November 8, 1994, by UN Security Council Resolution 955.

[16] *Prosecutor v. Jean-Paul Akayesu* (Case No. ICTR-96–4), Trial Chamber Judgment, ICTR-96–4-T, September 2, 1998 (henceforth "*Akayesu* Trial Judgment").

[17] *Akayesu* TC, ¶673(iv). In addition, the judgment notes that *Inkotanyi* means literally "warriors" and at the time was a term commonly used to refer to the soldiers of the Rwandan Patriotic Front (¶147).

Second, and most important for this chapter, the Trial Chamber made conspicuous claims about the causal effects of one of the defendant's speeches:

> The Chamber is of the opinion that there is a causal relationship between Akayesu's speeches at the gathering of 19 April 1994 and the ensuing widespread massacres of Tutsi in Taba. (*Akayesu* TC, ¶673(vii))[18]

In finding Akayesu guilty of direct and public incitement to commit genocide, the ICTR Trial Chamber saw it as pertinent that Akayesu's call to arms "was indeed successful and did lead to the destruction of a great number of Tutsi in the commune of Taba" (*Akayesu* TC, ¶673(vii)). Furthermore, *Akayesu* went beyond mere findings of fact about the circumstances of the case to seemingly elevate the causality to a legal requirement to prove incitement, stating that "there must be proof of a *possible causal link* between the statement made by the Accused during the said meeting and the beginning of the killings" (*Akayesu* Trial Judgment ¶349; my emphasis).[19]

Subsequent ICG cases at the ICTR have referenced and amplified the causal element established in *Akayesu*. For instance, the *Ruggiu* Trial Judgment in 2000, in a case where the defendant pleaded guilty to the charge of ICG, found that "RTLM broadcasters, managerial and editorial staff bear full responsibility for the 1994 massacre of Tutsis and Hutu opposition party members" (*Ruggiu* Trial Judgment, ¶44(xiii)), and the judgment quotes the defendant's admission that "there was a direct link with what I said and their deaths" (¶45). Yet no trial grounded liability for ICG in the causal effects of speech acts more than did *Prosecutor v. Ferdinand Nahimana, Jean-Bosco Barayagwisa, Hassan Ngeze*,[20] also known as the "Media Trial." The three defendants in this case were all owners of major Rwandan media outlets: Ferdinand Nahimana and Jean-Bosco Barayagwisa were both government ministers and founders of the main independent radio station, Radio Télévision Libre des Milles Collines (RTLM), and Ngeze was the owner and editor of *Kangura*,[21] a widely distributed Rwandan newspaper. All were convicted in 2003 of ICG in a verdict that constructed its case for incitement upon the causal connection between speeches and radio broadcasts and subsequent public violence. The judgment affirms a causal connection between speech acts and genocidal killings no less than sixteen times using language such as:

> Many of the individuals specifically named in RTLM broadcasts after 6 April 1994 were subsequently killed. . . . While the extent of causation by RTLM broadcasts in these killings may have varied somewhat, depending on the circumstances of these

18 The public address was given at the village of Gishyeshye.

19 On the causation element specifically in *Akayesu*, see Wallenstein (2001).

20 For legal commentary on the Media Trial, see Davidson (2004); Gordon (2005, 2010, 2012); MacKinnon (2009); Maravilla (2008); Orentlicher (2005); Zahar (2005).

21 Literally, "Wake Others Up!"

> killings, the Chamber finds that a causal connection has been established by the evidence. (¶482)
>
> Without a firearm, machete or any physical weapon, he [Nahimana] caused the deaths of thousands of innocent civilians. (¶1099)

In response to the defense's request for proof of the connection between RTLM broadcasts and acts of genocide, *Nahimana* identified three types of evidence. First, a number of Tutsi individuals specifically mentioned by name in RTLM broadcasts prior to April 6, 1994, were subsequently killed (¶478). That broadcasts motivated listeners to take action was proven by the testimony of one witness who reported being accosted in the street by an attacker who referred to the content of an RLTM broadcast (¶479). The final indication of the nexus between broadcasts and killings could be found in the threat perceived by individuals who had been named in RTLM broadcasts (¶479). *Nahimana* referenced *Akayesu*'s factual finding of a causal relationship between the defendant's speech and widespread massacres, and, in the legal findings section, the judgment (mistakenly) stated that the *Akayesu* judgment established causation as an element of the crime. A few sentences later, the *Nahimana* Trial Chamber backtracked, reaffirming the conventional view that causation is "not requisite to a finding of incitement."

What was the mechanism through which propaganda exerted its causal force? *Nahimana* invoked Nuremberg's hypodermic needle metaphor in which the propagandist injects poison into the minds of a civilian population. The Media Trial verdict explicitly cited *Streicher* (*Nahimana* TC ¶981) as it sought to comprehend the consequences of the publications and broadcasts of the three accused:

> RTLM "spread petrol throughout the country little by little, so that one day it would be able to set fire to the whole country." This is the poison described in the Streicher judgement. (¶1078)
>
> He [Ngeze] poisoned the minds of his readers, and by words and deeds caused the death of thousands of innocent civilians. (¶1101)[22]

In 2007, the ICTR Appeals Chamber reversed a number of the Trial Chamber's findings.[23] It overturned the conviction for ICG against the defendant Barayagwisa on the grounds that he was no longer in a position of superior responsibility at the station after April 6, 1994, when the genocide began. Second, and more important, the Appeals Chamber established a clear and binding precedent on the temporality of ICG, declaring that RTLM broadcasts could not have substantially contributed to the commission of acts of genocide *prior* to the start of the actual genocide.[24]

22 In addition: "The ethnic hatred that permeates *Kangura* had the effect of poison, as evidenced by the testimony of the witnesses (*Nahimana* TC ¶243)."

23 *Prosecutor v. Ferdinand Nahimana, Jean-Bosco Barayagwisa, Hassan Ngeze* (Case No. ICTR-99–52); Appeals Chamber Judgment, ICTR-99–52-A, November 28, 2007. ("*Nahimana* Appeal Judgment").

24 *Nahimana* Appeal Judgment, ¶728 et passim. Note especially: "The Appeals Chamber thus finds that, although it is clear that RTLM broadcasts between 1 January and 6 April 1994 incited ethnic hatred, it has not been established that they directly and publicly incited the commission of genocide" (¶754). At

According to this new temporality requirement, the crime of ICG could be committed only in the context of an ongoing genocide, and in this way the ICTR echoed the "imminence" requirement of *Brandenburg*. The Appeals Chamber rejected the Trial Chamber's evidence of a link between RTLM broadcasts and acts of genocide for the time period preceding April 6, 1994, declaring such evidence "at the very least, tenuous" (¶513). The 2007 decision confirmed the convictions against Nahimana and Ngeze for ICG, and did not challenge the Trial Chamber's legal reasoning on the significance of causation in establishing the crime of ICG. Indeed, the imminence requirement introduced by the Appeals Chamber could be said to have reinforced the centrality of causation.

ICTR verdicts in ICG cases have continued in this vein – for instance, in the 2008 conviction of Rwandan musician Simon Bikindi on the basis of his calls to violence made over a public address system while genocide was occurring.[25] However, the Bikindi judgment refrained from the strong references to causation seen previously in *Nahimana*. While the Trial Chamber stated that Bikindi's "songs inspired action" (¶252), and that "broadcasts of Bikindi's songs had an amplifying effect on the genocide" (¶264), the defendant was not convicted on the basis of his songs or broadcasts, but rather because of his explicit and public calls to eliminate Tutsis that he made in person. This change in emphasis might have resulted in part from a different bench of judges, but could also been the outcome of the different evidentiary basis of the case, and the judgment observes that one witness did not testify to any causal link between Bikindi's speech to a crowd and a subsequent killing, as had been claimed in the initial indictment (¶127). According to Gordon (2010, 623), the Tribunal implicitly confirmed the imminence criterion formulated earlier in *Nahimana* when it absolved Bikindi of liability for anti-Tutsi songs written well before the genocide, stating that, "for words to constitute incitement they must be uttered at, or very near, the time of genocidal violence" (*Bikindi* Trial Judgment, ¶255, ¶421).

The ICTR's (albeit changeable) emphasis on causation as an element of actus reus in ICG cases gives rise to a number of concerns, starting with first principles; namely, as an inchoate crime, the consequences of inciting speech acts are immaterial to the crime's conceptualization and punishment. In contesting centuries of established legal precedent on inchoate crimes, the Tribunal tied itself in analytical knots, perhaps best illustrated in the following passage in *Nahimana*:

> With regard to causation, the Chamber explicitly recalls that incitement is a crime regardless of whether it has the effect it intends to have. In determining whether

¶775, however, the Appeals Chamber found that articles published in the newspaper *Kangura* between January and April 4, 1994 (the onset of the genocide), by the accused Ngeze did constitute ICG. Therefore we could say that the *Nahimana* AC decision is somewhat ambivalent on the temporality criterion.

25 For a cogent discussion of the *Bikindi* Judgment, see Gordon (2010).

> communications represent an intent to cause genocide and thereby constitute incitement, the Chamber considers it significant that in fact genocide occurred. (¶1029)

The second sentence of this paragraph appears to be a non sequitur, or at the least it contradicts the sentence before it, and placing the two statements sequentially defies the principle of logical coherence. This logical flaw in determining intent has knock-on effects, and the *Nahimana* decision exhibits further confusion in the number of disparate models of causation it puts in play. In descending order of robustness, it begins with a "specific and causal connection" (¶949), but also concedes that "the extent of causation by RTLM broadcasts in these killings may have varied somewhat" (¶482), and eventually acknowledges that RTLM broadcasts may not have been the immediate proximate cause of killings and that there may have been a number of intervening factors in addition to the communication (¶952). Add to this the prior *Akayesu* Trial Chamber's insistence on an undefined probability, or "proof of a possible causal link" (¶349), and it is not unfair to say that there is a regrettable lack of clarity and consistency in the ICTR's conceptualization of the role of causation in determining intent in ICG cases.

Other legal observers have also found the ICTR's reasoning on ICG wanting (see Zahar 2005). In a noteworthy edited collection, *Propaganda, War Crimes Trials and International Law* (Dojčinović 2011), Susan Benesch (2011, 254) lucidly identifies the ways in which the "ghost of causation" has haunted the international law of ICG. She observes that in ICG cases, ICTR judges have made stirring pronouncements on causation, even when such pronouncements are neither required by the law nor justified by the circumstantial evidence presented before the Tribunal. On the causal nexus between speech acts and subsequent violence, she recognizes the problem:

> It is difficult to prove such a nexus, since the effect of speech on large groups of people is hard to measure, [is] poorly understood, and is only one of a constellation of forces that affect why people act as they do. (Benesch 2011, 257)

In the place of unfounded claims about the consequences of speeches and broadcasts, Benesch (262), pace *Brandenburg*, formulates a framework for assessing the *likelihood* that a speech act could have resulted in genocide, based on the context of the speech act and the foreseeability that the speech act would have genocidal consequences. Space does not allow me to evaluate Benesch's framework in detail here, but it does seem to offer a more detailed set of criteria for evaluating the degree of risk of speech acts.

III. SOCIAL FACTS AND FABRICATIONS OF LEGAL CAUSATION

> There is something which is at the moment of uttering being done by the person uttering.
>
> J. L. Austin (1962, 12)

The question I would like to turn to now is, given the ICTR Trial Chamber's insistence on the need to show causation in proving ICG, what empirical verification might exist for a causal link between speech acts and violent acts? In recent years, a number of social scientists have conducted empirical studies and quantitative analyses that provide a mixed assessment of the international tribunal's account of the role of propaganda and the media in 1994 Rwanda. It is fair to say that the weight of evidence seems to be against the Tribunal's claims regarding media effects (see also Carver 2000).

The most critical assessment of the ICTR's case law on ICG has come from researchers who have conducted interviews with perpetrators and ascertained that propaganda was quite low on the list of motivating factors in the genocide. In 2000, Rwandan cultural anthropologist Charles Mironko (2007) conducted 100 interviews in Rwandan prisons with self-confessed perpetrators of the genocide. Mironko draws a distinction between two distinct audiences of RLTM – unemployed urban youth and rural peasants – and he found that an overwhelming majority of low-level peasant perpetrators reported not having radio reception in the rural areas. Where perpetrators did have access to radio coverage, the two audiences processed the RLTM broadcasts in different ways, and the messages inciting the population to violent acts were plainer to urban youth who were already armed and organized into *Interahamwe* militias. In his interviews, Mironko (2007, 134) learned that many ordinary peasants either did not receive RTLM's messages or did not necessarily interpret them in the way they might have been intended. Further, they viewed the radio as alien, external to their social milieu and "as a medium for the urban, the educated, and the elite." Mironko therefore urges caution in ascribing a causal link between RTLM broadcasts and genocidal killings: "this information alone did not cause them to kill" (134).

Scott Straus's (2006, 2007) research on the relationship between radio and violence in Rwanda both corroborates and extends Mironko's study. Straus (2007, 614) starts by pointing out that the hypodermic needle model of propaganda used by both the International Military Tribunal and the ICTR has been discredited by four decades of empirical political communication research. He proceeds to identify a number of flaws in the ICTR's reasoning and fact-finding: RLTM's coverage was very uneven, especially in rural areas, and only 10 percent of the population owned a radio in 1994; the initial violence did not correspond with areas of broadcast coverage; and the most extreme and inflammatory broadcasts came after most of the killings had been carried out.[26]

Straus complements his impressive quantitative analysis with 200 perpetrator interviews, and the results of these interviews substantiate Mironko's observations. Radio listeners did not necessarily internalize the elements of anti-Tutsi propaganda, and, perhaps most crucially, no respondent cited the radio broadcasts as

[26] Although Straus (2007, 616) acknowledges that many persons might listen to the same radio.

the most important reason for participation in the genocide. Instead, the primary reasons they gave were face-to-face interactions with an authority figure such as a mayor, or recruitment by groups of men who went from house to house (Straus 2007, 626). To the direct question "Did the radio lead you to take part in the attacks?" 85 percent of Straus's respondents said "no."[27] Like Mironko, Straus infers that the radio broadcasts functioned as a device to coordinate attacks and were meant primarily for local authorities who played the main role in mobilizing citizens directly (628–629): "Radio did not cause the genocide or have direct, massive effects. Rather, radio emboldened hard-liners and reinforced face-to-face mobilization" (631).

Economist David Yanagizawa-Drott (2014) dissents from the emerging social science consensus on the basis of his econometric model and tests using a nationwide village-level data set on radio coverage and prosecutions for genocide. Acknowledging that only about 20 percent of the Rwandan population received RTLM broadcasts from the two transmitters in the country, Yanagizawa-Drott finds that RTLM coverage increased participation in violence by a statistically significant margin. Media effects were most marked where the Hutu population was large and the Tutsi population relatively small [Table 7], and where a village or town had full rather than partial radio coverage [Table 5]. In a bold conclusion, he estimates that radio caused approximately 10 percent of the genocidal violence, corresponding to at least 51,000 deaths (Yanagizawa-Drott 2014, 1947).

How do we account for the divergences in these social science studies? Part of the difference may lie in the different methodologies used, since the main contrast seems to be between qualitative research based on interviews and econometric models.[28] There may also exist other reasons worth considering. While Yanagizawa-Drott's statistical modeling appears to be well formulated and ought to temper any outright skepticism of media effects, it also contains some questionable assumptions. In the absence of any direct measure of the participation rate in the genocide, Yanagizawa-Drott's model turns to a proxy measure: the prosecution rates for violence provided by Rwanda's National Service of Gacaca Jurisdictions. Prosecution rates, however, may not be a reliable indicator of actual participation. In postgenocide Rwanda, where rule of law is inconsistent, prosecutions may be patchy and erratic and focus more on certain parts of the country (e.g., urban areas, the capital Kigali, etc.) and pass over others. Marked regional variations in prosecution rates for the same criminal acts are found even in advanced industrial nations.[29]

27 This raises the thorny question of unconscious motivation and the degree to which propaganda and speeches function subliminally to shape behavior without the social actor being aware.

28 For another economic model of the effects of hate speech, see McAdams and Dharmapala (2005).

29 For the United States, see the Bureau of Justice Statistics: http://bjs.ojp.usdoj.gov/fjsrc/var.cfm?t=new. See also "Federal Prosecutors: Wide Variation Found in Handling of Criminal Referrals for Prosecution," A TRAC Special Report, January 24, 2003. http://trac.syr.edu/tracreports/pros/ausa_pctdecG.html.

Furthermore, and more problematic for Yanagizawa-Drott's analysis, prosecution rates may be intimately associated with radio coverage; that is, it could be that there were more prosecutions in areas of radio coverage because both are associated with urban areas. It could be that there was just as much or more genocidal violence in rural areas that were not reached by radio broadcasts and that went unprosecuted. We just don't know. Treating variables as independent and then measuring the degree of correlation and causation between them, when in fact the variables are dependent upon one another, is what economists call an endogeneity problem. Such design flaws, if not addressed satisfactorily, may be fatal to a study. Finally, there are a number of important independent variables omitted from Yanagizawa-Drott's design, especially the presence and involvement of the Rwandan Army, the principal government institution that directed and coordinated the violence.

Whichever explanation is most likely, we can say that the empirical evidence on the effect of propaganda is mixed, and that the stronger claims made by ICTR judges for a connection between speech acts and violent acts seem to rest on shaky foundations. We could go a step further and say that social science research points to other ways of understanding the role of RLTM and radio during the genocide.[30] Space does not allow me to develop the argument fully here, but it could well be that the radio served less as an initiator of the violence than as an ex post facto legitimating device that mattered most to political elites once the majority of killings had already taken place. It could well be that the primary role of the radio was to justify and to condone, not to instigate, violence.

There is compelling evidence to substantiate this post facto accomplice theory of radio propaganda. Straus (2007, 622) analyzes the timing of the most inflammatory RTLM broadcasts, and most of these occurred after May 7, 1994, by which time most of the killing had already occurred. Broadcasts in the earlier "high genocide" period of April 6 to May 7 were not explicitly genocidal and instead encouraged Rwandans to "be strong," "remain vigilant," and "be heroic." This leads Straus (2007) to infer that RTLM did not spark the violence in the initial instance, but rather validated it after the mass killing had mostly ended. Support for this interpretation can be identified in the *Nahimana* TC judgment when it refers to an RTLM broadcast after a notorious massacre in a mosque in Kivugiza that "accepted, condoned and publicly presented the killing of hundreds of people in a mosque as normal" (¶416). We should at least consider the possibility that the criminal responsibility of the owners and broadcasters of RTLM might lie in how they sought to normalize and legitimize violence. If that were so, then the relevant "mode of liability" in international criminal law terms would be "aiding and abetting" genocide, rather than instigation, incitement, or direct commission.[31]

30 Generally on the relationship between social science and law, see Mertz (2008).

31 See Cryer, Friman, Robinson, and Wilmshurst (2010, 379–380) on distinguishing among instigation, incitement, and aiding and abetting. Cryer cites the *Orić* TC Judgment at ¶271, which states that

IV. LEGAL REALISM AT INTERNATIONAL CRIMINAL TRIBUNALS

Thus far, this chapter has been concerned with the causal effects of speeches in the ICTR's determination of ICG, assessing the judges' claims in terms of the social science research on media effects in Rwanda. It is also worth considering how and why international criminal law got into this predicament in the first place. This calls for a new legal realist approach to international tribunals, one that takes seriously the values and attitudes that motivate the main legal actors in the criminal process and the unique character of international crimes like genocide. What would induce professional judges to apparently abandon centuries of convention on the law of inchoate crimes and require proof of a causal connection between speech acts and the crime of genocide, when there is no legal requirement to do so?

In looking for clues to explain a sudden rupture in legal reasoning, it can be fruitful to look for the places in the text of judicial decisions where the logic breaks down. I have already identified one such place in the *Nahimana* TC judgment earlier in this chapter, and returning to consider this paragraph in full is highly instructive:

> With regard to causation, the Chamber explicitly recalls that incitement is a crime regardless of whether it has the effect it intends to have. In determining whether communications represent an intent to cause genocide and thereby constitute incitement, the Chamber considers it significant that in fact genocide occurred. *That the media intended to have this effect is evidenced in part by the fact that it did have this effect.* (¶1029; my emphasis)

I have already commented on sentences one and two, but sentence three engages in a perplexing reverse logic, where proof of intention is discovered ("in part") in the consequences of a speech act.[32] Can intentions in fact be read off from subsequent acts? It can at times, for instance when individual A encourages individual B to commit a crime and B commits the crime in the way that A intended. And yet this is not an infallible method, since one can think of many other examples where a speech act is highly ambivalent and leads to one outcome, when another may have been intended by the speaker.[33] In such cases, the subsequent effect of speech, or

instigation "requires some kind of influencing the principal perpetrator ... [but] does not necessarily presuppose that the original idea or plan to commit the crime was generated by the instigator. ... However, if the principal perpetrator ... has definitely decided to commit the crime, further encouragement or moral support may merely, though still, qualify as aiding and abetting."

32 The *Nahimana* Appeals Chamber did not find this reasoning erroneous on the grounds that in some circumstances, the fact "that a speech leads to acts of genocide could be an indication that in that particular context the speech was understood to be an incitement to commit genocide and that this was indeed the intent of the author of the speech" (¶709).

33 In a notorious British case, teenager Derek Bentley was hanged in 1953 for the murder of a police officer who was shot by Bentley's accomplice, Christopher Craig, then aged 16. When confronted by police officers during a burglary, Bentley was alleged to have called out to Craig, "Let him have it, Chris." In 1998, Bentley was granted a posthumous pardon by the highest criminal appeals court in England and Wales. See Judgment of England and Wales Court of Appeal (Criminal Division) in *R v.*

what J. L. Austin (1962, 101–131) called the "perlocutionary" aspect of a speech act, is in fact a false guide to subjective intention.

What matters here, however, is not whether effects (always, or even sometimes) prove intentions beyond reasonable doubt, but that the ICTR judges believed this to be so, and felt the need to accentuate this point in their justification of causation in determining ICG. As a result, it seems that the key to understanding the function of causation in the reasoning of the ICTR lies in the problem of proving special intent to commit genocide, a particularly arduous exercise that has vexed jurists at a number of international tribunals. This matters for ICG cases because the type of intention in direct and public incitement to commit genocide must be *special intent*, not just any common-garden variety criminal intent. In international criminal law, special intent calls for a higher-order purpose above and beyond merely the intention to commit a prohibited act. This greater burden of proof for special intent constitutes the main reason why many defendants have been acquitted of genocide, especially at the International Criminal Tribunal for the Former Yugoslavia (e.g., Brđanin, Gvero, Jelisić, Krajišnik, Krstić, and Stakić).

From my prior interviews (Wilson 2011), it is safe to say that by the time that Nahimana and his codefendants came to trial in 2001, there was a great deal of prosecutorial anxiety in the two ad hoc international tribunals regarding the inordinately high standard of proving special intent in international criminal law. The most likely explanation is that the quest for a causal connection between speech acts and genocidal acts arose from the uncertainty of prosecutors regarding their ability to prove the genocidal intent of speech acts beyond reasonable doubt. They led evidence on the consequences of speeches and broadcasts in the hope that if they could prove that others committed genocidal acts after a speech, then the speech in question must have constituted incitement to commit genocide because it was interpreted and acted upon in this way by the audience. Susan Benesch (2011, 254) writes, "No prosecution for incitement to genocide to date has led evidence that speech *caused* thousands of deaths: only evidence that speech was made, juxtaposed with separate pieces of evidence of mass violence afterwards [her emphasis]." Benesch is technically correct, but her statement does not entirely acknowledge the thrust of prosecutorial strategy. In cases where propaganda features prominently, prosecutors are in fact very keen to establish "the connection between the leadership's desires and the acts of those on the ground," as one prosecutor, speaking anonymously, told a journalist from *Balkan Insight* (Ahmetasević 2010).

Generally, in international criminal tribunals, the Office of the Prosecutor adopts a cautious and rather indirect strategy when representing the role of war propaganda in the media. While prosecutors may not have introduced evidence directly positing a nexus between speeches and criminal acts, and they have not rested their entire

Derek William Bentley (Deceased) [1998] EWCA Crim 2516, 1998. See Duncan Campbell, "Justice at Last, 45 Years Too Late," *The Guardian*, July 31, 1998.

case for special intent on demonstrating this connection, their courtroom presentation of evidence often exhibits a discernible arc that ultimately comes to rest on an assertion of a causal relationship. In case after case at the ICTY and ICTR, and most recently in the prosecution's closing arguments against Vojislav Šešelj at the ICTY, prosecutors have led evidence in the courtroom on a speech – on its content and interpretation – and then immediately introduced witness evidence on violent acts committed in the aftermath of the speech, thereby hoping to establish by contiguity in space and time a necessary connection between the two events. Through repeated use of chronology, prosecutors have sought to take advantage of a cognitive predisposition (found, I would expect, even among professional international judges) to comprehend contiguity in space and time as proof of a necessary connection between two or more events.

Evidence from a prior survey I conducted of prosecutors, judges, defense attorneys, and expert witnesses at the ICTY suggests that these groups are not entirely confident about this endeavor.[34] The survey was primarily concerned with the use of historical evidence and the expert witness testimony of historians, but we included a question that asked whether the respondent agreed with the statement that historians (from both the prosecution and the defense) had provided important information on "the hidden meanings of political leaders' speeches and statements" at the ICTY: with only 41 percent in agreement with the statement, this element had the lowest approval rating of any of our categories. By comparison, 69 percent of respondents thought that ICTY historians had provided important information on "the authority structures of political parties" and 66 percent valued the information provided on "regional or municipal histories." Of course one needs to handle these results carefully: the ICTY and the ICTR are two different tribunals. At the same time, their jurisprudence is binding on one another, they shared the same Chief Prosecutor and Rules of Procedure and Evidence for the first ten years, and many judges moved between the two tribunals. Also, the low opinion of expert witness evidence on political leaders' speeches may indicate an appraisal of the quality of defense and prosecution experts' reports and testimony on propaganda and speech making, rather than an outright rejection of the relevance of political leaders' speeches for understanding international crimes.

Despite the skepticism expressed by ICTY staff regarding the value of evidence on the meaning of political leaders' speeches, judges at the ICTR have maintained that proof of intention in ICG cases can be discovered in part by reference to violations that occur afterward. Why would international judges promote this line of reasoning? Part of the reason lies, I would maintain, in the difficulty international judges have encountered in distinguishing the crime of hate speech from direct and public incitement to commit genocide. In the abstract, the conventional wisdom is quite

[34] Survey conducted in 2009 (N = 75), MOE = 11.9%. For a fuller explanation of the survey methods and outcomes, see Wilson (2011) and Wardak, Corin, and Wilson (2011).

straightforward: hate speech is commonly understood as derogatory speech exhibiting racial ethnic or religious bias, often linked to a program of persecution, whereas incitement to commit genocide requires that the speech act be clearly directed toward destroying a protected group in whole or in part. In a number of judgments, international jurists have declared that derogatory language, including even extremely unpleasant and bellicose statements, is not sufficient to demonstrate special intent to commit genocide. The Appeals Chamber in *Nahimana* made the following distinction:

> The Appeals Chamber considers that there is a difference between hate speech in general (or inciting discrimination or violence) and direct and public incitement to commit genocide. Direct incitement to commit genocide assumes that the speech is a direct appeal to commit an act referred to in Article 2(2) of the Statute; it has to be more than a mere vague or indirect suggestion. In most cases, direct and public incitement to commit genocide can be preceded or accompanied by hate speech but only direct and public incitement to commit genocide is prohibited under Article 2(3)(c) of the Statute. (*Nahimana* AC ¶692)[35]

The statement that incitement has to go beyond "mere vague or indirect suggestion" has echoes of *Brandenburg*, which found that incitement must go beyond "mere advocacy." Yet as in *Brandenburg* and the US law of incitement, the threshold between mere advocacy and incitement to imminent lawless action is difficult to define a priori, and each case presents a unique fact pattern. In certain cases, ICTY judges have ruled that discriminatory speech, even of an extreme nature, is not in itself an indication of genocidal intent, and that such speech must be clearly directed toward an avowedly genocidal outcome to be considered evidence of special intent.

In a pivotal early case at the ICTY, the Trial Chamber in *Jelisić* (1998) considered the case of a defendant, Goran Jelisić, who called himself the "Serb Adolf" and admitted that he came to the camp to kill Muslims (whom he insulted as "*balijas*" or "Turks"). Eyewitnesses reported "statements by the respondent that he wanted to rid the world of the Muslims, announcements of his quota of daily killings, and his desire to sterilise Muslims in order to prevent proliferation of the group" (*Jelisić* Appeals Chamber ¶66). Were speech acts such as these on the part of Goran Jelisić evidence of genocidal mens rea, or rather "mere advocacy"? According to the Trial Chamber, they showed only discriminatory intent and a disturbed personality, not special intent to commit genocide, and, crucially, Jelisić was acquitted of genocide on the grounds that the prosecution had failed to demonstrate that Jelisić was aware of, committed to, and acting under superior orders in furtherance of a wider policy of extermination of Bosnian Muslims.[36] The Appeals Chamber upheld this reasoning,

[35] Cryer et al. (2010, 381) cites ICTR Appeals Chamber in *Nahimana* as noting that simple "'hate speech' may not be enough; the incitement must be to commit genocide, although that call need not be express, so long as it is direct."

[36] *Prosecutor v. Goran Jelisić*, Trial Chamber Judgment, IT-95-10-T, December 14, 1999. ("*Jelisić* Trial Judgment"). See ¶¶98–105.

although it noted, en passant, that the evidence of the defendant's utterances presented before the Trial Chamber "could have provided the basis for a reasonable Chamber to find beyond a reasonable doubt that the respondent had the intent to destroy the Muslim group in Brčko" (*Jelisić* Appeals Judgment ¶68).

The precedent set in *Jelisić* was echoed and expanded in various ways in subsequent judgments. In 2004, the Appeals Chamber in *Krstić* found that the use of disparaging language by the accused could not be seen as an indication of genocidal intent:

> Further, at the Appeals hearing the Prosecution emphasised – as evidence of Krstić's genocidal intent – the Trial Chamber's findings of incidents in which he was heard to use derogatory language in relation to the Bosnian Muslims. The Trial Chamber accepted that "this type of charged language is commonplace amongst military personnel during war." The Appeals Chamber agrees with this assessment and finds that no weight can be placed upon Radislav Krstić's use of derogatory language in establishing his genocidal intent. (¶130)

While one can accept that derogatory language by General Krstić is in itself not evidence of genocidal intent, to state that "no weight" can be placed upon his speech constitutes a cavalier dismissal of an undeniable indicator of Krstić's state of mind during the Srebrenica massacre (an event now classified as "genocide" by both the ICTY and the International Court of Justice).[37]

At around the same time, in the *Brđanin* case, the ICTY Trial Chamber noted the extreme nature of Radoslav Brđanin's speeches:

> By his public statements the Accused created fear and hatred between Bosnian Serbs on the one hand and Bosnian Muslims and Bosnian Croats on the other hand, inciting the ethnic groups against each other. The Accused repeatedly used derogatory language to refer to non-Serbs, calling them "Balijas" (Muslims), "Ustaša" (Croats), "Šiptar" (Albanians), "vermin," "scum," "infidel," and "second rate people." (2004, ¶325)
>
> Moreover, he publicly suggested a campaign of retaliatory ethnicity-based murder, declaring that two Muslims would be killed in Banja Luka for every Serb killed in Sarajevo. (¶329)

The defendant Radoslav Brđanin's incendiary public statements were articulated at a time of all-out war between groups in Bosnia and had a "disastrous impact" according to the Trial Chamber, but the Tribunal did not see them as proof of the requisite mens rea, and Brđanin was acquitted of genocide and complicity in genocide.[38] The key question here for those seeking consistency in the legal

[37] On the finding of the Srebrenica genocide at the ICTY, see the TC and AC judgments in *Krstić*, and the TC judgment in *Popović et al.* At the ICJ, see Application of the Convention on the Prevention and Punishment of the Crime of Genocide (*Bosnia and Herzegovina v. Serbia and Montenegro*), Judgment of February 26, 2007.

[38] *Brđanin* Trial Judgment ¶330. Brđanin was convicted of persecution and other crimes against humanity. He was not charged with ICG, but with committing genocide and with complicity to commit genocide as part of a joint criminal enterprise.

distinction between hate speech and special intent to commit genocide is: when does derogatory speech cross the line from discriminatory intent[39] into genocidal intent? Stated more concretely, were Radoslav Brđanin's references to "vermin" and "scum" and his calls to kill Muslims really so unlike Ferdinand Nahimana's statements about "*inyenzi*," or "cockroaches" (deemed indicative of genocidal intent)? Part of the answer lies in the context of each speech act (that is, a widespread and systematic attack on a civilian population with intent to destry a protected group, in whole or in part), but the requisite link between speech acts and context still remains unelucidated and opaque in international criminal law.

Then there is the opposite problem: given that judges have allowed the "direct" in "direct and public incitement" to include euphemistic, veiled, or coded calls to exterminate groups, when does insulting language cease to be genocidal? It is understandable that international courts would struggle to define this line clearly, conceptually and a priori. Again, much of the determination of whether a speech act illustrates genocidal intent will rely upon specific circumstances and context, and the demonstrable effect seems to have become the most important feature of how international tribunals go about contextualizing a speech act.

In concluding, there is much to be gained by a legal realist approach that unearths the ways in which international criminal court decisions result as much from the quotidian dimensions of the law – the courtroom conventions, rules of procedure and evidence, and assumptions and beliefs of legal actors – as they do from the black letter of the law and established legal reasoning. Attention to organizational culture – an often overlooked dimension of international law – can allow us to explain how legal thinking changes suddenly and unexpectedly, and why time-honored conventions are overturned. Through a better comprehension of the motivations and subjective thought processes of key legal actors (i.e., their intent!) as they grappled with hard cases where incitement was charged, social science might contribute to a fuller understanding of why international law sometimes makes claims about human behavior that are not necessarily borne out by the evidence.

REFERENCES

Ahmetasević, Nidzara. 2010. "Hague Recognizes Propaganda's Role in Srebrenica Genocide." *Balkan Insight*, July 7. Accessed July 1, 2012. http://www.balkaninsight.com/en/article/hague-recognises-propaganda-s-role-in-srebrenica-genocide/.

Alexander, Larry, and Kimberly Kessler. 1997. "Mens Rea and Inchoate Crimes." *Journal of Criminal Law and Criminology* 87: 1138–1193.

Austin, J. L. 1962. *How to Do Things with Words*. London: Oxford University Press.

Benesch, Susan. 2011. "The Ghost of Causation in International Speech Crime Cases." In *Propaganda, War Crimes Trials and International Law: From Speakers' Corner to War Crimes*, edited by Predrag Dojčinović, 254–268. Abingdon and New York: Routledge.

[39] Discriminatory intent is a requirement in some crimes against humanity, such as the crime of persecution.

Cahill, Michael T. 2012. "Defining Inchoate Crimes: An Incomplete Attempt." *Ohio State Journal of Criminal Law* 9: 751–759.

Carver, Richard. 2000. "Broadcasting and Political Transition: Rwanda and Beyond." In *African Broadcast Cultures: Radio in Transition*, edited by Richard Fardon and Graham Furniss, 188–197. Cape Town: David Philip.

Cassese, Antonio. 2008. *International Criminal Law*. 2nd ed. Oxford: Oxford University Press.

Chrétien, Jean-Pierre, J. F. Dupaquier, M. Kabanda, and J. Ngarambe. 1995. *Rwanda: Les Médias du Génocide*. Paris: Karthala.

Clarke, Kamari. 2009. *Fictions of Justice: The International Criminal Court and the Challenge of Legal Pluralism in Sub-Saharan Africa*. New York: Cambridge University Press.

Cryer, Robert, Hakan Friman, Darryl Robinson, and Elizabeth Wilmshurst. 2010. *An Introduction to International Criminal Law and Procedure*. 2nd ed. Cambridge: Cambridge University Press.

Davidson, Ron. 2004. "The International Criminal Tribunal for Rwanda's Decision in *The Prosecutor v. Ferdinand Nahimana et al.*: The Past, Present, and Future of International Incitement Law." *Leiden Journal of International Law* 17(3): 505–519.

Des Forges, Alison. 1999. "Propaganda and Practice." In *Leave None to Tell the Story: Genocide in Rwanda*, by Alison Des Forges. New York: Human Rights Watch (March).

Dojčinović, Predrag, ed. 2011. *Propaganda, War Crimes Trials and International Law: From Speakers' Corner to War Crimes*. Abingdon and New York: Routledge.

Eastwood, Margaret. 2011. "Hitler's Notorious Jew-Baiter: The Prosecution of Julius Streicher." In *Propaganda, War Crimes Trials and International Law: From Speakers' Corner to War Crimes*, edited by Predrag Dojčinović, 203–230. Abingdon and New York: Routledge.

Gey, Steven. 2010. "The Brandenburg Paradigm and Other First Amendments." *University of Pennsylvania Journal of Constitutional Law* 12: 971–1052.

Gordon, Gregory S. 2005. "A War of Media, Words, Newspapers, and Radio Stations: The ICTR Media Trial Verdict and a New Chapter in the International Law of Hate Speech." *Virginia Journal International Law* 45(139): 1–60.

Gordon, Gregory S. 2008. "From Incitement to Indictment? Prosecuting Iran's President for Advocating Israel's Destruction and Piecing Together Incitement Law's Emerging Analytical Framework." *Journal of Criminal Law & Criminology* 98(3): 853–920.

Gordon, Gregory S. 2010. "Music and Genocide: Harmonizing Coherence, Freedom and Nonviolence in Incitement Law." *Santa Clara Law Review* 50: 607–646.

Gordon, Gregory S. 2012. "Formulating a New Atrocity Speech Offense: Incitement to Commit War Crimes." *Loyola University Chicago Law Journal* 43: 281–316.

Hagan, John. 2003. *Justice in the Balkans: Prosecuting War Crimes in the Hague Tribunal*. Chicago: University of Chicago Press.

Healy, Thomas. 2009. "Brandenburg in a Time of Terror." *Notre Dame Law Review* 84: 655–731.

Kearney, Michael G. 2007. *The Prohibition of Propaganda for War in International Law*. Oxford: Oxford University Press.

Kellow, Christine, and H. Leslie Steeves. 1998. "The Role of Radio in the Rwandan Genocide." *Journal of Communication* 48(3): 107–128.

Kelsall, Tim. 2009. *Culture under Cross-Examination: International Justice and the Special Court for Sierra Leone*. Cambridge: Cambridge University Press.

La Mort, Justin. 2009. "The Soundtrack to Genocide in the Bikindi Trial to Protect Free Speech and Uphold the Promise of Never Again." *Interdisciplinary Journal of Human Rights Law* 4(1): 43–66.

Li, Darryl. 2004. "Echoes of Violence: Considerations on Radio and Genocide in Rwanda." *Journal of Genocide Research* 6(1): 9–28.

MacKinnon, Catharine A. 2009. "International Decision: *Prosecutor v. Nahimana, Barayagwiza, and Ngeze.*" *American Journal of International Law* 98(2): 325–330.

Maravilla, Christopher Scott. 2008. "Hate Speech as a War Crime: Public and Direct Incitement to Genocide in International Law." *Tulsa Journal of International & Comparative Law* 17: 113–617.

McAdams, Richard H., and Dhammika Dharmapala. 2005. "Words That Kill? An Economic Model of the Influence of Speech on Behavior (with Particular Reference to Hate Speech)." *Journal of Legal Studies* 34(1): 1–45.

Mendel, Toby. 2006. *Study on International Standards Relating to Incitement to Genocide or Racial Hatred.* Report for the UN Special Advisor on the Prevention of Genocide (April).

Mertz, Elizabeth, ed. 2008. *The Role of Social Science in Law.* Farnham, UK, and Burlington, VT: Ashgate.

Mironko, Charles. 2007. "The Effect of RTLM's Rhetoric of Ethnic Hatred in Rural Rwanda." In *The Media and the Rwanda Genocide*, edited by Allan Thompson, 125–135. London: Pluto Press.

Nuijten, Monique, and Gerhard Anders, eds. 2009. *Corruption and the Secret of Law: A Legal Anthropological Perspective.* Farnham, UK, and Burlington, VT: Ashgate.

Oberschall, Anthony. 2010. "Vojislav Seselj's Nationalist Propaganda: Contents, Techniques, Aims and Impacts, 1990–1994." An Expert Report for the United Nations International Criminal Tribunal for the Former Yugoslavia. November 2007.

Orentlicher, Diane. 2005. "Criminalizing Hate Speech in the Crucible of Trial: *Prosecutor v. Nahimana.*" *New England Journal of International and Comparative Law* 12(17): 1–34.

Pavlakis, Christoforos. 2008. *The Role of the "Hate Media" in Rwanda's Genocide.* Norderstedt, Germany: Druck und Bindung.

Rikhof, Joseph. 2005. "Hate Speech and International Criminal Law: The Mugesera Decision by the Supreme Court of Canada." *Journal of International Criminal Justice* 3(5): 1121–1133.

Ruzindana, Mathias. 2011. "The Challenges of Understanding Kinyarwanda Key Terms Used to Instigate the 1994 Genocide in Rwanda." In *Propaganda, War Crimes Trials and International Law: From Speakers' Corner to War Crimes*, edited by Predrag Dojčinović, 145–170. Abingdon and New York: Routledge.

Schabas, William. 1999. "International Decision: *Mugesera v. Minister of Citizenship and Immigration.*" *American Journal of International Law* 93: 529–533.

Schabas, William. 2000. "Hate Speech in Rwanda: The Road to Genocide." *McGill Law Journal* 46(141): 1–33.

Straus, Scott. 2006. *The Order of Genocide: Race, Power, and War in Rwanda.* Ithaca, NY: Cornell University Press.

Straus, Scott. 2007. "What Is the Relationship between Hate Radio and Violence? Rethinking Rwanda's 'Radio Machete.'" *Politics & Society* 35(4): 609–637.

Surdukowski, Jay. 2004. "Is Poetry a War Crime? Reckoning for Radovan Karadzic the Poet-Warrior." *Michigan Journal of International Law* 26: 673–699.

Taylor, Telford. 1992. *The Anatomy of the Nuremberg Trials: A Personal Memoir.* Boston: Little, Brown and Co.

Thompson, Allan, ed. 2007. *The Media and the Rwanda Genocide.* London: Pluto Press.

Timmermann, Wibke Kristin. 2005. "The Relationship between Hate Propaganda and Incitement to Genocide: A New Trend in International Law towards Criminalization of Hate Propaganda?" *Leiden Journal of International Law* 18(2): 257–282.

Timmermann, Wibke Kristin. 2006. "Incitement in International Law." *International Review of the Red Cross* 88(864): 823–852.

Wallenstein, Joshua. 2001. "Punishing Words: An Analysis of the Necessity of the Element of Causation in Prosecutions for Incitement to Genocide." *Stanford Law Review* 54(2): 351–398.

Wardak, Ahmad W., Andrew Corin, and Richard A. Wilson. 2011. "Surveying History at the International Criminal Tribunal for the Former Yugoslavia." *Journal of Eurasian Law* 4(1): 1–39.

Wilson, Richard Ashby. 2011. *Writing History in International Criminal Trials*. Cambridge: Cambridge University Press.

Yanagizawa-Drott, David. 2014. "Propaganda and Conflict: Evidence from the Rwandan Genocide."*Quarterly Journal of Economics*. 129(4): 1947–1994.

Zahar, Alexander. 2005. "The ICTR's 'Media' Judgment and the Reinvention of 'Direct' and Public Incitement to Commit Genocide." *Criminal Law Forum* 16: 33–48.

LEGAL CASES CITED

Application of the Convention on the Prevention and Punishment of the Crime of Genocide (*Bosnia and Herzegovina v. Serbia and Montenegro*). International Court of Justice. Judgment of February 26, 2007.

Brandenburg v. Ohio, 395 U.S. 444 (1969).

Chaplinsky v. State of New Hampshire, 315 U.S. 568 (1942).

Mugesera v. Canada (Minister of Citizenship and Immigration) (F.C.A.), 2003 FCA 325, (2003), [2004] 1 F.C.R. 3.

Prosecutor v. Jean-Paul Akayesu (Case No. ICTR-96-4) Trial Chamber Judgment, ICTR-96-4-T, September 2, 1998 ("*Akayesu* Trial Judgment").

Prosecutor v. Simon Bikindi (Case No. ICTR-01-72) Trial Chamber Judgment, ICTR-01-72-T, December 2, 2008 ("*Bikindi* Trial Judgment"). Judgment on Appeal, ICTR-01-72-A, March 18, 2010 ("*Bikindi* Appeals Judgment").

Prosecutor v. Radoslav Brđanin (Case No. IT-99-36) Trial Chamber Judgment, IT-99-36-T, September 1, 2004 ("*Brđanin* Trial Judgment").

Prosecutor v. Goran Jelisić (Case No. IT-95-10) Trial Chamber Judgment, IT-95-10-T, December 14, 1999 ("*Jelisić* Trial Judgment"). Appeals Chamber Judgment, IT-95-10-A.5, July 2001 ("*Jelisić* Appeals Judgment").

Prosecutor v. Radovan Karadžić (Case No. IT-95-5/18-PT) Third Amended Indictment, February 27, 2009.

Prosecutor v. Radislav Krstić (Case No. IT-98-33) Trial Chamber Judgment, IT-98–33-T, August 2, 2001 ("*Krstić* Trial Judgment"). Appeals Chamber Judgment, IT-98–33-A, April 19, 2004 ("*Krstić* Appeals Judgment").

Prosecutor v. Alfred Musema (Case No. ICTR-96-13) Trial Chamber Judgment, ICTR-96-13-T, January 27, 2000 ("*Musema* Trial Judgment").

Prosecutor v. Ferdinand Nahimana, Jean-Bosco Barayagwisa, Hassan Ngeze (Case No. ICTR-99-52) Trial Chamber Judgment, ICTR-99-52-T, December 3, 2003 ("*Nahimana* Trial Judgment"). Judgment on Appeal, ICTR-99-52-A, November 28, 2007 ("*Nahimana* Appeals Judgment").

Prosecutor v. Eliézer Niyitegeka (Case No. ICTR-96-14) Trial Chamber Judgment, ICTR-96-14-T, May 16, 2003 ("*Niyitegeka* Trial Judgment").

Prosecutor v. Vujadin Popović et al. (Case No. IT-05-88) Trial Chamber Judgment, IT-05–88-T, June 10, 2010 ("*Popović* Trial Judgment").

Prosecutor v. Georges Ruggiu (Case No. ICTR-97-32-I) Trial Chamber Judgment, ICTR-97-32-I, June 1, 2000 ("*Ruggiu* Trial Judgment").

Prosecutor v. Georges Anderson Rutuganda (Case No. ICTR-96-3) Trial Chamber Judgment, ICTR-96-3-T, December 6, 1999 ("*Rutuganda* Trial Judgment").

Prosecutor v. Vojislav Šešelj (Case No. IT-03-67) Third Amended Indictment, December 7, 2007.

Prosecutor v. Duško Tadić (Case No. IT-94-1) Trial Chamber Judgment, IT-94-1-T, May 7, 1997 ("*Tadić* Trial Judgment"). Judgment on Appeal, IT-94-1-A, July 15, 1999 ("*Tadić* Appeals Judgment").

R v. Derek William Bentley (Deceased). Judgment of England and Wales Court of Appeal (Criminal Division) [1998] EWCA Crim 2516, 1998.

Schenck v. United States, 249 U.S. 47 (1919).

Trial of the Major War Criminals before the International Military Tribunal, Nuremberg, November 14, 1945–October 1, 1946 (Section on Julius Streicher; part 22, pp. 182, 501).

Index

37777517R00171

Made in the USA
Lexington, KY
30 April 2019